Lewis B. Hershey,
Mr. Selective Service

For forms of government let fools contest;
Whate'er is best administer'd is best.

Alexander Pope

Qui desiderat pacem, praeparet bellum.

Vegetius

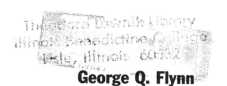

George Q. Flynn

LEWIS B. HERSHEY, MR. SELECTIVE SERVICE

University of North Carolina Press

Chapel Hill and London

© 1985 The University of North Carolina Press

Manufactured in the United States of America

Library of Congress Cataloging in Publication Data

Flynn, George Q.
Lewis B. Hershey, Mr. Selective Service

Bibliography: p.
Includes index.
1. Hershey, Lewis Blaine, 1893—   2. Generals—
United States—Biography.   3. United States. Army—
Biography.   4. Military service, Compulsory—United States
—History—20th century.   I. Title.   II. Title: Mister
Selective Service, Lewis B. Hershey.
U55.H38F59   1985   355.2′25′0924 [B]   84-10397
ISBN 0-8078-1621-3

Frontispiece: Hershey as Lt. General in 1960's,
courtesy of Hershey Family

For Paul A. Reising, 1909–1980
and
Lillian Reising

Contents

Illustrations

Acknowledgments

Writing a biography of a public figure recently deceased creates problems which can be overcome only with the aid of many people. This work would have been impossible except for the cooperation of the Hershey children, in particular Gilbert Hershey and Kathryn Hershey Layne. Colonel and Mrs. Gilbert Hershey opened their own fine collection of material to me and provided charming hospitality during my research. Similarly, Kathryn Hershey Layne revealed her material to me and consented to several interviews. Dozens of Hershey's colleagues in government also were willing to help. Most of them are listed in the bibliography, but a special note of thanks must go to Colonel John W. Barber of the Selective Service System for finding material. The Hershey Papers are held by the Military History Institute at Carlisle Barracks, Pennsylvania. My work at this installation was made easy through the cooperation of its archivist, Richard Sommers. Similar thanks go to the librarians and archivist at the Library of Congress, especially Margaret Melun; to Frederick W. Pernell at the National Archives; and to the Yale Library, the Franklin D. Roosevelt Library at Hyde Park, the John F. Kennedy Library in Boston, the Harry S Truman Library in Missouri, the Dwight D. Eisenhower Library in Kansas, and the Lyndon B. Johnson Library in Texas. Throughout my research I benefited immensely from the kind hospitality of several people: Paul and Cilla Reising in Boston, Norman and Gertrude Melun and Lawrence and Barbara Henneberger and Elizabeth Denny in the Washington area, Colonel and Mrs. William Averill in Tupelo, Mississippi, Colonel and Mrs. Frank Kossa in Louisville, Margaret Rowdybush in Florida, Professor and Mrs. Don Zimmer and John W. McClellan in Angola, Indiana, Colonel Frank Keesling in San Francisco, Cathy and James C. Otto in Newark, Ohio, and Dr. Kenneth McGill in Abilene, Kansas. At the Texas Tech Library, which provided considerable assistance, special thanks are due Paul Young and Gloria Lyerla. James Patterson of Brown University and Alwyn Barr, Chester Pach and Ben Newcomb of Texas Tech read parts of the manuscript and offered useful criticism. For my typing I relied upon Joan Weldon and Casey Wallace. Mary Reising Flynn again provided a proper home atmosphere for scholarship. Sharon Wood and Dennis Edwards introduced me to the magic of computer writing. Margaret and Mary Flynn helped proof-read. Dan Flores helped with the illustrations. At the University of North Carolina Press I received excellent assistance from Lewis Bateman and Gwen Duffey. One would have thought I was a basketball star.

Portions of Chapter V originally appeared in *Military Affairs*, 47, no. 1 (Feb. 1983) and are reproduced with permission of the American Military Institute. Other sections of the same chapter appear in the *Journal of Negro History* and also are used here with the permission of that journal.

The cost of my research was augmented by a faculty development leave and a grant from the Arts and Science Research Council at Texas Tech. The Southwest Collection provided technical aid for interviews.

Naturally, none of the above-mentioned individuals is in any way responsible for the final shape of the material. I can only hope that the finished product will provide them some satisfaction for their assistance.

Prologue

he students at UCLA crowded into the hall, anxious to get a close view. The bane of their college careers was scheduled to appear for a talk entitled "Age Talks with Youth," an overdue topic for a man who had been tormenting them for so long. By October 1970 his fangs had been extracted by President Nixon, but the students were still curious, bitter, and angry.

Slowly, with the uncertain gait of a half-blind, half-deaf seventy-seven-year-old, an elderly gentleman took the stage. With his white hair in an unfashionable crewcut and wearing an out-of-style blue suit, complemented by scuffed shoes, he looked like a refugee from a park bench. Although a retired four-star general, he wore no uniform and no ribbons. The audience of over a thousand, already restless, was confused by his appearance. To relieve the tension Robert Elias, a student leader who had organized the talk, walked to the podium and introduced General Lewis Blaine Hershey, recently retired head of the Selective Service System. Here was the man who had directed the iniquitous draft for the past thirty years.

To many of these students Hershey was the arch symbol of the government's criminal adventure in Vietnam, which had already taken the lives of over 40,000 Americans and untold numbers of Asians. Elias had expected a few radicals to attend. To prevent violence, several members of the campus security force took up stations backstage. Hershey had spoken to hostile audiences before, but in the last year of his administration he had tried to avoid confrontations because death threats had been issued. Now, having lost all authority for the draft, as well as his FBI guardians, Hershey had accepted Elias's invitation.

The heckling began before Hershey could open his mouth. Several of the students had come with their own prepared statements and had no intention of listening to Hershey. Elias made the situation worse by trying to browbeat the hecklers into submission. When Hershey finally obtained the microphone, he displayed a high degree of sang-froid. As the boos escalated, he announced, "I feel that I am being welcomed, each in their own way." He had always been noted for his crackerbarrel wit in testimony before Congress, but such an attitude would not serve him now. When several students shouted profanities at him, he replied, "I'll probably regret the part that I've had . . . to keep this boy in college." A student then asked how he felt after killing so many men and babies. Hershey responded by explaining that he did not run the war and that "this is flattery that I just simply can't stand." He explained that he was merely doing his duty. Another student raised the precedent of Nuremberg, where Nazis had claimed only to be doing their duty. Hershey, missing the point of the analogy, insisted that the United States did not follow the Nuremberg precedents in domestic law. For those dissatisfied with the draft, he recommended lobbying Congress, rather than rioting.

The student criticism left him unimpressed. "It is easy to know what is wrong when you are ignorant," he explained. "My six-year-old grandchild knows everything is wrong, but she can't fix anything." These statements only enraged the crowd further. Someone began to shout that he should shoot his grandchild.

Around the auditorium several students jumped up to make political statements. Hershey continued to take the uproar calmly, but he wondered if any system would work when "some people who are taking all the benefits won't keep their mouths shut." This reply struck home to many students who had enjoyed draft deferments while others, not so fortunate, went to die in Asia. The scene rapidly lost all semblance of order. One student jumped up and spoke: "I'd like to—uh—like I'm thinking and I'm looking at you, and like you're death personified. . . . Like I don't want to talk to you because you're in the past, and we're here, and we're now, and we're alive. . . . You're a good German. . . . Everybody here is so mad at you, that if they saw you on the street and didn't have just respect for your age, and, knowing that things are going to happen naturally, they'd rip you off . . . and I think I'm rational I kinda have pity, because you can't make sense of what I'm saying right now, but like people here make sense." Some sense, muttered Hershey.

Faced with this type of statement in an environment supposedly dedicated to reasoned discourse, Hershey began a withdrawal. He expressed an understanding of his audience. "I expect such tactics," he admitted, "because you are frustrated. It is easier to be mad at a person than at a cause." But he still had faith in youth. He simply did not believe that those denouncing him at UCLA represented youth, or "the America that I know." The uproar continued and Hershey left the stage, returning to his room in the Statler Hotel.

The question left unanswered was whether the America that Hershey knew, the America he had grown old serving, still existed. If it did, how could he explain such treatment of a man who had spent most of his life in its service? Having worked in a position of national authority under six different presidents, Hershey thought he deserved something better. In the beginning it had all been much easier to understand loyalty, duty, and patriotism.[1]

Lewis B. Hershey,
Mr. Selective Service

I. The Mold

Some people called it "the heartland." Others referred to it as Mid-America, the home of the "silent majority," as they said in the 1960's. Whatever the epithet, it was a region rich in human resources, a region which had produced Abraham Lincoln, and Carl Sandburg, but also Joe McCarthy and the Ku Klux Klan. Lewis B. Hershey was born on 12 September 1893 in the northeast corner of Indiana.

The land had beauty—rolling hills, over a hundred lakes, and maples, oaks, and elms. Nestled throughout were hundred-acre farms. The farmers worked hard to raise corn, soybeans, some cattle, and a few hogs. The land was neat; the people were patriotic. Steuben County boasted of having sent more soldiers to fight for the Union than any other county its size. A 90-foot column in honor of the Civil War dead rose in the middle of Angola, the county seat.

The world of 1893 still paraded in the robe of liberalism, but signs of fraying had appeared around the edges. In England an independent Labour party was formed with socialist goals. In Paris the hero of Suez, Ferdinand de Lesseps, was fined over scandals in Panama. In the United States a severe economic panic greeted President Grover Cleveland as he began his second term. Seeking to stem the crisis, Cleveland attacked the Sherman Silver Purchase Act and thereby helped to split his Democratic party. With 20 percent of the work force idle, men paused to listen when radicals spoke.

But few radicals spoke in Steuben County. Although hardly the romantic scene painted in pious platitudes by James Whitcomb Riley, this region did not suffer industrial depression. Life was hard enough without belching furnaces, immigration, and radicals. The Hershey farm had barely a hundred acres; the house was heated by one woodstove in the living room. The other five rooms were all small—and crowded, with ten adults. Water came from an outdoor pump and was heated over the woodstove. Rainwater caught in a reservoir filled the washbasin for the occasional scrub.[1]

The natural beauty of the region escaped the notice of people who struggled over its dirt roads. These people were as homogeneous as the landscape. White Anglo-Saxon Protestants associated with each other at the local Masonic Lodge, and sent their children to one-room school houses where they were taught the virtues of Republicanism, Protestantism, and patriotism. The Fourth of July remained the most sacred day of the year. In urban America people might be questioning the assertion that this nation was "the last best hope of mankind," but certitude remained in Steuben County. There were few extremes of wealth and poverty, and seldom was an alien to be seen.

The Hersheys had roots as deep as most families in America. Ironically, Lewis, who was later called a pillar of the establishment, traced his ancestry back to some of the most uncompromising rebels in European history. The Hersh family of Appenzell, Switzerland, had embraced the Anabaptist cause during the Reformation. These followers of Zwingli viewed the Bible as the one standard for life, and they refused any service to the state. From this clan Christian Hersche came to Lancaster, Pennsylvania, in 1708. The family name was Americanized to Hershey. In the pre-Revolutionary War period George Hershey moved to the region of Geneva Falls, New York. Surrounded by his coreligionists, he married, and subsequently fathered George R. Hershey. Like innumerable other men, this grandfather of Lewis sought his fortune in the new West. In 1849 he took his wife, Joanna L. Freleigh, to northern Indiana. A stonemason by vocation and a lifelong Democrat by avocation, George Hershey eventually had ten children. Lewis's father, Latta Freleigh Hershey, was born near Fremont in 1858.[2]

Like many western travelers, George Hershey left his religious commitment behind in New York. He and his sons were manual laborers with little formal education, although Latta did manage to teach himself to read and write a clumsy hand. On his mother's side Lewis was descended from the family of Nelson Hutchins, which also moved from Seneca Falls, New York, to Indiana in the nineteenth century. Nelson's daughter Francis married Lewis Richardson, an Irish immigrant and common laborer. Their daughter, Rosetta Richardson, married Latta Hershey in 1879. From this marriage came two sons: Russ in 1882, and Lewis in 1893. Lewis was named after his maternal grandfather and received his middle name from George Hershey, who had been smitten with James G. Blaine's presidential candidacy in 1884.[3]

The Hershey clan had no pretensions of gentry status. When he married in 1879, Latta Hershey turned from stonemasonry and an occasional job on the railroads to farming. Beginning as a tenant, he finally saved enough to buy eighty-two acres near the even smaller tract of his parents. When his first son was born in 1882, Latta seemed to be making his mark in the community. After a few years he added his eighty-two acres to his father's fifty and moved back home to farm the entire plot. This strapping six-footer, with a glib tongue and a willingness to accept hard work, seemed destined for prosperity. But almost overnight a series of tragedies struck the family. In 1897 Rosetta Hershey fell ill with lung congestion, probably tuberculosis. She lingered until 14 February 1898. The next summer George Hershey died, and four years later Joanna Hershey followed her husband. The expense of these illnesses and funerals added to the burden of two motherless sons. As a partial solution to his problems, Latta invited his sister-in-law, Alma Richardson, to move in and help raise the boys.[4]

Growing up on a farm used to be the common heritage of most Americans, and the virtues of such an experience later became romanticized in tales told in urban America. Lewis Hershey never accepted the romance and never felt the lure of the soil. At the turn of the century a small farm in northeastern Indiana was an isolated place. The roads were bad, and few families had telephones. Getting the mail meant traveling five miles. Most of the day was spent in work. Lewis, as the younger child, had the responsibility for feeding the hogs and tending the horse and cattle. Latta took care of milking the cows. The land was too hilly for a tractor, even had they been able to afford one. Money, in small quantities, came from corn, hogs, and a few cattle. For the most part, the Hershey farm was a subsistence operation.[5]

The relative isolation did help Lewis develop a strong sense of family. His father provided the adult model during these formative years. Latta Hershey was a big, brawny man, with red hair and a ready tongue. Although almost illiterate, he had the typical American faith in education as the key to social progress. As Russ seemed to have no interests outside the farm, Latta concentrated on convincing Lewis of the virtues of schooling. Lewis responded to the encouragement and viewed his father as a natural leader—a view endorsed by neighbors, who eventually elected him county sheriff.

Lewis and his father developed a kind of special closeness which often occurs in motherless homes. The boy had hardly started school when he was helping his father in his job as township assessor. Convincing local farmers to answer dozens of questions on the size of their farms and types of crops was no easy task. From his father Lewis received a lesson in the work ethic and a view of local politics. As Latta became more prominent in the community, he took Lewis with him to Masonic meetings. More important, Latta became a pillar of the local Republican establishment. He made a point of taking the eight-year-old Lewis with him to township caucuses and county conventions. Here the boy saw how politics worked in rural America, with different opinions being compromised in debate. As Lewis recalled in later years, "Whatever political tendencies I may have developed, I trace directly to the training which I received, most of it subconsciously, from him".[6]

Boyhood recreation in rural Indiana consisted primarily of self-organized games. Lewis and his young friends would take to the woods on weekends for games of mock war, with corncobs as ammunition. There was always the water to provide diversion, so they swam, boated, and fished. Bathing suits were a luxury disdained by these young roughnecks. The lakes offered up perch, trout, sunfish, and bass, but Lewis never considered himself a true fisherman. A nibble on his line disturbed his general tranquility. The outdoor life agreed with him, and by age thirteen he stood six feet, well above the average for the day. He inherited his father's red hair and added his own freckles. Despite the usual boyhood diseases such as mumps, whooping cough, and measles, he enjoyed robust health as a youth and for most of his life.[7]

The all-boy play soon evolved naturally into more mature social activities. Lewis had some trouble making the adjustment because his rapid growth had left him a bit clumsy. He never felt at home on the dance floor but was more comfortable holding attention through his considerable vocal abilities. At many a dance he could be found on the sidelines, regaling an audience with stories or provoking a debate on some insignificant political issue. During the Chautauqua visit he and his friends gathered to hear Alice Nielson sing and Horace Fletcher speak on the virtues of good nutrition. At night an opera was performed.[8]

Despite the veneer of Victorian morals imposed by the adult community, these youths of rural Indiana enjoyed a robust sex life. Sex education came from one's peers, and the empirical approach was most popular. Lewis seemed to have more than his share of female company, attracted by his physique and his glib tongue. The boys spent much time plotting stratagems which would end in sexual delights. Ample opportunities for such activities presented themselves; the woods were convenient, and hayrides were always pleasant. The adults seemed to hold a rather loose reign, allowing young people to stay out until 3:00 or 4:00 in the morning.[9]

Lewis began his formal education in March 1899 at Hell's Point, a one-room schoolhouse located only 250 yards from his home. His father expected him to do well. Fortunately, he had the aptitude for schoolwork and the negative incentive of disliking farm labor. His teachers recognized his above-average talent. Equally fortunate, the curriculum in Indiana at this time catered to Lewis's voracious reading habits. The Indiana State Series of readers offered the students challenging stories about patriotism in John G. Whittier's "Barbara Frietchie," about constancy in "Bruce and the Spider," and about duty in "The Leak in the Dike." Young scholars imbibed rustic sentimentality from James Whitcomb Riley. Longfellow and Browning selections were also prominent in the readers. Lewis's favorites included "Horatius," by Thomas Babington Macaulay, "How the Spartans Fought at Thermopylae," and various essays by Ralph Waldo Emerson. The reading series was designed to generate good morals, duty, honor, patriotism, loyalty, and charity. As an adult, Lewis remained fond of these stories, and he read them to his children.[10]

After moving successfully through a curriculum which included courses in spelling, reading, writing, grammar, arithmetic, geography, history, and deportment, in 1905 Lewis took a special exam for placement in high school. He was under the age for admittance, but his report cards from Mrs. Hazel M. Rodgers revealed straight perfection in 1906, except for a 99 in deportment. He was the obvious choice to write the graduating essay. Appropriately, he wrote on "success," quoting liberally from Bayard Taylor's writing on the self-made man. Lewis told his fellow students to "hitch your wagon to a star," have high standards, stay faithful in your task. Spouting such Horatio Algerisms, young Lewis Hershey moved on to high school.[11]

Although the vast majority of students ended their formal education before the eighth grade, Lewis, with his father's encouragement, enrolled at Fremont High School. It was about five and one-half miles from the farm to Fremont. The high school had a total enrollment of twenty-four students when Lewis entered; the school building consisted of one big assembly hall and a few small classrooms. Two teachers were responsible for the entire curriculum. Recitation was the favored method of instruction. Lewis took three years of Latin, two of algebra, one and one-half of geometry, four of English, and three of history. The progressive education theories of John Dewey had not yet seeped into northeast Indiana.

Lewis made outstanding marks in all of his subjects. He consistently averaged in the 90's and did particularly well in math, although history was his favorite subject. The reading curriculum contained large doses of the classics. Much emphasis was placed on oral skills. Two literary societies, the Emersonians and the Albaians, were supported by this tiny student body. Lewis joined the Emersonians and soon became editor of their monthly collection of essays, orations, and recitations. He also engaged in public speaking and debate under the direction of Mrs. Nellie Ball Reed. His one failure came when he tried out for the high school basketball team—the coach turned him down despite his six-foot height. When he graduated in 1910, he was again chosen to deliver the graduation speech.

His teachers and his father encouraged him to attend college, but Lewis found his life becoming more complicated.[12] Perhaps the biggest complication was the increasing importance of Ellen Dygert. The Dygert family had come to Indiana from Virginia. Ellen's parents, George and Emily Dygert, boasted prominent relatives such as a grandfather, Joseph Johnson, who was governor of Virginia from 1852 to 1856, and Newton Whiting Gilbert, Ellen's uncle, who had served as lieutenant governor of Indiana, a congressman in 1905, and acting governor-general of the Philippines. The Dygerts considered themselves socially superior to farmers such as the Hersheys. Lewis had met Ellen at school in 1907.[13] Although not beautiful, Ellen attracted boys with her quiet confidence. She knew her family had some claim to distinction. She had a serious personality (her mother once remarked that Ellen never cried after her infancy) and, unlike the other young girls within Lewis's view, she had no time for silliness and weakness.[14]

The explanation for their mutual attraction seems difficult to pinpoint. True, Lewis also considered himself rather serious and mature beyond his years, yet his personality was much more gregarious than Ellen's. Whatever the explanation, they soon began seeing each other on a regular basis. Unfortunately for Lewis, Ellen's family, who had lived on a farm east of Angola, decided to move into the county seat. This meant Ellen had to attend Angola High School in 1908. Although Lewis was disappointed, Ellen looked forward to the move to town, having already rejected the farm as too boring. In a day when telephones were luxuries, the two maintained their relationship by mail. Lewis wrote almost weekly.[15]

After having established that Ellen was no "dam-o-crat," Lewis saw fit to lecture her on the female company she was keeping. At least one of her friends had the reputation of being "loose" with boys. He also lectured on more intimate subjects, sometimes at the cost of pain. Ellen warned him that she still had her Masonic pin, "on which you hurt yourself so badly. It is all ready for the next fellow who puts his hand there." But it was still all "dearest," and "loving," by the end of 1909. They enjoyed the Christmas vacation together and skated on the lakes.[16]

As 1910 began the two seemed secure in their affection, but it was literally a star-crossed year. Haley's Comet streaked across the sky on 4 May, making its first appearance in seventy-five years. Lewis had many obligations as his high school graduation drew near. For graduation Ellen bought him cuff links and a stick pin for $3. He looked very impressive in his new suit giving the valedictory address.[17]

A few weeks after his graduation Lewis finally impressed the Dygerts with the seriousness of his intentions. Ironically, he made his case thanks to an unfortunate accident which had nearly cost him and Ellen their lives. He took her out in the family rig for a ride in the country and decided to play the hero by racing the rig with Ellen sitting in his lap. One hit with his whip, however, caused the horse to bolt. In short order the harness separated and the entire rig turned over. Lewis was able to jump clear and sustained only a cut on his head. Ellen was not so lucky; her foot was badly injured. He immediately carried her into a nearby house and found a physician. Ellen's aunt and uncle were summoned, and a call was placed to Mrs. Dygert in Angola. Mother Dygert insisted that the sedated Ellen return home that very night. Lewis assumed full responsibility when they arrived at the Dygert home at 4:00 A.M. He explained the accident and promised to pay the medical expenses. For the next week he called daily to check on Ellen's progress. The Dygerts were impressed by the way he handled the accident.[18]

The relationship continued to follow an uneven course for the next two years, while Ellen was finishing high school. They saw each other frequently, but neither remained immune to other opportunities. Lewis met new girls at his high school and at Tri-State College. Since he had little money, the idea of marriage seldom entered his mind. As for Ellen, she was already restless with the parochialism of Angola and looking for more adventure before settling down. Her chance came in 1912, when she graduated from high school. Her uncle, Newton Gilbert, had invited her to the Philippines for an extended visit.[19] On 9 June 1913 she left Angola for her big adventure. Ellen lived in Manila from September 1913 until July 1914, and she admitted to Lewis that she did not know "whether I would be contented to come back for any length of time to the quietness and uneventfulness of Steuben County."[20]

Lewis had kept busy during Ellen's absence. Even before she departed he maintained an active correspondence with half a dozen young women, all of whom seemed smitten with his maturity and wisdom. Hazel, Shirley, Carrie, Mabel, Irene, and others insured that his nights would not be lonely. Once he stepped on another man's toes with his flirtations and found himself challenged to a duel.[21]

Despite this female attention, Lewis suffered from depression in Ellen's absence. Her letters left him little reason to be confident about their future together. He seems to have rejected any thought of marriage. With false bravado he urged his friend Paul to play the field and not be trapped by one female. The best thing to do was concentrate on finding a means of livelihood outside of farming. As for women, that problem would take care of itself in time.[22]

After high school graduation Hershey's career opportunities were limited. One easy option was a teaching career. Obtaining a teaching job in rural Indiana before 1910 merely required certification by examination. In 1910, however, the legislature in Indianapolis passed a law requiring at least three months of college, a high school diploma, and a certification exam.

If Lewis was going to teach, he would have to find some way to attend college for three months. Fortunately, a nearby college offered a special three-month teaching course during the summer. Tri-State College in Angola was a small private school established in 1883 by businessmen to provide vocational education. The catalog explained that Tri-State wanted to help students "find their bearings, to know what to do as a life's work." In what was hardly a break with the past, the trustees emphasized that "individual drill is an indispensable condition to successful teaching." They criticized other colleges which were requiring fewer than a dozen recitations per term. Tri-State, in contrast, promised to provide daily drills. The school endeavored to "give a year's discipline in a year." The faculty consisted of about ten men and women. Only two of them held doctorates, but a few had Columbia M.A.'s.[23] Tri-State offered a variety of degree programs. Modern notions of freshman, sophomore, junior, and senior levels were not applied. The three-month summer course covered four subjects: elementary psychology, methods of teaching, grammar, and physiology. The bachelor of science in Pedagogy required thirty-six credits over four years and provided permanent certification for high school teaching. The degree required courses in foreign languages, math, English, science, history, economics, philosophy, and nineteen elective hours.[24]

Early in June 1910 Hershey and his father rode over to Angola to inquire about admission. They were somewhat surprised that no one was around on Saturday, but, after a few inquiries, they ended up at the home of Lester B. Rogers, head of the department of education. Rogers had his M.A. from Columbia and was one of the more promising faculty members at Tri-State. He gave the Hersheys a friendly reception. If Lewis could come up with $15 by the following week, he could begin his three-month program. The following week Lewis returned with his money and began school. He found a room to rent for $1 per week only two blocks from the campus and, for $3, bought a meal ticket at Watson's Restaurant.[25]

During the summer Hershey took four courses. Professor Rogers taught him teaching methods. William A. Fox, another Columbia M.A., taught psychology. Hershey enjoyed this course and began a lifelong interest in psychology. The text used was by Professor William James of Harvard, who had helped to create a new way of viewing human psychology. Professor Frederick Starr, another popular instructor, taught grammar, a review of a subject that Hershey had recently studied in high school. Despite the heavy schedule, his limited funds, and the social life of Angola, Hershey raced through the special course. By September he was eligible to teach, and he accepted a position at Dewey School in Jamestown Township, Steuben County.[26]

Hershey's main recommendation for the job was his size. County supervisors wanted big teachers to provide some discipline in these small rural schools. Teaching in a one-room school in rural Indiana also constituted an intellectual challenge. For a monthly salary of $45 Hershey was required to teach the following subjects: orthography, reading, writing, arithmetic, geography, grammar, language, physiology, U.S. history, literature, music, drawing, and finally, scientific temperance.[27]

This task was herculean. He had fifteen students in six different grades, and he had to conduct the classes simultaneously in one room with one blackboard. If everyone showed up (which was unlikely, because the older boys were still helping to bring in the crop), he also had the problem of maintaining discipline. Generally a good shaking took care of the problems, but occasionally he might use a switch to cure swearing habits. At odd intervals he managed to teach. He organized the students by grades and gave the older ones assignments in reading and writing. With a fine commitment to basics, he insisted that the younger students read aloud at least twice a day. Yet not even John Dewey himself could have made marble out of mud. Most of Hershey's students left school after the fifth grade, undoubtedly having imbibed enough scientific temperance to satisfy themselves and their parents.[28]

Despite these setbacks, Hershey found satisfaction in his time at Dewey. He also impressed the county supervisor, who offered him certification for another twelve months of teaching. But Lewis had saved enough money to reenter Tri-State and, fortunately, by 1912 his father had been elected sheriff. The pay was meager, just over $1,000 a year, but the job included living quarters at the county jail in Angola. Latta offered his son a new opportunity: on 1 January 1913, he hired him as a deputy and provided space at the jail.

For the next two years Lewis had a small income and free board while attending Tri-State.[29] His full-time degree program included the normal courses in chemistry, physics, English, math, and history, but also involved heavy concentrations in German and Latin. He read Cicero, Livy, Caesar, and Horace. For a school that boasted of its vocational orientation, Tri-State was still loaded with the elite requirements of a nineteenth-century college. From 1910 through 1914 Hershey attended thirteen quarters of school. Although originally enrolled in what was called the classical course, in 1912 he switched over to insure that he would have enough credits for the shorter degree in pedagogy.

As financing remained tied to his father's two-year term as sheriff, Lewis was hedging his bets.[30] Although not a "grind," he was a whiz at math and also did well in the humanities. His grades for history, German, biology, philosophy, and chemistry were always in the ninetieth percentile.[31]

Besides doing well with the books, Lewis also became active in extracurricular activities. He was an early version of what became known as a Big Man on Campus. The long hikes to and from Dewey School had prepared him for another try at basketball. The sport at this time was hardly played in the racehorse style which was later identified with the "Hustling Hoosiers." It resembled indoor brawling more than anything else. Lewis made the team and made good use of his bulky frame by providing body blocks on the opposition and snaring rebounds. The scoring was usually below thirty points, and Lewis left many a game with sprained fingers and bruised legs.[32]

He also coached the Tri-State girls' basketball team and became a leading member of the two literary and debating clubs: the Emersonians and the Crescents. In one debate he upheld the negative side of the question: "Resolved, that woman suffrage should be adopted by the Constitution." In his argument he expressed a point of view that he maintained for most of his life. He argued that the ballot would lessen women's influence, rather than increase it. Women already possessed great natural influence in the field of morals. Hershey insisted that when one sex was pitted against the other, the downfall of civilization was near. Women should make their influence felt through their moral power over men. They would be ill suited to the political arena.[33]

Although hardly a first-rate academic institution, Tri-State did provide an opportunity for an ambitious student to master the basics in what then passed for a classical education. Hershey also learned from his experiences in sports and debate. Yet he was hardly the Student Prince at Heidelberg. Angola was a small (under 4,000), parochial, and dry town. The students frequently made a night out of visiting the train station to watch the tourists arrive for vacations at the lakes. But Lewis had other activities to keep him busy, including his work as deputy sheriff. When he graduated with honors in the summer of 1914, with a B.A. degree and a degree in pedagogy, several options were open to him.[34]

At twenty-one, a college graduate, Lewis seemed above average in maturity and talents. He worked at local politics, helping his father win reelection. The work as deputy sheriff provided Lewis with a new experience. Although Steuben County harbored no desperadoes, he was kept active serving papers and subpoenas for testimony, hauling in the local drunks, and breaking up fights. He found the job valuable experience, because he saw several different facets of the human animal. Graduate work in education or law appealed to him, but he lacked funds. Since he had his degree and a ticket into public school teaching, he decided to follow this path of least resistance. Perhaps something else would turn up in the future.[35]

Flint High School needed a principal. The prospect of a career in Flint, "just a place where a few roads crossed each other," hardly stirred his soul, but he took the job. As principal Hershey had responsibility for enforcing county regulations. These rules said much about the ideals of rural Indiana in 1914–16. Students were required to spend no fewer than fifteen minutes each day on writing and spelling. No student was permitted to leave the grounds during recess. Neither student nor teacher was permitted to use tobacco or chewing gum. "Habitual users of cigarettes will not be graduated from high school or grade school," warned the regulations. The rooms were to be kept at 68 to 72 degrees but filled with fresh air during breaks. The county board commended talented teachers who dared to conduct "classes without the textbook in their hands." Teachers were warned not "to keep company with pupils of their room, or with pupils of other rooms in the same school," because such behavior "tend[s] to disorganize and cause unfavorable comment."[36]

At both Dewey and Flint schools Hershey demonstrated a clear aptitude for his job. His program became so popular that parents who had sent their children to bigger schools in neighboring townships decided to return them to Flint. One young woman, who had started teaching at Flint without much self-confidence, thanked him for sympathy and advice which pulled her through. When Hershey was later called for active duty with the National Guard, his students were distraught. Several threatened to quit school unless he returned immediately. When a rumor arose that he would not be back in 1916, the township commissioner made every effort to change Hershey's mind by offering him an additional $25 a month.[37]

Increasingly the community began recognizing Hershey's distinctive abilities. He impressed both sexes with his optimistic disposition. Young women looked upon him as a father figure; young men considered him a natural organizer. With such praise ringing in his ears, it was no wonder that Hershey had confidence in his abilities. Yet he still remained unsure of his role in life. Like Ellen, he had little interest in remaining in Angola and no interest whatever in farming. Politics attracted his attention, and his talents seemed well suited for this game, but he had neither the money not the state connections to advance very rapidly. Teaching suited his bookish inclinations and his gregarious personality. Here again, however, his options were limited, with only a bachelor's degree from Tri-State. If he wished to move beyond rural schools, he would have to take graduate degrees. He could afford to invest the time, but the money to live away from home was not available. One other option remained—a military career through the Indiana National Guard.[38]

The guard had grown rapidly after the labor riots of 1877. Indeed, limited state funds were often supplemented by business donations to sustain this agency for civil order. Membership grew in the late nineteenth century because of the enthusiasm of many Civil War veterans. The guard also served as a fraternal organization, providing fellowship, social activities, and athletic competition. After the Militia Act of 1903 and provision for annual appropriations from Congress, the guard seemed on a solid foundation as a national reserve force. Not until America's entry into World War I, however, did it overcome chronic shortages of men and money.[39]

Angola sponsored Company B, 1st Battalion, 3rd Infantry Regiment of the Indiana National Guard. It was a small organization, consistently undermanned and undertrained, but in a small town such as Angola it represented one of the few institutions with ties to a world of adventure. While such links appealed to young Hershey, he was also influenced by other considerations. In February 1911 Ellen had informed him of her plans to visit Uncle Newton in the Philippines. On 16 February he traveled to Angola and took the oath. Since he was only seventeen years old, he first obtained his father's permission. Although hardly the equivalent of joining the French foreign legion, the gesture was influenced by Ellen's decision and by Lewis's desire to achieve a visible sign of manhood.[40]

Membership in the guard was a mixed blessing. He had to travel five miles into Angola to attend the weekly meetings, but he gloried in his uniform and enjoyed the male camaraderie. For the most part the duty was not onerous. Weekly drills were supplemented by occasional visits to the rifle range. Hershey did better at pasting targets than at firing a rifle. The pay of ten cents per drill provided little incentive, but the guard did offer occasional adventure. Each summer the boys entrained for ten days in camp near bustling Indianapolis.[41]

Lewis once traveled to Indianapolis for more serious duty. The governor had declared martial law in response to labor unrest, and in November 1913 the guard, true to its calling, came in to keep order. The troops camped outside of town and waited as arbitration took place. Hershey warned his relatives that, if negotiations failed, the guard would probably take over the town. When he took out a scout squad of six men for a brief reconnoiter, he was surprised at their unfriendly reception from the citizens. With only 2,000 troops on duty and 300,000 citizens to deal with, Hershey became apprehensive about his task. Fortunately, the strike was soon settled, and his unit returned to its desultory drill in Angola.[42]

Despite his failures as a marksman, Lewis made rapid progress within the ranks. His physical size, plus his general organizational talents, served him well. On 10 June 1912 he was promoted to corporal, and in May 1913 he received his sergeant stripes. Not satisfied, he aimed at a commission as a second lieutenant. Under state law this grade was filled through election by members of the company. To exploit an opening in the summer of 1913, Lewis began using the political savvy he had picked up from his father. The competition for the office was vigorous and included the captain's brother. Lewis Kosch became Hershey's campaign manager. All of Hershey's friends in the company, some of whom had not been to drill for months, received notes encouraging them to show up for the vote and offering them free board at the jail. After nine ballots, these efforts paid off. Hershey obtained a majority and his lieutenancy; his commission was dated 17 June 1913.[43]

For the next few years, while finishing school at Tri-State and teaching, Lewis remained active in the guard. Jesse Covell was the captain and in command, but Hershey became an active assistant. His job entailed responsibility for obtaining uniforms and equipment for all men in the unit. He also began a task which later became his specialty: recruitment. Then, and later, it proved a frustrating job.[44]

While Hershey was busy organizing Company B, President Woodrow Wilson was busy organizing Mexico. The Mexican Revolution of 1910 had upset the orderly, if expensive, dictatorship of Porfirio Diaz. In his place had appeared the charismatic Francisco Madero. In the turmoil of the revolutionary settlement Madero died at the hands of one of his generals, Victoriano Huerta. Into this cockpit of controversy stepped Wilson, dedicated to insuring that the Mexican people received the honest, democratic government he thought they so richly deserved. Refusing to recognize the murderous Huerta, the United States provided arms for Venustiano Carranza, another rebel leader. After military intervention at Veracruz and a conference of Argentina, Brazil, and Chile, Huerta had had enough. To Wilson's disappointment, however, Carranza proved just as unsatisfactory. When a new rebel general, Pancho Villa, appeared in the field, Wilson at first offered his support. He soon changed his mind after Villa began raiding border towns and killing American citizens. By 1916 Wilson had convinced Carranza of the wisdom of allowing General Jack Pershing and 15,000 American soldiers to seek out Villa in northern Mexico. As a supplement to this expedition, Wilson also decided to federalize several National Guard units for border duty along the Rio Grande. The Indiana National Guard had the dubious distinction of being one of the units activated.

Hershey, a loyal Republican, had little affection for Woodrow Wilson, but from the environs of northeast Indiana the messy turmoil with Mexico appeared more serious than it was. One of Hershey's girlfriends asked him to bring her an Indian blanket and "one of Villa's brain pieces;" such were the sentiments which sent Americans to the border. The order to activate came on 19 June 1916. With all the efficiency of the Keystone Kops, Company B prepared to defend the country against Mexican bandits. Hershey supervised the posting of handbills throughout the county calling for volunteers. Much cheering was heard, but few recruits appeared. When his unit marched to entrain on 24 June, the company remained three men under strength. As though to make up for their lack of valor, the townspeople of Angola turned out to give the boys a rousing sendoff. Two bands played martial music, sometimes simultaneously, as Lieutenant Hershey left Angola on the first great adventure of his life.[45]

After a few days in Indianapolis to join up with the 1st Battalion, Hershey and his unit boarded a train for the trip south. Leaving St. Louis, he had his first view of the American South, a land he had learned of through Civil War literature. The large number of blacks impressed him, as did the fertility of the soil. The troop train moved south at a leisurely 40 miles per hour, and the enthusiasm of the civilian population grew as the troops neared the border. Every crossroads in Texas seemed to have a crowd of flagwavers who frequently provided fresh produce for the boys. By 11 July the troops had reached Harlingen and immediately pushed on to their camp at Llano Grande. As they attempted clumsily to detrain, the first rain in thirteen months began to fall.[46]

In the next several weeks Hershey grew a mustache and fell in love with army life. The land between Harlingen and McAllen on the Rio Grande in southeast Texas is one of the more unlikely tourist spots on the face of the earth. The temperature in the summer averages in the nineties; mosquitoes plague all warm-blooded creatures. In dry weather the soil generates dust storms; in wet, a quagmire. Poverty abounds. To make matters worse, the troops had been sent down with little planning. The absence of a water supply at camp made sanitation a problem. Pit latrines became dicey in the heat. The men lacked tents, cots, cooking utensils, and other essential items. Hershey lamented the "utter unpreparedness" of the nation. "It makes a person wonder," he wrote, "what in the world the U.S. would do if they were faced by a real invasion by a real country." No ammunition had been issued, but, upon reflection, Hershey thought this was the safer course. The danger from Mexicans seemed more remote than danger from armed recruits.[47]

Soon the people back home in Angola began to hear rumors of the confusion on the border. Hershey wrote to the local paper in hopes of correcting some of the disillusionment and ending some of the rumors. He admitted that conditions were not what they should be, but he insisted that the blame for such problems rested not on the War Department, or on the guard, but upon the American people. Politicians had insisted that the nation could face any emergency by a "clarion call to arms." The one big lesson of this expedition, wrote Hershey, was that such an approach would not work. If the citizens of Indiana had paid more attention to the militia, the existing shortages would not have arisen. But, like other Americans, Hoosiers forgot that they had citizen soldiers. Many of the men on the border had come to the conclusion that "there is one way to take care of the defense question and that is by universal military service of some kind." Already Hershey had become totally disillusioned with the voluntary system of raising troops.[48]

Within a few days the camp had a source of clean water and Hershey ended his diet of lemonade. While most of his colleagues continued to grouse in the traditional manner of soldiers everywhere, Hershey counted his blessings: "I have enjoyed every hour, and would not change places with any man, woman, or child in the state of Indiana." He even enjoyed the climate, especially the cool nights and warm days. The campfires with the sound of off-key singing appealed to his sense of fellowship. He literally pitied the boys back home who had passed up this opportunity. They had missed a wonderful chance to prove their manhood. In his diary he expressed confidence that he would measure up to the needs of the hour. The tour would be a test of whether he could soldier for a living.[49]

In contrast to his colleagues from Indiana and most Texans, Hershey refused to swallow a racist stereotype of Mexicans. He rejected the popular notion that Pancho Villa represented all Mexicans. To become more knowledgeable about local problems he began studying Spanish. His social forays (an occasional dance at the Mercedes Hotel) brought him into contact with Mexican girls. To his surprise, he found a self-satisfaction among Mexicans, despite their poverty, that seemed absent among more affluent Anglos. He did some superficial research and noted the poverty and large families. He concluded that only education could uplift these people. Not realizing that they were American born in many cases, he insisted that U.S. citizenship was out of the question as long as they could not speak English.[50]

In campfire colloquia, the troops discussed subjects later to be of more than passing concern to Hershey. Someone wanted deferments from military service for all college men. Hershey agreed that college was a good thing, but he considered it preposterous to offer students immunity from military service. The college man was just an ordinary citizen and owed his country as much as anyone else. Education, he explained, "should be training in living and if going to college does not train him in living, and one essential in this life is patriotism, then it were better for civilization in general that he had never gone to college at all."[51] Hershey became convinced that a tour in the service would help top off any education.

He obtained more and more responsibility for his unit. When Captain Covell took leave, Hershey, already a first lieutenant, assumed command. Just as he began to enjoy the command, however, the colonel picked him to return to Indiana.[52] In late August and September Hershey assumed duties as a recruiting officer for southern Indiana, with headquarters in New Albany. This town, across the Ohio River from Louisville, proved a stony soil for Hershey's recruiting seeds. The general apathy of the populace also convinced him that only "a national degradation" would wake America to the need for building up the army.[53] He rented rooms for $3 a week, paid 25 cents each day for his meals, found an office at the YMCA, and waited in vain for recruits. The interest in Mexico waned. Hershey blamed "extreme individualism—all attention directed to the promotion of private fortunes and private interests." By 3 October he had managed to find four recruits. In desperation Hershey hired a band and speakers to promote enlistment, but he still found little military interest in this community, which he described as filled with too many German-Americans. His attitude toward volunteer service would be long conditioned by this failure in New Albany.[54] Hershey had joined the guard to relieve his own romantic frustration and to seek adventure, but now he came to believe it had all been an act of patriotism.

He was soon distracted by the 1916 presidential race between President Wilson and Charles Evans Hughes, his Republican challenger. Hershey traveled down to Hodgenville, Kentucky, the site of Lincoln's birth, to hear President Wilson. The president spoke forcefully, but Hershey remained a Hughes man. Besides having learned Republicanism from birth, Hershey opposed the Democrats in 1916 because of their vacillating policy on preparedness. His own recruiting efforts were being undercut by announcements from Washington that 15,000 National Guardsmen were soon to be sent home. The major drawing card in the recruiting game had been a free trip south. Now the War Department had withdrawn this prospect. Finally, on 23 September, Hershey traveled up to Indianapolis to hear candidate Hughes. Not surprisingly, Hershey was favorably impressed with his sincerity and naturalness, in contrast to Wilson's artificiality.[55]

With recruits nonexistent and the War Department committed to reducing tension with Mexico, Hershey was not surprised on 9 October 1916 to receive orders to close his office and return to Texas. Before returning, however, he visited his family in Angola. By 23 October he was headed back to the Mexican border. The camp at Llano Grande had improved since his departure; the tents now had wood floors, and everyone slept in cots. Hershey, with renewed affection for the border, expressed a willingness to stay the winter.[56]

Few of his comrades shared such enthusiasm for the area. The main problem was the absence of any threat from Mexico and the resultant boredom of camp life. Hershey blamed the morale crisis on the inactivity and on using volunteers. On 18 November, when word arrived that the unit would soon be returning home, Hershey had mixed feelings and even hoped he would be the last to leave, but he was on the train on 4 December as it headed toward Houston. The return to Indiana took the men through New Orleans. Having already smuggled liquor onto the train, the troops were in a fine mood to enjoy this wide-open city. Hershey, Covell, and Kosch took advantage of a layover to tour the Paris of the New World.[57]

After New Orleans the troops headed home. Hershey did not expect much of a reception from the citizens of Indiana, and he was not disappointed. The governor did provide a reception on 11 December. Badges commemorating border service were handed out to the accompaniment of several longwinded addresses. William Dudley Foulke read what Hershey called a "well composed and appropriate ode" for the occasion. As the troops marched through the semi-deserted streets, Hershey reflected: "Either we must pass laws that shall provide for some form of compulsory training or we will be compelled to about face and dispense with our armaments altogether." If the nation chose disarmament, he felt it would be a clear sign of "decadence."[58]

This tour of the border contributed greatly to Hershey's maturity. He had demonstrated his ability to shoulder the responsibility of military duty in the field. Thanks to Covell's frequent absences, he had several chances to command troops. He became something of a father figure, loaning them money and writing their letters home for them.

Hershey discovered that he immensely enjoyed this type of life. The experience had also convinced him that the American public could be shaken out of its apathy toward world events only by the most direct action. Preparedness had been a sham. His association with the voluntary system of recruitment left him convinced of the need for some sort of compulsory draft. Finally, although always sympathetic to the National Guard, he realized that a military career would require his transfer to the regular forces.[59] But an appointment to the army seemed very unlikely in January 1917. Instead, he decided to enter graduate school at Indiana University.[60]

The idea of attending graduate school had first occurred to Hershey in September 1916, during a visit to the campus. Recruiting was a bust, and he was having serious doubts about his future in the military service. The army had its allurements "and were I younger I am sure I would give it more serious consideration." He recognized, however, that his age and his "love of politics" made him unfit for the army. After canvasing his options, he decided to continue his education. His old professor at Tri-State, W. O. Bailey, cooperated by sending transcripts and a letter of recommendation to the dean of education.[61] On 29 January Hershey left Angola again to assume a new role.

Indiana University had been founded in 1820 as a multipurpose institution for the entire state. By 1917 it had grown from a sleepy midwestern school to a thriving academic community of 2,000 students. Several of its graduate programs enjoyed high reputations. The Bloomington area, bordering on Brown County, remains one of the most appealing regions in the state, covered with trees, rolling hills, and quiet brooks. When Lewis Hershey stepped off the train in Bloomington he was twenty-four years old and still looking for a career. Carrying introductions from his county superintendent of education, he made his way to the dean's office. Dean H. L. Smith gave the budding student permission to take whatever courses he wished and to enroll for up to eighteen hours, a rather heavy load of graduate work.[62]

Ellen, who had returned home and renewed her romance with Lewis, had doubts about his new adventure; she expressed reluctance to see him leave Angola and set up house among all the pretty coeds. Aunt Alma and Latta wanted him to return and take up farming. But Lewis soon became absorbed in the routine and challenge of his six courses— four in education, plus Spanish and economics. Despite the heavy responsibility, he was confident that "so long as my health and eyes are alright, I can carry any subject I have if the majority of the class can." His course in the history of education appealed to him because the professor's ideas were "modern and progressive." His other education courses included one on crime and penology, another on educational psychology, and one on secondary education. As usual, he made excellent grades.[63]

Not even the most diligent student, however, could shun all recreation. Hershey tried the Christian Church social but did not stay long. More entertaining were the basketball games. After watching Indiana beat Butler 18-9, Hershey criticized the team for wild running and wild shooting.[64]

Above all, he read. The opportunity for serious reading in education, which in turn led to self-analysis, was IU's main contribution to Hershey's development. His readings in educational psychology, especially the works of William James, continued to influence him in later life. He came to accept fully the unified notion of personality which James propounded. He read on history and educational methods.[65] His grades were good but, before he could finish the semester, outside events upset his plans.[66]

The world took on a new stridency in the spring of 1917. The outbreak of a European war in 1914 had caused barely a murmur in the secure little world of Indiana. True, President Wilson had proclaimed neutrality, a move much applauded in an isolationist-inclined Midwest. Hershey and his friends in the guard disliked Wilson, not because of his neutrality, but because of his refusal to promote preparedness. By 1917, events seemed to be pulling the recently reelected Wilson into a European maelstrom. On 1 February the German High Command announced the resumption of unrestricted submarine warfare. Since Wilson had warned in May 1916 that such a resumption would lead to severance of relations, few were surprised when he took this step on 3 February. Americans then waited for the dropping of the other shoe—a declaration of war. Weeks passed, however, with no sign that Wilson would take that step. Then, on 1 March, the government released the text of a telegram by German Foreign Secretary Arthur Zimmermann to his ambassador in Mexico. The message proposed an alliance with Mexico in the event that the United States declared war on Germany. After bitter debate Congress approved the arming of American merchant ships. Wilson's call for war seemed imminent.

Such events distracted Hershey from graduate school. In Angola his National Guard unit had resumed drills and expected to be federalized in the near future. Hershey could not merely sit on the sidelines in what might be the great event of the century. He immediately inquired as to what part of his coursework could be salvaged if he had to rejoin his unit. He convinced the university to promote a military drill unit among the students, and once again he was disappointed in the reaction of civilians to military needs. On 7 March, after considerable promotion, only 130 men showed up for drill. Hershey felt this was another sign of the dearth of patriotism. "I fear for my land," he sermonized, "when this represents their flower of manhood." As for himself, with a naivete which trench warfare was curing among Europeans, Hershey looked forward to American involvement. When offered a teaching job for the fall, he rejected it out of hand because he had other plans.[67]

II. A Military Career, 1917–36

March 1917 passed without a declaration of war. Lewis Hershey kept active with the drills at Indiana University and had his military kit sent to him. The future was filled with uncertainty, but he felt that the war scare had been good for the country. The awakening of America might at least lead to preparedness which would provide safety for the future. Uncertainty ended for Hershey and millions of others when Wilson sent a message to Congress on 2 April asking for a declaration of war.[1] On 4 April Hershey left Bloomington with vague hopes that he might someday return to finish work on his master's degree.[2]

The Indiana National Guard was not called to federal duty for six months. Hershey kept busy by promoting enlistments in his unit, traveling throughout the region and giving talks on why men should join the National Guard. Occasionally his off-key baritone would join in the chorus of a popular ditty: "We're the boys from old Angola—We'll help humanity—to whip the German Kaiser—So the World will have democracy—and life in Peace and Freedom." Despite the high spirits, recruitment again proved slow.[3] Hershey's zeal for service, at the expense of schooling and sweetheart, proved the exception in 1917.

On 18 May Congress passed the Selective Service Act, requiring registration and service from all men between ages twenty-one and thirty. Wilson euphemistically called this "mass volunteering," but Hershey knew better. He approved of the draft because the voluntary approach had failed; time and again he had been unable to find recruits. Now he saw that the draft might fail as well. His stomach turned at the many claims for exemptions on what he considered "ludicrous grounds." Such claims proved his conclusion that the war was needed. "When that spirit of responsibility dodging is abroad to so large an extent," he wrote sententiously, "it certainly seems that only a war with all its horrors can awake us to our obligations."[4]

Waiting for Washington to make up its mind and federalize the guard, Hershey spent his time in drilling and in polishing equipment.[5] By 9 August he had taken his physical in South Bend. He stood 72½ inches tall and weighed 172 pounds. At last, on 10 August, he was mustered into United States service. Next came shots for smallpox and typhoid, French lessons, and additional shots.[6]

Hershey was happy when orders finally arrived. His unit was being sent first to Indianapolis and then to Camp Shelby, outside Hattiesburg, Mississippi. A crowd gathered on 10 September to see the unit off. The boys entrained for Indianapolis, consoled by box lunches provided by the ladies of the Christian Church. Considering the general shortage of military clothing, belts, bayonets, and cots, they were lucky to get the lunches. After a short stop in Indianapolis for bayonet practice and work with horses, the unit was converted to the 137th Field Artillery, 38th Division, National Guard of the United States and sent to Mississippi.[7]

The conversion to artillery appealed to Hershey, although he had never touched a cannon until his arrival at Shelby. Even here such weapons were a rare commodity. His entire regiment of over 1,000 men had only two guns and six caissons. Each battery had three horses. He was assigned as a reconnaissance officer for Battery C. After two weeks' work he had become so enamoured of his new role that he wrote: "An officer should have no time of his own, he is entitled to none. . . . The extent to which you can surrender yourself to your duty in a large measure determines your worth."

Fine words, but Hershey was already thinking of nonmilitary matters. He had written his father on the advisability of investing some of his pay in farmland around Angola.[8] If the war ended quickly, he had hopes of returning to Indiana University to finish his graduate work. But even more important to Hershey than a farm or graduate work was his on again, off again relationship with Ellen. The time had come to put his private life in order.[9]

Hershey never did buy the farm, nor did he return to graduate school. He did marry Ellen Dygert. For Ellen, life had become more prosaic since her trip to the Philippines. She returned to Angola and took classes at Tri-State in 1914–15 but did not take a degree. As Lewis began teaching, Ellen became desperate to escape Angola. Marriage seemed an unlikely exit. Lewis had little money saved; furthermore, his attitude toward marriage was practical in the extreme. He considered marriage perpetual and had no wish to take such a decisive step until his expectations were greater. Ellen became irritated at this practicality. In 1916 she was twenty-four years old, receiving solicitations from a matrimonial agency and worrying about the danger of spinsterhood. Her old friends had left the single state. While Lewis was in Texas, Ellen found a job as an assistant to the local surgeon. The work proved so fascinating that in 1917 she decided to enter nursing school in Chicago. With only single girls allowed in nurse's training and Lewis's commitment to graduate school, prospects of marriage began to fade.[10]

Among other things, however, America's entry into the war had a significant effect on the Hershey romance. When Lewis prepared to depart for training in Mississippi, Ellen offered encouragement. Still exhibiting the romantic view which had carried her through the Philippine adventure, she rejoiced in his marching off to war. In her mind he was leaving to play an active role "in a mighty conflict that no one knows when or how it will end. . . . I can't believe your part will be a small one for I believe that you have it in you to do things that count." Lewis shared this sense of adventure, but he also hoped to keep Ellen secure at her training in Chicago. He sent her an occasional check to help with expenses.[11]

Although he had departed for war without proposing, Hershey soon began to reconsider. In what must go down in history as one of the least romantic proposals ever made, he wrote to Ellen on 30 October 1917, explaining his decision by referring to, of all things, a recent congressional enactment of insurance for soldiers. He wanted to take advantage of the insurance and wanted to name Ellen as his beneficiary. The law, however, prohibited him from naming her unless she was his wife. As he lamely explained, "I will admit that it may seem a rather sordid reason for speaking of matrimony, but I believe you are entitled to some consideration." He thought it best to take precautions which would net her $75 a month in the event of his death.[12]

Ellen had waited a long time for this proposal and had no inclination to reject it, however "sordid" the tone. She telegraphed her plans to arrive in Jackson, Mississippi, on 29 November. Lewis immediately purchased the license. When Ellen arrived, Lewis took her straight to the First Christian Church and to the consummation of a relationship which had been seven years in fruition. The next day they left for a honeymoon in New Orleans. By 2 December Ellen was on the Panama Limited, headed back to Chicago and school. The marriage was kept secret from nursing school officials.[13]

Lewis returned to his full-time military duty. He attended classes on the firing of the famous French 75mm. As the mild but damp Mississippi winter hit the camp, the army was ill prepared. Many men continued to live in tents, and the supply of winter clothing was inadequate. Altogether Hershey felt that only Charles Dickens "could describe the madhouse." In March the troops began instruction in the use of gas masks. A French officer appeared to lecture them on the features of German artillery. Hershey's performance in camp was superior, and he was selected as one of the first officers to attend the ten-week course at the army's School of Fire in Fort Sill, Oklahoma.[14] The School of Fire had the reputation of being a vigorous test for young officers. Work began at 7:00 A.M. and continued until 11:00 P.M. The officers were constantly at firing points and engaging in physical training under the violent Oklahoma sun, where temperatures could reach 115 degrees. Besides firing, the troops had to attend classes requiring mathematical problem-solving.[15]

Despite these rumored rigors, Hershey arrived in Oklahoma on 23 March in high spirits. As for the school, he believed "that the big idea is not to lose your goat and I have decided to keep mine firmly tied." Soon he was doing so well that he expected to be selected as an instructor for future classes. For recreation there was always the city of Lawton. The town had grown up around the base and was so depressing that Hershey admitted he even began to find Indian women attractive.[16] In his spare time he reflected on the sloppy way in which America had mobilized. He was gratified, however, that Indiana had closed all breweries, distilleries, and saloons. He hoped it would be a permanent measure, and that the people would be educated to insist upon enforcement of prohibition.[17]

Time moved quickly at Fort Sill, but Hershey remained impatient. He was being considered for promotion to the rank of captain. He fired artillery problems, visited Lawton, played golf, and saw his first game of polo. While returning from the firing range one day he had an accident. Riding in the back of a truck, he attempted to jump off while the vehicle was slowing down. As he tried to swing free from the gate, his heel caught. The wheel of the truck passed over his left leg. Amazingly, he felt no pain and managed to rise to his feet and stagger to the sidewalk. His leg then began to ache. Friends carried him to the infirmary but found no one on duty. He then walked home unaided and took a hot bath. Finally the medical officer arrived to inspect the damage wrought by a two-ton truck. To his surprise, the leg was not broken. The next morning Hershey found his leg black and blue and stiff, but it soon was as good as new. Although his good fortune was difficult to explain, he became convinced that his new vegetarian diet had helped save him from a nasty break.[18]

A few days later, on 27 May, he received an official wire from the War Department announcing his promotion to the rank of captain. On 29 May he graduated from the School of Fire and departed for Angola. At home by 1 June, he and Ellen sent out official announcements of their marriage. Ellen had now given up hopes of a nursing career because of a continuing problem with her feet. While at home, Hershey visited with friends and pushed patriotism. He was happy to see that many former pacifists had changed their tunes. On 8 June he boarded the train for his return to Camp Shelby without Ellen.[19]

Hershey assumed duties as the division personnel officer. He was ready to go to war. At twenty-four he was the picture of health, carrying 179 pounds lightly on his broad frame. His physical examination revealed a steady pulse of 72, a robust heartbeat, and generally sound health. There were no after-effects from his accident. Rumors began circulating that the unit would soon be heading for Europe. Hershey prepared his trunk locker and bedroll for immediate departure, but— as was so often the case—he found himself waiting around. He was now regimental adjutant for the 137th and had the responsibility of training the 344 new recruits who came into the unit. He sold his horse, paid off his bonds, made out an allotment of $175 per month for Ellen and stood ready to depart. On 9 September the unit finally left for New York.[20]

Arriving at Camp Mills, Long Island, on 12 September, the young man from rural Indiana experienced a sense of dislocation. The Statue of Liberty, the Singer and Woolworth skyscrapers, were "in many ways the most imposing sight[s] I had ever seen." After reaching Camp Mills the men immediately headed for the bright lights. With $90 in his pocket Hershey rode into town and took a room at the Hotel Madison. Strolling through the city he was overwhelmed with the vast number of houses and buildings and with the alien population. "New York is large, very large," he wrote, and "she is just as Jewish as she is large." For the next few days he continued his inspection of New York. The more he saw, the less he liked, and the more he became convinced of the virtues of small-town America. He visited Chinatown, Little Italy, the Bowery ghettos "alive with Jews." The streets were littered with paper and fruit peelings. He enjoyed his visit to the Metropolitan Museum of Art, but New York did not seem a safe place.[21] He worried as the evil influence of the city seemed to be affecting his unit. He condemned fellow officers who disgraced themselves by riotous living. Night after night the men engaged in wild parties where illegal liquor flowed. Hershey could not understand how "those who have for thirty years or more lived a normal, decent existence" would now go crazy with fast women.[22]

Hershey cursed the delay in embarkation. Not only was it undermining morality in the unit, but it was also preventing him from reaching the war before the fighting ended. In the summer of 1918 the Germans had been thrown back at the Second Battle of the Marne. Field Marshal Ferdinand Foch had launched a counteroffensive with newly arrived American troops. As Hershey sat around in New York, American units attacked on both sides of the St. Mihiel salient. The United States was finally making a contribution, much to Hershey's gratification. He remained disturbed at the lethargy of the American masses, unaccustomed as they were "to thinking in national terms, let alone international." The war was changing America. "Personally," he wrote from the safety of New York, "I am a strong believer in the ultimate good that shall arise from the war, no matter how long it may be prolonged." Hershey was infected with Wilson's idealism. Although he denied expecting the war to end all wars, he did think it would "remove many of the superficial things that have over-crowded our existence."[23]

On a cloudy 29 September he shipped out with his unit on the liner Aquitania. No crowds cluttered the dock as the ship pulled out, but Hershey, with his Sam Browne belt and overseas cap firmly in place, felt very settled about the world. Remaining settled proved difficult during the crossing. Although German submarines were no longer a menace, the weather in the North Atlantic was foul. Not far from its landfall in England, the liner made news by cutting through the destroyer U.S.S. Shaw, with the loss of fifteen seamen but no damage to the liner. In Southampton Hershey spent twenty-four hours exploring. The exotic sights in camp intrigued the young soldier from Angola: Scottish officers running around in kilts, British officers with a superficial air. He never did develop a rapport with his British colleagues, whom he found "clingers to many things that to us appear trifling."[24]

While Hershey was still on the high seas, the German and Austrian governments appealed to President Wilson for an armistice. On 4 October the Central Powers accepted the Fourteen Points as a basis for peace. The war, however, continued for several weeks as notes were exchanged. At the same time the Allies continued their advance against a rapidly disintegrating German army.

These issues were played out far above the perspective of Captain Hershey. He arrived at Le Havre, France, on 11 October and immediately formed a good opinion of the rolling farmland and the narrow streets, compared to the "over systematized plots" of American cities. He reported to a French artillery school at Mauron, Morbihan. This region of southern Brittany was his home for several weeks. For four hours in the morning and two in the afternoon he went to school with the French 75mm. In his spare time he visited the cathedral at Vannes and began to read the history of the country. He hoped to be at the front soon.[25]

Hershey's enthusiasm for battle seems archaic to the modern mind, but he had been trained for battle. This conflict was the first international event in his life. It had taken him out of a vocational rut and given some larger purpose to his life. His experience pointed to engaging the enemy in battle, yet fate then tossed him a joker. On 30 October he awoke with a sore throat and fever; his tonsils felt swollen. At the infirmary his problem was diagnosed as diphtheria. The remedy included several shots with an antitoxin, and for the next twenty-four hours he became delirious with a high fever. By 2 November he was much improved and slept well, but he had to stay in the hospital. In a state of profound frustration he heard the news of the German surrender. On November 11 at 11:00 A.M. all fighting ceased. Hershey had missed the fighting, a disappointment which would irritate him for the rest of his life. Now he reconciled himself to the thought that several major problems remained unsettled. "If allied armies are stationed in Germany or even left here," he wrote, "the problem of discipline has not as yet begun." Perhaps he could still find a role for himself.[26]

As thousands of American boys raced to the embarkation ports, Hershey decided to see Europe. This decision reflected a sense of adventure and ambition rather remarkable in a recently married man. With most of the troops desperate to return home and with the American public clamoring for immediate demobilization, the appearance of a young, capable officer seeking to extend his tour was unusual. Hershey's unit received orders on 29 November 1918 to prepare for embarkation. With good recommendations from his regimental commanders, Hershey finally succeeded in obtaining a transfer to American Expeditionary Headquarters at Brest, with the assignment of transportation officer. From 9 December 1918 to 21 September 1919 he worked at providing shipping for the thousands of American troops seeking passage home.[27]

Duty in Brest was not a soft assignment. The harbor itself was a majestic sight, with high rocks rising on both sides of the channel and forming a great arch embracing the bay. The city rose on terraces from the docks. Hershey, at first impressed with the lush fields of Brittany, soon discovered why everything seemed lush. Brest, he complained, "has only two kinds of days: rainy and misty." For most of the year he worked in a sea of muck. It was hectic work, embarking 100,000 troops in fifteen days on one occasion. He watched famous people pass through the harbor, including President Wilson, Secretary of War Baker, and General Pershing, as the peace conference began in January 1919. Hershey's hours depended upon the availability of ships. Many of the troop ships were too big to reach the dock, so troops had to be taken out by tenders.[28]

Storms provided a challenge to loading men, but he soon became bored. The entire process seemed oversystematized. For days on end no boat would appear in the harbor. Hershey filled his off-duty hours with an occasional game of basketball at the local YMCA, one of the few places where he could take a shower. The girls of the Red Cross unit proved very congenial, and dances were held at the officer's club. Within a matter of weeks several of his old friends from the Indiana National Guard had arrived in Brest. Lewis F. Kosch swung a transfer and joined Hershey in the transportation office. The two finally ventured beyond the sheltered existence of the YMCA and officer's clubs. On 24 December Hershey dined for the first time at a small French restaurant. With a vegetarian diet and limited ability in French, Hershey dined modestly on consomme, bread, fried potatoes, small peas, and celery salad.[29]

Hershey disliked the typical American doughboy who raced back home, cursing France and its culture. He felt that such an attitude was the result of trying to see France through American eyes. "America is young," he wrote, "and has a badly overgrown case of ego." She had much to learn from France and from the recent conflict. Hershey now set about learning as much as he could. He began reading European history and studying French. On a more practical level, he opened a bank account with 600 francs.[30] Increasingly, he mingled with the natives. His first associations occurred during dances sponsored by the officer's club. American women were scarce but French women plentiful. He became a regular patron.[31]

As Hershey became more accustomed to the language and the food, his quarters in a tin-roofed temporary building seemed less and less suitable. Several of his fellow officers had moved in with local families who were eager to supplement their incomes with boarders.[32] Could this Indiana farmboy, who not only refused to eat meat but also disapproved of drinking and smoking, live with a French family? He decided to try.[33] In February 1919 he and Kosch sought out a suitable French family. After obtaining a recommendation from the YMCA, they visited the home of Joseph Hirsch, an agent of a Zurich insurance company who lived at 98 Rue de Liam with his wife and their three teenage children—Marguerite Marie, Pierre, and Marie Therese. The charm of the family and the coincidental similarities in family names led Hershey to accept their accommodations. He took a room on the fourth floor. To help with the house Madame Hirsch employed two maids, one of whom served Hershey a continental breakfast each morning. None of the Hirsches spoke English.[34]

The Hirsch family must have had occasional second thoughts about their new boarder. The huge red-haired American seemed to have odd habits, abstaining from tobacco, alcohol, and meat. Yet in the ensuing months the family came to adopt him. Hershey, for his part, was never the same after his life with the Hirsches. At first he was somewhat shocked at the women drinking and smoking and the riotous behavior of the children, but eventually he came to respect their sense of play as "wholesome." Soon he joined them in fishing, tennis, and attending local musical plays. Although he continued his abstentions, he began to appreciate the French view of wine as a natural accompaniment to any meal. Hershey wondered whether any family in Angola would have opened its doors to a stranger as the Hirsches had opened their home to him. The French lacked the American hustle and bustle, but "I am convinced that much of our hustle gets us nowhere that we want to be."[35]

Above all, Hershey began to lose some of his native prudery. Like many American men, he had learned to wrap sex in plain brown paper, to accept a double standard. At first he was slightly shocked at the frankness with which the French, especially the females, approached this taboo topic. Not only did they wear revealing bathing suits at the beach, but they thought nothing improper about visiting the hotel rooms of young men. At one hotel the girls had rooms on the same floor as the young officers. "This would be an impossible situation in the States," Hershey explained. On mixed social occasions Hershey was startled to see postcards that in America would be labeled obscene, such as Big Bertha Krupp squatting over the channel at Calais, defecating shells on the English. He attended a French comedy which presented an adulterous relationship as acceptable.[36]

At first shocked at the French attitude and convinced that it would never work in the States, Hershey eventually came to applaud the lack of hypocrisy. Above all, he was amazed at the French sense of play. He hardly became a libertine as a consequence of this exposure to French life, but his views became a bit less narrow. As he wrote after witnessing a drinking party which would have been called the work of the Devil in Angola: "The older I grow, the less ability I have in deciding some of these weighty questions."[37]

Life with the Hirsches had its charm, but Hershey had stayed over to see more of Europe than the rocky coast of Brest. On 14 May 1919 he took leave with Kosch to visit the rest of the country. They headed by train toward the City of Lights, arrived at Gare Montparnasse on 15 May and took rooms at the Hotel du Louvre. Like men the world over, Hershey admired the physical beauty of Paris as his bus tour wound its way around the Place de la Concorde, the Arch de Triomphe, the Eiffel Tower (still unfinished), and, outside the city, to Versailles. Jostling with other tourists, he pushed his way into the Folies Bergère at night and was disappointed with the show. Walking back to the hotel, they fought off female prostitutes, male solicitors, and peddlers of dirty books.[38]

The tourists soon left by the Gare de L'Est for the north of France and the battlefields. From Chateau Thierry to Epernay, to Chalons and Verdun, they found scenes fresh with reminders of battle. Rheims Cathedral was in ruins. Carnage surrounded the Verdun fortress. For miles their train rolled through deserted country, wrecked cities. The scene greatly impressed Hershey. He became convinced that no price was too great to pay to insure that war was fought on some other nation's territory. This attitude was reinforced when he passed into Germany at Coblenz and Cologne and found little evidence of conflict. After a brief trip to Bonn, Brussels, and a trip to Waterloo field, their tour took them by way of Ypres and Arras back to Paris. Even the secular Hershey was impressed with "the awe to be had as one walks about under [Notre Dame's] high domes." In late May Hershey returned to his room with the Hirsches where he immediately fell ill. The medic suggested that he may have picked up venereal disease while on leave. Hershey scoffed at the idea and cured himself with Epsom salts.[39]

In August Hershey again took leave to visit England and Ireland. Rolling into Victoria Station, he booked a room at the Washington Inn and set out to see the sights. After a quick view of Parliament, Buckingham Palace, St. Paul's, and Westminster, he booked passage on 1 September for Edinburgh. Although impressed by this Scottish city, he pressed on to Ireland. In Dublin he found the station alive with "dirty, yelling urchins, thin faced women and red nosed men." Eventually finding a room at the Abbotsford Hotel, he took a tour of Trinity College and attended a vaudeville show at the Hippodrome. Soon he was deep in conversation with a Sinn Feiner on the subject of Irish independence. Without settling the problem, he embarked on the Royal Mail Packet for the trip back to England and thence to France. By 6 September he was home in Brest.[40]

The European tour left Hershey with several convictions about the course of American foreign policy and the prospects for his own future. Like many of his generation, he had looked upon America's entry into the war as a blessing which would provide unity and spiritual renewal to a country threatened with the rot of materialism. His failure to reach the front, to engage in this alleged noble endeavor, left him with guilt feelings. He had little doubt that there would be a future need for the army.[41]

As negotiations dragged on through the first part of 1919, Hershey became increasingly dubious over prospects for permanent peace. He especially distrusted Wilson's attempts to appeal over the heads of Allied officials to the people, as in the case of Italians. Such gestures would only split the Allied cause. When the terms of the treaty appeared in May he wondered about its practicality. It put Germany on its knees, but it needed "firmness in carrying out its provisions." The Allies won by force, and that force had to be maintained, because already Germans were speaking of revenge.

Could such force be sustained? Would the United States play a role?[42] Hershey admitted that the war had changed the United States, had made her a world power. Yet he wondered if she had changed enough. In an editorial written for the Angola newspaper he sought to identify the problem. He warned that to demobilize immediately would be to lose the fruits of victory. Germany would remain a factor in international affairs. "The war," he wrote, "should have taught us that there is but one method of raising an army in peace or in war and that is one which entails universal and compulsory service." The day of America's aloofness from the world was over. This new position would require that Americans awaken to the need for universal military service. Unlike Wilson, Hershey had little expectation that this conflict had ended all wars. The great lesson of the war should be to remain prepared for the next one.[43] But Hershey was casting his words upon the water. Americans had already decided to give up their conscription and their large army.

With the expectation of future conflicts and at the constant urging of Ellen, who had failed in attempts to join him in Europe, Lewis made his decision to seek a commission in the regular army. Although in July he had been pessimistic about his chances, his confidence returned as he packed his gear to leave Brest. Even if he met disappointment at the hands of the regular army board, he was sure something would turn up. There would always be the farm waiting for him back in Angola.[44]

Hershey's tour in Europe had convinced him that he could compete successfully with other candidates for the regular army. His superiors at Brest agreed. Lt. Col. F. F. Jewett, his commanding officer, was glad to recommend him for such a commission. According to Jewett, Hershey had shown "foresight and planning, insight, initiative, and devotion and good judgment." All of these traits recommended him for even more responsible duty.[45] With orders to sail for home on 15 September, Hershey spent his few remaining days in France enjoying the company of the Hirsch family. For one of the few times in his life, he became sentimental. The Hirsches had taken him in as a true member of the family. A champagne party was arranged to commemorate his sailing. After being bumped off his initial ship, he set sail on the Von Steuben, departing Brest for New York on 21 September with 2,275 troops. After a rough trip, the ship docked in a fog at New York Harbor on 28 September. Hershey stepped off to meet Ellen and begin his campaign to remain in the United States Army.[46]

Hershey returned to an America undergoing rapid change. The census report would soon indicate a large increase in the number of Americans living in urban areas. New York, rather than Angola, was becoming the model of the future community. As his ship landed, he read of labor unrest throughout the land. A general strike in Seattle had been crushed by the vigorous action of Socialist Mayor Ole Hansen. Strikes continued in the coal mines. Anarchists predicted more violence, and Bolsheviks predicted a sovietized America. President Wilson, traveling the country to defend his beleaguered treaty, was on the verge of physical collapse. On 2 October he suffered a stroke but remained in the White House, politically impotent, for another year. Prohibition settled over the country, and Warren G. Harding spoke of the need to rid the country of "nostrums" and to adopt "normalcy" as a guide. The economy plunged into recession as European nations cut back on their purchases.

These events occurred as Hershey awaited action on his regular army commission. He and Ellen moved to Camp Dix, New Jersey. Many of his fellow officers had already been discharged, but Hershey remained optimistic. The gossip at headquarters predicted a need for artillery officers. The process dragged on, however, and he was happy finally to receive orders assigning him to duty with the 10th Field Artillery, 3rd Division, at Camp Pike, Arkansas. Stopping to visit the folks in Angola, he was immediately deputized by his father to bring in a local character accused of "making indecent exposure of his person." Such was the fate of the returning hero.[47]

On 15 October Hershey headed for Camp Pike via St. Louis and Little Rock. As he prepared to take up his new assignment, he reflected on the meaning of the last few years for America and the world. Many Americans feared that the current labor unrest was a prelude to revolution. In November coal miners walked out of the pits. Hershey felt the government should act vigorously, with troops if necessary, to end their strike. As for the Communist agitators, "these people, male or female," he wrote, "must be changed radically or eliminated." "If it means fighting," he wrote, "let's have it out." Hershey applauded Governor Calvin Coolidge of Massachusetts for refusing to buckle under to a striking police force in Boston. Yet Hershey disagreed with predictions of a revolutionary outbreak in May 1920. Such an event seemed "miles and miles away" to him. He felt that the body politic was more endangered from internal selfishness than from the work of outside agitators.[48]

Hershey had little sympathy for this new age of materialism, this Jazz Age. At Camp Pike he heard the music which gave the decade its name, played by "a party of duskies from Memphis." He compared the noise to a brawl in the kitchen with stove lids, pots, and pans all sharing in the orchestra. Although personally still a confirmed teetotaler, he now doubted the wisdom of Prohibition. After his tour in Europe he decided that drinking should be left to personal choice. Observing the enforcement of the act for several months, he concluded that nothing had changed, despite the law.[49]

The political scene was more encouraging to a lifelong Republican. Wilson, with vague statements about running again despite his physical disabilities, was proving an embarrassment to the Democrats. The firing of Secretary of State Robert Lansing was another sign of the Democrats' disarray. Wet and dry factions in the party were at odds. But the results of the Republican convention disappointed Hershey. Committed to a pro-League stand and to progressive Republicanism, he was dissatisfied at the selection of Harding, a man "so closely allied with the politicians." The Democratic ticket seemed even weaker. Hershey viewed the vice-presidential nomination of Franklin D. Roosevelt as "heart balm for the mystic portion of rampant Democracy."[50] Sending his absentee ballot home to Angola, Hershey predicted a Republican victory, not because Harding was a worldbeater but because he was "safe" and the country was tired of Wilson's idealism. As Hershey expected, there was no "solemn referendum" on the League. Harding straddled the issue and carried over 60 percent of the popular vote.

How would these changes effect Captain Hershey, now stuck in Arkansas?[51] He took up his new assignment at Camp Pike, a rather rundown establishment in 1920. Life as a peacetime soldier in the United States between wars seldom rose to the level of tedium. Enlisted men found their way into the army as a last resort. With few officers around, the men took much time to perform useless tasks. Hershey began duty as mess officer, later becoming supply officer and eventually CO for a battery. In his spare time he enrolled at the camp college, took twenty-three weeks of Spanish and also passed courses in military law and administration. And he played polo.[52] For a change of pace he frequently joined the boys for a game of basketball at the camp gym. For light recreation, while awaiting the rare recruit, he read military history, including the memoirs of U. S. Grant.[53] At Camp Pike, on a monthly paycheck of $276.85, the Hersheys finally set up housekeeping and waited for news of Lewis's R.A. application.

As the delay grew longer, he tried to prepare Ellen for disappointment. He had put in his original application on 2 March 1919, while still in Europe. Now, in July 1920, he decided to reapply, in hopes of ending the uncertainty. He took a calculated gamble by insisting upon a regular commission at his present rank of captain. There followed a battery of tests on geography, history, English, natural science, and mathematics. The next step was a physical examination which found him in excellent health. A board of officers under Colonel Mark Wheeler interviewed Hershey along with eighty other candidates for regular commissions. On 29 July 1920 the board of review recommended favorably on his application but reduced his rank to first lieutenant. The final selecting board, however, approved his application for captaincy on 17 August 1920, despite what one officer called a colorless record. After eighteen months of waiting, Lewis B. Hershey was a captain in the regular army. Ellen was elated, but they saved the celebration for another pending event.[54]

At 4:00 A.M. on the morning of 13 November 1920, Ellen went into labor. She was admitted to the post hospital and, after a rather difficult period, finally delivered a healthy baby girl. Both Ellen and Lewis had hoped their first child would be a boy, but they were grateful for a healthy and lively girl, whom they named Kathryn. As he took stock after the birth of his first child, Hershey admitted that his estate seemed meager, but it had been immeasurably blessed by the addition of this young lady with "good health and inexpensive habits."[55]

Prospects for improving the estate looked unpromising in 1920, despite his appointment. With a deepening recession, Congress turned its knife once again on the military. Pay and strength cuts made recruiting men even more difficult. The volunteers who did appear were "illiterate, unAmericanized . . . some insane."[56] Hershey was beginning a career which would have little prospect of advancement for the next twenty years. The Hersheys became part of that small group of army families who transferred from one barren military post to another during the 1920's and 1930's. Frequently their quarters consisted of half a barracks building with one faucet, as at Fort Pike. The shortage of officers and wars insured that Hershey would spend much of his time on what were called fatigue tests. Pay remained low, and the general population looked down upon the professional soldier. The glamour of wartime duty seemed a distant dream.

And so began the grand tour of military posts, taking the Hersheys to such picturesque spots as Fort Sill, Fort Lewis, Fort Bliss, Fort Leavenworth, with an intermediate stop at Arkadelphia. On 25 July 1921 Hershey learned that the entire 3rd Division was to transfer to Camp Lewis, outside Tacoma, Washington. As this trip would relieve him of his current duty as mess officer, a position he detested, he received it gratefully. Although the unit was not due to leave until 15 September, the Hersheys took leave and boarded a train for the West on 12 September. Travel by train in the 1920's meant accepting certain inconveniences. Connections were frequently missed because trains generally ran three or more hours behind schedule. Travelers could spend hours waiting in dusty terminals, only to find that all berths had been taken. On this particular trip the glorious scenery of the Badlands and the Rockies, all new to the Hersheys, helped distract from the inconveniences.[57]

The country surrounding Camp Lewis offered new vistas to the Mid-westerners. Mount Rainier loomed on the horizon as part of the beautiful Cascade Range. The lush vegetation, nourished by the almost constant rain, provided a stark contrast to previous assignments in Texas and Oklahoma. There were also changes in the racial climate. While awaiting the arrival of his unit, Hershey attended a football game between the post team and the University of Washington. Not only did the collegians win the game by a score of 24–0, but they almost provoked a riot by using black players. Hershey noted that "slant eyed personages are as common here as hooks are in the city of New York."[58]

On 17 October Hershey received orders appointing him battery supply officer for the 10th Field Artillery, 3rd Division. The unit participated in normal training, which involved firing on the range and providing cadre for National Guard units which came for instruction. To his annoyance, his superiors had already marked him out as an outstanding administrator, a rare commodity in this ragtailed army. His ability with mathematics also earned him the dubious honor of serving as pay officer. Talent with the pen led to assignment as personnel officer, where he struggled to prepare reports for Washington on information he was sure was not needed. Occasionally he had opportunities to serve as counsel in general courts-martial. He became rather proficient at this task and sometimes regretted not having gone to law school.[59]

Despite the different climate and geography, Camp Lewis resembled Camp Pike in that the officers had much idle time. The rhythm of Hershey's own routine shifted in November 1921, when a second child arrived. Gilbert Richardson Hershey was born on 12 November. On Thanksgiving Day Hershey escorted Ellen to religious services at the post chapel, making one of his infrequent appearances at that station.[60] On weekends the family piled into the Ford to tour the beautiful Northwest. The car, however, broke down with tiresome regularity. After several misadventures they decided to enjoy sights closer to home, such as the buxom Mme. Schumann-Heink singing patriotic songs at the Tacoma theater. One had to conserve funds with a monthly pay check of only $266.50.[61]

Even this modest pay depended upon politicians in Washington. Hershey had welcomed the election of a Republican administration but, after two years of Harding, problems appeared. Hershey felt that these problems were caused by Congress, rather than by the President. To his mind, "the organization and system is so throttling that the fault lies not with the individual members." Committees on appropriations and on finance stuck their noses into matters more properly dealt with by the military affairs committee.[62]

Congressional failing became vivid to Hershey when the issue of military appropriations arose in 1922. The new law cut the number of authorized personnel.[63] Hershey wondered at the folly of such a policy when the world situation remained so unstable. The Washington disarmament conference of 1922 appeared to contribute some stability, but Hershey found it difficult to gauge what the United States had gained or lost in the various treaties. The nation had achieved naval parity with England through the Five Power Naval Treaty; Japan had been set back, and Hershey doubted that she would remain long content with her inferior stakes. He felt that the United States should look to its interests in the Far East. As for Europe, France continued to suffer from chronic political instability. Her weaknesses shook the foundation of the Versailles settlement. France was, after all, the major power responsible for executing the treaty system. Britain, which also had responsibilities, had her own problems with a rebellion in Ireland.[64]

With these larger issues still unresolved, Hershey learned of a new assignment. The normal career pattern for artillery officers required attendance at the Field Artillery School in Fort Sill. In July 1922 he received news of his assignment. Originally he planned to drive by way of Canada, but once again the Ford acted up. On the day of departure he loaded the family, the car, and his goods on a train heading for Portland, then east to Pocatello, and on to Salt Lake City. The train crossed the Continental Divide at the Tennessee Pass and went through the Royal Gorge, an inspiring sight to Hershey. He arrived at Fort Sill on 7 September, a few days before his twenty-ninth birthday.[65]

For artillery officers Fort Sill meant drills, field exercises, and, above all, school. Nothing seemed more disconcerting to these mature officers than the prospect of becoming students again, being forced to renew acquaintance with books and study habits. A climate of gloom hovered perpetually over this dusty fort in southwestern Oklahoma. Hershey had few good things to say about his classroom teachers. First, he found theoretical discussion a poor substitute for firing weapons. Second, the instructors posed as petty tyrants. Many of them had little ability as teachers, droning on with all the variety of a metronome. Despite his complaints, Hershey performed well at the school. Unlike many of his fellow students, he had confidence in his mathematical ability. After several weeks of training, including firing 8-inch and 155mm canons, he established himself as thirty-second in a class of

124. His final report called his performance average but described him as a "good officer." [66]

Unlike many of his fellow career officers, Hershey refused to allow his busy schedule to blunt his interest in politics and world events. He was upset by the failure of an Indiana clerk to provide him with an absentee ballot during the 1922 congressional elections. Hershey expected the Democrats to rebound after the Harding landslide of 1920, but he resented his own failure to help stem the tide. The resurgence of Democrats in 1922 was a natural development, but it was undoubtedly helped by the problems of the Harding administration and the obvious failure of Prohibition. The flourishing of hijackers, safe-crackers, and embezzlers also convinced Hershey that some change was needed. [67]

Neither the national nor the international scene satisfied him. The dream of Hershey's generation, that the Great War was a prelude to a golden age, seemed even more elusive. "The war to end war," he wrote, "has been but an incubator to breed rather than inhibit. Europe is on the very brink of an abyss." Germany owed reparations but could not pay. Hershey felt the American attitude toward France was entirely mistaken. The United States refused to cut her debt payments, but was more understanding with the German debt to France. When France occupied the Ruhr in January 1923, Hershey could not understand the American criticism. "Sometimes," he declared, "one wonders which side of the war we fought on." [68]

The national scene proved equally disappointing. Not only had the Democrats regained power in Congress, but the scandals of Harding's administration were now trickling out of Washington. Albert Fall, secretary of the interior, would be convicted for squandering national petroleum reserves at Teapot Dome, Wyoming, in exchange for personal gain. Repeatedly Congress turned its back on the needs of national defense. The increasing number of pacifists who dreamed of a crusade for peace similar to the earlier crusade for war were, in Hershey's opinion, ignoring human nature. [69]

Hershey's own future appeared as cloudy as did that of the country. As he concluded his schooling at Fort Sill, he gave thought to his next assignment. With two small children, he hoped to find an ROTC assignment close to Angola. He had now spent over five years at the rank of captain. All signs indicated that he would probably spend many more years at this grade. On 14 June 1923, graduation day at Fort Sill, Hershey accepted his certificate with orders in his pocket assigning him to the ROTC cadre at Ohio State University. [70]

Few assignments could have been more pleasing. Not only was he to work close to his home in Indiana, but the type of work fit his tempera-

ment. He could combine his love of teaching with his commitment to
the military life. He rented a big old house at 548 Vermont Place.[71] But
being close to relatives was a two-edged sword. It proved comforting
to have Ellen's parents around when another son, George Frederick
was born on 9 September 1923, and when Ellen Margaret made her
appearance on 10 June 1926. But no sooner had Hershey moved into his
new home in Columbus than problems arose. Mr. Dygert suffered a series of financial reverses. With Lewis's approval, Ellen decided to cash
in their bonds and loan $1,000 to her father. The farmboy with poor
prospects had proved his worth. Newton, Ellen's brother, a sailor in
the merchant marine, was missing at sea and a presumed suicide.
Lewis's relatives also suffered misfortune during this period; Russ's
barn burned down, and Latta lost a bid for reelection as sheriff. To
make matters worse, Ellen began to suffer from a series of physical
disabilities which would plague her for the rest of her life.[72]

Such distractions failed to affect Hershey's performance in his new
assignment. Although not many students enrolled for ROTC, those
who did included such future luminaries as Curtis LeMay and Oscar W.
Griswold. Hershey enjoyed the contact with young men, although he
found his commanding officer "too officious." When the cadets became
interested in playing polo, Hershey became the coach. In his spare
time he took several military correspondence courses, including those
of the Command and General Staff College. During the summer his
duty took him to Fort Knox, Kentucky, to command cadet training programs and instruct National Guard units.[73]

When his four-year tour drew to a close, Hershey expected a less
pleasant field assignment. He was not disappointed. The War Department ordered him to report for duty on 1 July 1927 with the 1st Battalion, 82nd Field Artillery Brigade, stationed at Fort Bliss, Texas. He
was made commanding officer of Battery "A," 1st Battalion. Fort Bliss
was an old, established army post located on the outskirts of El Paso, a
border town nestled against the Rio Grande and surrounded by tree-
less mountains and desert. The units spent much of their time in field
exercises along the turbulent border with Mexico, a nation still struggling to achieve domestic tranquility.

The Hershey clan, now numbering six, traveled down to Fort Bliss
in the summer of 1927. Although they were assigned adequate post
housing, the family had problems adjusting to Texas. Ellen found the
climate debilitating. Despite the dry air, her lungs constantly gave her
trouble. She began to spend more and more time in bed. As Lewis had
to spend most of his time in the field, the children lacked a firm hand.
Most of the time Ellen supervised and managed the home, but she felt
inadequate to deal with the children's problems. Kathryn, Gilbert, and

George had trouble in Texas schools. Lewis began tutoring his children during his free time, but he was often in the field. Above all he urged Ellen to keep the children reading in their spare time.[74]

Despite the dust and family problems, duty at Fort Bliss had a certain appeal for Hershey. Once again, after a hiatus of many years, he was in charge of troops. Being stationed near the Mexican border from 1927 to 1929 provided some excitement and relief from the boredom of garrison duty. Mexico continued to struggle over its revolutionary settlement. Plutarco Calles had become president in 1924. He immediately instituted drastic agrarian and educational reforms which involved conflict with large landowners and the Roman Catholic church. Insurrections broke out in October 1927 and periodically for the next few years. The northern provinces were filled with rebel armies and federal troops. In 1929 rebellions were led by Jesus Maria Aguirre and Gonzalo Escobar. With these conflicts so close to American settlements, the War Department insisted that the units at Bliss make periodic excursions along the border to provide protection.

Hershey no sooner arrived at Bliss than he took to the field with the 82nd F.A. Battalion and the 1st Calvary for war games. The units marched out of Bliss for the southwest part of Texas, through such scenic delights as Sierra Blanca, Hot Wells, Lobo, and Valentine. The troops began their war games in the dusty terrain dominated by the Davis Mountains on the northeast and the Sierra Vieja Mountains on the southwest. Hershey's unit marched an average of twenty-five miles in six hours, with dust storms swirling around the ranks. At night torrential rains washed over the camp. The war games seemed hopelessly confused, and Hershey had problems carrying out assignments. His unit had only 20 percent of its authorized strength, but the experience gained seemed to make the exercise worthwhile.[75]

This pattern of constant maneuvers and field exercises continued during Hershey's entire stay at Bliss. He had a brush with real combat in 1929. Mexican rebels again raised the flag of revolution in the north, and American ranchers along the border in New Mexico and Arizona began screaming for protection from marauders. When a war scare erupted in Juarez in April, the 82nd and the 7th Cavalry crossed the Rio Grande. After blundering about in the sand for a day and reaching Nona, both units returned to the United States and headed west toward Columbus, New Mexico. On and on through the dust they marched, through Hachita, toward Douglas, Arizona. But Hershey saw no rebels and began to think all the marching was a bit insane. At Douglas, American troops watched from north of the border as federal units of Mexico used planes to root out the rebels. General Escobar was soon captured. As he wrote to his father, Hershey felt that the rebellion was over and that no threat existed toward the United States as long as the administration continued its policy of readiness. "If they come down hard on the first one that comes across or fires across the line," he wrote, "there will be no trouble."[76]

During his stay at Fort Bliss Hershey also suffered a serious physical setback. He had escaped crippling at Fort Sill earlier, but now he experienced an injury which was a threat to his future as a military officer. During the 1920's his enthusiasm for polo had grown almost into an obsession. His coaching at Ohio State had helped improve his game. Not unexpectedly, he became an active rider on the polo team at Fort Bliss. He had taken his share of spills and suffered from bruises, but on 9 November 1927, during a game in the First Cavalry Tournament, in the midst of a melee an opponent struck Hershey in the face with a polo mallet. He uttered a cry and fell to the ground, clutching his eye. Captain Milton W. Hall, a medical officer, raced to the fallen Hershey and examined the injury. The right eyelid had a lacerated wound. The eyeball had suffered contusion, and the iris appeared ruptured. After a short stay at the post hospital, Hershey returned to duty. Vision in his right eye was permanently impaired. Treatment continued, but he would never see more than shadows with that eye. This handicap, which involved a loss of depth perception, was a difficult hurdle for an artillery officer to overcome.[77]

In spite of this injury, Hershey performed well in his troop duty assignment at Fort Bliss. His efficiency reports showed superior performance in all categories, with the exception of military bearing and physical activity. His men seemed devoted to him, and he was rated an "ideal battery commander." His superiors strongly recommended him for assignment to the next class at the Command and General Staff College (C & GS), Fort Leavenworth, Kansas.[78]

With another four-year tour drawing to a close, Hershey realized that his hopes for advancement depended upon attending C&GS. Waiting for orders seemed a major part of army life to the Hersheys, although in this case they did not wait long. In the summer he learned of his selection for the class starting in August 1931. With a sense of relief and expectation Hershey packed his family into a newly purchased but second-hand seven-passenger Packard and took a month's leave. On June 3 they began a 6,000-mile odyssey which took them around the Gulf of Mexico, through Florida, to Washington, D.C., into New England, across into Canada, and finally home to Angola.[79]

Command and General Staff College presented Hershey with the challenge of competing with officers from all different branches of the army. This school was an essential hurdle for those officers aspiring to field-grade rank. Failure here, or even a poor showing, would probably mean early retirement in the rank of captain or perhaps major. Hershey welcomed the challenge, confident as always of his abilities as a student. His ratings throughout the course were excellent to superior in all categories. Colonel Russell P. Reeder, his instructor, called him "quiet and industrious, practical, energetic and loyal." In his spare time he became sponsor of the local Boy Scout troop. This duty involved refereeing and coaching the boys in football, basketball, and baseball.[80]

Hershey graduated from C & GS on 5 June 1933. According to the normal cycle of assignments, he was due for an overseas tour, but normal cycles did not prevail in an America wracked by severe economic crisis. The Great Depression had been deepening for several years. Unemployment now stood at one third of the work-force; banks were closing across the country. Herbert Hoover had left the presidency to a chorus of jeers. Franklin D. Roosevelt offered the country a "New Deal" and assured people that "the only thing we have to fear is fear itself." In rapid succession a bewildering series of federal agencies were created to get people working again. The Civilian Conservation Corps was designed to provide temporary employment for 250,000 young men between the ages of eighteen and twenty-five. These men left the crowded cities and took up quarters in camps established across the country for work in reforestation, flood control projects, and other tasks. Military officers were to establish the camps and provide general supervision. Orders immediately went out to corral all casual officers for temporary duty with the CCC.

The net swept across the country and ensnared Lewis Hershey. The day after graduation from C&GS he received orders assigning him as quartermaster in the Arkadelphia subdistrict of the Arkansas CCC program. To complicate matters, he already had orders to report to the August 1933 class of the Army War College in Washington, D.C. In June, to his surprise, he was heading for Arkansas. The people around Arkadelphia had not noticed the onset of the Great Depression, for they had lived most of their lives in depression. This area southwest of Little Rock contained a large population of poor blacks and poor white farmers. To make the assignment even more distasteful, Hershey had little enthusiasm for Roosevelt's relief program. He disliked any reckless expenditure of public money for relief, feeling that the government was squandering money "on needless work for the unemployed."[81]

Leaving Ellen with the children at Leavenworth helped to further sour Hershey on his new assignment. His orders read that he was to proceed to Kierks, Graysonia, and Willow, Arkansas, "for the purpose of determining work camp sites for the C.C.C." He was given a $5 per diem and the use of a new Dodge truck. Speed was essential, because the recruits were expected any day; campsites had to be selected and then built. Once more Hershey found himself stuck with a quartermaster's task. In this case, however, his job was rather more complex than it would have been on an established army post. He raced around a district, covering 400 square miles, buying all of the supplies needed to build and service the camps. Setting up headquarters in a hotel room rented for 75 cents a day, he made the rounds of lumber stores, dairy farmers, and other local suppliers. There was a certain fascination in spending $5,000 of the government's money. There was also the challenge of playing the role of purchaser, carpenter, foreman, and architect. But Hershey's mind kept straying back to his family.[82] To his relief, orders arrived, detaching him from this temporary duty and returning him to the Army War College.[83]

Hershey's selection for the Army War College (AWC) in Washington came as a surprise to some of his colleagues. Captains had not previously been picked for this school, which prepared men for service on the General Staff. Rarely did an officer go immediately from C&GS to AWC. General George S. Simonds, the AWC commandant, was personally involved in opening the door to captains. Since promotions moved with glacial slowness during the 1920's and 1930's, such a step seemed logical. Being picked as one of the first captains, however, put additional pressure on Hershey. As General Simonds wrote, "I trust that you will personally prove that my judgment was sound."[84] But Hershey was moving in very fast company, with full colonels as classmates. The roll revealed the names of Omar Bradley, Jonathan Wainwright, and William Halsey. The work proved strenuous, with much emphasis upon research and oral presentations.[85]

While at the War College Hershey continued his research into a problem which had long attracted his attention—the psychological dimension of leadership. At Leavenworth he had written an elaborate study on "Fear as a Factor in Leadership Problems." The insights he had gained in this earlier research served him well at the AWC. Using a wide range of sources, stretching from Plutarch through William James and Karl Menninger to the writings of William Allen White, Hershey concluded that control of fear was an essential requirement of leadership. He also insisted that punishment to generate fear represented a failing in existing military doctrine. Even more disturbing, officers seemed strikingly illiterate on the subject of emotional behavior. To the assistant commandant at the Army War College, Hershey reiterated the need to correct this glaring defect in training. He felt that the army should study civilian methods and incorporate training in this field. Officers should be assigned to civilian schools and industry to study what was being done. The assistant commandant found these recommendations interesting, but nothing was done to implement them. Instead, the army continued to believe that strong leadership could overcome all emotional problems. Such thinking led logically to the later indifference of military leaders to men suffering from battle fatigue in World War II.[86]

At the end of his tour, in June 1934, Hershey evaluated the Army War College. While praising the scope of his courses and the high level of teaching, he was disappointed that the school failed to invite experts from the civilian world, "unhandicapped by official status," to discuss foreign affairs. He also urged that the school invite a competent civilian psychologist to lecture on personality traits and psychology.[87]

The school's evaluation of Hershey proved more generous. His academic work was rated superior, but he received only a satisfactory mark in his military bearing and neatness, a failing which accompanied him throughout his career. In a final summation, Major General Simonds wrote that Hershey was "a serious, agreeable officer, rapid, accurate in his work and open minded." Yet, despite this superior academic performance, Simonds ended his evaluation with the pregnant notation that Hershey was "qualified for duty with civilian components." In an age when line command remained the sine qua non of success, such words were disappointing. Undoubtedly Hershey's vision problem—his eye was useless—and his unmilitary bearing told against him for field command. Yet, serving with civilian components might have its own rewards.[88]

Upon graduation, Hershey finally received an overseas assignment. On 14 August 1934 he reported for duty with the supply section of army headquarters at Fort Shafter, Hawaii. As assistant to the G-4, Hershey again found himself saddled with staff work. As expected, he performed well. Finally, on 1 July 1935, the War Department promoted Hershey to the rank of major. He had been fifteen years a captain in the regular army; he was now forty-one years old. His children were growing up. He kept at the task of self-improvement, attending a nondegree program on Pacific relations at the University of Hawaii. Regardless of his competence and industry, however, he had little chance for further advancement. The strength of the army remained low, and the isolationism of the 1930's promised little expansion. Without a West Point pedigree, Hershey had few illusions about his future. When orders arrived in May 1936 to report to the personnel branch of the General Staff in Washington, Hershey read this as a terminal assignment, a prelude to retirement.[89]

Before returning to Washington and planning for a civilian future, however, he decided to take leave and tour the world with his family. Because he was not traveling under orders, Hershey had to mortgage his life insurance policy to finance the trip. Using second-class accommodations, the family sailed west from Honolulu on June 5. Their first port of call was Japan. For the next several days Hershey observed the culture of this new power in Asia. Although many young men were in uniform, he was not impressed with the smartness of their appearance. But a visit to Kyoto and a ferry ride on the Inland Sea brought home to him the naval strength Japan had amassed in recent years.[90]

Japan had made clear her intentions of playing the major role in the future development of Asia. In 1931 she had stripped Manchuria from the feeble grasp of a China torn by revolution. Chiang Kai-shek and his Kuomintang still sought to modernize China. The youth of China resented Japan's aspirations and attempts to usurp the Middle Kingdom's traditional Asian leadership role. Few Chinese had accepted the Manchurian coup as final. Chiang's government took slight solace from the nonrecognition policy formulated by Secretary of State Henry Stimson in 1931. Japan, aware of her tenuous hold on Manchuria and of the dangers of Communist influence in China, began planning a swift action in the north to protect vital resources. Into this cockpit of intrigue and military ambitions traveled Hershey with the naive eyes of a typical American.

On 20 June the family traveled north through Korea, which, Hershey felt, had no future except "as a part of Japan." Adopting the pose of a latter-day Cecil Rhodes, Hershey felt that Koreans had lost their right to self-government because "they stood in the way of an awakened people and because they lacked the capacity to govern themselves." These same pro-Japanese sympathies accompanied Hershey as he moved north to Mukden and northern China. "There is a tragedy being enacted in North China," he wrote, but "I do not believe we are interested enough to fight about it and fighting is the only thing that will influence the situation." Ancient China impressed itself on the touring Hersheys. Lewis wondered about China's ability to feed and support the masses of humanity that pressed around him, constantly seeking alms. He was relieved to sail on 3 July.[91]

The Empress of Asia sailed for the Philippines with an ailing Ellen Hershey on board. Ellen continued to complain of illness, but the tour proceeded in relentless fashion. After a few days in Manila, they shipped back to Hong Kong, where Ellen entered the hospital for observation. After a few days' rest she was ready to travel again. On 11 July their ship, the Corfu, sailed toward Singapore. The family enjoyed this bastion of the British Empire in the East, although its impregnability would be detroyed by the Japanese in 1942. But in 1936, still basking in the rays of an imperial sun already declining, Singapore's culture of soccer, cricket, and tennis, its botanical gardens and lovely shops appealed to the tourists. On 17 July the Hersheys sailed again, through the Straits of Malacca into the Andaman Sea. Their destinations: Ceylon, and then Bombay. They jumped from one pebble of British civilization to another in their tour of the East, ignoring the native cultures of the interior.[92]

All too soon it was back to the ship and a foul-weather run to Aden, through the Suez Canal, and into the Victoria Hotel in Cairo. Hershey, who closely guarded his purse, felt he was being cheated by the various hands constantly outstretched before him. In the next few days they visited the bazaars, Gizeh and the pyramids, explored excavations, and toured museums. The spectacle of Egypt could be enervating, however. The merchants were the most persistent in the world, haranguing and embarrassing tourists into unwanted purchases. Fortunately, Hershey found a guide who was able to drive off the merchants and the beggars with wild waves of his flyswitch. After the boys had climbed the pyramids, adding their share of erosion to the decay of ages, the family boarded a ship for Europe.[93]

The mild climate of the Mediterranean greeted them on their return to a more familiar civilization. After a brief stop at Malta they reached Marseilles, where Hershey sought to book passage home. He finally found third-class accommodations on the Aquitania sailing on 9 September. In the meantime, the Hersheys soaked up the culture of southern France and toured Italy. The Riviera glistened with wealth outside their train as they traveled to Venice, where Hershey haggled over the price of a gondola ride. Their whirlwind tour completed, the family headed back to the United States and Lewis Hershey headed to his new assignment.[94]

Hershey at age four, 1897 (courtesy of Hershey family)

The Hershey family and homestead, 1901; Aunt Alma, Lewis, Latta, Russ (courtesy of Hershey family)

Teenage clown, 1908 (courtesy of Hershey family)

High school valedictorian, May 1910 (courtesy of Hershey family)

Schoolmaster, 1911 (courtesy of Hershey family)

Basketball player at Tri-State College, 1913 (courtesy of Hershey family)

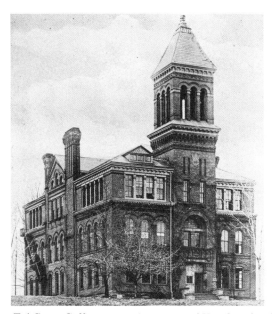

Tri-State College, 1913 (courtesy of Hershey family)

Lieutenant in the National Guard, 1913 (courtesy of Hershey family)

Polo player in the 1920's (courtesy of Hershey family)

Home with the family, Fort Bliss, ca. 1928 (courtesy of Hershey family)

On maneuvers in the Southwest, ca. 1928 (courtesy of Hershey family)

III. New Horizons

Hershey began duty in Washington in September 1936 as a mature, confident officer. He had traveled far from rural Indiana in his forty-three years. Some of the confidence came from his physical appearance. Six feet tall, he carried 200 pounds on a hulking frame with broad chest and shoulders. Despite having only one good eye, he glowed with good health to the top of his red crewcut. He could draw on his physical strength for the energy needed to work long hours at any task.

To these physical talents and keenness of mind he added an abnormal amount of self-discipline. His approach to his schoolwork, the decision to adopt a vegetarian diet and maintain it in the midst of French cuisine, and his approach to marriage all spoke of rigorous self-control. Nothing displeased him more than to see a man ruled by his emotions. As a young man of twenty-three he wrote, "I have tried in many cases to keep from showing my feelings, this has formed a habit that is gaining considerable strength." [1]

Hershey always emphasized his lack of pretense, yet he did cultivate an image—that of a homespun midwestern farmboy. People in Washington usually identified him as a rural teacher or farmer. In fact, Hershey was no more a farmer than was Franklin D. Roosevelt. In both cases the pose served a larger purpose—putting people at ease. Like Roosevelt, Hershey was a master at human relations. He genuinely liked people, and his gregarious nature was not insincere. Throughout his career he spun funny tales in a manner made famous by Herb Shriner. The jokes usually depended on self-deprecation or an ironic twist. Neither sexual innuendos nor sophistication found a place in Hershey's stories. Ellen always thought he acted like an "overgrown kid." [2]

Hershey's attitude toward material wealth was humanely ambiguous. He had little drive to accumulate money for its own sake, but he was acutely conscious of his finances. On the one hand he was generous to friends and relatives in need, and he was considered a soft touch for a loan in his old units. He assumed responsibility for the financial care of his relatives in Angola, paying for hospitalizations, nursing care, and rent for elderly relatives. Yet he paid careful attention to his cash flow. During his travels he would embarrass the family by lengthy arguments with taxidrivers, gondoliers, and waitresses. When traveling for the government in the line of duty he always took the cheap ticket, even when he was entitled to first-class accommodations. In dealing with landlords or with utility companies he wrote at length to debate sums of less than $10. He resented the thought of anyone taking advantage of him.[3]

His devotion to Ellen never wavered during their long marriage. In a career which required frequent and long absences and in an age grown more receptive to adultery, Hershey remained constant, "unalterably opposed" to divorce. When asked late in his career who "exercised the greatest influence upon your professional career," he named Ellen without hesitation. Their relationship had an almost childlike quality of affection about it. On special occasions he would compose poems expressing his undying love and admiration. Although a flop as a "do-it-yourself" man, he took pride in his washing, ironing, and grasscutting. When Ellen was ill (a frequent occurrence in later life), he cooked the meals and became a master of leftover stew. Ellen handled the daily and monthly expenses, but Lewis made the big financial decisions. As a father he was frequently absent. While the children were growing up at Fort Bliss, he spent much time in the field. In general, he encouraged them to assume self-responsibility and self-direction.[4]

Despite many opportunities, he retained conventional tastes in food and drink. With the end of Prohibition he took an occasional social drink. His vegetarian experiment, which lasted until the 1930's, had always met with the disapproval of his family. Ellen found it an embarrassment while dining out and an inconvenience at home. He eventually gave it up without comment, but he remained satisfied with typical American fare such as fried chicken, cold roast beef, corn muffins, and fried potatoes. For dessert he preferred apple or chocolate pie.[5]

"I am quite sure," he wrote, "that one of the philosophies that we should live by is to find hobbies and interests that are time consuming enough to make us forget some of the unpleasant things that come to all of us at all times." Unfortunately, he never mastered this philosophy. Early in his career he enjoyed a rare musical show. As his work load increased in 1940, his recreational reading was limited to snippets of news magazines or current affairs. Going to movies took too much time, so he turned instead to the radio. He and Ellen spent many hours listening to Jack Benny, Charlie McCarthy, and Eddie Cantor. With the advent of television he became a fan of the major news shows, "Face the Nation," "Meet the Press," and others. For relaxation there was always Lawrence Welk. When asked by a biographical publication to list his hobbies, he facetiously replied: "collecting medals and awards."[6]

In fact, his work consumed his entire attention after 1940. "Much of my joy in labor," he wrote, "is in the fact that it prevents idleness." At his office by 8:30, he would spend the morning in conferences and staff studies. Lunch might involve sending out for a cheeseburger or cottage cheese and fruit to eat at his desk. On more leisurely days he would stroll down to the cafeteria in headquarters to dine with clerks and other personnel. After lunch he generally had several speaking engagements and interviews with his staff. He welcomed visitors from behind a huge desk surrounded by flags from each of the states, symbolizing the federated nature of the Selective Service System. When he left the office at 5:00 his briefcase invariably contained several staff studies or pending bills to peruse at home. By 11:00 P.M. he was in bed.[7]

Like most public men, Hershey had an active rather than a contemplative mind. He seldom reflected upon the meaning of his life. Toward the end of his public career, however, he articulated a cyclical view of history, tracing the average age of great civilizations of the past through the following steps: "from bondage to spiritual faith; from spiritual faith to great courage; from courage to liberty; from liberty to abundance; from abundance to selfishness; from selfishness to complacency; from complacency to apathy; from apathy to dependence; from dependence back again to bondage." America, he felt, had reached the level of abundance and stood poised on the brink of selfishness. There had been many significant changes in his own lifetime, but the changes had been in material things "that are merely furniture on the stage of life, at best, and perhaps obstructions to stumble over at worst."[8]

For Hershey the key to breaking out of the historical cycle could not be found in mechanical achievements. The only salvation possible was the salvation of the race or nation in this world. The key to salvation was improving knowledge in human relations.[9] For a period he thought psychology might be the answer to the problem of national redemption, but Hershey always tended toward fatalism, even while insisting that he was an optimist. Accepting the inevitable became a mark of his mature life. Despite the inevitable he fought, illogically, to retain some optimism. Nature, in Hershey's view, was working out his destiny with little aid from him. Yet he could also insist that a man's life was the result of his own actions: "I think each day we build the house in which we are to live because day-by-day, week-by-week, we forge the chain of the habits which are to bind us."[10]

This juvenile jumble of contradictory ideas became more consistent when he discussed political and social problems. Throughout his life he

espoused a faith in agrarianism and echoed the sentiments of Thomas
Jefferson; yet Hershey had little personal love of farming. Rather, he
considered farming valuable because of the alleged virtues of independence and oneness with nature which it conveyed. He knew at first
hand that "the poetry of rural life" had its drawbacks, but, the farm
and local community were essential to the health of the nation. Such
institutions led to a federated polity.[11]

In Hershey's mind, the key to America's republicanism was decentralized government. In the local community people learned and
practiced the virtues of cooperation and assumed the responsibility of
citizenship. In the twentieth century big government and a communi-
cations revolution were threatening to destroy village life. The rise of
central government meant the demise of local responsibility and the
atrophy of virtues which developed good citizenship. Individuals would
simply let Washington take care of their problems. Hershey found
such a trend dangerous. He preferred to allow the local community to
make its own mistakes, so errors would be restricted. Errors made in
a centralized system, however, would flow out to the entire nation.[12]

Another key to good government, Hershey felt, whether in the local
community or in the nation, was leadership. During his military career
he had many opportunities to observe inept leadership. Some of his superior officers confused leadership with smallmindedness. For Hershey the truly effective leader was able to "grasp essentials and, from
them, work the details. But our pygmies with much ado begin at details and end there."[13] On the national political scene, Hershey saw few
examples of true leadership.

While attending Command and General Staff College, he sharpened
his ideas on leadership by extensive reading in behavioral psychology.
Drawing upon the studies by Josiah Morse (*The Psychology and Neu-
rology of Fear*), George Humphrey (*The Story of Man's Mind*), George
A. Dorsey (*Hows and Whys of Human Behavior*), William James
(*Psychology*), Sigmund Freud (*The Ego and the Id*), Karl A. Menninger (*The Human Mind*), and Edward W. Lazell (*The Anatomy of
Emotion*), Hershey traced the growth of the new psychology, which
rejected a strict duality of mind and body. He adopted the monist views
expressed by James and others. To Hershey, the science of psychology
could help the leader control fear by understanding the operations of
the subconscious. The effective leader understood the causes of fear
and was able to help the individual transcend the problem.[14]

Hershey believed in leadership but had suspicions about great men.
After watching George Bernard Shaw's *Man and Superman*, he reflected that only "about one in a thousand has a career that is worth
allowing the freedom of earth." He never considered himself one of

those supermen, but he did believe that leadership was a matter of practicing certain principles. He summarized the formula with the initials WALK. "Work" created the opportunity for leadership. "Adaptability," or the ability to roll with the punches, was essential. "Loyalty" toward the men and organization would be reciprocated. "Knowledge" of the job was the last element in this formula. Above all, Hershey felt that the effective leader knew how to delegate authority, how to avoid meddling with those below him. This view seemed particularly unmilitaristic, at odds with the blood-and-guts theory propounded by such soldiers as George Patton. Hershey's leadership formula seemed most suited for dealing with civilian institutions.[15]

As he began his new assignment with the general staff of the War Department, he had a chance to test these principles. For all he knew and expected, this assignment would be his last. Normally a general staff assignment lasted four years, but Hershey had less than three years to retirement. "I was a little concerned," he wrote his father, "for I could not understand the detail when I knew that I was not eligible for the entire four years." He added prophetically, "Many things may occur before that time [retirement] so I am not worrying about that now."[16]

The War Department in 1936 still operated under the restrictions created by a climate of pacifism and isolationism. America had tasted European wine in 1917 and found it bitter. During the 1920's the country had sunk its ships and cut its armed forces to under 250,000. Congress had placed heavy budgetary restrictions on defense spending. Planning for war remained an exceedingly unpopular pastime for the American public. Despite these problems, the army had to be ready to expand rapidly in an emergency.

The National Defense Act of 1920 had authorized the War Department to prepare plans for mobilization. Although nothing significant was done for several years, the planners had precedents on conscription. The Draft Act of 1917 had been the brainchild of General Enoch H. Crowder, who had drawn inspiration from a study by General James Oakes of Illinois. The disaster of the draft during the Civil War had prompted Oakes to offer in 1866 a series of principles which should guide future conscription: an end to all bounties paid to volunteers, an end to distinctions between volunteers and draftees, an end to hiring substitutes, and no blanket exemptions or deferments for classes or occupations. All enforcement of the draft law was to be taken out of the hands of the army and given to the Department of Justice. He also urged—and this was most significant for the future—that the selection of draftees be made the responsibility of local boards made up of civilian neighbors. In 1917 Crowder adopted most of Oakes's ideas. Local boards were established and paid by the government. The system had proven successful, although there were major complaints when blanket deferments were extended to certain industries. This system provided the basis for army planning in the 1920's.[17]

Given the antiwar climate in Congress and the nation, planning proceeded slowly. In 1926 the secretaries of war and navy exchanged letters creating a Joint Army-Navy Selective Service Committee (JAN-SSC), which was to function under the chief of staff, G-1, and be responsible for updating mobilization plans. The committee consisted of several army officers who had been active in the draft organization of World War I, plus a few naval officers. By 1932 the committee had taken several significant steps. A bill creating a new Selective Service System had been drawn up, together with regulations to implement the system. More important, a group of reserve officers, called selective service specialists, was being recruited. The adjutants general of the states were asked to develop plans for implementing the draft at their level. Finally, a publicity organization was being established to help sell the need for a draft.[18]

In selecting members for the special commissions, the army turned to local elites. Through an old boy network which included the state adjutants general and the Junior Chambers of Commerce, the JAN-SSC sought out young, patriotic men of wealth and local influence. These men were offered commissions consistent with their ages. Almost uniformly the men had no prior military experience but were recognized for their ability and standing in the community. This cadre would provide the nucleus for the national headquarters of Selective Service. In 1935 the men began receiving correspondence courses and attending annual conferences to discuss planning. Even before Hershey's arrival the JANSSC was a very active organization, with many principles of the draft already established.[19]

By 1936 American isolationism appeared less and less realistic. Adolf Hitler announced a two-year compulsory military service plan for all Germans. He denounced the Locarno Pact and marched his troops into the Rhineland. Italy proceeded to mop up its conquest of Ethiopia and sign the Rome-Berlin Axis. In Spain, General Francisco Franco raised the banner of rebellion while France and England promised nonintervention. In the Far East, Japan signed an anti-Communist pact while several young military officers assassinated a moderate finance minister and others. But the United States Congress deliberated and extended the neutrality act prohibiting loans, credits, or arms to belligerents. Franklin D. Roosevelt on 14 August at Chautauqua, New York, announced: "I hate war."

While Hershey expected an assignment in Washington as part of his normal rotation, he did not expect that he would be working with Selective Service planning. The assignment, however, seemed perfectly natural. Major John Lucas of G-1 had observed Hershey's work as a battalion executive officer at Fort Bliss in 1929 and 1931. Lucas recognized Hershey's talents at management and personnel. Even more significantly, Colonel Sandiford Jarman, who had taken over as secretary of the JANSSC in 1934, was looking for a replacement. Jarman and Hershey had been in the same War College class. Jarman recalled that Hershey had originally come from the National Guard, an outfit which had to play a big role in the conscription plan. The secretary of the JANSSC had to be someone who could deal with civilian reservists and state officials, especially the adjutants general. Hershey had no sooner arrived in Washington than he was detailed to work with the JANSSC as executive secretary. The entire operation, which consisted of two officers and two clerks, was under the G-1 office of the chief of staff.[20]

Much work had been done before Hershey's arrival. Officers had been earmarked, correspondence courses drafted, a few conferences held, a draft bill prepared. When Hershey appeared, the plans moved from paper to people. For the first time the JANSSC was authorized money, some $10,000, to promote training of the reserve units. Annual conferences were scheduled at four different locations: Washington, New Orleans, Chicago, and San Francisco. For the first time National Guard officers began attending these training conferences. Hershey began cultivating the adjutants general who controlled the guard and who advised the governors on military matters.[21]

Hershey traveled throughout the country, attending as many of the training conferences as possible. His task took finesse; the men who had been earmarked were still civilians. Over the next four years Hershey succeeded in winning their loyalty and affection. Unlike the regular army officers they had dealt with in the past, Hershey was not mired in military protocol. He was more a Scout leader than a martinet. He tried to view problems through the eyes of a civilian draftee. Could the average draftee understand what was required of him? Would the system be easily understood by the draftee's parents? At all times he emphasized the need to keep the system so simple that the man in the street would have little trouble comprehending how it worked. People had to go into the draft because they saw it as their duty, or because peer and community pressure would insist upon it. The important role of local boards flowed directly from this need to have the system accepted.[22] A public opinion poll of 8 Feburary 1937 revealed that 56 percent opposed requiring young men to serve six months in the army or navy.[23]

But Hershey could not do his job solely in Washington or at annual conferences. He had to get out into the country to organize state units which would be ready to work with the national Selective Service headquarters. During this assignment he spent untold hours traveling by train across the country. He rode coach class and carried his lunch in a bag.[24] The War Department finally upped his per diem from $2 to $5. In February 1937 he traveled to the conference in New Orleans. While in town he took time off to attend several of the Mardi Gras balls. In late April and early May he supervised the conference held in San Francisco. Although pleased with the training, he was disappointed because of the absence of regular army and navy officers.[25]

By 1938 the JANSSC consisted of a half-dozen officers serving under the chief of staff. The committee spent most of its time overseeing the training of seventy reserve army officers, eight navy reservists and two marines. Almost every state AG office had now allotted a staff officer to train with the committee. There was no legal justification for selective service. A draft bill creating a Selective Service System was approved by the secretaries of war and navy in October, but there would be no effort to secure passage of the bill unless "conditions change materially." In an emergency, the bill would go to Congress; if passed, reserve officers would enter active duty to staff national headquarters. The 250 National Guard officers in the states, those who had taken extension courses and attended conferences, would become the nucleus for the state headquarters. Such was the plan. The state personnel situation, however, continued to worry Hershey. "The problem of mobilizing civilian sentiment and effort in the support of war," he explained, "must be handled inevitably through the Governors of the several states." Unfortunately, the state adjutants general lacked funds for sending staff members to training conferences.[26]

In 1938 Hitler annexed Austria and made demands on Czechoslovakia; Japan renewed its war against China. And Hershey struggled with a draft organization which most Americans thought unnecessary. When news of draft planning leaked out in newspaper reports, the War Department was upset. Hershey's superiors feared that Congress would order an end to such activity. A Gallup poll of December 1938 reported only 37 percent favoring one year of compulsory military service. Hershey and his organization had to keep under cover. Officially the United States was suppose to rely upon volunteers in the event of war.[27]

During 1939 Hershey tightened up the mobilization program, insisting that earmarked officers attend training conferences or take extension courses. As he wrote to one major, "My responsibilities to the government make it necessary that the limited number of commissions allotted to this organization be given to those who can and do contribute most toward planning and training for emergency." He also revised the extension courses, moving from an academic format to more practical exercises. He worked closely with state officials to insure that they had a detailed plan to complement the national effort. He wanted each state to have a plan, but he praised diversity. As the states had different jobs, their organizations should be different. "No one in Washington," he insisted, "is as well qualified as you are to decide what means should be taken to carry out the functions devolving upon the state headquarters in Massachusetts during an emergency." National headquarters had the task of formulating and interpreting the basic law, but he expected each state headquarters to divide the state into local board areas best suited to their problems. As a rule he felt every local board should represent a certain number of voting precincts.[28]

Hershey also had to grapple with men who wanted to expand the mission of the draft. Leo M. Cherne, a New York economist, prepared an organizational plan which showed Selective Service headquarters establishing priorities for the use of civilian labor. Hershey hastened to reject this idea. Besides deferring men because of occupations, Hershey insisted that Selective Service "has no responsibilities . . . for any other priorities in connection with labor." He reminded Cherne that the current Selective Service plan did not include using conscription as a means of staffing industry. Hershey thought any reference to "work or fight" would be inappropriate and unfortunate. He had enough problems without having to face irate unions. "Perhaps laziness," he wrote, "has led me to prefer to think of the Selective Service agency as [having] a minimum of connection with the procurement of men for industry."[29]

Although insisting to friends that "I am struggling along in a pick and shovel job which some individuals with more imagination than accuracy have extended materially," his work had reshaped much of the plan. He was instrumental in enlisting the aid of the adjutants general and the National Guard units. He tightened up the extension course and dropped officers who were unable to stay current in their work. Regional conferences were held on a regular basis; mobilization exercises were conducted. State plans had been drawn up and approved or revised. He had done much, and the press began to take notice.[30]

In September 1939 *Look* magazine ran a story on the army's plan for mobilization, including several pictures of recruiting posters. A few weeks later Drew Pearson went visiting in the War Department to check rumors of a plan for the draft. After several false starts, he ended up interviewing Major Hershey. To Pearson, Hershey at first looked "dangerously Prussian." Hershey admitted the existence of a plan but blandly insisted that he personally did not want any draft. "I'm a Hoosier and an isolationist," he informed the reporter, "and I believe we should keep out of other people's troubles." After spending most of his public career privately decrying American isolationism and lack of preparedness, Hershey now offered another line to the press. Pearson went away somewhat reassured and wrote a complimentary column.[31]

Events in Europe soon made such equivocations unnecessary. Hitler's attack on Poland on 1 September 1939 was followed by the rapid occupation of that country, accomplished with the aid of the Soviet Union. A declaration of war by England and France widened the scope of the contest. After hesitating for several months, Hitler struck in the West. First he secured his source of iron ore by taking over Norway. Then, in a series of rapid thrusts through Belgium and the Netherlands, the German army destroyed the Anglo-French army which had been waiting behind defensive positions. Using lightning tank attacks through the Ardennes, Hitler's armies broke the French will to resist. On 22 June 1940 France signed an armistice. Britain was left to fight alone.

Americans watched these events with a growing sense of unreality. The mighty coalition which had frustrated imperial Germany earlier in the century had been brushed aside in a matter of weeks by Hitler. France had fallen, and already German planes were pounding England on a daily basis. Most of the assumptions that had guided American attitudes toward Europe were shattered in 1940. President Roosevelt's hopes of providing arms to help England and France seemed outdated, and he took additional steps to prepare America for a larger role. Henry L. Stimson and Frank Knox, two Republicans who supported more vigorous American involvement in the war, accepted appointments as secretaries of war and navy, respectively. In May, Roosevelt requested additional funds to complement the $3 billion already appropriated for national defense, and he recommended a production program of 50,000 planes a year. Still hoping to avoid sending Americans boys into combat, and facing a reelection campaign against Wendell Willkie, Roosevelt also arranged for the shipment of 50 overaged destroyers to aid England.

These events were unfolding just as Hershey's tour with the chief of staff was coming to a close. His time for retirement had arrived. His own planning provided that the director of the Selective Service System should be a civilian. When he traveled to San Francisco in May 1940 he began making plans for life in the civilian world he had left in 1917. Blind in one eye and forty-six years old, his planning seemed prudent. He arranged to see the head of the New York offices of the Hearst newspaper chain. The Hearst corporation offered Hershey a job as a labor consultant to management with a starting salary of

$25,000—almost $20,000 more than his army salary. Despite the money, Hershey equivocated. He felt it would be foolish to leave the army until the international situation had become clear. In addition, he hated the thought of leaving the service without having reached the rank of colonel. But he left the door open for reconsideration later in the year.[32]

The War Department now informed him that, rather than retirement, his next assignment would be with an artillery unit at Fort Knox, starting 30 June 1940. As Hershey's train traveled back across the country from San Francisco to Washington, the government seemed to be repeating the mistakes of 1914. Although President Roosevelt had called for a massive expansion of the armed forces, Hershey considered the President's message alarmist in nature. "I fear," he wrote, "the country has too many people who have been led to believe we should go to war now—without either cause or means." There seemed little the United States could do at the moment to change the scene in Europe. For Hershey, the best solution would be for the country to put its own house in order, and a good first step would be to adopt military training.[33]

Although Congress had responded to Roosevelt's call for revision of the neutrality law, support for national conscription remained weak. A Gallup poll of 29 January 1940 asked respondents whether the Constitution should be changed "to require a national vote before Congress could draft men for service overseas." Over 60 percent of the sample approved of the idea. The events in Europe during the spring, however, had a dramatic effect on public opinion. As Hitler's armies pushed across the Netherlands, Belgium, and northern France, polls recorded an about-face on the draft issue. On 2 June 50 percent of the sample approved of having "every able-bodied young man 20 years old . . . serve in the army, navy, or the air force for one year." After the armistice in France and before the Battle of Britain began, 67 percent approved of a draft of twenty-year-olds for one year. With every bombing raid in England, American support for conscription became more pronounced.[34]

President Roosevelt still hesitated to request a draft bill from Congress. His reluctance to support Selective Service was at one with his hope to restrict American involvement to material aid. Furthermore, he was running for reelection in 1940. The third-term issue had already been raised by the Republicans. During the campaign Roosevelt promised that American boys would not be asked to fight in foreign wars. He could hardly be an enthusiast for Selective Service and simultaneously campaign on a noninvolvement theme.[35]

The War Department, ready with a Selective Service bill, waited impatiently. Hershey and others in the military fully expected Congress to repeat its 1917 pattern and call for volunteers before moving to the drastic expedient of conscription. General Marshall concentrated all of his congressional efforts on obtaining an increase in military appropriations. Into this vacuum stepped a dynamo named Grenville Clark, a New York lawyer and personal friend of President Roosevelt's. Clark had been active in the promotion of conscription during World War I. The old preparedness organization of 1917, called the Military Training Camp Association, spawned a policy committee in 1940. Led by Clark, the group consisted of such men as Elihu Root, Jr., General John M. Palmer, Colonel William J. Donovan, Archie Roosevelt, Henry L. Stimson, and Julius Ochs Adler of the *New York Times*. After Roosevelt announced his plan for military expansion in May 1940, Clark wrote of the need for conscription, informing President Roosevelt that, if he did not act, the MTCA would prepare a draft bill and submit it to Congress.[36]

Faced with the prospect of Clark introducing a bill which might be inconsistent with War Department plans, Roosevelt ordered General Marshall to establish liaison with the civilian lobby. To fill this role Marshall decided he needed Hershey more in Washington that in an artillery unit at Fort Knox. Line officers were scarce in 1940, but manpower mobilizers were even more valuable. Throughout his tour in Washington Hershey had impressed his superiors. They rated his value to the service in the following terms: "inestimable in procurement of manpower either by volunteer effort or the draft." Hershey was also valuable because of the relationships he had established throughout the nation. Over 400 prominent citizens looked upon him as the natural leader of the draft organization. Typical were comments of 27 March 1940: "Resolved, that the Adjutant General's Association of the United States recognize very thoroughly the most competent and efficient service rendered by Major Lewis B. Hershey . . . and . . . we can only wish that Major Hershey might be kept on this duty for a greater length of time."[37]

Hershey now assumed responsibility for dealing with the civilian lobby. In late May, General Palmer of Clark's group arrived in Washington to see Marshall. Major Hershey met Palmer at the train and attended a conference with the chief of staff. Marshall remained reluctant to involve the War Department in an issue he thought premature and certain to cause political problems in Congress, but he did authorize Hershey and two other officers to meet with the Clark group. Hershey understood clearly that Marshall would disown him if the meeting became known to the press. Acting under Marshall's instructions, Hershey provided Clark with information on the JANSSC plan, including training plans for the National Guard and the reserves. Clark informed Hershey that the lobby was drafting a conscription bill for introduction in Congress but would welcome aid and advice from the War Department.[38]

In the next few weeks the draft issue became more pressing and problems arose. Clark had visions of using the draft as a means of total manpower mobilization. Hershey explained that the War Department felt an initial registration of all men eighteen to sixty-five years old was undesirable because of administrative problems. The army plan called for a maximum registration at one time of 12 million men. He had no objection to requiring all from eighteen to sixty-five to register, but he wanted more latitude on when they would be asked to do so. Hershey felt that Clark was seeking to do too much at one time, and that a more limited approach would have a better chance of meeting with Congressional and public approval.[39] He was acutely aware that President Roosevelt had not yet endorsed conscription. On 20 June 1940 Representative James W. Wadsworth (R, N.Y.) and Senator Edward R. Burke (D, Nebr.) introduced a draft bill in Congress. Not until 23 August did Roosevelt officially endorse the bill.[40]

During July and August 1940 Congress debated the Burke-Wadsworth Selective Service bill and Lewis Hershey developed a national reputation. For the first time he was in the national spotlight. Not only was he in the right place at the right time, but he was uniquely prepared to play a major role in the debate. For the past four years he had become familiar with the nuts and bolts of the proposed Selective Service plan—indeed, he had helped shape it. This experience provided him with technical information and with arguments to defend the plan. Soon the press was writing of the "big stooped-shoulder fellow with the massive red-topped hair," the homespun manner, and the look of a dirt farmer. He was constantly in demand during the hearings. Congressmen enjoyed his tendency to illustrate a point through a folksy story or a backwoods metaphor.[41]

Hershey approached the congressional debate over Selective Service with a keen sense of politics. Unlike some fellow officers, he had never neglected national political events during his military career. As secretary of the JANSSC he had, on a few occasions, informed congressmen of War Department planning.[42] Now, in testimony before both the House and Senate Military Affairs Committees, he explained what he had been doing over the past four years. To the surprise of some congressmen, Hershey explained that the JANSSC had already established an organization which reached down into the states and was ready to become operational as soon as the bill was passed. He went over the mechanics of registration, classification, the quota system for each state, the deferments planned, and the cost. Several congressmen suggested that the plan might be improved by providing legal deferments for certain groups, such as married men and physicians. Hershey argued that such deferments would best be left to the authority of the president.

When asked about the enforcement system of the plan, Hershey offered a philosophy of decentralization which remained unrevised throughout his career. Decisions on the draftee should be made by his neighbors, who were most familiar with any personal problems. The integrity of the local board would be guaranteed by the mothers of draftees, who would police deferments to insure equality of treatment. Draft dodging would be unpopular because of peer and community pressure. Although Hershey insisted that legal prosecution under the act should be handled by the Justice Department, ultimate enforcement of the act had to be by public opinion. Without such public support, he had no hope of success. As for those who feared military control of the draft, Hershey offered words of reassurance. "This organization operates like a civilian organization," he insisted. "There is nothing military about it."[43]

There was some truth to this statement, in that Hershey was a very unmilitary regular officer and the staff positions were filled with reserve officers recently recruited. The local boards, of course, would be staffed by civilians. But to say that there was "nothing military" about the draft was disingenuous. In fact, the chief civilian, the president of the United States, had little to do with the details of the Selective Service bill. Franklin D. Roosevelt pursued a cautious policy toward manpower mobilization. The draft bill had originated with outsiders. Yet by August Roosevelt saw that European events had weakened American isolationism. Polls indicated support for greater preparedness, and General Marshall and Secretary Stimson both argued strongly for presidential support of the draft bill.

At this late stage in the debate, Roosevelt sought to impress his own thinking, vague as it was, on the draft. On 27 August he designated a special committee under Frederick H. Osborn to coordinate the planning of the JANSSC. Besides Osborn, the committee consisted of W. H. Draper, Joseph P. Harris, Floyd W. Reeves, Wayne Coy, and Channing H. Tobias. The next day the group met with Hershey and other members of the JANSSC. Hershey had little trouble with the presidential committee; the only substantive issue which emerged revolved around whether or not to use the postal system to handle the first draft registration. Hershey opposed this idea because it would cost money to pay these officials, preferring instead to use county election officials, who would volunteer and would keep the operation on a local level. With Postmaster General James Farley's support, Hershey won this argument. The committee officially cleared all proclamations and regulations submitted to the president, but it did little to change the program Hershey promoted.[44]

On 16 September 1940 Lieutenant Colonel Hershey, newly promoted to enhance his testimony, looked on with satisfaction as President Roosevelt signed the Selective Service Act. The law had imperfections: it required only one year of training for a maximum of 900,000 draftees. But Hershey was surprised and delighted that any law had passed during peacetime. Congressional changes were minor. Overall, he felt that the law would not interfere with the execution of the draft plan he had been practicing over the past two years. The character of the system was to be shaped by regulations, rather than by the basic law. These regulations—Hershey's regulations—were already drafted and needed only presidential approval.[45]

Later, when explaining the success of the draft, Hershey emphasized three facts. First, the system was decentralized and incorporated the services of state officials, especially governors, who might have been critics of a centralized federal scheme. Second, the law left details to the operating agency's regulations. This broad delegation allowed the system a flexibility needed in establishing such a new organization. Finally, the system benefited from being run by the same men who had planned it for several years. Hershey and his colleagues literally had the system on an operational basis before FDR signed the law. Lists of names for appointments to local draft boards and appeal boards existed before the law passed; similarly, registration forms had already been mailed out.[46]

Roosevelt continued to play only a minor role in shaping the character of the Selective Service System. For the most part he merely signed executive orders authorizing Hershey to issue regulations. The Osborn committee and the War Department gave casual attention to the regulations Hershey sent to Roosevelt. On 21 September Roosevelt issued a statement, drafted by Hershey, to all governors, calling upon them to appoint as local board members men who had the confidence of the local community. "The procurement and training of our manpower under proper administration, fairly and without fear or favor," the president wrote, "is undoubtedly the most important single factor in our entire program of national defense." To carry out the initial program Roosevelt authorized Hershey "to perform all duties in connection with the administration of the Selective Service law." This duty included overseeing the appointment of local board members, board physicians, appeal agents, and others. Roosevelt did qualify his order by requesting that Negroes be appointed to boards in the South, and that labor gain some representation in large industrial centers. Neither of these qualifications had any effect.[47]

Despite the preparation, the Selective Service System had problems in the first few days. In Milwaukee one local board was involved in selling deferments. More common was the tendency of a few governors to appoint members of their own party. Hershey worked hard to keep the system free from political partisanship, but he had trouble coping with Governor Lauren D. Dickinson of Michigan, who turned over the appointment of board members to the Republican machine. Roosevelt had little authority to reverse the governor's decision. The Osborn committee, on Hershey's recommendation, had refused to require that local boards reflect different interest groups.[48]

Because the Selective Service System was decentralized, President Roosevelt had only limited control over staffing. Before signing his letter to the governors, Roosevelt approached Hershey and the Osborn committee to see if something could be done about insuring organized labor some representation. Hershey and the JANSSC refused to cooperate and insisted that local boards must not be "a collection of special interests." Osborn and Secretary of War Stimson both supported Hershey's position, and Roosevelt gave up the idea. In ideal form, Hershey saw the local boards as representing the neighbors of the man to be inducted. The law required only that the local board official be over thirty-six and a resident of the county. The system insured representation of local elites. Board members tended to be judges, bankers, or merchants. The state director often obtained names for the governor by writing the local Kiwanis club, the National Grange, and the Chamber of Commerce. Veterans' organizations also supplied eligible names. The boards were never envisioned as containing a cross-section of the community.[49]

Complaints soon poured into the White House. Senator William H. Smathers complained about one New Jersey county where Governor Arthur H. Moore had appointed all Republicans or anti–New Deal Democrats. General Edwin M. Watson, Roosevelt's military aide, wanted Hershey to hold up these appointments. Similarly, R. J. Thomas of the CIO and union leaders in Michigan complained about the governor's refusal to pick representatives from labor. Sidney Hillman at the War Production Board also complained at the shoddy treatment of labor. Hoping to defuse the issue, Hershey and his state representatives met with union officials and local political leaders in Michigan. After conversations with an aide of John L. Lewis, Hershey was satisfied that the miners' boss agreed on the virtue of keeping local boards independent. As a concession, however, the statewide boards of appeal were to have members from labor, management, and agriculture.[50]

Besides dealing with political controversy, Hershey also had to arrange for the initial registration and classification of draftees. The law called for the registration and classification of all men ages twenty-one to thirty-six at a time and place fixed by the president. Roosevelt wanted the registration before the November election. Hershey arranged for county and state election officials to man some 125,000 registration sites and, on 16 October, approximately 16,400,000 young men provided their names and addresses for the draft. Once the local boards were established, registration cards were forwarded to them. The boards then assigned each registrant a number.

The next step took place at the national level. Hershey arranged for a random drawing of 10,000 numbers to cover the maximum registration in each board area and to establish the order of call for the registrants. On 29 October Franklin D. Roosevelt appeared at national headquarters with Secretaries Stimson and Knox for the drawing of the first number. After a few remarks on the methods of the draft (which Hershey thought inaccurate), the president stood aside as a blindfolded Stimson drew the first number.[51] When the drawing was finished, Hershey was surprised to discover that six numbers were missing. Quickly Hershey wrote those numbers on slips of paper and allowed reporters to pick them out of the bowl. The draft was now officially in business.[52]

But would it work? Public opinion had changed on the draft issue during the summer of 1940. By 30 August some 71 percent of a Gallup sample indicated approval of drafting men between ages twenty-one and thirty-one for one year. Yet some opposition continued among those who feared regimentation. College officials wondered at the future of their institutions if male students were removed.[53]

Hershey's engaging public style convinced Secretary Stimson and Undersecretary Robert Patterson that he was a valuable asset in representing the draft to the public. Hershey traveled to New York, where he regaled the Conference of Mayors about the key roles each of them would play in the new system. He reassured the university community, but he refused to console educators with support for blanket deferments for teachers and students.[54] When a few educators suggested that the army draft men from the ranks of the unemployed, rather than interrupting a young man's education, Hershey explained that "this army must be democratic." By 29 December 1940, 92 percent of a national sample thought the draft was being handled fairly.[55]

The autumn of 1940 was a decisive period in Hershey's career. His reputation spread beyond the military and into the halls of Congress, into the White House and among the press. He was constantly sought out by politicians and reporters, who applauded his lack of militaristic traits and his rustic manner. On 25 October, at the urging of Secretary Stimson, Roosevelt promoted Hershey to the rank of brigadier general. Hershey took his new image in stride. To an old schoolmate he admitted concern over European events, but surprisingly he added: "I have remained through it all an isolationist. I cannot see where we should participate in some of the events that are taking place in this world." He was reluctant to jump into war to save the British.[56]

The Selective Service Act authorized the president to appoint a director, directly responsible to the president, to administer it. Hershey and the JANSSC had presumed that this director would be civilian. As he explained to one of his friends in North Carolina, "I look for the military to be out of it." Yet several congressmen and many state officials kept telling him that he was best qualified for the post. Congress had even inserted a provision in the law which allowed a military officer to serve as director without prejudicing his status in the armed forces.[57]

But President Roosevelt shared with most Americans a concern over the separation of military and civilian powers. When Secretary Stimson had approached the president to obtain a temporary authorization for Hershey to launch the system, Roosevelt had demurred at first. He insisted that he had no intention of assigning an unknown officer to act in an area of such political importance. Instead, he wanted the attorney general to oversee all appointments to local and appeal boards. Such a requirement reflected Roosevelt's general ignorance of a law he had done little to draft, for the numerous appointments could not possibly be checked without mobilizing the entire Federal Bureau of Investigation. Stimson explained the problem, and Attorney General Robert Jackson supported him. Roosevelt had no choice but to make a temporary delegation of power. He hoped to avoid criticism by trying to keep the order secret, but by law such executive orders had to be published in the *Federal Register*.[58]

President Roosevelt had allowed events to force his hand. The Selective Service Act had been generated outside the White House, although the Osborn committee had provided some screening. Now Roosevelt had a Selective Service System but no idea who should be made its director. His unfamiliarity with the provisions of the system insured that he would select a director on political and philosophical grounds. He turned to Harold Smith, the director of the budget, for assistance. The Osborn committee, impressed with Hershey's work, had recommended him. Several congressional leaders, including Senator Henry Cabot Lodge and Congressmen Morris Sheppard and Emanuel Celler, also endorsed Hershey. Sheppard wrote: "I know of no officer of the army who has greater natural ability and aptitude in the handling of legislation." [59]

In addition to Hershey, other army officers were also being pushed. The list included General Douglas MacArthur, Ulysses S. Grant III, and Major General Allen Gullion, the current judge advocate general of the army. [60] The president thought that Gullion was probably better qualified than Hershey, but Smith insisted that many people still opposed conscription, and that civil rights would be an issue. Smith convinced the president that a civilian would be a better choice under such circumstances. Roosevelt suggested Robert Hutchins (president of the University of Chicago) and several other academic leaders, but he finally settled on University of Wisconsin President Clarence Dykstra. As a professor of political science, an expert on city government, a former president of the National Municipal League, and a confirmed liberal, Dykstra seemed ideal for the post. When he came to Washington and met with Stimson and Hershey, both were impressed with the educator's self-confidence. On 12 October Dykstra accepted the post. Hershey then became a brigadier general and deputy director. [61]

Like Stimson, Hershey found Dykstra a bit liberal and aggressive but down to earth in most of his ideas. Rather than becoming despondent over a lost opportunity, Hershey threw his full support behind the new chief. Aware of the considerable public fear of the military, Hershey was not surprised when he was passed over. He established a fine working relationship with Dykstra, made easier by Dykstra's willingness to accept Hershey as the real manager of Selective Service. Dykstra permitted operations to proceed according to existing plans. Indeed, his single contribution to Selective Service was to urge Roosevelt to reject various congressional proposals for amending the law. After this modest contribution and some minor roles in dealing with conscientious objectors, Dykstra began to phase himself out of operations, encouraged by bad health and by discontent at the University of Wisconsin. [62] Officially his resignation became effective on 1 April 1941, but he had ceased to run the organization even earlier. [63]

Lewis Hershey became acting director in April. In reality, he had always been acting director. Working a 42½ hour week in the old Potomac Park Apartments, with no air conditioning and faulty heating, Hershey and his staff struggled to iron out problems with the draft. Reporters noticed how smoothly Selective Service operated even in Dykstra's absence. Russell Gore, a columnist, explained that this was because Hershey, who "looks more like a dirt farmer or the country school teacher," was an expert on mobilization and had the support of Congress. [64]

Although President Roosevelt had not considered Hershey a leading candidate for the job, the general now became tied to the directorship with bonds which endured for thirty years. Roosevelt accepted the situation with considerable reluctance, still believng that a civilian should hold the office. Harold Smith supported and encouraged this notion, pointing out that Hershey would be too easily manipulated by the War Department. James Rowe, a White House aide, disliked Hershey's reliance on decentralization. Roosevelt's problem was finding someone who would accept the job and also meet with Stimson's approval. Into the White House came letters from Governor Sam H. Jones of Louisiana, Congressman Louis Ludlow of Indiana, Senator Claude Pepper of Florida, Hugh Johnson, the old New Dealer, and Channing H. Tobias, a prominent black leader, all urging the appointment of Hershey as the man most able to do the job. Arthur Krock of the *New York Times* warned against putting a New Dealer in a position with such power. Hershey seemed suited to deal with both civilian and military officials.[65]

Hershey refused to lobby for the post. He did not even visit the White House while his future was being debated. Despite this self-effacement, on 31 July 1941 Roosevelt appointed him director of Selective Service, with responsibility for mobilizing millions of Americans. The Hershey family held a modest celebration. Ellen Margaret asked if her dad would get Dykstra's salary of $10,000 a year.[66]

Hershey assumed authority eight months before the United States went to war. Over the next five years he presided over the drafting of 10,110,104 men into the armed forces. The induction of such numbers insured that Hershey would have extensive dealings with Congress, the president, and the War Department. The War Department in particular sought to push Hershey toward certain goals while he was pulled in other directions by the needs of the civilian economy. While many officials entered Washington during the war to help mobilize society, few survived the complex controversies over priorities, the rivalry between military demands and civilian needs. Hershey not only survived, but flourished.

The style Hershey brought to his job contributed to his success as a wartime administrator. Unlike many of his peers, he had little interest in cultivating a role as statesman. Instead, he approached his new job with an air of naturalness and even casualness. Reporters warmed to this unmilitary general who conducted press conferences as though conversing over a cracker barrel at the neighborhood store. With his gold-rimmed glasses dangling off one ear, he rivaled President Roosevelt in playing with the press. In May 1941 reporters asked him if the boys recently drafted would be out in a year, as the law had promised.

Hershey disdained prophecy but warned that, in this weather, a farmer would be wise to get in his hay. Senator Robert Taft, a Republican leader, remarked, "Hershey has his feet pretty firmly on the ground."[67] When discussing changing deferment policies, Hershey explained, "I am noted in this country for making contradictory statements, and I am perfectly willing to make one any time the country needs it." "Policy," he explained, "is a high sounding word and usually amounts to how are we going to answer someone's letter."[68]

Even before the Japanese attacked Pearl Harbor, Hershey presumed a conflict was inevitable. In January 1941 he announced to the press: "We are a nation at war." In his opinion this meant that, besides providing men for the armed forces, the system was to support the nation's agricultural and industrial economies by individual deferments. Although these additional tasks were only dimly outlined in the law creating his agency, Hershey became committed to them during the war. Indeed, he soon conceived of Selective Service as an agency for planning so that every man, woman, and child could play a role in national defense.[69]

Above all, Hershey believed that the Selective Service System was "an application of practical democracy." The right of the community to decide who should serve he considered "the very essence of democracy." He wanted simplicity and openness in the operation, with maximum delegation of authority to local draft boards. As he said, the draft should be "so simple that even the crooks will say, 'I'll be patriotic and register just like all the other guys.'" In contrast to the World War I draft, under Hershey the local boards had full power of classification and deferment. Thousands of individual volunteers, operating in their own communities, decided which of their neighbors would go to war. Hershey envisioned the local boards as little schools in how democracy functioned during a national emergency. Finally, and most pragmatically, this decentralized approach would fragment problems and deflect opposition to the draft. The system worked, Hershey insisted, because "6,443 local centers absorb the shock." "I would have been gone months ago," he explained, "if every criticism aimed at the System had been aimed at me."[70]

Hershey directed Selective Service out of a nondescript brick building on the corner of 21st and C Streets, N.W. The men who staffed headquarters came from the cadre who had worked with Hershey in the system's planning. Commissions were granted to these men and to some at the state headquarters. Hershey explained to General Marshall: "I am . . . convinced that the War Department will always find it to its advantage to have Selective Service administered by individuals who are familiar with problems of the military forces." Soon Hershey had built an organization which offered him complete loyalty. Few defections occurred during the war.[71]

The recordkeeping task alone was formidable. In 1940 national headquarters mailed out some 85 million pieces of printed material to the local boards. As registrants filled out forms, other government agencies came running to Selective Service seeking data. In one three-month period Hershey received a million requests for information. He had no time to answer these requests and simultaneously to oversee the draft. He was also concerned about the confidentiality of Selective Service records. In August 1942 a House bill sought to open the records of registrants to public scrutiny. Hershey accepted the need to post the names of registrants and their classification numbers, but he fought against opening the file because it would "tend to encourage certain busybodies and meddlesome individuals" to disturb the operation of the boards.[72] He made an exception, however, when approached by law enforcement agencies. In March 1941 he wrote, "It should be the policy of the S.S.S. to cooperate with law enforcement officials as much as possible." When the Office of Strategic Services and the Federal Bureau of Investigation sought access to specific personal files, he cooperated.[73]

Hershey did not fit into the role of a Washington bureaucrat. He left the capital whenever he could, visiting the thirteen regional offices, state headquarters, and local boards. As he explained, "I can always learn far more out of Washington than I do here." He traveled in civilian clothes and occasionally paid a surprise visit to state headquarters. Although committed to decentralization, he still insisted that state headquarters remain loyal to national policy. Decentralization existed, but no one doubted who was the boss. When a state official decided to take his complaints to the press rather than keep them in the system, Hershey removed the malcontent.[74]

The key element of the system was the local board, which represented Hershey's troops in the field. When a 1941 Gallup poll revealed that 93 percent of the public believed the draft was being handled fairly, Hershey gave the credit to the local boards. He boasted to Congress that local boards "need not pay any attention to 99 percent of the things we sent out. . . . It is a good thing they do not have to."[75] Such freedom, however, led to inconsistent deferment policies—a problem which would resurface in the 1960's. Hershey admitted that some inconsistency existed, but he insisted that no two cases were identical. Inconsistency was supposed to be minimized through monitoring by regional and state officials and by a liberal appeal procedure. Hershey also promoted consistency by sending optional guidelines to the local boards. But he argued that some inconsistency was the price of decentralization: "I have said many times I would rather have stupidity in the local boards than at National Headquarters."[76] He was still saying the same thing twenty years later.

On several occasions, during the war and later, Congress sought to pay local board members. Hershey always fought this idea, believing that the best-qualified men were willing to serve without pay. Such a volunteer approach insured that boards were filled with men already wealthy enough to expend their time freely. The system excluded the average wage earner, but this was precisely Hershey's intent. By having recognized leaders on the board, the system drew upon existing systems of deference within the community to enhance the draft's credibility. In Hershey's mind the local boards were comparable to local courts. The public expected judges to be fair and estimable men who would apply the law in an evenhanded manner.[77]

Draftees who felt abused by their local boards had the right of appeal. Appeal boards existed at the state level and at national headquarters. Theoretically, one appeal board existed for every twenty local boards, covering some 70,000 registrants. The national appeal board was supposedly under the authority of President Roosevelt; in fact, it was handled out of national headquarters.[78] Yet, even with a system of appeals, some men refused to cooperate with the law. Some 12,000 men worked in Civilian Public Service camps operated by Selective Service. Others refused to register. During the war there were a half-million cases of delinquency.[79]

With 10 million draftees inducted and a mere 16,000 convicted of draft dodging, the problem hardly interfered with Hershey's work. Yet he always took a firm stand on the issue. For those convicted of avoiding the draft, Hershey insisted that parole be conditioned upon accepting induction. The felony carried a maximum punishment of five years in prison, but Hershey feared that if a man were sentenced to only two years and then released he would be avoiding his duty. "I have always believed," he told state directors, "that it is not right to permit a man by his actions to continue to be of no damned good to the country and atone for it in less than the time the war lasts." When the culprit was released from jail, he was again called for induction. Indeed, prison wardens had authority to register felons without their signatures.[80]

Hershey rejected any direct enforcement role for his agency. He argued throughout the war that enforcement should be in the hands of the Department of Justice, "the civilian part of the Government."[81] He also rejected the use of vigilantes to coerce people into registering for the draft. The American Legion volunteered its members to check on slackers, but Hershey demurred. Late in the war Mayor LaGuardia of New York asked Selective Service to use the draft to induct gamblers. Again Hershey refused to cooperate,[82] insisting that the Selective Service "is not the agency which prosecutes violaters of the law or its regulations."[83] Without assuming a police function, Hershey had enough of a challenge simply running Selective Service while the nation was at peace.

The Selective Service System depended upon good relations with Congress. Hershey had already demonstrated remarkable finesse during the passage of the Burke-Wadsworth Act in 1940, and he considered maintaining good congressional relations to be one of the most important responsibilities of his office. In an average day during the war he might receive anywhere from 25 to 200 inquiries from Congress. This volume of mail continued even after he established Colonel Frank Keesling and others as legislative liaison officials. Keeping Congress informed and content consumed much of Hershey's time.[84]

Congressional sensitivity to Selective Service was inevitable, given the nature of the draft. Taking millions of young men away from their families, their schools, and their jobs was bound to generate complaints, many of which found their way to Congress. The decentralization of the system, the wide power of local boards to make deferments, and the absence of uniform standards all contributed to complaints in early 1941. On 5 May Senator Arthur H. Vandenberg introduced a resolution calling for an investigation of Selective Service by a special committee of five senators. Vandenberg was disturbed by complaints that different standards were being used for deferments. His proposal did not get far. The Senate Military Affairs Committee, under Robert R. Reynolds, considered itself the watchdog of the new agency and wanted no help from ad hoc groups.

Despite complaints, a Gallup poll on 23 May 1941 revealed that 93 percent of the sample thought the draft had been handled fairly.[85] Hershey, nevertheless, admitted that the law needed some revision. It required every man between ages twenty-one and thirty-six to register, but reports from induction stations revealed that older men usually flunked the physical exam. By March 1941 Hershey began studying the possibility of deferring men by age groups. As he explained to the secretaries of navy and war, the system had classified about 5 million of the total 16.5 million registered. Of those classified, the age group twenty-one to twenty-seven had generated 77 percent of all eventual inductees; only 12 percent were men over thirty, yet this older group was generating most of the public relations problems. Taking older men meant disturbing marriages and interrupting established careers.

Hershey recommended that the age liability remain twenty-one to thirty-six, but that the president be authorized to defer older men.[86]

Both Frank Knox and Henry Stimson agreed with Hershey's arguments for a discretionary age deferment. Surprisingly, the White House reacted coolly. Rather than have the president request this power, Harold Smith suggested that Hershey make a direct appeal to Congress. Hershey submitted a bill on 10 May which gave the president the power to defer men by age groups. Congress soon used the occasion for a full review of the system.[87]

Several hundred thousand men had been drafted since October 1940 and senators had many questions for Hershey when he appeared before a committee to urge an amendment allowing the president to defer all men over twenty-eight. "I think after the middle 20's the ability to learn things that involve physical aptitude and coordination of mind and muscle falls off rather rapidly," Hershey announced to Chairman Robert R. Reynolds.[88] The Senate Military Affairs Committee had little objection to the bill and supported the plan to defer every man who had reached his twenty-seventh birthday on or before 16 October 1940.

Several senators, however, had questions about the forthcoming second registration, scheduled for 1 July. Some 820,000 men who had turned twenty-one since October 1940 were expected to register. Hershey explained that these new registrants would probably be put at the bottom of the existing list. Neither Senator John C. Gurney nor Senator Edwin C. Johnson liked this proposal. They insisted that Congress had intended the new registrants to be intermingled with the old ones, thereby reducing the liability of all men in the pool. Hershey saw several problems with the Gurney approach. Such an integration would require a new national drawing to establish a new order of call. He would have to ask local boards to establish new serial numbers for all of the men. "If we had a drawing in each place," he explained, "and the damn thing reeks with criticism, it is not going to be on anybody except me." Gurney, however, was adamant and drew support from Chairman Reynolds. Hershey had little choice but to agree.[89]

Hershey had less trouble before the House Military Affairs Committee, where the focus of the discussion remained on the amendment to authorize the president to defer men over twenty-eight. A few congressmen suggested limiting induction to men eighteen to twenty-three. Hershey rejected this approach. The country was staffing a fighting army which would sustain casualties. Therefore, he explained, "I do not think it is biologically sound to put that loss to too restricted an age group." As for spelling out the deferment in the law, Hershey felt such a procedure would be too inflexible; he preferred to allow the president to make the decision.[90]

As Congress voted to grant this power of deferment, the war expanded dramatically. German troops massed on the Soviet border, preparing to launch Operation Barbarossa, as Hershey urged President Roosevelt to establish a new draft call for fiscal year 1941–42. Roosevelt signed the executive order on 28 June, six days after the German invasion of the Soviet Union. The order directed the induction of not more than 900,000 men. On 17 July Hershey gathered several dignitaries for the second national lottery. Secretary of the Navy Frank Knox stepped aside to allow the first capsules to be drawn by a group of draftees on leave for the occasion. "Tonight," Hershey announced, "we are gathered here to witness a ceremony . . . that is symbolic of our American democracy." The entire affair represented another public relations triumph for Hershey. He basked in the glow of a Gallup poll revealing that the public approved of the handling of the draft. The respite, however, was only a lull before the storm.[91]

With the German invasion of the Soviet Union and the increasing success of Nazi submarines in the Atlantic, America drew closer to war. Yet within a few months the thousands of draftees who had been inducted in October 1940 were due to return home, their twelve-month tours completed. Neither President Roosevelt nor General Marshall felt the nation should permit such trained troops to return to civilian life, given the current state of international tensions. The draft law had limited the total number of men who could be inducted to 900,000 at a time. The law also limited service to twelve months, unless Congress should declare the national security imperiled. Finally, the law prohibited the use of draftees outside the western hemisphere. Revising these provisions would not be easy. On the question of overseas duty, May, July, and August polls revealed consistent opposition. On the question of extending the tour beyond one year there was more public support. In April 65 percent of those polled felt the men should be kept only one year, but by 22 July some 50 percent accepted the need for a longer tour. Although there was no strong public sentiment for changing the law, events in Europe, and General Marshall's arguments, required that revision be attempted.[92]

In July Hershey again went to Congress. He had always been dubious about the restrictions in the original law, though he had accepted what he could get in September 1940. Now, on 24 July 1941, he appeared before the Senate Military Affairs Committee to argue for an emergency bill giving the president authority to retain draftees on active duty. Hershey argued that if the men in training since 1940 were released, the nation would be naked to its enemies. "If we could let everyone come home, nothing would better suit a man who grew up in the Midwest like I did," he explained, but "we can't shut our eyes and change the course of the desert." "I try to integrate my boys' best interest," he testified, "with the best interest of the nation in the long run." The national interest required that the draftees stay on duty.[93] For Hershey, the real issue was whether or not the nation faced an emergency. The president had decided that these trained units should not be deactivated because it would take another year to get them ready again.[94]

As Congress debated this issue, public opinion remained clearly divided. On 6 August a Gallup poll found 50 percent for extending the tour but 45 percent in favor of release. When the House voted on 12 August, the extension issue passed by one vote, 203–202. The narrow victory clearly reflected indecision about America's role in the European conflict. Finally, on 18 August Congress passed, and President Roosevelt signed, a compromise measure which extended the tour of draftees to eighteen months.[95]

The compromise failed to satisfy Hershey. He explained to the press that releasing men after eighteen months meant an increase in the numbers called up. He expected calls to increase to some 70,000 a month. As for the morale of the draftee, Hershey insisted "there is nothing wrong with the young folks if some of the parents would just leave them alone." At a rally for National Youth Day at the Commodore Hotel in New York, where he shared the platform with Douglas Fairbanks, Jr., Ethel Barrymore, and other Hollywood stars, Hershey told the audience that they had to "break down the barriers between groups which are stratifying" and "bring to the community the unity of all of its citizens." The overflow crowd, however, was more interested in seeing the stars. Hershey departed unnoticed at 10:00 P.M.[96]

While Hershey roamed the country promoting national unity to indifferent audiences, military planners in Tokyo were putting the finishing touches on the plan for a surprise attack on Pearl Harbor. Diplomatic negotiations continued between the United States and Japan, but an unseen clock ticked away the remaining hours of peace. Congress continued to debate whether draftees could be sent outside the western hemisphere. Soon they would be serving in every corner of the globe. In later years comparing stories about what one was doing when Pearl Harbor was attacked became a popular parlor game. Few Americans in Honolulu on the morning of 7 December 1941 were playing games. Japanese fighters and bombers streaked across the sky, leaving death and destruction in their wake.

IV. Drafting for World War II

Hershey was riding the Union Pacific Railroad from Salt Lake City to Boise. He planned to address a meeting of local board members on the night of 7 December. While talking with Governor Nels H. Smith of Wyoming, he was startled to hear the conductor run through the car announcing that Japanese planes were attacking Pearl Harbor. Hershey assured the conductor that he must mean the Philippines. Like most Americans, Hershey was surprised at the audacity of the Japanese. When the train reached Boise, he faced questions from the press. Although pleading ignorance on military matters, he warned the public that only a shortage of equipment would now limit the rate at which men would be inducted. Congress, "with not much more than a twist of the wrist," could lower the age limit and end dependency deferments and other restrictions on the draft. He cancelled the rest of his tour and the next morning rode the City of Portland toward the east and new responsibility.[1]

Upon his return to headquarters Hershey immediately announced "that all requirements of the armed forces [will] be met without delay." He called for a reexamination for induction of all twenty-one to twenty-eight-year olds who had been deferred and insisted that all industrial, professional, and other deferments be cut. The administration planned to amend the law to provide for registration of all men from ages eighteen to sixty-five, but to limit liability to those from nineteen to forty-five.[2]

Yet at a press conference on 11 December Hershey tried to play down the need for any drastic surgery in the law. When asked about expanding the present pool, he admitted that expansion might be needed, but he insisted the best approach would be to provide broad, flexible authority to the president so that he could focus on one age group or another. Hershey expected to obtain about 3 million men from the currently liable group between ages twenty-one and twenty-eight, but he favored registration of all men up to age sixty-five. He had no idea when he would have to draft older men.[3] All job deferments would now have to be reconsidered. To build up an army of 10 million (a figure tossed about by some military leaders) he would have to "invade homes" and upset the social structure of the nation.[4]

Congress responded with dispatch to the crisis. By 13 December joint resolutions had removed the restriction on men serving outside the western hemisphere and had extended the period of duty to include "the duration of the war and six months after its termination." These measures passed without debate. The administration's bill, calling for registration of all males from eighteen to sixty-five and making those nineteen to forty-four liable for induction, received more deliberation. Chairman Andrew J. May of the House Military Affairs Committee and others worried about registering eighteen-year-olds. Drafting such youngsters would break up homes and deprive the boys of their educations. Hershey argued vigorously for registration; eventually these young men would have to be drafted. When congressmen questioned the need to register men over age forty-five, Hershey justified a broad registration in terms of its psychological effect on the nation.[5]

Hershey argued that the real purpose of the bill was national unity. "I happen to be one of those individuals," he explained, "who believe that there isn't any military, there isn't any economic, there isn't any industrial, there is no psychological situation. They are all a part of one situation, just like a human being is an integrated thing." For those disturbed about taking men under twenty-one, Hershey pointed out that of a total of 2,778,000 Civil War enlistments, some 2,159,000 were of soldiers twenty-one and younger. On 20 December 1941 the act passed Congress and was signed by President Roosevelt. An unprecedented amount of power had been delegated, under pressure of war, to the president. This power, in turn, was soon delegated to Brigadier General Hershey.[6]

The president proclaimed 15 February as the day for registering all men twenty years old and between thirty-six and forty-five. Local boards handled the registration. The new names went to the bottom of the existing reservoir of eligibles, which was drying up.[7] To determine the order of call for this third registration, Hershey held another festival with the fishbowl. He decided upon green capsules as a nice touch in honor of St. Patrick's Day. The Irish War Veterans served as ushers, and Hershey announced the numbers on national radio. On 17 March a blindfolded Secretary Stimson selected the first number. Following Stimson came Secretary Knox, Congressman Andrew May and Senator James Wadsworth. On two occasions the dignitaries came up with duplicate numbers, much to Hershey's embarrassment.[8]

On 19 March the president called for registration of men ages forty-five to sixty-four. Since there would be no immediate inductions from this age group, the fishbowl was put in storage, but registration was held on 27 April. Among the new registrants were President Roosevelt and many members of the White House staff. On 22 May the president finally called for registration of men eighteen to twenty years of age. After this event, on 30 June 1942, each man had to register upon reaching eighteen years of age. The order of call would now be based on date of birth, rather than upon lottery—for which Hershey gave thanks.[9]

At a press conference on 16 January Hershey expressed optimism that the new registrants would provide ample manpower to furnish the army of 3.6 million men which Stimson had originally requested. The age group between twenty and forty-four could provide 9 million men. By the middle of 1942, however, the War Department wanted an army of 7.2 million. This increase, combined with excessive deferments for dependency and occupations, plus a high rate of physical rejections, forced Hershey to reassess his pool. By summer 1942 he was urging the president to issue a proclamation allowing Selective Service to draft from the eighteen- to twenty-year-old group, which totaled some 3,125,000 men.[10]

Unfortunately, these younger men, while registered, were not liable for induction under the current Selective Service law. All signs indicated that such a liability would provoke considerable congressional opposition. A poll of 12 May 1941 found 51 percent favoring a change in the law to allow for induction of those eighteen to twenty-one, but 44 percent still opposed the idea. Undismayed, Hershey told several audiences: "We have never had a war in which it was not necessary to draft boys of eighteen and nineteen, and I expect we'll have to take them in this one."[11]

Hershey had to come up with some means of convincing Congress and the public of the virtues of drafting eighteen-year-olds. The strategy he adopted involved an "either-or" routine. Without the power to draft eighteen year olds, Hershey informed Congress that in the near future he would have to induct between 1 and 1.5 million married men. In September he predicted that some 10 million men would be in the armed forces by the end of 1943. He ordered local boards to begin calling childless married men in December 1942. Even more disturbing, he warned that if Congress did not authorize the drafting of eighteen-year-olds he would start inducting fathers by October 1943.[12]

Forty-three million men ages eighteen to sixty-five were registered, but Hershey could take only 27 million, those between twenty and forty-five. The army needed 7.5 million by mid-1943. Men under twenty were already being recruited into the service as volunteers, and Hershey wanted to replace this hit-or-miss volunteering with the draft. If Congress authorized the draft of eighteen-year-olds, he could produce an additional 800,000 to 900,000 soldiers by December. The real issue was to find young men who could "jump from planes without breaking ankles, to drive tanks in 130 degree temperature, to swim ashore."[13]

A few days after the November elections Congress passed the bill amending the draft law to allow induction of eighteen- to twenty-year-olds. On 18 November Roosevelt ordered registration of all youths who had turned eighteen since 1 July. Hershey's manpower pool was now complete, covering for registration all men from eighteen to sixty-five and for induction all from eighteen to forty-five.[14]

Hershey still faced other problems, however, including the task of avoiding partisan politics. A lifelong Republican, he worked well with Franklin D. Roosevelt during the war. During the 1930's Hershey had doubted the effectiveness of much New Deal legislation; he also disliked Roosevelt's approach to mobilization. Yet he had to "give the Devil his due." He soon came to appreciate that the president had uncanny political acumen and unparalleled skill in avoiding messy problems. As a military officer on detached duty, Hershey also recognized the need for loyalty to the commander-in-chief. When Senator Joseph L. Hill asked about the state of national leadership in July 1941, Hershey explained "Regardless of how we feel in an election, we must listen to our responsible heads now. . . . If we are going to get the ship to port, we have got to let the captain set the course."[15]

During the first year of the Selective Service Hershey had to struggle to keep his organization out of party politics. Not unexpectedly, many people wrote to the president seeking special draft deferments. Invariably President Roosevelt refused to intervene.[16] State election committees often sought the cooperation of local boards to obtain the names of registrants. Hershey refused permission, arguing that the system could not spare the time for such work.[17] By 1941 the White House decided that it would be best to "keep hands off" Selective Service appointments in order to preserve the integrity of the system.[18]

But keeping the White House out of the system merely allowed state and local politicians to move in. Hershey's emphasis on decentralization and local control insured that power would be exercised by local rather than national elites. In March 1941 newly elected governors began removing existing state directors to make room for their own men. Georgia Governor Eugene Talmadge began a purge of Selective Service personnel appointed by his predecessor. Hershey's reaction was consistent with his federal view of the system: if the governor wanted his own man, he should get him. Roosevelt insisted that Talmadge provide some reason for removing the state director, but Hershey successfully argued that the White House should go along with the governor as a matter of policy.[19] By 1942, however, Hershey himself began to draw the line. Governor Culbert L. Olson of California wanted to remove the state director and replace him with a friend. Hershey told him that to remove the current director would signal to the public that the system was nothing but a political football. The governor might be entitled to his own man, but Hershey refused to allow the system to appear blatantly political.[20]

Besides dealing with governors, Hershey had to struggle with federal agencies. As the United States became a full-scale belligerent, the need for total mobilization meant the draft would have to be coordinated with overall manpower requirements. The British Ministry of Labour, for example, could not "conceive of an orderly manpower policy unless the control over manpower, whether for military or industrial purposes, is lodged in a single responsible agency." Hershey himself finally recognized the need to coordinate the draft with civilian manpower needs, and he expressed a willingness to assume such responsibility early in 1942. Roosevelt, however, had other ideas.[21]

After Pearl Harbor several leaders in Washington began to argue for stronger manpower controls which would cover civilian labor as well as draftees. Paul McNutt, head of the Federal Security Agency, recommended on 26 January 1942 that Roosevelt appoint a civilian manpower mobilization board. Grenville Clark laid before Roosevelt the plan for a national service bill which allowed drafting for civilian jobs. Hershey wrote to Clark on 5 March 1942, agreeing with the "pressing need" for overall manpower allocations. Roosevelt finally responded by creating the War Manpower Commission on 18 April 1942. He appointed Paul McNutt as the chairman, and Hershey became a member. When reporters asked McNutt to clarify his relationship to Selective Service, he explained that the WMC would direct the system on whom to defer by groups, regions, and locations. When a reporter noted that Hershey had consistently opposed group deferments, McNutt rejoined: "Well, after all it is a question of where the determination of policy will be made." Hershey, to his dismay, was now working with McNutt.[22]

At the first meetings of the WMC Hershey pledged his cooperation and admitted that Selective Service needed someone to identify those industries where deferments were justified. The WMC soon replied with a long list of essential skills and jobs to guide local boards in deferment policy. Hershey was startled by the range of the lists, which covered many areas he considered unessential to the war effort, and he insisted that such information was merely advisory. The manpower scene became increasingly confused and, by autumn, public criticism reached a high pitch.[23]

During September and October 1942 Congress launched an investigation of the manpower problem. The issues included migration of labor, the drafting of eighteen-year-olds, and, finally, the question of national service. During several hearings congressmen repeatedly encouraged Hershey to act independently of McNutt, who had a poor reputation on the Hill. When asked about McNutt's power over Selective Service, Hershey at first insisted that it was purely an academic question, as he had found no conflict between his mission and McNutt's directives. He insisted that Selective Service was a service agency, not a policy agency. When pressed, however, Hershey admitted that the list of essential activities and critical occupations spawned by the WMC was rather formidable. Several congressmen worried at McNutt's power over the draft. Congressman John P. Thomas asked if Roosevelt planned to take Selective Service away from army officers and give it to civilian bureaucrats, "these swivel-chair patriots." Had not McNutt recommended to the president, he asked, that the Selective Service System be taken away from the army and put in his agency? Hershey replied incoherently: "I do not believe that anything I can say would add to the facts of the situation there."[24]

Behind Hershey's back, McNutt and Grenville Clark were urging just such a revision upon Roosevelt. In Clark's view Hershey had been "pretty consistently late because of his inability to grasp the size and seriousness of this war." He should be kept at Selective Service, but someone else (and McNutt felt he was well qualified) should be appointed to run a national service program. McNutt joined in lobbying either for a law or for executive reorganization which would give him more direct control over Hershey. The military should not be determining civilian manpower policy, McNutt insisted.[25] Secretary of War Stimson, however, argued that military manpower should be kept segregated from civilian manpower. Stimson had no wish to see his own special relationship with Hershey upset by the appointment of a civilian director of manpower. Several governors also wired Roosevelt, urging that Hershey be left in charge and that the system retain its decentralized character.[26]

Roosevelt knew that Hershey was better liked in Congress than McNutt, but something had to be done. Harold Smith, director of the budget, wrote Roosevelt: "Highly as I regard Hershey personally, a great mistake was made in letting a military man run Selective Service, so important an element in manpower. No matter how intellectual he may be on the subject, he is bound to be pushed in one direction and one direction only, and no matter how objective he may be, his career and promotion depend upon the Army." On 5 December 1942 Roosevelt issued an executive order placing the system under McNutt's control.[27]

Roosevelt's domestic solution to the manpower problem was doomed to failure. McNutt soon realized that he needed more power to insure that each local board would adopt the list of occupational deferments developed by the WMC. While Hershey would cooperate with McNutt

on many issues, there would be no compromise on the idea of decentralization. The new executive order authorized McNutt to issue directives to local boards, yet the law required that local boards retain autonomy on classification. One of Hershey's subordinates had jokingly
warned that all Selective Service personnel would now have to wear a
new insignia—"a Hershey bar with McNutts in it." Besides being a
bad pun, the statement was false. Hershey blandly informed all units
that the system would operate "as heretofore." His legal counsel assured him that he retained all of the powers and duties he had possessed before Roosevelt's order.[28]

While this new arrangement had little practical effect, Hershey was
still nettled, and he spent the next several months seeking a path out
of what he called "the bondage time." McNutt and his crowd had a very
poor reputation in Congress; critics called them too political, too pro-
labor, and too pro-civilian-economy. Hershey's headquarters, in contrast, were filled with men in uniform who fancied themselves a military unit committed solely to winning the war. The WMC depended for
its authority on an executive order, while Hershey had a statute behind him. Hershey now thought it contradictory to have the procurer
of manpower (SSS) united to an agency concerned with the use of manpower (WMC).[29] The most serious disagreement arose over the integrity of decentralization. Hershey wrote to McNutt: "I will not transmit
any order from you for classification." As a military officer, Hershey
also had doubts about the WMC's statement that protecting men in
critical jobs took priority over furnishing troops for the army.[30]

The solution to Hershey's problem appeared in the person of Frank
Keesling, a young, bright, and ambitious lawyer from California who
had joined headquarters during 1940. Keesling argued that the WMC
was unnecessary because Selective Service could force men into desirable occupations through the use of the draft. He used his position as
liaison man on the Hill to undermine McNutt and promote Hershey. In
February 1943 McNutt called for the induction of fathers. Congress
had little sympathy for taking such a step before all young single men
in war industry had been drafted. Congressman Paul J. Kilday of Texas
and Senator Burton Wheeler offered bills providing blanket deferments for married men. Keesling immediately tried to revise these
bills to free Hershey from the WMC. Although well aware of what
Keesling was doing, Hershey pretended ignorance in the event that he
might have to repudiate his ambitious aide. On 5 December Congress
passed a bill restricting the induction of pre–Pearl Harbor fathers and
limiting Roosevelt's delegation of draft authority to Hershey.[31]

Roosevelt, busy on a tour of the North African front, where American forces had recently been bloodied in battle, found the bill distaste-

ful. Secretary of Labor Frances Perkins, Attorney General Francis Biddle, Donald Nelson, director of the War Production Board, and McNutt all urged him to veto the measure. From more politically astute advisors, such as Sam Rosenman and Harry Hopkins, Roosevelt received other advice. The bill might well pass even over a veto. Furthermore, for Roosevelt to approve the draft of fathers would be a considerable political liability. The president, "after rather disgusted contemplation," signed the measure, although he considered its administrative restrictions silly.[32]

Hershey had freed himself from McNutt's control, but his battles with the executive branch were not over. No issue was filled with more political shoals than the problem of deferments for federal government officials. To preserve the integrity of the system Hershey had to avoid favoritism. He received help from Secretary of the Treasury Henry Morgenthau, who distrusted his fellow cabinet members when it came to asking for deferments and who sponsored an ad hoc group to recommend uniform policy on government deferments. Hershey was asked to write up a policy for the approval of the committee and submission to the president. His plan called for certification that the official was in a war-related job and was difficult to replace, and it limited the deferment to six months.[33] The secretary finally agreed to Hershey's proposal and sent it over to the president. In February 1942 Roosevelt released the Hershey memorandum with the statement that he wanted an "equitable and uniform" policy established according to the guidelines.[34]

By October 1942 some 5.5 million draft-age men were working in government jobs. In congressional testimony Hershey called this "a luxury that we cannot afford in the war." "I do not know," he insisted, "just how you are going to squeeze them out, but I am afraid you are going to have to." Congressman Dewey J. Short and Senator Millard E. Tydings needed little encouragement. Short complained about the thousands of young government officials crowding thirsty congressmen out of Washington cocktail lounges. Tydings kept Hershey busy checking lists of federal employees who were registered for the draft.[35]

Hershey faced a dilemma. On one side, Congress was determined to prevent government service from becoming a haven for draft dodgers. On the other, several members of the Roosevelt administration insisted upon protection for key officials. Secretary of the Interior Harold Ickes and Attorney General Francis Biddle were particularly interested in protecting their men. President Roosevelt at first seemed to favor the congressional position. On 17 November 1942 he issued a memorandum to the heads of departments and agencies calling for the cancellation of all employee deferments. Pressure within the cabinet soon led Roosevelt to reconsider his order. He explained to the press that, of the civilian workers in the federal government, some 60 percent were in defense-related jobs under the navy and army. Washington itself had very few deferred types.[36]

Congress was not satisfied, but Ickes and Biddle continued to press for protection of their key men. Biddle argued that the president should not delegate to Hershey the power to review such cases. In desperation, Roosevelt finally asked Sam Rosenman to assume this responsibility.[37] The entire issue of government deferments had become a political football, one which Hershey was happy to drop into Rosenman's lap.

Congress, to the end of the war, remained suspicious of draft dodgers in the government, yet as the war came to a close Hershey reported that the deferment trends in government were very close to those outside it. On 1 December 1944 more than 72 percent of all federal deferees were over thirty years of age. Of the 265,909 not physically disqualified, 80 percent were over thirty and less than 1 percent under twenty-six. Of the 2,452 under twenty-six and not physically disqualified, some 1,261 were employed by the navy and 624 by the War Department. The others were agents of the FBI or scientists. The federal service had not become a haven for draft dodgers.[38]

Given the variety of interests served by congressmen and the larger responsibilities of the executive branch, Hershey's conflicts were predictable. Less predictable, but no less important, were the battles he fought with the armed forces over the conduct of the draft system. During World War II Hershey was both a soldier and a civilian. Although on detached assignment, he remained officially a military officer. Wearing a uniform, however, did not make a military man. Senator Warren R. Austin explained to his colleagues: "I have come to consider General Hershey as having a civilian outlook, although technically he is an officer of the Regular Army." Hershey, according to Austin, "because of his civilian background and because of his long association . . . with the civilian officers connected with Selective Service, has very definitely the civilian outlook." But he also understood the military outlook, which made him "an ideal person to administer the Selective Service System." Hershey apparently fit the national ideal of citizen-soldier.[39]

Though Hershey was detached from the army for duty with Selective Service, he was not impervious to influences from the War Department—specifically, from Secretary of War Henry Stimson. Hershey knew that he owed his position and promotion to Stimson, and he had respect for the integrity of the secretary. This relationship placed limits on the independence of Hershey and his staff, which also consisted of military officers. Stimson, in turn, felt free to issue orders to Selective Service personnel.[40] Hershey considered the chief of staff, General George C. Marshall, a source of guidance. Although physically and legally separated from Marshall's office, Hershey still considered him a military superior. During the war Marshall's office rendered efficiency reports on General Hershey. On 11 September 1942 Marshall congratulated him on his achievements and invited him to seek advice and guidance "at any time that you believe I can be of help." Hershey replied that he often "wished for your counsel and guidance."[41]

When the draft bill was passed, most people assumed that civilian control had been established; Franklin D. Roosevelt supported this idea when he appointed a civilian as the first director. But by 1941 General Hershey had become director, and all of the key positions in the system were filled with army officers. Hershey was naturally sensitive to charges that the army controlled his agency. In October 1940 he issued a directive on the wearing of uniforms: "Since it is believed desirable that the entire emphasis be placed on the civilian nature of Selective Service," all officers assigned to the system "will neither wear uniforms at the state headquarters nor in the field." Hershey spent much time reassuring Congress that there were only three regular army officers in the entire system. When war came in December 1941 and the wearing of uniforms became required, Hershey explained that his men were civilians in disguise.[42]

The War Department appreciated the need to reassure the public over civilian control of the draft; but in practice the department sought close ties with the system. While publicly claiming a civilian role, Hershey privately agreed on the need for such ties. He requested that the War Department assign more soldiers to his operation.[43] In April 1941 he explained to General Marshall that it would "not be in the best interest of the War Department, Selective Service or the nation to relieve officers from key positions in Selective Service." The War Department would find "it to its advantage to have Selective Service administered by individuals who are familiar with the problems of the military forces."[44] Stimson agreed and wrote, "In the case of Selective Service work I have already held that it is not a purely civilian work but a work so closely connected with the army that my policy of taking away Army men from civilian duty does not apply."[45]

Hershey understood his special relationship with the army, yet dealing with the War Department could be a very frustrating experience. The provisions of the law and the regulations made Hershey's task appear simple. Theoretically, the president and the War Department decided on the size of the armed forces. The war and navy departments issued calls to Hershey sixty days in advance of the need for men. National headquarters broke down the calls by states. Each state received a draft call based on a percentage of the total number of registrants in 1-A status, after subtracting for men already in organized units such as the National Guard and the number already enlisted through volunteer recruitment. At the state level the calls were distributed to local boards, again on the basis of how many 1-A's were registered. Draft notices were sent out, and the men eventually reported to induction stations for examinations and oath-taking.

This neat design had little relation to reality. Perhaps the most basic problem confronting Hershey in seeking to fill the military calls was the constant change in the many variables with which he had to deal. Although people spoke of a manpower pool, Hershey had to deal with a manpower stream. The number of men available was in a constant state of flux, with men obtaining jobs and losing deferments for such things as dependency, defense jobs, and farming. Not only did the pool fluctuate, but the military calls also changed with alarming frequency. The size of the call depended upon the projected size of the army, which was debated and revised several times during the war. In addition, the success or failure of military recruitment programs affected both Hershey's pool and the size of the call. The War Department made the problem more complex by insisting upon separating calls by race, despite the provisions of the law. Finally, even after Hershey delivered the required number of draftees, a high percentage were rejected because of the physical and mental tests imposed at induction stations.[46]

To succeed in his task Hershey had to remain very flexible. He issued so many regulations, many of which countermanded earlier ones, that political cartoonists had a field day with him. While local boards complained about the frequent shifts in guidelines, Hershey was merely reflecting the shifts in national policy.[47] He had little effect on what was perhaps the most basic question facing the draft: the size of the armed forces.

This question of size was answered by Roosevelt, Stimson, and Marshall. Indeed, War Department planners made their projections with little attention to social and economic considerations on the home front. Using an occult method, army planners estimated that a total of 8 percent of the population was the maximum which could be mobilized for military service. This estimate projected a total of 9 million for the army and 3 million for the navy. Hershey played no role in determining these figures, but he consistently supported them.[48] In 1942, when asked about manpower needs of the armed forces, Hershey predicted that the total would approach 13 million. As this figure was far beyond what had been publicly admitted by either Roosevelt or Stimson, Hershey was criticized at a cabinet meeting for scaring the public. Roosevelt told Marshall that the army and marines total would be limited to 7.2 million up to the end of 1943. Yet Hershey stuck by his projection, which was predicated upon total mobilization.[49]

While agreeing with the need for a large armed force, Hershey disagreed with both the army and navy over how this force should be mobilized. Hershey believed the Selective Service System represented the most sensible and orderly means of obtaining men. The military services, in contrast, refused to depend entirely upon conscription. The navy in particular, supported by President Roosevelt, insisted on freedom to recruit. Before Pearl Harbor Hershey had tried to cooperate with such recruiting efforts. Stimson and Hershey signed a memorandum of understanding by which recruiters were forbidden from enlisting as a volunteer any draftee who had already received his induction notice. The agreement proved impossible to enforce. Admiral Chester W. Nimitz, in fact, issued a circular to draft boards instructing them to provide lists of men in 1-A classification to local navy recruiters. Hershey balked at this attempt to order his local boards around, but he tried to meet the armed forces halfway. As a compromise, he argued that local boards could prepare lists of 1-A men for recruiting agencies. Such agencies would then have thirty days or longer in which to recruit these men, but once the men had received induction notices, recruiters should not touch them. Nevertheless, old habits persisted.[50]

When the United States entered the war, the recruiting problem became even more serious. Thousands of young men, in a patriotic fervor to avenge Pearl Harbor, rushed to volunteer. Hershey patiently explained to Roosevelt, Stimson, and Knox that this enthusiasm was making a shambles of orderly manpower management. Most of the volunteers were already in the 1-A classification and would be drafted in the normal order of events; others were in key industrial positions, and their loss would seriously hamper the war economy. But both Knox and Stimson wanted to reap the effects of this enthusiasm before it waned.[51]

As a result of Roosevelt's attitude, supported by Stimson and Knox, the United States repeated the mistake of World War I. Instead of relying upon systematic procurement by Selective Service, the military pulled in men from all walks of life. By summer 1942 the War Manpower Commission realized that attempts at stabilizing employment in war plants was impossible so long as military recruitment continued. Finally, at a cabinet meeting on 4 December 1942, after McNutt and Nelson repeated Hershey's earlier arguments, the president agreed to end all voluntary enlistments. Roosevelt, however, allowed the military to continue recruiting men under eighteen and over thirty-eight. Hershey was thus confronted with an indeterminate pool of new draftees. By the end of the war Hershey complained that some 200,000 young men had been recruited into the air force cadet program and allowed to linger at home.[52]

Eliminating most recruiting did not end all of Hershey's headaches. From September 1940 through August 1945, some 22 million men between the ages of eighteen and thirty-seven were registered. Of this total, some 5 million were deferred for a variety of reasons; another 5 million were rejected as unfit. Hershey had to send twice as many men forward as the military actually used.[53]

Throughout the war Hershey fought to reduce the standards imposed on the draftee. As someone with impaired vision, he had sympathy for those in less than perfect health. Such men could make a contribution if the armed forces would use a more positive approach—if they would ask how a man might be utilized, rather than searching for his deficiencies. Hershey also felt that the mental requirements for service were unrealistic. If a man held down a regular job in civilian life, Hershey felt he had all of the physical and mental equipment needed to contribute in some way to the army or navy. Indeed, Hershey looked to the army as a means of improving the health of many American youngsters. Such reformist ideas met with consistent opposition from military leaders, who refused to consider any other mission than battle with the enemy. Yet, by presenting the problem in graphic detail and by constantly hammering at the loss of salvageable manpower, Hershey at least publicized the problem.

Hershey was astounded at the high rate of rejection—some 40 percent—for the first million draftees. Hershey concluded, "We are physically in a condition of which nationally we should be thoroughly ashamed." One-third of those rejected were turned down because of nutritional disabilities. He called for the induction of all men rejected on grounds of correctable mental deficiency, such as illiteracy, and for half of those with remedial physical problems. This proposal encountered stern opposition from both the War Department and professional psychiatrists.[54]

Meeting resistance from the armed forces, Hershey called upon each citizen to assume responsibility for making himself healthy to fight. When this naive idea had no effect, he began urging the federal government to assume responsibility for rehabilitation. The concept of equal sacrifice embodied in the Selective Service law was becoming a joke which might well destroy the draft system. Several senators and congressmen complained because men were being rejected because they did not have a fourth-grade education.[55] In enforcing a fourth-grade level of literacy, the system in two months deferred 91,919 registrants. Hershey feared that army psychiatrists "in their enthusiasm . . . push the pendulum to an unnatural position," rejecting men "no queerer than the rest of us."[56]

Hershey also sought help from Eleanor Roosevelt. He explained that many of the men physically and mentally disqualified from service could be rehabilitated, but that the Selective Service lacked the facilities for such a program. Soon the president found his wife aggressively promoting several elaborate rehabilitation schemes.[57] Roosevelt agreed that the army was the logical agency to correct defects, and Stimson finally met with Hershey to study the problem.[58]

On 10 October 1941 Hershey reported that 1 million men had been rejected for physical, mental, or educational defects out of some 2 million examined. Hershey proposed rehabilitation for men with VD, hernias, dental and vision problems. The individual could choose to have the service performed at home by a private physician, but the cost would be borne by the federal government. The next day Roosevelt issued a statement instructing Hershey to undertake such a program in cooperation with the army.[59]

Hershey immediately launched a pilot program in two states. Temporarily neglecting his Jeffersonianism, he now began planning a program of health care financed by the federal government.[60] The rehabilitation program, which had potential for evolving into a national health-care system, hardly left the ground despite Hershey's efforts. Stimson talked cooperation, but the army expected Selective Service to do most of the work. The issue was still being debated on 7 December 1941. After the Japanese attacked Pearl Harbor, the army immediately lowered physical and mental standards.

Nevertheless, throughout the war Hershey fought to reduce induction standards even further. He tried to explain to Stimson that "there are not enough Class 1-A men available under present standards to meet contemplated requirements of the armed forces." Local boards were raising hell at healthy young men being rejected because of illiteracy. Stimson finally conceded Hershey's point: effective 1 August 1942, the literacy standard was reduced to allow induction of anyone who could understand simple orders in English and who could absorb training, provided that this category did not exceed 10 percent of either white or black calls.[61]

But Hershey wanted more. As the rejection rate climbed in the summer of 1943, he again took his case to the president. Roosevelt, in late 1943, appointed a special committee headed by Admiral Ross McIntire to study the feasibility of lowering the standards. In February 1944, after two months of collecting data and despite a warning from Hershey that he would have to draft fathers if standards were not lowered, the committee supported Stimson. The report concluded that lowering physical standards would impair military efficiency. Rather than have that happen, the committee urged Hershey to draft fathers.[62]

As the manpower pool dried up in 1943, congressmen also became indignant about the high rejection rate. Neither politicians nor the public would tolerate young, seemingly healthy men staying home while fathers went to war. As the head of an agency largely dependent upon volunteers, Hershey was very sensitive to public attitudes.[63] By 1944 he reported that some 4 million men had been rejected because of physical or mental problems, which included educational deficiency. These figures prompted passage of a Senate resolution authorizing an investigation into the health of the nation.

Senator Claude Pepper headed a subcommittee of the Committee on Education and Labor to look into the fitness question. Hershey was the star witness. He made clear that the rejection of 4 million men insured that more fathers, scientists, and key workers would be drafted. Hershey blamed the educational establishment as well as high military standards for this state of affairs. "It is idle," he explained, "to talk of a democracy, in which each citizen had equal opportunities with every other citizen and equal responsibilities . . . unless these citizens, each and every one, are able, when the responsibility comes, to carry their part." He also complained at the narrow intellectual approach of schools following nineteenth-century models. With myriad labor-saving devices now in people's homes, the school had to train the body as well as the mind.[64]

But mental defects also caused rejections. No issue upset Hershey more than the rejection of almost 1 million of some 4 million 4-F's for defects above the neck. Some 750,000 men had been turned down for service because of psychiatric disorders ranging from emotional instability to paranoia. In World War I nervous and mental rejections had accounted for 12 percent of the total; by the end of World War II the percentage had climbed to 35.2.[65] As Hershey fancied himself something of a lay expert in psychology, he felt qualified to raise serious questions about mental barriers to fighting a war. The rise in rejections for mental disorder could be partially explained by the inability of Yankee psychologists to communicate with rural boys from the South. The armed forces test reflected a cultural bias, measuring intelligence only for those who had similar experiences. The draftees, however, came from varied cultural and social backgrounds and could not be forced into such a procrustean bed.[66]

Not surprisingly, Congress heard with a sense of outrage of the increasing numbers of rejectees. Especially upsetting was the politically dangerous trend of taking fathers away from their families while single men stayed home because of induction standards. One solution offered was to threaten to draft all 4-F's (physically disqualified) unless they went into critical defense jobs. Gallup polls revealed that 78 percent of the sample favored drafting 4-F's for war work. Testifying before a House committee in March 1944, Hershey complained that the 1.4 million 4-F's under age twenty-six were not contributing to war work. Neither he nor the armed forces, however, wanted responsibility for work battalions. Even President Roosevelt seemed to back away from such an approach. The 4-F's were scattered all over the country and possessed a great variety of skills; they could not simply be pushed into key jobs. Perhaps shortages could be made up by better utilization, rather than by drafting fathers.[67]

Hershey thought the armed services guilty of massive malutilization of manpower. Visiting one military installation, he found many strapping young men, individuals "who would have been welcomed by Frederick the Great in his Potsdam Guard," being trained as mechanics.[68] Secretary Stimson and Undersecretary Robert Patterson boasted of a tough-minded approach toward the draft. The country should be asked to sacrifice all peacetime conveniences for the war effort. Despite this public posture, Hershey found them quite willing to intercede in the draft process whenever it threatened special projects. Patterson called for a blanket deferment for men in the aluminum industry. Many young draft-eligible men were recruited into civil service jobs in the War Department, or into what became known as the Armed Services Training Program (ASTP), or into the enlisted reserves and the Reserves Officers Training Program. The army enlisted men and assigned them to inactive status in the reserves, where they could continue their schooling in specialized fields. In 1943 the War Department authorized the temporary transfer of certain specialists in the enlisted reserves to civilian jobs in nonferrous metal production.[69]

Hershey felt that such programs were destructive of public morale. While he was being forced to draft fathers, the army was taking young men and assigning them to enlisted reserve duty back in their old communities.[70] Although the president supported the army's desire to maintain men in training programs, to Hershey, the ASTP was a haven for draft dodgers and had been established "over my dead body."[71]

The navy proved equally irresponsible, also adopting the practice of enlisting bright young men and leaving them in school.[72] Hershey appreciated the need for deferments for trainees in shipyards and scientists in research laboratories, but many shipyards had deliberately hired men under twenty-five because they rated less pay. The navy claimed large numbers of job deferments at various installations; naval recruiters then moved into the same area to fill enlistment quotas. Hershey explained to a Knox aide, "Is it a fair conclusion that Selective Service should give no consideration to a 41A (job deferment request form) from a naval installation or naval contractor because of the fact that the navy itself gives no consideration to an occupational deferment when it interferes with their procurement objectives?"[73] Hershey insisted that the draft could furnish enough men for the navy, for over half of their so-called recruits were men who had already been notified of their draft selection.[74]

These problems arose because the army and the navy lacked faith in the draft as the sole means of solving their manpower problems. Then, in late 1943, the armed forces accused Hershey of failing to accomplish his primary mission—filling military manpower calls. Marshall and Stimson were anxious about the rate of troop buildup in England, as a prelude to the continental invasion. In December 1943 the army had some 7,400,000 men; the navy and marines had 2,700,000. Hershey expected all services to reach their authorized strength (7,700,000 for the army, 3,600,000 for the navy) by 1 July 1944. To reach this total, losses of 100,000 per month would also have to be replaced. Overall, Hershey expected to draft some 2 million men to fill military calls before July, but for the last three months of 1943 he had been coming up short on his monthly quotas. Congressional debate over exemptions for fathers confused local boards; high rejection rates also contributed to the problem. The army was at 90 percent of authorized strength.[75]

Hershey was optimistic for 1944. He would have to draft some of the 5 million fathers, the 1.8 million with farm deferments, and the millions in defense industries to fill the anticipated call through July. But with 500,000 young men reaching age eighteen during the period, he felt there would be no strain in meeting his responsibility. Major General Millard G. White, the G-1 at the office of the chief of staff, was equally sanguine. On 12 February 1944 White sent over a call for 145,000 white and 15,000 Negro inductees during April, warning that "should it be apparent during March that the ceiling of the army has been obtained, this call will be reduced accordingly." The army's chief manpower specialist was thinking in terms of reduced calls, yet within days the entire situation changed, and Hershey was confronted with a manufactured manpower crisis.[76]

On 26 February 1944 President Roosevelt informed Hershey that the Selective Service had failed to fill army monthly calls of 100,000 since October 1943. Roosevelt insisted that Hershey tighten up the draft system, squeeze more men out of the nation. All deferments should be immediately reviewed. Roosevelt saw no reason why men under age twenty-six should be considered critical workers. This sword fell on Hershey's head because Stimson and Marshall had convinced Roosevelt of a manpower crisis. Marshall was upset because the average age of soldiers had remained twenty-five, rather than becoming younger. There was no shortage on any battlefield and no problem in staffing the armies in the field, yet Roosevelt complained at the failure of the draft.[77]

The message threw a monkey wrench into an already confused manpower program. The president's call for ending most industrial deferments stunned McNutt and Donald Nelson, who predicted a collapse of the economy. Hershey immediately requested that all government agencies and private industries cooperate so that he could take 386,000 deferred men from agriculture and industry. Occupational deferments "must be drastically reduced and the requests for special treatment in certain activities must of necessity be withdrawn." This threat caused McNutt and Nelson to scurry to Roosevelt with warnings.[78]

Within a matter of days the crisis of hot air began to dissipate. Hershey had no sooner sent out emergency calls to local boards then he was forced to cancel them. General White finally explained to Stimson and Marshall that the army would soon be beyond its authorized strength, even without making up past shortages. On 7 April White explained that, due to fewer losses and a high rate of induction, "the Army has reached ceiling strength of 7,700,000." He wanted Hershey to drastically reduce the call for April. Hershey, who lacked Stimson's access to Roosevelt, argued that a sharp reduction would cause publicity problems, but the May call was cut from 110,000 to 75,000. Muttering to himself at this artificial panic, he instructed his boards to stop trying to fill previous shortfalls and to concentrate on finding men under twenty-six, even at the risk of not filling current calls.[79]

After White's note of April 1944, Hershey again became publicly optimistic about the manpower scene. He predicted in May that draft eligibles under twenty-six would fill his calls until the early fall. By September he opined that the men already classified 1-A and new eighteen-year-olds would supply all of his needs for the rest of 1944.[80] But manpower was a fickle field, and by December the entire scene had changed. Stimson and Marshall began calling for a national service law to cope with what they perceived as another manpower shortage. Having been made to look foolish in early 1944, Roosevelt was reluctant to throw himself into another manpower battle, but the German counterattack at Bastogne and the huge losses reported from the Battle of the Bulge changed his mind. In January 1945 Roosevelt authorized an increase in the army's manpower ceiling. Stimson quickly warned that the Selective Service would have to increase its March call from 80,000 to 100,000 men. All physically qualified men under thirty would probably have to be drafted. Hershey took much of this rhetoric with a grain of salt. Privately, he saw little need for national service; as for drafting every man under thirty, that idea would never win approval in Congress.[81]

Still, he had to go through the motions. He informed local boards in January that they must furnish 750,000 young men before 1 July 1945. He sent out guidelines which provided for withdrawal of men from war industries and from farms. Roosevelt now wanted a national service law that would draft all men under twenty-six. The new program immediately ran into congressional and industrial opposition. Congress had no intention of adopting a draft for civilian jobs, or of abandoning the special deferments for farmers, just as the war in Europe seemed about to end. Industrial and labor leaders agreed. Consequently, Hershey failed to fill these late calls.[82] The problem of conducting the draft while allowing the economy and society to function, however, had started in 1940, rather than in 1945.

V. Mobilizing the Economy and Society

Drafting men for the armed forces ensnared Hershey in the imbroglio of economic and social mobilization. The wartime economy depended for its labor upon the same manpower pool as Hershey depended upon for soldiers. Section 5(e) of the Selective Service Act read: "The president is authorized . . . to provide for the deferment from training and service . . . those men whose employment in industry, agriculture, or other occupations . . . is found . . . to be necessary to the maintenance of the national health, safety or interest." Hershey accepted the need for occupational deferments and social stability. There should be no revolution in sexual roles and race relations.

In all of the prewar planning for the draft, Hershey supported deferment for economic reasons, but he also supported a clause which prohibited the president from providing blanket deferments to workers. Such a procedure had been abused during World War I. The 1940 law provided for only individual deferments, and maintaining this standard became one of the most difficult problems Hershey faced. He was supposed not only to find men for the armed forces, but "to make a man available for service in the place where he can do the greatest good for the Nation."[1] Such a mandate was not clearly stated in the law, and Hershey eventually came to regret his assumption, but he realized the close connection between the draft and the civilian economy.

Despite his lack of a legislative mandate, Hershey looked upon his task as one of promoting national unity. He had viewed World War I as having provided an opportunity to renew the oneness of a nation being torn apart by material greed and selfish interest groups. Now envisioning the same opportunity, he hoped for a renewal of a golden age in which all Americans would work together under a banner of patriotism. Such an age existed only in Hershey's mind, but the image kept appearing in his rhetoric during 1941 and 1942. In an address to the Junior Chamber of Commerce on 20 June 1941, he explained that a man could serve his country just as effectively in the field or in the factory as in the armed services. The draft was "an excellent force for the solidification and unification of America." The management view, the labor view, and the farmer view were giving way to the national view.[2]

Yet strikes continued. Raised in an environment where few unions

existed, indoctrinated with the Republican philosophy of business virtues, Hershey had grown up with little appreciation for worker soli-
darity. His short duty as a strikebreaker with the Indiana National
Guard had not helped him to understand the workingman's position.
Now he controlled a weapon which could be used to break any strike.
Some local boards, based on elites, had a built-in anti-union bias. But
Hershey realized, earlier than many military men, that he would have
to work closely with unions if he hoped to promote national unity. Although he had no philosophical objection to drafting strikers, he considered it impractical and politically unwise. Yet he was not a free
agent. Gradually President Roosevelt and the War Department pushed
Hershey into the uncomfortable role of strikebreaker.

In January 1941 the workers at the Ryan Aircraft Company in San
Diego, a UAW local, threatened a strike. The company was producing
vital military aircraft. The local draft board chairman, Ralph B. Elm,
on his own initiative warned that the board would draft all strikers.
This gesture provoked the ire of labor leaders across the country, who
had been promised that the bill was not designed to destroy their organizations. The law did give the president the power to take over plants
which refused to cooperate with the government's war effort, yet the
statute also stipulated that "nothing herein shall be deemed to render
inapplicable existing State or Federal laws" concerning labor rights.[3]

Hershey immediately reined in the rambunctious Elm and his local
board and explained to reporters that a man's draft status did not depend on his availability for a specific job. Furthermore, a striking
worker had not, theoretically, left his job. Hershey insisted that changing the status of a draft registrant because he was on strike "is contrary to the intent of the law." Workers' rights had to be respected. In
fact, the strike never materialized, and the issue became temporarily
moot.[4]

Hershey's interpretation soon changed, for Secretary of War Stimson and President Roosevelt had a different interpretation of the draft
law. Stimson wanted the Selective Service to prevent strikes in war
plants. He called Hershey in for a chat and explained that, in the future, he should not "monkey" or interfere with threats by local boards.
President Roosevelt agreed.[5]

In June 1941, when workers at the North American Aviation Company of California went out on strike, Stimson directed Hershey to
prepare a statement calling for the reclassification of strikers "imped-
ing the national defense program." On 9 June Stimson cleared the message with President Roosevelt and then hustled Hershey to a pre-
arranged press conference to read it. Local draft boards were ordered
to reclassify immediately any deferred registrants in essential jobs

when "they have ceased to perform the jobs." Hershey now explained that a man could not expect to retain his deferment when he stopped working in the job which had earned him that status.[6]

Hershey took this initial step with reluctance. He disliked ordering his local boards to do anything, because to do so violated his principle of decentralization. Just as important, he knew that this action was fraught with political hazards. His system needed an image of impartiality, not a reputation as a tool for management. When the state director for Illinois explained that he had been telling his local boards to draft strikers for months, Hershey warned him that "we've been trying not to keep too far ahead of the administration."[7]

As Hershey anticipated, organized labor was outraged. Phil Murray of the Congress of Industrial Organizations had played a major role in Roosevelt's reelection in 1940; now he felt betrayed. Allen S. Haywood, a Murray aide, wrote Hershey that his order of 9 June represented a "very serious encroachment on the rights of labor." The National Labor Relations Act protected workers from retribution if they struck. Haywood urged Hershey to withdraw his order; President Roosevelt felt similar pressure.[8]

Faced with this opposition and with compromise brewing at the White House, Hershey retreated. In August he invited Haywood and Murray to a private conference. When another strike occurred at the Kearney Shipyards in New Jersey, Hershey instructed the state director to suspend action until notified. On 8 August Hershey issued orders that "registrants will not be reclassified pending clarification of the situation." When other strikes broke out, Hershey issued identical instructions. On 12 August he stated that strikers at the Kearney plant should not be reclassified because the company refused to accept the recommendations of the National Defense Mediation Board. Hershey later justified his actions by explaining that the president had declared the strike illegal.[9]

In early 1942 Hershey invited William Green and Phil Murray to appoint officials to act as "close contact and liaison" with Selective Service. These meetings were useful and led to several deferments for labor leaders. By 24 September, during a speech in Cleveland, Hershey declared his opposition to using the draft as a weapon against strikers, even in war plants. "I don't think the so-called strike situation is so bad," he explained, "that we have to consider such a step."[10]

John L. Lewis put this optimism to a sore test in 1943; when he took his United Mine Workers out of the coal mines and thumbed his nose at the entire nation. Lewis's demands and the arguments for and against them were debated within and without the administration. With the war effort threatened, Roosevelt privately cursed the labor leader.

Congress began debate on a bill (Smith-Connally) which made it a crime to strike in plants taken over by the president. Stimson, who viewed strikers as soldiers deserting their posts, urged the president to sign the bill. Yet, as others pointed out, throwing several thousand miners in jail would mine no coal. Roosevelt vetoed the bill but suggested that Congress pass a bill authorizing him to draft miners for noncombat duty.[11]

Hershey wanted no part of this struggle, but he was reluctantly pushed into it. When the Smith-Connally bill appeared in Congress, both houses invited Hershey to comment. He explained that the bill was not needed, as the existing draft law provided the power to reclassify strikers whenever the director considered the deferment unnecessary for the war effort. Congress nevertheless passed the bill, over Hershey's protest and Roosevelt's veto.[12]

From 1943 to the end of the war Hershey cooperated in fighting labor unrest. In December 1943 Stimson called upon Hershey to draft all strikers at the Western Electric plant in Baltimore, which the government was seizing. Hershey promised to comply and merely requested that Stimson provide the names of workers involved. When a transit strike occurred in Philadelphia in August 1944, Hershey again ordered local boards to call up the strikers for immediate preinduction examinations. In January 1945 he assured Governor Frank J. Lausche of Ohio that the Selective Service was moving to draft strikers at the Cleveland Electric Company. In May 1945 the secretary of the navy took over the San Francisco plant of the United Engineering Company. Hershey authorized local boards to terminate all deferments of strikers and to reclassify them as 1-A, to be ordered for immediate preinduction physicals. A similar order went out in July to local boards in Akron, to deal with strikers at the Goodyear Tire and Rubber Company. When local board members protested ("We should not be forced to become a strike-breaking agency"), Hershey threatened to replace the entire board.[13] Everyone had to sacrifice some rights during wartime. He could speak so forthrightly because he wore a uniform and claimed to only execute policy. Nevertheless, he had met with labor leaders to reassure them.

Convincing people to concede their rights proved a formidable task, made even more difficult by the array of special deferments which arose. Many years later the issue of draft equity would contribute to Hershey's downfall. This same issue had to be reckoned with during World War II. The law recognized and the planners understood that not all men liable for the draft would be inducted. Hershey had to administer the deferment program, but, as he admitted in 1943, "I hope you are not so naive as to believe that National Headquarters now or at any time in the future can determine deferment policy. Everybody in the world is in the deferment business." Hundreds of pressure groups sought to protect their pet projects.[14]

Trying to control deferments became a time-consuming task for Hershey. Upon the solution of this problem rested not merely the strength of the armed forces and the productivity of the war economy, but also public confidence in the fairness of the draft system and Hershey's own reputation. Despite plans for protecting essential workers, when the United States went to war large numbers of key workers rushed to volunteer. Others were taken from key jobs by local boards who refused to allow young, healthy, single men to stay at home while fathers were threatened. Hershey spent time in the next few years trying to recover from this initial confusion. In January 1942 the Selective Service System listed some 600,000 men as having occupational deferments. By February 1943 there were 1,000,000 with industrial deferments and another 379,000 with farm deferments. A year later industrial deferments had grown to 3,204,000 and farm deferments to 1,689,000. Although farm deferments began to shrink slightly, industrial deferments climbed to 4,256,455 in December 1944. By April 1945 the totals had declined to 3,664,001 for industry and 1,321,155 for farms. How these men were selected revealed the health of interest-group politics in the midst of war.[15]

In some ways Hershey contributed to his own problem with the deferment issue. He assumed in 1941 that the Selective Service would have an effect on manpower for the economy. Before Pearl Harbor he told local boards to consider the entire defense picture and not to take men needed in production. Hershey cooperated to help industry adjust to its newly expanded mission, yet this attitude soon came back to haunt him, as industry began a policy of indiscriminate requests and local boards became hesitant about challenging such deferments.[16]

After Pearl Harbor Hershey restated his deferment policies. Those who stayed in their jobs would have to be more carefully screened. An industry had to prove that the loss of a man would hinder war production. He expected all firms to begin a systematic inventory to see who could be replaced, and when. Hershey expected that all young men would eventually be replaced by women, older men, or 4-F's. He believed that industry could triple its workforce without becoming a haven for draft dodgers.[17]

In the ensuing few months Hershey issued several bulletins to guide local boards in dealing with occupational deferments. He established the following guidelines: 1) no group or class deferments could be made; 2) job deferments could be granted only by local boards based on national interest. Before granting a deferment, the local board should be sure of three things: 1) that the business was necessary to defense or national interest, 2) that the work the man was performing was essential, 3) that no replacement was available. The War Production Board and the procurement divisions of the armed forces sent Hershey information on key plants and industries which had to be protected. Hershey believed that local boards should make their own decisions. As he told a meeting of state directors in November 1944, "I think maybe you are going to have to do as I have told you so many times— know the bets and how to make them; know the rules and when to break them." [18]

A unified deferment plan which would deal fairly with the many components of the American economy—managers, workers, unions— and also generate sufficient manpower for the armed services was impossible, an administrative nightmare. Essential occupation lists mushroomed. There were thirty-four essential occupations in the repair and trade services alone. In some cases companies refused to ask for blanket deferments. And then there was the political pressure to provide blanket deferments to fathers and farmers. [19]

The debate over whether or not to draft fathers provided a clear lesson on the priorities of the American people in the midst of war. The law allowed the president to provide deferments "of those men in a status with respect to persons dependent upon them for support." Yet the same clause insisted that no deferment would be made except on an individual basis. Despite the law, fathers enjoyed a group deferment for most of the war. [20]

In 1941 some 70 percent of all classified men claimed deferment because of dependency. Defining dependency raised thorny issues about working wives and the degree of dependence of aunts and uncles. Hershey told the boards that the dependency had to be "in the natural course of events." Hershey worried in 1941 because the country had "40 percent of its young men twenty-one years old getting married within six weeks after registration." [21]

In early 1942 Hershey accepted the deferment of married men with dependents. Such men were deferred because "it is in the interest of the government to maintain, if possible, the family as the basic social unit." But privately he wrote, "We may be making mistakes on dependency deferment." On 20 March he announced that, in the future, occupations rather than family status would be the major consideration. A Gallup poll of 23 March indicated that 71 percent favored drafting men with dependents if these soldiers were needed to win the war. As Hershey explained to President Roosevelt, dependency now accounted for 65 percent of all deferments. War industries were complaining about the shortage of workers. By focusing on jobs rather than on dependency, Hershey hoped he could cause a "voluntary shifting" to essential jobs and relieve the shortage.[22]

Hershey was launching a work-or-fight program, and it provoked opposition. Several congressmen questioned his authority to force men into industry by threatening induction. Donald Nelson warned Hershey that such a shift in priorities required more groundwork or propaganda. Hershey retreated and told Congress that he would go slowly in calling married men. In July he established a new order of draft call: single men with no dependents first, single men with secondary dependents second, married men third, and married man with children last. By August there were 17 million men with dependency deferments.[23]

In September 1942 General Marshall insisted that the draft age be reduced to eighteen. In October Congress began hearings on such an amendment. The issue soon became tied to dependency deferments. When asked to distinguish between teenagers and married men without children, a poll sample favored drafting the latter by 47 percent to 43 percent.[24]

In both Senate and House hearings Hershey insisted that, even with the bill, he would still have to take married men through 1 January 1943. Congress wanted a system which would draft every single man before taking any married men, but Hershey warned that this requirement would be impossible to adopt in all areas. Furthermore, despite the polls, he advised that "public opinion is going to demand that married men do not hide behind wives and children." In some cases wives called local boards to report their husbands for induction. Constant emphasis upon protecting the family irritated Hershey. Lowering the draft age to eighteen might delay drafting married men for three or four months, but Hershey warned that they had better find jobs in the defense industry. On 13 November Congress passed the bill extending draft liability to men ages eighteen to forty-five.[25]

By early 1943 some 11,670,025 men were still being deferred for dependency alone. During the next twelve months Hershey continued to threaten to draft these men; the public and Congress continued to protest the taking of fathers while deferring single men for key jobs. The year was filled with contradictory statements and circular marches. When the dust finally cleared in December, Congress passed a law prohibiting the drafting of fathers with dependent children before the induction of all single men.[26]

Fathers, however, would still be needed. The armed forces required 11.3 million men by July 1944, and in December 1943 they had only 10.1 million. Hershey expected trouble. As he explained to his staff, "We must come up with words to explain why fathers are given deferments over skill." The real reason, of course, was the belief by Congress and the public that fathers were more valuable to society than single men, no matter what jobs they held.[27]

Hershey carried out his mandate as best he could. From 1 October 1943 to 1 February 1944, only 161,000 pre-Pearl Harbor fathers were drafted. The public resistance to such calls remained strong. (On 9 March 1944 a Gallup poll reported that some 75 percent of the sample still believed that single women should be drafted before fathers.) But Hershey was now faced with calls averaging some 250,000 per month, and to fill these he had to reduce the numbers in occupationally deferred categories.[28]

The largest group of such men, in farm labor, represented another special interest which enjoyed congressional protection. The story of farm deferments during World War II was a tale filled with the powerful agrarian myth of that atypical farmer, Thomas Jefferson. It was also a tale of political power as the farm lobby demonstrated that farmers would not allow a mere world war to distract them from their interest. Hershey, who contributed to the mythology by passing himself off as a former dirt farmer, approached the farmer with a keen sense of political realism.

A great deal of ink and rhetoric was used in arguing the merits of farm deferments from 1941 to 1945. What seems clear from the statistics is that these efforts were remarkably successful. It is less clear whether or not this special protection was needed. American food production reached new heights during each year of the war, and there was never any danger of a serious food shortage in the United States. At the same time, American farmers sent millions of tons of food abroad under the Lend-Lease Act. This production record was achieved with the cooperation of the Selective Service. In November 1942 only 15,523 men were deferred for farm work; by the following month some 136,678 were deferred. By 1 March 1944 agricultural deferments had peaked at 1,721,759. On 1 January 1945 three times as many men under age twenty-six were deferred for agriculture as for industry.[29]

The Selective Service Act had no sooner passed than some farmers began complaining about a shortage of workers. The draft had little to do with shortage of farmworkers at this time; rather, farm work was hard, with long hours and modest pay, and men had been leaving American farms for years before World War II. When new defense industries sprang up in 1939, they served as magnets for many young men who wanted better wages and hours. Although the coming of the draft had little effect on this phenomenon, the high visibility of the draft insured that it would receive some of the blame when agricultural states began finding it difficult to harvest crops.

On 26 May 1941 Secretary of Agriculture Claude Wickard informed

Hershey that the food supply was being threatened by a labor shortage. During the preceding twelve months farm labor had declined by 17.8 percent. Hershey tried to explain that these shortages arose because of the low wage scale in agriculture. If a true market economy had been operating, farmers would have been forced to raise wages to compete; instead, they complained to Washington. In congressional hearings during June 1941 several representatives began a campaign for special deferments for farm labor. Sensing the political wind, Hershey appeared sympathetic and argued that his background from a farm area enabled him to understand the problems.[30] He issued a memorandum on 4 December 1941 calling upon local boards to consider four factors in determining agricultural deferment: 1) the importance of the product; 2) the importance of the work performed; 3) the skill involved; 4) the shortage of labor in the area. These guidelines would remain in effect throughout the war.[31]

Yet men continued to leave farms, primarily because of the attractive opportunities in war industry. Congress became increasingly sensitive to calls for help from farm organizations. Senator Sheridan Downey pushed through a resolution for a special investigation into the farm labor problem. The War Manpower Commission responded by establishing a labor stabilization plan for the hard-hit dairy industry. A conversion scale was drafted based on the work required to care for one milk cow.[32]

Hershey never believed that farm labor was "irreplaceable," or that it should receive a blanket deferment. In February 1942 he explained to a House committee that the best approach was to balance the military calls with the needs of the civilian economy, including the farmer. "We cannot defer every farmer, every farmer's son, and every farmhand," he argued, "merely because the individual happens to be engaged in the occupation of farming." Farmers were volunteering for military duty and running to war industry.[33]

Congress, however, was not satisfied. With congressional protest growing, Hershey met with Secretary Wickard. They worked out a plan by which Wickard provided local boards with detailed information on the highly diversified labor needs of farming. County boards and agricultural agents were asked to advise on deferment requests. The plan seemed sound on paper, but it did little to quiet the incessant complaints from farm groups. As a stopgap measure Hershey authorized several temporary statewide delays in induction so farmers could harvest their crops. He explained that granting a blanket deferment to farmers meant attaching "a stigma to the farming industry which they could not easily eliminate."[34]

Concern about a stigma had little effect, and political pressures continued to build. Hershey's sense of realism soon surfaced. He explained to Congress in October that, if ordered to do so by the president, he would freeze essential workers on the farm by giving them the choice of remaining or being drafted. He remained adamantly against the idea of a blanket deferment for all farmers. He pointed to draft statistics indicating that while some 23 percent of registered men were in agriculture, only 14 percent of recent draftees came from the farm. Even if the Selective Service did not draft one farmer, the shortage would continue.[35]

Congress decided otherwise. To insure Hershey's tacit support, Senator Millard Tydings invited him to draft an amendment which would protect the farmer but not create problems for Selective Service. Colonel Frank Keesling, in conference with Hershey, drafted what became known as the Tydings amendment. As passed on 13 November 1942, the rider provided that every registrant found by a local board to "be necessary to and regularly engaged in an agricultural occupation or endeavor essential to the war effort, shall be deferred from training and service . . . until such time as a satisfactory replacement can be obtained." If any deferred person left his farm job, he would be subject to immediate reclassification and induction.[36]

Although Hershey still refused to admit that he had been party to a blanket deferment of farmers, he also realized that it would be impolitic to raise objections in the face of congressional pressure. He assured Congressman Forest A. Harness of Indiana that he knew of the tough problems facing farmers, because "I am one of them." The system had deferred over 600,000 farmers in only six weeks, yet he warned that Congress could not expect every farmer to stay on the farm. Local boards were supposed to consider essentiality, and leaving single men at home raised morale problems in communities. Such quibbling prompted Eugene D. Millikin of the Senate Committee on Agriculture to recommend a new law specifically deferring all farmers for one year. Manifesting a rather strange concept of the law, Hershey argued that public opinion would prevent compliance with such a discriminatory measure. "There is no use of me as an administrator," he insisted, "coming here and saying that I can carry out your will in the face of the will of the people."[37]

Could a nation of 130 million fail to support a military force of only 11 million men?[38] Despite Hershey's response, the drive for increased farm deferments continued. Senator John H. Bankhead complained to President Roosevelt about farmers being drafted. According to the advice of both the War Manpower Commission and the Department of Agriculture, subsistence farmers and men who produced commodities not needed for the war effort were not deferred. Even with this qualification, the Tydings amendment had led to the deferment of over 364,002 farmers by 31 January 1943. Hershey expected 3 million to be deferred by the end of the year.[39]

Congress decided more should be done. In February 1943 Bankhead and some forty other senators introduced a bill (S 729) to provide exemptions for all farmers regardless of whether they contributed to the war effort. Hershey fought vigorously against this measure, warning that he would soon be taking married men and fathers. If single farmers were left behind, the entire community would unite against the implementation of the draft. His system, relying as it did upon local consensus, would fall apart. Without the requirement that the farmer produce essential foodstuff and be irreplaceable, the bill provided a class exemption.[40]

The Bankhead bill died for lack of support in Congress. This defeat can be partially explained by vigorous opposition from both Hershey and Stimson. Also important was President Roosevelt's decision to establish a War Food Administration on 26 March 1943. The new agency promised to insure proper consideration to the role of food production in the war effort. Complaints still came to Congress, but the steam seemed to go out of the movement as farm deferments increased to some 1,721,759 by 1 March 1944.[41]

Unfortunately, for Hershey's morale, the fortunes of the war again threatened farmers. In 1944 General Eisenhower and General Marshall decided that they needed more men, and they had to be young men. President Roosevelt supported these requirements and on 25 February sent Hershey orders to review all job deferments. According to the president, Hershey had been too liberal, especially with farm deferments. He immediately began tightening up such deferments, and the Senate Committee on Agriculture called him in for an explanation. Hershey explained that he had "leaned over backwards" to protect farmers, but that the decision had now been taken out of his hands. He had to get young men. Seeking to smooth ruffled feathers, he admitted that "Congress can give me any directions it decides on where to get them." Congress encouraged him to get them from nonfarm sources.[42]

With the approval of the War Food Administration, Hershey replaced the war credit system and tightened up his guidelines on farm deferments. On 24 March he called upon local boards to review all agricultural deferments for men eighteen to twenty-five. These actions had a modest effect on the farm deferment rate. On 21 March 570,000 men under twenty-six had farm deferments; by 1 July the figure had dropped to a total of 474,081 out of a total farm-deferment pool of 1,641,396. Through 1 January 1945 the size of the under twenty-six group declined to 341,953—still three times the number of young men with industrial deferments.[43]

Testimony to the staying power of the farm lobby appeared in early 1945. In December 1944 the German counterstroke in the Ardennes had ruptured the complacency on the American homefront. The Germans had no sooner launched their attack than the Roosevelt administration called upon Hershey to increase his draft calls, particularly among men under twenty-six. The one remaining source of young men consisted of those deferred for farm work. Touching these farmers, Hershey predicted, would raise the ire of Congress. He recommended strategies to Roosevelt. The president might request Congress to amend the Tydings rider to apply only to farmers twenty-six and over; he might also state publicly those farm products which needed manpower. Hershey warned that, unless he was able to tap the younger farm deferment group, he would be forced to turn to older men, including fathers, to fill military calls.[44]

After consulting with advisors and considering the political implications of Hershey's suggestions, Roosevelt shoved the problem into the lap of James Byrnes, director of the Office of War Mobilization. On 2 January 1945 Byrnes instructed Hershey to draft young farmers because of the shortage of other sources and because the testimony of the War Food Administrator indicated that the loss of young farmers would not lead to a food crisis. As for the Tydings amendment, Byrnes reminded Hershey (who needed no reminding), it was never intended to be a blanket deferment. Hershey immediately sent Byrnes's letter to all local boards with instructions to order for pre-induction examination men in the deferred group.[45]

In the farm belt, the proverbial manure now hit the fan. No sooner had Hershey sent out his telegram than an invitation arrived from Congress to appear and explain this serious error. The farm bloc in the House demanded a conference with Byrnes, with War Food Administration Director Marvin Jones, and with Hershey. President Roosevelt decided, however, to allow the director of Selective Service to represent the entire administration. Hershey tried unsuccessfully to appease Congress. Over a hundred members of the House signed a statement expressing fear that Hershey's directive would endanger food production. Hershey replied that the Tydings amendment had to be reinterpreted in light of new war conditions; agriculture was no longer considered critical.[46]

The farm bloc ignored this argument. A special ad hoc committee representing 150 farm-state congressmen met to draft a resolution under the leadership of William Lemke of North Dakota. The resolution stated that local boards were breaking the law by ignoring the Tydings amendment and that Hershey "should be directed to comply with the intent and spirit as well as the letter" of this provision.[47]

In responding to this threat Hershey again displayed his political skill at backtracking. Attempting to undercut support for this resolution, he issued a "clarifying directive" on 22 January to all state directors. In this message he emphasized, with British understatement, that Congress had raised questions about his earlier message. Hershey now argued that his 3 January message did not "change or modify in any manner the Tydings amendment." His order had not called for the immediate induction of all farmers under twenty-six, but merely for them to be checked to establish how many would be eligible should he have to take them.[48]

Hershey's flimflam operation hardly resolved the basic problem. Local boards began to act as though the Tydings amendment had been suspended. Word reached Congress from the farm belt, and Congress reached for Hershey. He explained that his recent directives did not abrogate the Tydings amendment. Despite the political risk, Hershey now publicly rejected the view that the amendment provided a blanket deferment for farmers. In a radio address on 1 February 1945 he insisted that the Tydings amendment merely required local boards to consider such factors as what was produced, how essential it was, and how irreplaceable the young farmer was. Local boards could draft as many young farmers as needed to fill calls. Unfortunately for Hershey, Congress had no sympathy with this interpretation. A joint resolution was introduced by Congressman Lemke calling for a special congressional committee to investigate whether officials were breaking the law by drafting young farmers.[49] In April the Lemke resolution passed both houses.[50]

Hershey's only recourse now was to appeal to the new president. On 12 April 1945 Franklin D. Roosevelt had died in office, a victim of heart disease. President Harry S Truman had little preparation for assuming direction of the manpower problem. On the issue of farm deferments, however, he had some personal experience. As a senator from Missouri, he had received letters from several of his rural constituents complaining about the loss of their young workers. Truman responded sympathetically. His own brother had just lost his last young farmhand, but he had insisted that "the Selective Service Board is the absolute authority on the procedure which they are following."[51]

Given this attitude, Hershey hoped that an appeal to the president would defeat the Lemke resolution. By April, with the war in Europe virtually over, 255,000 men under twenty-six still held farm deferments. All other job deferments for men under twenty-six (excluding merchant marine and foreign army duty) totaled only 30,000. The actual number of young farmers being inducted had not changed since the Byrnes letter of January, yet Congress had passed a resolution which threatened to usurp the decisionmaking power of local boards. On 27 April 1945 Hershey urged President Truman to veto the Lemke resolution. With surprising candor, Hershey concluded that, even if the resolution was signed, it would be applied by local boards according to their "good sense and judgment." As he told his state directors, "If I were on a local board and I could not take a man because he was essential, I could take him because he could be replaced or some other reason." Fortunately, this extraordinary concept of legality did not come to a test. President Truman vetoed the resolution on 3 May, a few days before the end of the war in Europe.[52]

In his role as director of the draft, Lewis Hershey had to deal with social institutions. The draft involved many social issues, from the role of women to the role of religion in society. Hershey's first and foremost job remained the filling of calls for military personnel, yet this mission was carried out under the influence of certain personal values and assumptions about American society. Although he worked under the law and presidential policy, he had considerable latitude on interpretation. His vision of American society exercised influence, especially on local boards. With conservative views on politics and social institutions, he sought ways in which to preserve society from unreasonable shocks.[53]

War was a man's business in 1941—so thought Hershey and most Americans. But the mobilization experience during World War II generated important changes in the economic position of American women.[54] Selective Service provided for the induction of males only, yet the law had no sooner passed in 1940 than female leaders, such as Dr. Minnie Maffett, Nellie L. Bok, and Helen D. Harbison of the American Association of University Women, approached Eleanor Roosevelt with ideas on how to expand the female role in the Selective Service System. She passed on such requests to her husband, who turned the problem over to Hershey. Hershey had no intention of allowing women to become decisionmakers in his system. In justifying this exclusion (which had not been required in the law) Hershey wrote, "Members under certain circumstances may find it necessary to check upon registrants for physical defects." He also explained that it was best to have on the boards outstanding male community leaders, men who were better suited "by reason of their knowledge of economic and business conditions to pass upon problems arising in connection with occupational deferments."[55]

To Hershey's surprise, this reply failed to mollify the women leaders. He then took a more compromising and ambiguous line. To Minnie L. Maffett, president of the National Federation of Business and Professional Women's Clubs, he explained that women were already serving in administrative positions, including the key job of clerk to local boards. Given the unsettled condition of the still-young draft system, he refused to make any major changes. He promised to "give more thought to using women on local and appeal boards." He continued to think about this question—until 1967.[56]

This reluctance to allow women into his organization did not mean that Hershey underestimated their potential contribution. In public and private utterances he stressed that women were particularly suited to the task of rekindling the national spirit. Although "the thoughts of a nation are in the custody of its men . . . the feelings of a country are controlled by its women." In Hershey's social philosophy, women legitimized the customs and behavior patterns of society, something infinitely more important than the written law. Women promoted national unity and morale by guarding the customs of the clan and nation.[57]

Worried about the poor physical condition of many young men rejected by the draft, Hershey repeated his pieties to Mrs. Roosevelt. Rehabilitation "is a task," he explained, "that must fall to the woman of America. Women's destiny has always been the keeping of the home, and it is in the home that the solution of these problems must begin."[58]

Yet when the manpower pool became strained from servicing both the armed forces and industrial expansion, Hershey and the public began to accept additional roles for women. By 1942 he was preaching the need for women to take jobs in war industry in order to relieve men for military service.[59] As early as January 1942 a poll reported that 68 percent of the public favored drafting single women between the ages of twenty-one and thirty-five for training in war jobs. Women themselves supported the idea by 73 percent. When the pollsters began couching their questions in the form of either drafting single women or drafting married men with families, the percentage shot up to 81 percent in September 1943.[60]

Despite public support, Hershey approached a female draft with extreme reluctance. When asked on 15 January 1941 for his plans to draft women, he insisted that he had none. He saw a female draft as an additional headache for a system already straining under the task of finding men for the military. By April 1942, however, he admitted to the president that the registration of women aged eighteen to sixty-five would "provide recognition that women are considered as having an equal place with men in . . . our national war effort."[61]

Roosevelt liked the idea, but Hershey, upon further reflection, realized that such a symbolic gesture would burden his system without delivering significant results. By May 1942 he had reversed himself. He wrote to the director of the budget, "I believe it is unnecessary and

inadvisable to enact legislation at this time for the compulsory registration of women."[62] In 1943 he explained to reporters that drafting
women was not his job. In 1944, when HR 4906, a bill to draft women
between twenty and thirty-five, was introduced in Congress, Hershey
strongly opposed it. He admitted that Selective Service could do the
job, but he favored such a program only as the last step, after the
armed forces had failed to utilize the many limited-service men and
men thirty-eight to forty-five who had not yet served. Congress rejected the bill.[63]

While Hershey's social philosophy on the role of women underwent
little transition during the war, the same could not be said of his attitude toward the role of black Americans. Hershey grew up in a racist
society. Living in the northeast corner of rural Indiana provided some
shelter from the more glaring manifestations of this racism; as there
were few blacks or foreigners in the county, so there were few social
and legal devices to insure white supremacy. Hershey had accepted
the unspoken assumption of white supremacy, hardly conscious of
blacks.

His first exposure to a sizable black population occurred when he
was assigned to Fort Shelby, Mississippi, before World War I. Seeing
blacks within the Deep South, bowed down within a tight system of
social control, Hershey had little trouble accepting local prejudices.
Like many Northerners, he felt that the white South should be allowed
its own system of handling blacks. The system in rural Mississippi in
1917 consisted of a reign of terror for any black who stepped out of
line. Several blacks were burned alive during the year of Hershey's
training.[64]

During World War I Hershey saw little reason to change his views
on the race question. In Washington, D.C., Ellen wrote him of a recent
race riot, blaming the entire affair on the new equality being offered to
blacks. His own observations from Brest confirmed Ellen's opinion.
"With white officers," Hershey explained, "the colored soldier does
better, but at best he is a soldier with limitations sharply defined."
After returning to the United States and taking up duty at Camp Pike,
Arkansas, he wrote sententiously in his diary on the race question: "I
cannot but feel that the solution of the world's problems will come
sooner when it is accepted that there are lines of demarcation we must
observe."[65]

Yet while Hershey remained rather narrow in his outlook, the nation
was changing. The change occurred primarily on the surface, as black
migration to the North increased Negro voting strength. The rise of
Hitler with his notions of Aryan supermen created an embarrassment
for American advocates of white supremacy. The obvious contradiction

between the theoretical commitment to equality and the Jim Crow system was becoming harder to ignore.

The difficulty emerged clearly in the debate over the draft law in 1940. Here was a measure calling for all citizens to sacrifice equally for the defense of the nation. Black leaders from the National Association for the Advancement of Colored People and the *Pittsburgh Courier* testified in August 1940 against any color line in the draft. Roosevelt placed racial equality very low on his ladder of priorities, but black leaders such as William White and Mary McLeod Bethune rejected a Jim Crow draft system. When these considerations were added to the facile political ability of FDR to say one thing and do another, no one was surprised that the draft law passed with a clause rejecting Jim Crow. Section 4(a) insisted that the selection of men should be "in an impartial manner," and, even more clearly, "that in the selection and training of men under this Act, and in the interpretation and execution of the provisions of this Act, there shall be no discrimination against any person on account of race or color."[66]

Much like Prohibition in the 1920's, this provision against racial discrimination largely remained a dead letter. The law was no sooner on the books than the Roosevelt administration sought means of permitting "local mores" to continue. As Congress completed work on the draft law, members of the Negro community sought assurances from Roosevelt that the letter of the law would be followed. James Rowe, a White House aide, warned that his political mail and the black press both indicated black sensitivity to the draft issue. Roosevelt needed no reminding that there would be an election in November.[67]

Even before the first registration on 16 October black leaders began to complain over the failure of the Selective Service to appoint members of their race to the agency. Roosevelt sent these complaints on to Hershey for reply. Because Hershey's entire approach to the system had been to build upon the participation of local elites as designated by the governors, the system insured a low representation for blacks. He informed the Reverend A. L. Gilmore, president of the Black Ministerial Alliance in Memphis, "I regret that this office cannot assist you, since it is the responsibility of the Governor of each state to set up the necessary registration machinery and personnel."[68]

This attitude failed to satisfy William White, who immediately telegraphed President Roosevelt, urging him to inform all governors that the success of the draft depended upon public confidence. This confidence could come only if, in areas with large black populations, blacks obtained representation on local boards. With Hershey's aid, Undersecretary of War Robert Patterson replied to White that Congress, in passing the law, had sought to place responsibility on the local level.

The president had urged the governors to appoint only men in whom the community had confidence. The War Department had hoped that the governors would pay attention to the needs of their black communities through black appointments. This hope remained, but Patterson insisted that the final responsibility remained with the governors. Patterson assured White that Hershey was doing what he could "through consolidation and suggestion" to insure that local boards were representative of their communities.[69]

In fact, Hershey played a charade. On 26 September the White House advisory board on Selective Service, which included Channing Tobias, a black moderate, asked Hershey how many blacks were serving in local positions. Hershey had little information on the question, but he soon learned that the president expected some help in pacifying black leaders. Hershey handed out an empty gesture. He made long-distance calls to the adjutants general of several states, explaining that his action had been prompted by black pressure on Roosevelt to override gubernatorial appointments. "We stalled that," he boasted, "but I had to promise to call the Adjutants General in the south to find out what was happening. We don't want to do anything that will embarrass you," he insisted. Hershey's main purpose in the exercise was not to increase black participation in the system but to "placate" Roosevelt's critics.[70] In fact, nothing changed.

Complementing this ploy, on 9 October the War Department issued a policy statement which promised a segregated military force. Blacks would be inducted on the basis of their percentage of the eligible population, but they would go into black units and would be trained separately but equally. With the armed forces committed to Jim Crow, black leaders now felt it even more essential to obtain some representation within the Selective Service. James Rowe urged Roosevelt to appoint Channing Tobias as a special assistant to the director. Unfortunately, Tobias became ill; Roosevelt then turned to Campbell C. Johnson, who was the executive secretary of a Washington branch of the YMCA, a former faculty member at Howard University, and a reserve officer.[71]

With Roosevelt's approval, Campbell Johnson joined Selective Service headquarters to oversee the interest of black draftees. His reception was cool. Some renegades from the Ku Klux Klan painted the toilet seats black in the men's room at national headquarters. Hershey himself disliked having a man with such a narrow assignment, and he insisted that Johnson assume responsibilities for other areas.[72]

As anticipated, Johnson was no radical. Indeed, Hershey called him a realist—and since the general fancied realism as one of his own special virtues, this was high praise. Whatever his virtues, Johnson could do little to change the way Selective Service operated. As early as 13 November 1940 he urged Hershey to order state directors to appoint a Negro to each board of appeal in areas with heavy Negro populations. This recommendation met with opposition from the staff, which insisted that the appeal boards were not supposed to represent economic and social groupings. Hershey had accepted the Johnson appointment as a gesture for the president, but he had no intention of making any other change in the system.[73]

Occasionally Major Johnson went to a trouble spot in the South to calm the waters, and on one occasion Hershey addressed a gathering of blacks and reassured them of their great contribution in the war effort. By 1944, when Edward N. Wilson, the registrar at Morgan State College, complained at blacks being the victims of white supremacy, Hershey could blithely reply: "The manner in which the 6,442 local boards throughout the country have exercised their function of selection has served to strengthen the confidence of all citizens, and particularly Negro citizens, in the increasing realization of our democratic aims."[74]

Hershey took pride in his record, but when the final tally emerged, only 250 Negroes served on local boards in the entire nation. Only three southern states (Virginia, North Carolina, and Kentucky) had black local board members. Another 30 blacks served as appeal agents, and 620 worked in advisory capacities. After the war Johnson gave a summary report to a meeting of state directors. To Hershey's satisfaction Johnson concluded that the system had carried out Hershey's hope "that we could operate with fairness and equal justice among all our registrants." Hershey was well aware that racial discrimination had continued during the war, in clear violation of the law, but he blamed the problems on the armed forces.[75]

Compared to many in the armed forces, Hershey did appear enlightened on the race issue. When the draft began in 1940, blacks represented about 10.6 percent of the total population, or 12.8 million. Of the 32.4 million men who were registered during the war, blacks made up 3.4 million. During the war some 1,074,083 blacks were inducted and another 80,637 enlisted. Of all inductions, blacks represented some 10.7 percent. Given the early commitment of Roosevelt and the armed forces to taking blacks in proportion to their percentage of the population, the results seemed gratifying. Indeed, Johnson was gratified; Hershey was gratified. Yet the figures hid a system of racial quotas which amounted to a violation of the law.[76]

The decision to adopt a Jim Crow system of inductions for the armed forces prompted little debate in 1940. The entire South lived by such a code, and whites considered it a permanent arrangement. When a member of the University of Chicago Roundtable asked Hershey whether blacks would be segregated, he made it clear that this would indeed be the policy. The peacetime army had been a Jim Crow army, and the Secretary of War Henry Stimson was committed to maintaining such a policy. Even black leaders had little hope of ending it. The most they could obtain from President Roosevelt was a promise in October 1940 that blacks would be inducted on the basis of their proportion in the general population and would be allowed opportunities to serve in all branches.[77]

A problem soon emerged. If the armed forces were to maintain separate units in training and in combat, filling these units would require special racially defined draft calls—but making draft calls on the basis of race violated the provisions of the law. The armed forces brushed this technicality aside. At first President Roosevelt seemed embarrassed by this consequence of the policy he had approved on 9 October. General George C. Marshall explained that such calls were needed to insure that the number of black draftees sent forward corresponded to the rather limited number of openings in the authorized black units.[78]

Roosevelt still wanted some means of avoiding calls by race. Marshall responded on 26 October by calling each corps area commander. He ordered them to keep quiet on the earlier racial call and to notify the governors of a total "without reference to color." Unfortunately, as Marshall explained to the president, "the general content of these instructions has been known to many people for some time." Marshall suggested that the army might manipulate numbers so that the first racial call for blacks was higher than the promised 10 percent.[79]

Hershey, unlike Roosevelt, accepted the racial calls as nothing more than a logical outgrowth of the principle of a segregated army. At a conference with the War Department on 20 November 1940, representatives from Marshall's office assured Hershey that they planned to authorize 10 percent of all draft calls for blacks by 1 July 1941. Unfortunately, the black calls would not be 10 percent each month, because of the absence of training facilities and cadres for these Jim Crow units.[80]

Within a matter of weeks Hershey became aware that such racial calls created problems for his system. In several states officials wanted to place black calls only on local boards with large black populations. In other states officials pointed to the anti-discriminatory clause in the law as justification for ignoring such racial calls. National headquarters now began a process of hair-splitting which, Hershey hoped, would satisfy both the law and the army. Baird V. Helfrich, the legal advisor to Selective Service, admitted to state directors that the presidential statement calling for equality of treatment for blacks in the draft and the Selective Service law itself meant that "there shall be no discrimination against any person on account of race or color." Neither national headquarters nor any state headquarters had the authority to call upon local boards for a specified number of men by race. Boards were to fill calls on the basis of order number sequence, not race. Helfrich warned that such racial quotas would create innumerable political and public relations problems.[81]

After having made what amounted to an airtight case against racial quotas, Helfrich began explaining how to live with racism. National headquarters felt that the problem of segregation was a problem for the army at induction, rather than for the Selective Service in selection. If local boards selected men without regard to race, the army could delay the induction of blacks until the proper units were ready. Selection was theoretically nondiscriminatory, but induction was by race. Unfortunately, such a solution made little difference to blacks, who found themselves in a veritable limbo after receiving a draft notice with no job security and no date of induction.[82]

Despite the legal jargon and the convoluted casuistry, by 1941 Hershey committed the system to implementing the racial quota system adopted by the army. He justified this cooperation by pointing to the general acceptance of a Jim Crow army, to Roosevelt's acquiescence in Stimson's program, and to the need to mobilize the armed forces during a time of national crisis. The race question was too complex to be solved during such an emergency. At the time he saw no alternative, and he had no strong feeling for carrying out the letter of the law. Indeed, he threatened those who tried to obey it. Ernest L. Averill, the state director in Connecticut, was a civilian who insisted that the law prohibited racial calls. He sent blacks to induction stations on the basis of their sequence number, whereupon the military officers at the induction stations returned the blacks to the local boards. Hershey warned Averill that any "Director and Local Board member who sent blacks to induction [without authorization] would be subject to suspension."[83]

The entire situation seemed to be getting out of hand. As racial quotas went into effect, many liberal groups began protesting to the president. The army continued to drag its feet on organizing black units into which these draftees could be taken. By autumn 1941 the army still had fewer than 5,000 blacks in organized units. P. L. Prattis, editor of the *Pittsburgh Courier*, complained to the president that the Selective Service was engaged in racism. To Stimson and Roosevelt, Hershey explained that he had tried to cooperate with the army by adopting racial drafts, to allow the army time to prepare. He warned the president, "It is obvious we must sooner or later come to the procedure of requisitioning and delivering men in the sequence of their order numbers without regard to color." In response, the adjutant general of the army replied that present organizations and facilities made it impossible to change the rate of black inductions. Induction stations would continue to turn away any surplus blacks.[84]

In January 1942 the problem worsened. Some 30,000 blacks were classified 1-A. These men, claimed Campbell Johnson, had been passed over "in violation of the spirit of the Selective Service law." Johnson, of course, had it wrong: blacks had been passed over despite the letter of the law, but in sympathy with the spirit of the times. Blacks represented 10.7 percent of all registrants, yet less than 6 percent of the army was black. The marines, who took only volunteers, were refusing all Negro applications. The navy had a few blacks serving as messmen.[85]

Johnson urged Hershey to force the military to take more blacks, but his words had little effect. Hershey knew Stimson was immovable, and that the nation could ill afford a major conflict between the draft and the armed forces. By January 1943 blacks represented 10.6 percent of the total registrants, yet the army had inducted only 375,059, the navy 19,790, and the marines 639. Negroes in the armed forces now stood at a mere 5.9 percent, far below the proportion promised by Roosevelt. More disturbing, Hershey had on hand some 300,000 Negro registrants in 1-A classification who were not being called. In the South a serious problem had arisen because married whites were being drafted while single Negroes remained at home. Congressmen were complaining.[86]

By 1 September 1944 some 19 percent of the entire registrant pool was black. The backlog was growing and creating serious problems in local areas. Stimson heard these cries of anguish with total indifference. He explained to Hershey that the current calls represented replacement needs for fighting units; since these units were almost all white, black inductees could not be used. Stimson felt that it would be unwise simply to draft large numbers of blacks, and Hershey had to accept the situation. Privately, he made a deal with the G-1 to keep the Negro calls at the 5 percent rate.[87]

Hershey failed to budge the armed forces on the issue of racial calls or to insure that the services lived up to the earlier agreement to take 10 percent, but he did manage to avoid one racial problem which the services sought to drop into his lap. In addition to sending up troops on the basis of racial quotas, Stimson wanted Hershey to be responsible for deciding the race of the draftee. The sordid game of determining race by percentages of blood, or ancestry, had been characteristic of the South for some time. Hershey had no intention of allowing his agency to become involved in such an exercise. In his opinion, if a man had been accepted as white in his community, "it would be unwise for the local board to disrupt the mode of life which has become so well established." If the induction station complained, let the army handle the problem.[88]

Again the armed forces refused to cooperate. Induction stations returned questionable cases to the local boards. Hershey insisted that boards simply accept the racial claim of each draftee unless strong evidence emerged to challenge it. In mid-1944 he informed the army that, in case of conflict over race, local boards would send the man forward with the race section left blank. Within a month induction stations were again returning such men to local boards. Hershey now took his case directly to the secretary of war. One district court had already ruled that local boards had no authority to determine race. Stimson refused to cooperate, but Hershey decided to stand firm. On 28 August he instructed local boards that, in cases of dispute, they should merely use the race claimed by the registrant. The War Department finally capitulated and agreed not to reject a man without conclusive proof refuting his racial claim.[89]

Threat of court action had helped Hershey, in that instance, but the courts were less helpful on the issue of racial calls. The practice of taking men on the basis of race seemed a clear violation of the Selective Service law and of several articles of the Constitution, yet the courts refused to assert their authority over the draft system. During World War II the courts refused to accept a case until the draftee failed to step forward to accept induction. This attitude put all administrative actions of the system beyond the pale of judicial review. Nothing in the 1940 law precluded judicial review, but the courts acted with wartime restraint.[90]

Few better illustrations exist of how the court can cooperate with a national emergency than the case dealing with racial quotas. On 28 September 1942 Winfred W. Lynn of New York City, on the advice of his lawyer brother Conrad, refused to report for induction as ordered. After being reported as a delinquent and approached by the Federal Bureau of Investigation, Winfred issued a statement admitting his delinquency but insisting that the draft discriminated against black Americans and that the quota system used by local boards violated the Selective Service law, the Fifth Amendment (on due process), and the Fourteenth Amendment (on equal protection).[91]

Hershey agreed with many of these legal points, but he feared that the *Lynn* case might prove the undoing of his draft system. With the American Civil Liberties Union involved, he worried that a white registrant might also bring suit on grounds that he had been taken too early because of the quota system. If the courts decided that blacks had to be taken by order number, in Mississippi only blacks would be

called for several months. The armed forces obviously needed to end
their system of racial calls.[92]

Winfred Lynn obtained a temporary writ against the draft order. On
4 December the district court of New York revoked the writ on the
grounds that Lynn had first to submit himself to induction in order to
obtain standing in court. Lynn submitted to induction on 19 December
and immediately sought another writ. The Justice Department, however, succeeded in using several technical points to delay a hearing for
months. A subsequent district court decision upheld his draft as legal.
Lynn then appealed to the circuit court, which, on 2 February 1944,
upheld the government's position. The court's reasoning proved rather
fatuous: Lynn had failed to prove he was inducted under a racist call.
Though Lynn had already been moved to Europe, his lawyers took an
appeal to the Supreme Court, which on 29 May 1944, ruled that the
case was moot. Lynn was suing his original camp commander, who no
longer had authority over a soldier stationed in Europe.[93]

Hershey could breathe easier after this case of judicial railroading.
He was thankful for his narrow escape from judicial interference. As
he wrote to Attorney General Francis Biddle, the cooperation of the
Justice Department and the denial of certiorari was a "most satisfactory solution to that problem." Lynn's opinion of the solution went un-
recorded.[94]

Blacks were only one minority group affected by the draft. Hershey
had more problems in coping with an even smaller minority group.
During World War II almost 12,000 American male citizens identified
themselves as conscientious objectors to war and accepted alternate
service in Civilian Public Service camps. The Selective Service Act of
1940, Section 5(g), announced that "nothing contained in this act shall
be construed to require any person to be subject to combatant training
and service in the land or naval forces of the United States, who, by
reason of religious training and belief, is conscientiously opposed to
participation in war in any form." The act provided for alternate service for such CO's. This alternate service program came under Hershey's direction.[95]

There was irony in having Hershey assume responsibility for defining "religion" and "conscience" in the execution of the draft law. Hershey's ancestors were Mennonites, people so deeply opposed to war
that they had fled Europe rather than face conscription. This religious
enthusiasm had waned among the Hersheys by the time Lewis was
born; he never attended church with any regularity, and he was an indifferent Mason. But he had been exposed to religion and ethics in his
early years. His schooling included a considerable dose of the King
James Version of the Bible, besides the official morality inculcated by a

community of homogeneous Christians. From this experience Hershey fashioned a personal creed which drew eclectically from Greek stoicism, humanitarian ethics, American individualism, and deism. He had little time for the technicalities of theology or the formalism of a church.[96] Suddenly, in 1941, he found himself responsible for dealing with a profoundly ethical question.

In some ways the treatment of CO's during World War II represented a liberalization of earlier approaches. During World War I such status was granted by law only to members of traditional peace churches (Quakers, Brethren, and Mennonites), and little change was expected as the 1940 law was being drafted. Pacifism had no support in Congress. Secretary of War Stimson rebuffed an attempt by Roger Baldwin of the American Civil Liberties Union to discuss protection "for the rights of conscience in the draft bill." In January 1940 a Gallup poll asked what should be done with CO's if the nation went to war. Only 13.2 percent of respondents recommended exemption from military duty; 9 percent wanted them shot or put in jail, and 24 percent wanted to force them to fight. Some 37 percent recommended noncombat military service. In November 1940, two months after the law passed, a group of CO's refused to register and were sentenced to one year in jail. The public approved this punishment, although 21 percent felt it was not severe enough.[97]

Hershey was more liberal. The new draft bill of 1940 required that a CO belong to a traditional peace church, but Hershey, while testifying before Congress, supported a change to cover individual CO's.[98] In preparing a final draft of the bill, he discussed the treatment of CO's with the peace churches. The enforcement provision of the bill was drafted after consultation with Paul Comly French of the Society of Friends. After the passage of the bill Hershey invited the peace churches to submit a plan for alternate service. "As no one in the government service has given much thought to this problem," he explained, the peace churches should make "concrete and specific suggestions."[99]

The National Service Board for Religious Objectors (NSBRO), a secretariat for the peace churches headed by Paul French, recommended that the alternate service camps be run by the churches. There was some dispute over who would pay for the upkeep of the camps, and the peace churches did not envision paying for the upkeep of nonmembers. Yet, if the government funded the program, the churches could expect tighter control. Hershey finally allowed the NSBRO to organize and finance the camps, but he retained final authority over assignments and work projects. Some disagreement was inevitable. The draft had as its primary mission the furnishing of men for the armed forces; the peace churches, in contrast, were concerned with preserving the right of individual conscience while the rest of the nation fought what would be called a total war.[100]

Roosevelt allowed Hershey full freedom to run the alternate service program. On 6 February 1941 the president issued an executive order establishing the CO program and approving Hershey's plan. When the director of the budget, Harold Smith, urged the president to give more study to this delegation of power, Roosevelt replied, "We need action." Like other eligible citizens, the CO first registered with the Selective Service. Hershey instructed local boards not to use the CO claim if another deferred category could be justified. He met with several religious groups to explain how they might comply with the law without violating their consciences.[101]

Hershey approached the problem with a surprisingly tolerant spirit, making it clear to all local boards that objectors should receive the same consideration as non-objectors. As for the unenviable task of determining the sincerity of objectors, Hershey sympathized but refused to issue an official definition, a task he considered "impossible." In February 1941 he announced obscurely that "the judgment of individual conscience opposed to the national will should be given consideration and allowed a form of cooperation consistent with its judgments if they are the results of religious training and belief." The entire CO program had to be seen as an "experiment . . . to find out whether our democracy is big enough to preserve minority rights in a time of national emergency." He also argued pragmatically that the program would relieve the armed forces of thousands of malcontents.[102]

Whatever the rhetoric, the test of the program came through implementation, especially after 7 December 1941. Controversy was insured by a program in which the churches provided financial support and low-level management while the Selective Service controlled major policy decisions. The NSBRO could select camp directors and staff, recommend assignments, and even carry on religious and recreational programs, but Hershey retained the final authority on what work should be done, and on assignments. Although the law clearly stated that CO's must "be assigned to work of national importance under civilian direction," to insure that the program remained consistent with his own ideas Hershey picked an old National Guard crony, Lt. Col. Lewis Kosch, to supervise the camps. Hershey assured Kosch, "You will be in no way handicapped by rules or policy heretofore established."[103]

The CO program became defined by actions taken in individual cases. If the local board refused to grant the individual his claim of CO status, he was entitled to a hearing by a Justice Department official. If the board disagreed with this hearing officer's findings, the individual could appeal his case to the state appeal board. If refused, but not unanimously, by this board, the individual could then appeal to a presidential board. Such an appeal during World War II meant taking it to General Hershey, by presidential delegation.

Hershey took an active interest in appeals and stamped many decisions with his own outlook. In implementing the system he frequently had to overcome resistance by local board members. Coming from chambers of commerce and veterans' organizations, the men had little sympathy for the CO. To minimize difficulties, Hershey insisted that the boards give full details of the appeal procedure to all: "It is not the province of the local board to decide that all of these individuals must serve in the armed forces—the law provides otherwise." When Roger Baldwin complained at local board treatment of CO's, Hershey replied that every appeal received careful consideration by his headquarters.[104]

In acting upon appeals Hershey used his own definition of religion: "any and all influences which have contributed to the consistent endeavor to live the good life may be classed as 'religious training.'" Thus the applicant did not have to prove membership in a religious organization. In the appeal of Louis F. Doucette in 1941 Hershey overruled his own appeal panel. The panel had refused CO status to Doucette on the grounds that he was a Roman Catholic, whose officials denied teaching conscientious objection to the war. Hershey refused to accept church officials' denial that individual members could adopt pacifist ideas. There might be some disagreement on whether the individual was sincere in his belief, but if the facts supported him, he should not be denied CO status because the Catholic church had no official teaching supporting his claim.[105]

Hershey's interpretation, consistent with his personal philosophy, focused upon the individual conscience rather than on the formal teaching of any church. Yet the individual had to base his claim on more than personal ideas. "I must be satisfied," he wrote, "that the objection is based on 'religious training and belief' which contemplates recognition of some source of all existence, which, whatever the type of conception, is Divine because it is the Source of all things." But he also explained that "each case should be considered individually and no one presidential appeal decision can be considered binding precedent." He consistently rejected claims which rested solely on social philosophy, but he refused to demand a tightly drawn definition of religious training and belief.[106]

Whether Hershey was criticized for being narrow or broad in his interpretation of the law depended upon who was criticizing him. Clearly, however, his appeal decisions tended to support CO claims.

Presidential board actions were consistently more liberal than were those of local boards and appeal boards. Of 1,558 CO cases appealed, some 52 percent of appellants were placed in 1-A by local boards; 40 percent were placed in 1-A by the appeal boards; 9.8 percent were placed in 1-A by presidential board action. Of some 63,051 cases from October 1940 to September 1945, local boards approved CO deferments at a rate of 17.2 percent. Hershey's board approved them at a 36.5 percent rate, dealing only with cases rejected by local boards.[107]

Besides defining who was eligible, Hershey also faced the task of finding work or alternate service for the CO's. The law provided that they were to be "assigned to work of national importance." The NSBRO pressed to gain control over what work should be done, and Hershey did grant the organization the right to veto certain projects. (After all, the board was expected to spend several million dollars on the program.) But Hershey was always committed to insuring that the projects would involve some inconvenience and sacrifice for the CO. He should be moved away from his home and should not engage in educational projects which would give him "every opportunity to spread the doctrine of pacifism to our youth in its formative period."[108]

Requests poured into headquarters for the assignment of CO's to dairy farms and other private projects. Hershey agreed to these assignments, but with misgivings. Selective Service required that employers pay the "going wage" in order to avoid charges of exploiting labor, yet the sight of a CO making money might enrage public opinion. Since Hershey was committed to a "no pay" principle as part of his "equal sacrifice" idea, he had to develop some means of controlling the money earned. At first he agreed that the money should go to the NSBRO to defray camp expenses. The comptroller general, however, ruled that all funds earned had to revert to the treasury. NSBRO, for its part, objected to CO wages being used to support the war. Hershey finally drew up a compromise whereby the money, eventually some $1,225,000, would be held in a special Treasury account. The CO only received a $15 monthly cash allowance for clothing and incidentals.[109]

In addition to the pay issue, Hershey faced complaints from the CO's, from the NSBRO, and from Congress that the work assigned to the camps was not of "national importance." In Hershey's private opinion, the program had a political and social purpose, rather than a material one. Somehow these men had to be engaged in work which took them away from their homes and also convinced Congress and the public that the sacrifice was commensurate with avoiding military service. Achieving these social and political objectives frequently meant sacrificing efficiency. Many of the men performed manual tasks far below their educational levels, but Hershey felt that this was the price paid for the program's existence. He reassured such CO's that "men who have been exposed to considerable formal education have found their souls on the seas, on the mountains, in the forests, or even on the handle of a shovel." In time, CO's performed very useful work: as guinea pigs in health and dietary projects, fighting forest fires, and as aides in mental institutions.[110]

Representatives from the peace churches disputed Hershey's arguments. In May 1943 Clarence E. Pickett, the executive secretary of the American Friends Service Committee, complained to President Roosevelt about Hershey, a military officer, dominating the administration of the camps. The same year Ernest Angell and Paul J. Furnas of the NSBRO and Oswald G. Villard of the ACLU made the same complaint. Late in the war even Attorney General Francis Biddle urged that the president place all appeals in the hands of civilians.[111]

Hershey mounted a successful defense against these charges. Circuit court decisions held that he had been detached from military service; hence the Selective Service System was under civilian control. (Hershey claimed civilian status even as he sat testifying in uniform before congressional committees.) If he withdrew from the program, Hershey argued, it would merely put control "in the hands of individuals who by refusal to accept responsibility to government have created the original problem." If the peace churches withdrew their support, as a few threatened to do, Hershey promised to take over all of the camps. Under no circumstances would he relinquish final approval of projects.[112]

President Roosevelt, eager to avoid the problem, supported Hershey's position, accepting Hershey's contention that the work was under civilian direction. There were no military personnel at the camps, and the CO's remained under the jurisdiction of the civil courts. The president felt that Hershey was doing a fine job.[113]

Hershey had more trouble deflecting opposition from anti-CO forces. To one mother, who had lost a son in combat, he tried to explain why the CO remained at home while other boys went into battle. The entire nation should feel proud, he wrote, "that we today live in a country where the small minority can enjoy freedom of conscience and not be placed in concentration camps on account of their belief." To Congress, Hershey explained that the men were doing jobs selected by other government agencies. The CO's lived in remote areas, received no pay, and were not being pampered. In February 1943 when a bill emerged in the Senate to end the CO classification, Hershey successfully fought its passage.[114]

When individual rebels in the camps caused problems, Hershey sought to defuse the issue without generating publicity and without

creating a martyr complex. To one young man who left camp because
he refused to accept forced labor, Hershey explained the dangers of
this philosophy. Having accepted certain privileges by being a member
of society, the individual could no longer reject society's right to demand service. As military service involved the preservation of society,
the obligation to serve was basic. Alternate service, Hershey explained, was not a right guaranteed by the Constitution but "an indulgence extended to a few." The young man must follow his conscience,
but Hershey warned that refusal to accept alternate service might well
lead to the end of the indulgence.[115]

When reason and administrative solutions proved useless, Hershey
was willing to prosecute. Violation of the law carried a penalty provision of five years or a $10,000 fine or both. During the war the Justice
Department reported 16,000 convictions through 30 June 1946. Of
these, some 6,000 involved conscientious objectors, but only one-third
were due to refusal to report to CO camps. Hershey was quite willing
to use the Justice Department to enforce the law. When riots broke out
at several camps, he immediately requested FBI intervention. When
the Justice Department decided in September 1946 not to prosecute
a deserter from a CPS camp because he had served almost twenty
months and the war was over, Hershey was upset. He argued that,
unless the man was prosecuted, mass desertions from the camps would
occur.[116]

With the end of the war in Europe in May 1945, Hershey faced the
problem of ending alternate service. He argued that the CO's should
be released at the same relative rate as veterans. On 25 May Hershey
announced his CO release plan to the press. It duplicated the system
used by the armed forces, in which men were granted points toward
discharge by virtue of their length of service, number of dependents,
and other factors.[117]

In seeking to implement the plan he ran into opposition from all
sides. Congress, veterans' organizations, the War Department, and
the CO's all found his plan objectionable. More embarrassing, Hershey
had devised the plan without consulting the president. Harry S Truman, who had assumed office on 12 April, admitted that he found the
entire CO idea incomprehensible. When Francis Biddle urged the
president to take a more active interest, Truman turned to Samuel
Rosenman, an old New Dealer, for advice. Rosenman warned that
"this would be a very inopportune time to change our policy." Reform
might be misconstrued by the public as a softening of attitude which
would "increase a feeling that the war is over."[118]

Rosenman was right—any change in the CO program was bound to
provoke controversy. A New Jersey local board wired Hershey that

the release plan was "contemptible" and his action "despicable." In June, Undersecretary of War Robert Patterson informed Hershey that the War Department disapproved of the plan because it would promote the false notion that the war was over. Congressman Arthur Winstead (D, Miss.), who had originally introduced a bill legalizing Hershey's plan, reversed himself and introduced a bill specifically prohibiting the use of a point system for CO release.[119]

At first Hershey fought for his original plan. He reminded Patterson that the law gave Selective Service responsibility over CO's, without need for War Department approval. The CO's had done their duty under the law—without pay, family allowances, veterans' benefits, reemployment rights, insurance benefits, debt deferments, compensation, or pensions. Hershey felt that these men were entitled to release under the same conditions as soldiers. Such a release would not provide veterans with competition for jobs, because the CO had no reemployment rights. The number of CO's to be released was only seventy-five a month, hardly enough to create a morale problem in the army. He concluded, "I can see no reason why they should be discriminated against," after having done their duty under the law.[120]

He soon began to see reasons. The House Military Affairs Committee reported out the Winstead bill (HR 3772), which prohibited the implementation of his plan. Above all, Hershey was a political realist. He knew it would be courting disaster to plunge ahead with a release program in the face of opposition, even though Congress had recessed without acting on the bill. He met with members of the congressional committee and agreed not to use the point system. Rather, he would discharge CO's only on the basis of physical disability, undue hardship, age, and length of service. The new plan called for the release of men over forty with over two years of service, then moved to those over thirty-eight, and so on, down the list. This new plan began in the fall of 1945. Hershey explained, "We don't think this plan will create a public relations problem." Taking no chances, he waited until February 1946 to announce it to the press.[121]

The shift in public climate brought about by the collapse of Japan in September 1945 allowed Hershey to begin releases. A poll of 6 September indicated that 43 percent felt all CO's should be released; another 40 percent favored releasing all those who had done useful work. By 31 January 1946 Hershey had released 44.7 percent of the 12,000 under Selective Service control during the war. In contrast, the armed forces had released 60.6 percent of its strength for all causes since November 1940. The war was over, yet most of the CO's remained in camps. Hershey admitted the justice of NSBRO complaints and strove to bring the CO rate into line with that of the armed forces. In fact,

Selective Service released the last inmate of the camps only on 30 March 1947.[122]

Yet the demobilization of CO's represented only a minor part of Hershey's role in returning men to American society. He had worked to insure that the society would remain stable and its values secure. In addition to drafting men for the armed forces, Hershey now had the job of helping men return to civilian occupations.

*The fishbowl lottery of World War II, ca. 1940 (courtesy of the Military
History Institute, Carlisle Barracks, Pennsylvania)*

A quick snack for a busy man, ca. 1943 (courtesy of Hershey family)

Work with the War Manpower Commission, 6 April 1942. Front Row, L–R: Donald M. Nelson, War Production Board; Claude R. Wickard, Secty of Agriculture; Paul V. McNutt, Chairman; Frances Perkins, Secty of Labor; James V. Forrestal, Navy Dept.
Back Row, L–R: Wendell Lund, WPB; Goldthwaite H. Dorr, War Dept.; Gen. Lewis B. Hershey, Selective Service Director; Arthur J. Altmeyer, Executive Officer; Arthur S. Fleming, Civil Service Commission; and Fowler V. Harper, Deputy Chairman (courtesy of the Military History Institute, Carlisle Barracks, Pennsylvania)

Visiting the White House with Paul McNutt, 1942 (courtesy of the Military History Institute, Carlisle Barracks, Pennsylvania)

MAJ. GEN. LEWIS B. HERSHEY

For an A-1 army
In 1-A trim,
Selective Service
Selected him
To present free rides
To the front and fame,
In sort of a glorified
Numbers game.
You feel a draft?
You'd better check.
It's That Man breathing
On your neck.
—ETHEL JACOBSON.

A subject of national cartoonists, 1943 (reprinted from The Saturday
Evening Post, © *1943 The Curtis Publishing Company)*

"Hershey will, Hershey won't, Hershey will——"

Cartoon on the father draft, 7 August 1943 (reprinted from The Saturday Evening Post, *© 1943 The Curtis Publishing Company)*

Cartoon on the father draft, 11 August 1943 (permission of Jim Berryman and the Washington Evening Star)

Cartoon on draft confusion, 2 September 1943 (permission of Jim Berryman and the Washington Evening Star)

Cartoon on deferment problems, 28 February 1944 (permission of Jim Berryman and the Washington Evening Star)

Something Is Cooking

Cartoon on national service, 18 March 1944 (permission of Jim Berryman and the Washington Evening Star)

Cartoon on draft confusion, 12 April 1944 (permission of Jim Berryman and the Washington Evening Star)

Cartoon on draft confusion, 18 April 1944 (permission of Joseph Parrish and the Chicago Tribune, *copyright 1944)*

"*Tune in WJZ, Joe! Hershey's changed his mind again!*"

Cartoon on the postwar draft, February 1946 (permission from Esquire, *February 1946, © 1946 by Esquire Associates*

Chapter VI. Demobilization

Americans could hardly wait for the war to end. As the last German offensive collapsed in December 1944, they turned their attention to demobilization, to finding a peacetime job. Hershey viewed the ending of the war with more mixed feelings. A conservative Republican and a believer in decentralization, he had misgivings about the concentration of federal power that had escalated during the war. In an address on 20 May 1945 (Citizenship Day) he emphasized that "peace does not need these centralized controls. It will not be wise to continue them."[1] But he also had strong convictions about the important role of the United States in the postwar world.

He was dismayed that Americans repeatedly and rapidly disarmed after a fight. While calling for a dismantling of federal agencies, Hershey at the same time insisted upon the retention of a large standing army: "To be strong will require that all citizens, not just a few, be trained to defend their country if it should be attacked." America would need troops to maintain her position in the world. "I don't know whether we want to be policing all over the world or not," he argued, "but as a citizen and a father, I have a right to demand that my kid in Japan is either supported or taken out of there."[2]

Here was Hershey's problem: he disliked a strong central government, yet he saw the need for a strong military establishment. His midwestern heritage pulled him toward an insular view, but his own experience had convinced him of America's new role in the world. Such a role could not be sustained without adequate manpower, which meant either universal military training or a continuation of the draft. In addition, Hershey had a natural desire to see his agency continue to flourish. He had a paternalistic affection for the draft apparatus which he had nurtured through its infancy and into wartime adulthood. Since his system represented a triumph of decentralization, he could argue simultaneously for dismantling of wartime agencies and for retaining the draft apparatus. His thinking mixed logic and self-interest.

However inconsistent, these ideas guided him in confronting the problem of demobilization, which first became acute during 1944. The draft had caught up with the expanding needs of the armed forces, and by spring the army was asking Hershey merely to maintain strength levels through replacements. On the international scene, Italy had left the war, and Eisenhower was preparing to lead a giant taskforce in the invasion of Europe. Hershey anticipated the collapse of the enemy, but he insisted that the nation should adopt a system of universal military training to provide for any future war. He also hoped that troops would be demobilized at a rate which would permit their absorption into the economy without creating serious dislocation.[3]

Such sentiments sounded fairly conventional, but Hershey disturbed people when he insisted that men be kept in the armed forces until there were enough civilian jobs to accommodate veterans. He saw no need to rush the troops home "into some kind of a WPA." In August 1944 Hershey announced that the war with Germany would be over before the first snow in Europe, and that 2 million men would soon be returning to the United States. At a Denver press conference he explained, "The numbers discharged in any one area at any one time should be limited and should be based on the capacity of the community to absorb the numbers demobilized." He insisted, "It is cheaper to keep men in the army than it is to set up an agency to take care of them when they are released."[4]

Such remarks provoked controversy. Opponents of Roosevelt speculated about the involvement of New Dealers, with their penchant for manipulating lives for the sake of economic objectives. But the most embarrassing criticism came from Governor Thomas Dewey of New York, the recently nominated Republican candidate for the presidency. In the midst of a lackluster campaign against a popular incumbent, Dewey exploited Hershey's remark, quoting Hershey as evidence that the Roosevelt administration had plans for keeping the boys in khaki even after the war was over. In Congress Senator O'Mahoney rose to explain that Hershey had no authority to speak on demobilization policy. The Indianapolis *News* complained, "Hershey talks too much."[5]

At the White House the president considered removing Hershey from office. Undersecretary Patterson agreed that Hershey talked too much and wanted him replaced. Secretary Stimson, while sympathizing with Patterson, was reluctant to fire Hershey because putting in a new man would mean "delays and chaos." Instead, Stimson recommended that Hershey be scolded and told to keep his mouth shut. Roosevelt continued to wish he had appointed a civilian, but Stimson wanted to give Hershey another chance.[6]

In early October Hershey arrived at the White House for a chat with presidential aide Jonathan Daniels, who explained that the president was upset. On 13 October Hershey penned an apology of sorts, explaining that his Denver remarks had been in reply to an hypothetical question in an area where he had limited knowledge. As for Dewey's tactics, Hershey insisted that he had run the draft independent of partisan politics. As a military officer, he refused to become involved in any election campaign, although he admitted he was a Republican. "I plan to continue to vote," he wrote, "as I believe that to be my right and duty." If the president was dissatisfied, Hershey offered to resign.[7] After winning the November election, the president wrote to Hershey calling for an end to "speculative public statements by responsible military and civilian public officials at home and abroad indicating an early termination of the war." Such remarks, the president added, would only hurt wartime morale.[8]

Hershey had stubbed his toe by advocating a slow return of veterans. He also courted unpopularity by promoting the continuation of the Selective Service System. Martin Agronsky, a leading radio reporter, asked Hershey on 27 May 1944 whether his work was almost over. Hershey insisted that his biggest job remained: "the returning once again to civilian life . . . [of] the men who so bravely have fought for their country's victory."[9] If Selective Service could assume responsibility for the return of veterans to American society, and if the president and Congress approved a peacetime universal military training program, Hershey had an indefinite future in Washington.[10] But these were big "ifs."

Establishing a role for Selective Service in the demobilization of troops proved more difficult than Hershey had imagined. Section 7(b) of the Selective Service Act asserted the right of every draftee to be returned to his old job or to one of "like seniority, status and pay." Section 7(g) authorized the director of Selective Service to aid veterans seeking to return to their old jobs or to find new jobs. The system had a Veterans' Personnel Division at each state headquarters. At each local board one member assumed the duty of reemployment committeeman. In his interpretation of the law, Hershey insisted that the veteran should not lose seniority and should not be discharged from his job without cause within one year.[11]

Separations occurred during the war, but the numbers amounted to a mere trickle. From September 1940 to February 1945 Selective Service estimated that only some 75,000 veterans required reemployment aid. Hershey cooperated with existing government agencies to place these men in defense jobs. In September 1943 he issued a Reemployment Bulletin which emphasized the importance of clearing all job assignments with the United States Employment Service. The Veterans' Employment Service interviewed men at separation points and sought to channel them into vital jobs.[12]

On 24 February 1944 President Roosevelt established a Retraining and Reemployment Administration (RRA) to coordinate all aid for veterans. Hershey became one of three members of the board. Even after the GI Bill of Rights passed on 22 June and Frank T. Hines, head of the Veterans' Bureau, was made coordinator of RRA, Hershey continued to play a major role. His agency had been first in the field in dealing with returning veterans. As an operating agency with a far-flung network of volunteers, Hershey's words were translated into action. The local draft boards included important members of the business community.[13]

Before the trickle of returning veterans became a flood, before other government agencies divined a role, and before unions recognized possible problems, Hershey had a system in operation and had articulated an elaborate interpretation of veterans' rights. In his memos Hershey stressed that local boards had a "moral and legal" obligation to aid veterans. This aid included much more than merely educating the men to their rights under the law. If a man's old job had disappeared, the board should seek to fit him into a new position. If the employer refused to cooperate, Hershey would go to court to enforce a veteran's reemployment rights.[14]

By autumn 1944 the number of veterans returning each month had climbed to 50,000. As the problem became more burdensome, a number of challenges to Hershey's control arose. Perhaps his biggest rival was General Frank T. Hines. Hershey had made it clear to Hines as early as 15 March 1944 that Selective Service would brook no rivals in veterans' reemployment. To Congress, Hershey explained that Hines and the Veterans' Bureau had just begun thinking about a problem that Selective Service had been handling for four years.[15] In November he informed the state directors that "as long as our volunteers are convinced we are doing important work we will be safe." Other agencies might complain, but Hershey promised: "As long as we have the responsibility, I am not checking in my guns until I see something done to change it."[16]

Hines and budget director Harold Smith both hoped that Roosevelt would change Hershey's mind. Judge Samuel Rosenman explained to the president that veterans' reemployment was becoming a problem area. Hershey's zeal and his interpretation of the law were upsetting labor unions and making Hines a supernumerary. But during the election Roosevelt had little time to consider this problem; in fact, he even seemed sympathetic to Hershey's interpretation of the role of Selective Service. On 28 October Roosevelt praised the local boards for their work, adding, "There is another task which must be discharged with equal efficiency by the Selective Service System—that is to aid veterans in obtaining reemployment on discharge." With such a presidential mandate, Hershey had little trouble keeping Hines in his place.[17]

Overcoming union opposition, however, was more difficult. Hershey interpreted the law in a manner guaranteed to raise opposition from American labor. The law conferred reemployment rights on all men inducted after 1 May 1940. The veteran was entitled to reinstatement in his former position or a position of like seniority and status. If an employer refused to acknowledge these rights, the veteran could file suit in district court without cost. These principles were never seriously disputed, but in putting them into practice Hershey committed the system to other ideas which were not spelled out in the law.[18]

To help provide guidance for local board members, the Selective Service issued a veterans' handbook in September 1945. The *Veterans' Assistance Program Handbook* stated that veterans were entitled to any automatic pay increases given solely on the basis of length of service. It also ruled that union membership or any other condition not specifically enumerated in the law could not be required of a veteran before reinstatement.[19] The veteran was entitled to reinstatement even if it meant displacing an older civilian worker who had more seniority. Most important, "This right of reemployment," wrote Hershey, "would prevail as against all other employees, regardless of seniority or length of service, except other veterans having superior claims."[20]

Organized labor woke up to the problem of super-seniority in the summer of 1945, after Hershey had been using the principle for months. Speaking to the National UAW-CIO War Veterans' Conference on 6 April 1944, he insisted that Congress wanted the veteran to receive such priority. Such a radical view of reemployment disturbed Secretary of Labor Frances Perkins, a friend of unions. In her opinion, the super-seniority interpretation would create serious problems. Nevertheless, she refused to criticize Hershey: "You know how much I admire all of the work that you have done in Selective Service and how much confidence I have in your breadth of judgment, particularly on labor matters."[21]

Union officials lacked such confidence and challenged Hershey's interpretation of the law. In a public debate with Robert J. Watt of the AFL on 6 April 1945, Hershey reiterated his belief that the intent of the law was to set veterans apart as a special class because they had contributed more than others. Hershey promised to stand firm unless Congress revised the law or the courts declared him wrong. Ted F. Silvey of the CIO argued that unions had helped Congress write this section of the law, and that they knew more about its interpretation than did General Hershey.[22]

Hershey refused to budge. He interpreted Section 8 of the law to mean that a returning veteran "who meets all of the reemployment conditions of eligibility required by the statute, has an absolute right to be restored to his former position or a position of like seniority, status and pay."[23] Ted Silvey and M. H. Hedges of the AFL accused Hershey of trying to start a fight between veterans and civilian workers. These arguments left Hershey unmoved. As for the seniority system, if it could not "adapt itself to a wholly different situation . . . [it] is obviously going to die off anyway." Why is seniority so flexible, he asked, that it can exempt presidents, vice-presidents, recording secretaries, treasurers, and stewards in order to maintain the union, but "to maintain the greater union, the one the flag flies over, we can't bend it?"[24]

Given the sensitive issues involved and the importance of the union vote to Democratic victories, Hershey was not surprised when reemployment became a political football. The departments of labor and justice both had reservations about Hershey's interpretation.[25] As President Truman busied himself with the Japanese surrender, he was distracted by the reemployment problem. Harold Smith, one of the few holdovers from the Roosevelt administration, argued against allowing Hershey to preempt responsibility for veterans. Truman "agreed most emphatically," according to Smith. The White House informed the House Committee on Appropriations that Selective Service did not need more money because it had only a limited role to play in reemployment.[26]

Smith immediately conveyed Truman's desires, but Hershey refused to retreat gracefully. With Congress soon to begin debating an extension of the draft, helping veterans was a strong argument for the perpetuation of his organization. On 25 October 1945 he wrote Truman of his grave concern that the government was letting down the boys who had fought, failing in "the solemn obligations which a grateful nation owes to its returning veterans." Some 1,250,000 veterans per month were being demobilized. Smith had cut Selective Service's budget request to a point where some 1,500 employees would have to be released. Hershey begged the president to restore the sums cut, but Truman thought otherwise. On 2 November 1945 the president informed Hershey that the veterans' work of the SSS had to stop.[27] The Secretary of Labor would now be responsible for clarifying reemployment rights of veterans; Hershey was to be shunted aside.

With demobilization issues wrenched from his hands, Hershey seemed once again at a dead end. The beginning of World War II had found him contemplating retirement at the modest rank of major. Through good fortune and talent he had made a major contribution to victory, although not on the battlefield. Like many other Americans, he discovered that his war work had become the center of his life. His schedule was hectic. He roamed the country by car and train to hold the hands of state and local officials. In Washington he left for the office early in the morning and worked through lunch while munching on a cheeseburger and sipping hot tea. When he returned home late in the evening, with a briefcase bulging with more work, Ellen had already retired. He heated some food and was in bed by 11:00. The demands of his office crowded out his responsibilities as father and husband. The children grew up in his absence.[28]

As an officer with one of the most demanding jobs in Washington, he should not have had to worry about private finances, yet Hershey's salary of $10,000 a year never seemed adequate to cover his expenses. Clothing, feeding, and educating four teenagers absorbed most of his funds. Hershey also had to care for several aged relatives. To add to his burden, Ellen continued to suffer from chronic illness. Throughout her life she had problems with her respiratory system and required several operations.[29]

The war years, however, were not all work, family problems, and illnesses for Hershey. As a man of importance in national mobilization he enjoyed several privileges. No longer did he use second-rate hotels and second-rate travel. He received VIP treatment, took tours of tank plants, met mayors and governors. He and Ellen had the attraction of the active Washington social scene. Such social mixing appealed little to Hershey, but Ellen considered this one of the most appealing parts of military life.[30]

During the war Americans rewarded Hershey for doing a fine job in a thankless position. Accolades began to pour over his head with its rapidly greying hair. Tri-State College and Ohio State University presented him with honorary degrees. After the war recognition came from the army and navy in the form of distinguished service medals. President Truman surprised Hershey with an award from the army during ceremonies at the White House on 21 January 1946. In October the American Legion presented distinguished service awards to Hershey, J. Edgar Hoover, Cordell Hull, and Bob Hope. In February 1947 Columbia University presented Hershey and ten other military leaders with honorary law degrees. Dr. Frank D. Fackenthal, acting president of the university, cited Hershey for his vital work in balancing the needs of military forces against the preservation of the economic and social life of the nation.[31]

Inducting 14 million men into the armed forces deserved acknowledgment, but even more significant was the technique used to accomplish this task. Hershey managed to fulfill his mission while maintaining an unprecedented degree of public support. During the Civil War men had rioted over the draft; in contrast, Hershey grew in public esteem during World War II. The press held him in affection. His folksy style and skill at dodging questions by telling funny stories won him the admiration of even the cynical Washington press corps.[32] Throughout the war pollsters asked whether the public thought the draft was being handled fairly. From a high of 92 percent in December 1940, the Selective Service never dropped below 75 percent in its approval rating. In May 1942 George Gallup wrote that Hershey deserved the major credit for setting up a system which had won approval from virtually every segment of American society: "Few programs in the Nation's history have ever received such widespread favorable reaction from the people as the handling of the Selective Service draft."[33]

This success in public relations came despite the militarization of the draft. Most Americans in 1940 had agreed with the president that the draft system should be kept in civilian hands. The draft system did use civilian draft boards, but Hershey's entire headquarters was dominated by men in uniform. On the state level another 600 officers held positions. The original law called for establishing civilian appeal boards, but ultimately these boards were also manned by military officers. This character of the draft failed to provoke civilian revolt for several reasons. First, the advent of war disposed many congressmen and citizens to lay aside their distrust of the military, at least for the duration. Second, Hershey's own unmilitary personality and bearing, his down-home idiom, combined to reassure citizens distrustful of a man on horseback. Finally, the civilians on the local boards helped create the image of the Selective Service as nonmilitary in character, even while higher positions were manned by men in uniform. As one scholar has written, "The capturing of the Selective Service System stood as the Army's easiest victory of the Second World War."[34]

Besides maintaining the military character of the system, Hershey also avoided overdirection from civilian agencies, including Congress. The brief period of servitude under the War Manpower Commission had very little effect on his independence of operation; McNutt and his civilians soon went down in the flames of political opposition, while Hershey flew on. Except for the Tydings amendment, providing deferments for farmers, Hershey was also successful in deflecting congressional attempts to overdirect his operation. He argued consistently and successfully that all problems of the draft were best handled through administration, rather than through legislation.[35]

The achievement of which Hershey was proudest was the triumph of his philosophy of decentralization. When a military audience after the war asked him why he had not adopted a system of regional draft boards to avoid some of his problems, Hershey replied that such an approach was "diametrically opposed to what I believe." His philosophy, implemented throughout the war, was to have the local citizen "do the unpleasant thing." Of all the sanctions which made the draft work, Hershey was convinced that the most powerful one was community opinion. This opinion could function only if decisionmaking remained localized. Such an approach, he emphasized, "is fundamentally sound and in accordance with the highest tradition of American democracy." Whatever the problems and mistakes of mobilization, Hershey never doubted the wisdom of his Jeffersonian approach to the draft.[36]

Hershey had no illusions about the infallibility of his own work. For years after the war he was bitter at how he had allowed the army, his own branch, to waste manpower. The armed forces inducted men and then immediately sent them to civilian duty as members of the enlisted reserve. The army also rejected too many men. Hershey predicted that in any future war the military leaders would not be permitted to be so choosy. As for the specialist training programs of the army and navy, Hershey felt they were both a mistake.[37]

The civilian economy also failed to properly utilize manpower. Hershey had regrets over the excessive concern for dependency deferments, which had caused many problems in meeting quotas. He also found fault with the job deferment system—too many industries used their power to hoard labor. He recalled taking a tour of one shipyard by riding in an aerial bucket. He had noticed only three men moving in the entire workforce of 600 men. Farm deferments had been used in a disgraceful manner to protect young healthy boys. All of these problems convinced Hershey that in the future there would have to be a central procurement agency for military and civilian manpower.[38] He had resented the notion during World War II, but only because McNutt had been in charge.

Perhaps the most profound lesson Hershey drew from his experience was that the United States was a sick society. During World War II over 5 million citizens were rejected for service because of physical or mental problems. Some of this problem was due to unrealistic standards, but by 1943 Hershey realized that something more fundamental was being revealed. The entire experience convinced him that "no American child should come to adult life with physical or mental defects or conditions which can be prevented or corrected at an early age." The nation had "to provide a system that will bring to the youth of America the opportunity to guard their health, to develop their bodies so that they will be prepared to accept all of the responsibilities of citizenship," he informed the American Association for Health, Physical Education and Recreation.[39]

Yet when the war ended and Congress began hearings on several proposals to improve the nation's health, Hershey began to trim his sails. When called before the House Committee on Agriculture to testify for a bill setting up a school lunch program, Hershey sounded like a Jeffersonian: he was torn between his awareness of a national problem and his fear of a national solution. He could simultaneously support something as regimented and as centralized as a universal military training program while being suspicious of something as innocuous as a federal school lunch plan. While he agreed that the federal government had some responsibility, "I probably don't go as far as many people do in the execution. I believe in the establishment of a policy nationally, supervision in the States and execution in the community."[40] In other words, he believed the Selective Service model was appropriate for all situations.

Hershey hoped his ideas would serve as guides for the nation's future, even as his own future became more problematic. An increasing number of congressmen were calling for the dismantling of the Selective Service, causing Hershey some concern. His military career had skyrocketed during the war. From 1940, when he had given serious consideration to retirement as a major, he had become a national figure, promoted to brigadier general on 25 October 1940 and major general on 16 April 1942. Now, with the war over, Hershey had to fight for his own survival in the army, as well as for the survival of his agency.

Regardless of his civilian clothes and detached duty, Hershey was on assignment as a military officer during the war. Although he reported to the president, the War Department made out his efficiency reports. The army felt that Hershey was doing a good job in a unique position for an officer.[41] In May 1945 General Thomas T. Handy wrote of Hershey's work: "From the record and by general reputation, Hershey is an exceptionally intelligent and talented officer; shrewd, cool and resourceful." Handy admitted that no intelligent military comparison could be made to Hershey's work—a fact that created problems for Hershey when the army began demobilizing its officers. The regular army had fewer and fewer slots for general officers, especially those with unique talents.[42]

Hershey suspected that the army had no use for him in 1946. Major General W. S. Paul of G-1 wrote in April, explaining the problems. The army had to cut back on general officers, and all commanders had submitted merit lists for retention. Based on Hershey's ranking on the lists, Paul predicted a bleak future. Hershey had had feelers from civilian businesses seeking his services, but he had never seriously considered voluntary retirement. Anyway, the question might become moot if he failed his physical exam. The strain of war duty had taken its toll on his already damaged eye; by 1944 he began experiencing pain, probably brought about by stress and overwork. The cellular structure of the eye began to change, and infection (acute iridocyclitis) developed. Although advised to have the eye removed before the infection spread, Hershey put off the operation.[43]

In September 1946 the army instructed Hershey to report before a disposition board to be considered for retirement. In hopes of retrieving his health, he submitted to additional treatment by ophthalmologists at Walter Reed Hospital. His right eye had now developed chronic uveitis (infection of iris), and physicians feared sympathetic ophthalmia (infection) in his left eye. In early October the diseased eye was removed and Hershey was fitted with a prosthesis. He was only fifty-three years old. His permanent rank in the regular army was lieutenant colonel. When the retirement board convened on 20 November 1946, Hershey sat uncomfortably, still adjusting to the artificial right eye, which had the disconcerting habit of slipping out.[44]

Hershey realized that he had to make a strong case for retention. He insisted that he had no desire for retirement and that he was perfectly capable of carrying on his duties. Indeed, in the conduct of his office he spent from eight to fifteen hours each day reading reports. What surprised Hershey was that he should have been certified as fit for general duty in annual physicals from 1927 through 1945, whereas now, without warning, he was being labled unfit. Despite his recent eye problem, he was convinced that he still had a great capacity for work. "That a man with half his eyes can't get along just as well as some men with about half their head—inside—I don't agree," he told the board.[45]

Despite Hershey's vigorous defense, the board recommended that he be retired, considering him physically unfit for even limited service. Hershey, with no intention of allowing the verdict to stand, immediately began to pull strings in the War Department and at the White House. On 27 November the adjutant general of the army requested that the surgeon general reconsider the board's verdict, explaining that the president and the secretary of war both desired Hershey to remain in his position as director of Selective Service. The surgeon general was happy to amend the retirement board's finding to read "Major General Hershey is considered physically qualified for limited service following retirement." On 19 December the War Department issued orders announcing Hershey's retirement effective 31 December 1946. The same day the army issued orders recalling him to active duty effective 1 January 1947, to serve in his current position by direction of the president.[46]

Hershey was secure only as long as his agency survived. Congress did provide temporary extensions during 1945, but with the Japanese surrender in September an increasing number of people wanted to end Hershey's job. During 1945 Congress cut his budget. At hearings before the House Committee on Appropriations in September, Congressmen Clarence A. Cannon and Louis L. Ludlow argued that future military needs would be handled by volunteers. Hershey took strong exception, arguing that the country would need at least 2 million men in the army to cover occupation responsibilities and home defense. Cannon called such figures an "imperialistic prospect"; Hershey's budget was cut further.[47]

When state directors gathered in Washington for a conference during November 1945, Hershey tried to be optimistic, but the budget cuts required personnel reductions. The War Department was threatening to reduce its authorization of military personnel. Finally, and perhaps most important, President Truman had recommended to Congress a universal military training program. Hershey interpreted Truman's message as meaning that an agency would be needed to provide for registration, classification, and selection. What better agency to perform this duty than Selective Service? Hershey knew that his future depended largely upon the wishes of the new commander-in-chief.[48]

The two were cut from the same mold. Harry S Truman, thirty-third president of the United States, former senator from Missouri, had much in common with Lewis Hershey. Besides sharing a rural upbringing in the Midwest, both men had served in the National Guard during World War I and even had the same artillery background. Their personalities were very similar in that both detested sham and pretentiousness. They also understood and enjoyed political life. Finally, both had similar views of America's role in the world of 1945. As a great power, the United States could not pull back from commitments made during the war. The nation had to remain militarily strong and keep a wary eye on the ambitions of the Soviet Union.

President Roosevelt had been a distant aristocrat with little trust in military men and little time for Lewis Hershey. Things began to change when Truman unexpectedly assumed office. Hershey had the utmost confidence in President Truman's ability to fill the job thrust upon him.[49] Hershey also had close relations with Louis H. Renfrow and Harry Vaughan, two old political cronies of Truman's. Renfrow had started working for Selective Service as a political liaison man in 1944 and had a deep admiration for both Hershey and Truman. Similarly, General Vaughan, a military aide in the White House, had worked closely with Hershey on deferment questions when Truman was in the Senate.[50]

On 21 January 1946 Hershey brought to the White House fifty-four unpaid officials of the system. The president pinned them with Selective Service medals for jobs well done. In a surprise move, Truman also awarded Hershey the Army Distinguished Service Medal. In his remarks Truman praised the men for doing an outstanding job in an essential but unhappy task. He also promised that, after the induction job was over, "you will have, in all probability, a chance to help implement a military training program which has been recommended to the Congress." This was music to Hershey's ears, and the entire affair was a mutual admiration meeting. Hershey insisted upon pinning a medal on General Vaughan because of his great support for the system.[51]

The immediate problems facing Hershey involved continuing the draft to furnish replacements and developing a long-range program of universal military training. As the original draft law was scheduled to expire on 15 May 1945, Truman moved quickly for an extension. On 9 May he signed a bill extending the act to 15 May 1946. In August he ended all inductions for registrants twenty-six and over; in the same month the War Department reduced its calls to 50,000 a month. In October 1945 Truman began promoting a one-year military training requirement (UMT) for all young men. During this period of transition Hershey had to continue to fill calls for the armed forces, but he also hoped to find a role for his organization in the new defense system being constructed by the president. To survive, Hershey had to gain support from the War Department. Yet the army seemed more interested in returning to a volunteer system than in preserving Selective Service.[52]

On 7 September 1945 Truman had authorized recruitment of men from ages eighteen to thirty-seven. Once again the services dusted off their glamorous posters, revised their radio spots, and went forth seeking men in an indiscriminate manner. Hershey was furious at this move. He wrote Truman that Selective Service was continuing to draft men, but the bulk of draftees would have to come from the same pool as the volunteers.[53]

Hershey wanted a permanent extension of the draft during peacetime. The administration disagreed. Political opposition and public suspicion made peacetime conscription very unlikely. Furthermore, both Truman and the War Department preferred to adopt a system of universal military training, rather than the draft. This system would tap only the youngest men for one-year training. The army and navy refused to abandon their beloved recruiting. Throughout 1946 and part of 1947, Hershey's fight for an extension of the draft had to overcome congressional and public opposition and only lukewarm support from the administration.

Another major problem for Hershey, ironically, was the proposal for universal military training. Truman had strange reasons for calling for UMT. To Harold Smith, the director of the budget, Truman confessed that he was really opposed to military training. He would endorse UMT because he felt such a training program would do much to correct the glaring educational and physical defects revealed during the wartime draft. The army would be put in charge of the training because it was the only institution capable of handling the task. In Truman's mind, the task resembled more the work of a Civilian Conservation Corps than a program to militarize the nation.[54]

The president's approach appealed to Hershey. It might mean a continuation of his agency and an attack upon a glaring social problem which had disturbed him. The defects which had appeared so frequently during the wartime draft could be avoided in the future, he wrote, if a physical fitness program in early youth were supplemented with a program requiring every male youth to devote a minimum of one year to training for national preservation. Hershey felt that UMT run by the army would also be a training ground in democracy. In this belief he was at one with Truman, who had confided to Harold Smith that he planned to democratize the military by breaking up the cabals run by West Pointers and Annapolis men.[55]

For the next several months Hershey carried water on both shoulders. He continued to argue for a continuation of the draft, but he also endorsed the president's January 1946 call for UMT. Privately he had certain reservations about the UMT bill (S 1473). He disliked the decision to place the burden on men twenty-one or twenty-two years old, as they would already have begun their vocational and educational development. He preferred to take them at age eighteen.[56] But publicly he pulled no punches and endorsed UMT. In September 1946, at the annual conference of the National Guard Association, he warned that without UMT it would be impossible to expand the guard. To throw away our armed forces would only confuse and disillusion our friends. The "flight toward military impotence" in which the country was engaging had to end.[57]

In the next several months universal military training came in for considerable public scrutiny. Organized labor and other civilian groups opposed it; in addition, the plan suffered from the divided opinion among its friends. The War Department disliked the idea of training men for only six months and not taking them into active duty. The National Guard and the reserves wanted the UMT to serve as feeder to staff their units. Truman finally established a special advisory commission on universal training to cope with the many objections and plans. Hershey explained to Dr. Karl P. Compton, chairman of the advisory committee, that Selective Service was the perfect organization to handle procurement, training, and administration of UMT. The new plan required a decentralized civilian state-federal organization. Selective Service was just such an agency.[58]

Even as UMT was debated, Hershey also fought vigorously to insure the perpetuation of the military draft. In few battles was his political acumen so severely tested. In this campaign he found himself fighting against Congress, the president, and the armed forces—all of whom, for different reasons, were reluctant to perpetuate a system of peacetime conscription. The original law provided that the draft would become "inoperative and cease to apply after 15 May 1945." Yet with the war continuing in the Pacific there had been little debate over Public Law 54, which extended the draft to 15 May 1946. With the collapse of Japan in early August, however, Congress began calling for an immediate end of the draft.[59]

As draft opposition rose in Congress, Truman faced a quandary. To have the draft end immediately would create several problems. The reemployment rights of veterans would cease. More important, the armed forces would be unable to find adequate replacements to fulfill their occupation responsibilities. By July 1946 the armed forces would have 6 million men due for release, each with almost four years of service. Finding replacements would be impossible without the draft. As for future security, Truman felt the nation "dare not rely exclusively on volunteers." He admitted to Congressman Andrew J. May in August 1945 that continuing the draft was a headache. "I wish," he wrote, "it were possible for me to recommend that the drafting of men be stopped altogether and at once." Yet he concluded that a continuation of draft inductions was the only "safe and acceptable solution."[60]

Hershey played a major role in convincing Truman to continue the draft. Hershey explained to John W. Snyder, the new director of war mobilization and reconversion, that calls were running at 100,000 a month, but that the major source of men aged eighteen to twenty-nine would be gone by the end of the year. If calls were suspended entirely after VJ Day, it would be very difficult to restart the draft machinery. Yet men had to be found for replacements while universal military training was being debated. On 6 September 1945 the president decided to continue the draft until May 1946. Snyder informed Hershey that "your major recommendations are being carried out."[61]

In his state of the union address in January 1946, however, President Truman merely urged Congress to pass a universal military training program. After UMT passed, he would take up the draft issue. For the next several months Congress debated and refused to separate UMT from the problem of ending the draft. When the House Military Affairs Committee began considering a joint resolution to suspend all further draft inductions, Hershey was dismayed. He recommended that the president support an immediate extension of the draft for eighteen months, insisting that the president's hopes for UMT were tied to the survival of Selective Service, which provided the only feasible framework upon which to erect such a training program.[62]

Rather than meekly await his fate, Hershey launched a campaign for an indefinite extension of the draft, for eighteen months of service, for lower induction standards in the army and navy, and for the reinduction of veterans with less than eighteen months of service. Several members of the Senate subcommittee on demobilization were startled at Hershey's presumptuousness. The public blamed Congress because the troops were not coming home fast enough, and now Hershey wanted to draft more men. Senator Edwin C. Johnson gave Hershey notice that 15 May 1946 would bring the end of the draft.[63] The need for combat men was now over.

The attitude of the senators convinced Hershey that the system could survive only with support from the armed forces and the White House. The War Department still believed in voluntary recruitment and in universal military training as long-term solutions to their manpower problem, but in the short run they could not do without Hershey's draft. General Eisenhower, the newly appointed chief of staff, assured Hershey that the War Department believed Selective Service "must be continued." The army could not reduce the size of its calls. The recruitment program had proved inadequate, even with the negative incentive of the draft. If the threat of the draft was removed, volunteers would become very scarce.[64] Ike also promised to support a role for Selective Service in any registration, classification, and selection responsibility under UMT.[65]

Robert Patterson, the new secretary of war, wanted to sever all ties between the War Department and Selective Service.[66] Hershey and Patterson had different ideas of the ideal relationship between the two agencies. Hershey had long sought to have the best of both worlds: he wanted to seem like the civilian leader of a civilian agency when appearing before Congress and when criticizing the War Department; yet he sought the public relations bonus accruing to uniformed personnel. But, with the war now over, Patterson had a keener insight into the need for a new approach. As he explained to Hershey, the War Department believed that the "presence of commissioned military personnel within Selective Service impresses on the mind of the public the belief that the army is conducting the draft." Patterson felt it essential "to insure Selective Service be identified as an independent executive agency." Hershey disagreed. He felt the War Department was deserting Selective Service because the generals preferred volunteers.[67]

In early March the Senate Military Affairs Committee began hearings on a bill which anticipated the end of the draft by transferring the veterans' employment responsibility to the USES. According to Hershey, the pending bill would literally destroy the national defense. It would jeopardize the United Nations and signal to the entire world that the United States would depend upon mercenaries in the future. Without the draft, he continued, the United States would no longer wield worldwide influence, and the army would never reach its projected strength of 1.5 million by July. The blame for the erosion of American defense and for inviting a future war would rest with Congress if it passed such legislation.[68]

Senator Lyndon B. Johnson, the committee chairman, tried to interrupt Hershey. In his mind and in the minds of other senators, the issue of draft extension had been settled. The draft was to end on 15 May 1946. Now here was Hershey, raising a seemingly tangential issue. Hershey, refusing to limit his remarks, insisted that extension was the real question. Johnson finally asked Hershey whether he considered Selective Service to be a permanent government agency. Hershey replied "not necessarily," but the rest of his comments made clear that he did want a permanent extension.[69] Public opinion seemed to support him. A Gallup poll in March 1946 found 65 percent agreeing that Congress should continue the draft for another year; only 27 percent opposed the idea.[70]

Beginning on 20 March 1946 both the House and the Senate began hearings on draft extension. The administration, reluctantly conceding the failure of recruitment and UMT, now fell in behind Hershey. Patterson, Eisenhower, and General Carl Spaatz appeared before closed sessions of Congress to request an extension. Hershey's rhetoric was echoed by Ike, who now insisted that extension of the draft was needed to finish the task of the war and to live up to our commitments under the United Nations. He also recommended that the draft be extended indefinitely but admitted that he could live with less. With a requirement for 50,000 men per month, the army could anticipate only 10,000 volunteer enlistments per month without the draft.[71] Hershey still recommended an indefinite extension but he, too, was now willing to accept only twelve months.[72] Chairman Thomas and Senator Edwin C. Johnson refused to accept these arguments, accusing Hershey of favoring an impressed army and of using the draft as a hammer. Hershey resented "to the very bottom of my soul" any regimentation, but he also resented having "the poor and the willing" shoulder what should be a universal responsibility.[73]

Hershey argued that the draft was the only fair way of sharing the burden of citizenship equally. The United States was the richest nation in the world; as such, she was the envy of others and a likely prey for attack. All of these arguments, and more, made little impression on congressmen faced with reelection by the mothers and fathers of draft-age sons. When May arrived, the extension bill remained stuck in Congress. In fifteen days Hershey had to close shop.[74]

Only a few months earlier Winston Churchill had warned of an Iron Curtain descending over Europe and had called for a union of English-speaking people against the Soviet threat. Political instability continued in Europe, as Charles de Gaulle resigned as head of the French government and King Victor Emmanuel abdicated in Italy. With such international uncertainty Hershey found it hard to believe that his agency had only a week to live, and he did not intend to retire gracefully. "If we don't get an extension of the Act," he informed the cheering state directors, "section 8(g) [aid to veterans] is still there and unless somebody stops me, I intend to use that to the maximum, so let's be pretty clear that we are only talking about successive positions and not about the fact that this agency will quit business."[75]

Reacting to the international climate and the lobbying of Selective Service, the White House, and the War Department, Congress passed on 14 May a joint resolution which extended the draft for a mere forty-five days. To make matters worse, the bill (PL 159) prohibited the induction of fathers and changed the age liability to twenty to twenty-nine. Hershey immediately protested to Truman that these provisions would not do. First, removing the eighteen and nineteen-year-olds from the pool reduced it from 35,000 to 5,000 each month. Second, drafting men over twenty-six would be difficult and time consuming, resulting in many rejections for physical reasons. Truman agreed that the extension act was "bad legislation" and admitted signing it reluctantly because there was no alternative, but he hoped Congress would extend the draft system for a full year in its old form. "We must save what we can," Truman told the press, "from the near-wreckage of the Selective Service System." He warned that Hershey might have to redraft veterans to fill calls.[76]

Congress finally decided to bow to the wishes of the administration. As approved by Truman on 29 June Public Law 473 provided for an extension of the draft to 31 March 1947, or for nine more months. This new bill also returned liability to ages nineteen to forty-four, but it limited service to eighteen months. Veterans could be drafted only if they had not served overseas or had served less than six months. The bill also stripped Hershey of responsibility for veterans' reemployment.[77]

The administration, under the influence of the War Department, wanted no permanent draft system. President Truman still longed for UMT; the War Department, for its part, still hoped for an all-volunteer force. Congress still wanted an end to the politically embarrassing draft and to save all teenagers from the armed forces. Since no one wished to induct forty-four-year-old draftees, Truman informed Hershey that he should limit his calls to men nineteen through thirty-five.[78] Although General Eisenhower felt that "without Selective Service we could not have won World War II," in his heart he preferred volunteers. Major General W. S. Paul of G-1 in the War Department admitted that there had been an abrupt and continuing reduction in voluntary enlistments since early October 1946, but he was still confident that the army would reach its authorized strength by January. He told Hershey in early December that the War Department, "after careful consideration," expected to make no draft calls for January 1947.[79]

With ample evidence of myopia in the War Department, Hershey's only remaining hope for survival was the president. Hershey admitted that the extension of Selective Service "is a matter of policy to be determined by the President and the Congress," but he warned John Steelman, the new director of war mobilization and reconversion, that if UMT were not passed and if the draft could not be extended, he would recommend a law to provide for maintaining a skeleton system to care for the voluminous draft records. Even if UMT passed, the Selective Service could still serve to procure trainees.[80]

On 6 January 1947 President Truman dealt with the draft in his state of the union address. He called for passage of UMT and for a bill unifying the various components of the armed forces under a new cabinet-level Department of Defense. Hedging his bets against the failure of UMT, the president also recommended that the Selective Service be continued if the War Department requested such a continuation. American allies throughout the world watched carefully for signs that the nation was serious about assuming its new role of international policeman. In the eastern Mediterranean the Soviet Union applied pressure on Turkey; in Greece the British began withdrawing from a messy civil war. Hershey could not understand the willingness to scrap Selective Service under such conditions.

VII. Rearming and Korea

President Truman had many problems facing him in late January and February 1947. The extension of Selective Service had to compete with domestic inflation, with the international implications of British withdrawal from Greece, and with efforts to pass the bill creating the national military establishment. For guidance on Selective Service, Truman depended upon Secretary Robert Patterson and on James Forrestal, the secretary of the navy. He expected the secretaries to insist upon a draft extension if one was really needed. Patterson wrote on 31 January that, after much soul searching, he had concluded the president should not seek an extension. The army desired to rely on a volunteer system as soon as possible. Patterson admitted that this was a risky step, but he presented statistics which showed that, through enlistments and reenlistments, the army could obtain 20,000 men a month. Seeking to cover a retreat, he reserved the right to request renewal of the draft if voluntary enlistments failed.[1]

To insure the volunteer program's success, Patterson wanted $100 million to relieve a housing shortage for enlisted personnel, another $5 million for recruiting, and $45 million for pay raises. His recommendation was endorsed by Secretary Forrestal and by General Eisenhower. Both Patterson and Forrestal did endorse Hershey's request to continue a skeleton Selective Service organization even after inductions ended.[2]

Soon another voice entered the debate. General George C. Marshall had resigned as chief of staff in November 1945, to take on a special presidential mission to China. Truman had enormous respect for Marshall and had appointed him secretary of state in January 1947. When the president sought his views on draft extension, Marshall disagreed with Patterson's recommendations. "If there is the barest possibility that Selective Service must be resorted to in the future," he wrote, "then I believe it would be an error to allow the Act to expire in the hope that it might be subsequently reenacted when the need arises." He urged Truman to press for continuation of the act, even if no draft calls were made. As secretary of state, Marshall insisted that the extension "would have a highly salutary effect upon our relations with other nations during this period of negotiations over disarmament measures."[3]

There were so many arguments for and against Selective Service by now that Truman requested a summary from James E. Webb, the director of the budget. After pointing out that both the army and the navy had admitted the need for the draft from a purely numerical point of view, and that Marshall has stressed the international implications of nonextension, Webb concluded that the main motives for ending the draft rested upon considerations of public opinion and a desire to insure passage of UMT. But if the draft were not needed for national security, did this not weaken the argument for UMT? Also, would not some form of Selective Service be needed to operate UMT? Selective Service cost only a little over $2 million per month to run, whereas Patterson's replacement system would cost $550 million annually. Given these considerations, Webb recommended that the president request an extension of Selective Service until 30 June 1948, or until UMT was enacted.[4]

A strong case had been made for an extension of the draft, yet Truman decided to go along with Patterson. The president thought it best to concentrate on pushing UMT through Congress without the distraction provided by an unpopular draft. On 3 March he sent Congress a message justifying the end of the draft by pointing to the current military manpower scene. Both army and navy were still reducing force levels, so the only justification for renewal of the draft would be possible future shortages. But military officials were optimistic about voluntary recruitment. "Therefore," wrote Truman, "I recommend that no extension of Selective Service at this time be made." Throwing a bone to Hershey and other skeptics, Truman did recommend the creation of a new Office of Selective Service Records (OSSR) to preserve papers and conduct studies for future emergencies.[5]

James E. Webb asked Hershey for contingency plans if the draft died on 31 March. Hershey offered one plan for a standby organization to train state officials and prepare summary cards for remobilization; another plan called for a small group of specialists to work out of the executive office, closing boards and monitoring record storage. Complete termination would take nine months and cost $11 million. Yet Hershey could not refrain from insisting that "the cost of maintaining the Selective Service in some form is a very small premium for insuring national security." He recommended his first option to the president.[6]

At Truman's request, the Senate Armed Services Committee began debating a bill creating the Office of Selective Service Records to replace the draft. Several senators prodded Hershey to evaluate the presidential decision to end the draft during a tense time in international affairs. Hershey admitted preferring an extension of the draft to the OSSR bill, for he was concerned about being unable to resurrect his system if he lost all local board members. Even General Paul of the War Department testified that "it would be far simpler to have retained the skeleton organization, but the Commander-in-Chief did not see fit to do that, so I am in no position to say otherwise." This testimony irritated Truman, who fired off an inquiry to Patterson demanding to know what was going on. Had the War Department changed its mind? Patterson lamely replied that Paul had confused the issue of OSSR with the extension of the draft. There had been no change of mind; the draft was dead.[7]

A doleful group of state directors met with Hershey in Washington on 20 March 1947. In a moment of great emotion Hershey reiterated his deep feeling for the agency. Unlike other bureaucracies, the agency "did feel in unison and we were able to vibrate on a level even below our intellects." In a word, he admitted: "I think we have a soul." The Selective Service had demonstrated that the strength of democracy lay in its ability to delegate authority down to the community level, to make everyone a part of government.[8]

On 31 March 1947, as the Selective Service Act expired, Hershey visited the White House to watch President Truman sign a bill creating the Office of Selective Service Records. Hershey called upon all local boards to help headquarters draft a history of the successes and failures of the system to serve as a guide to future generations. He also badgered Congress for money to cover the liquidation of the system and the care of the records, which would be stored in fifty-four depots. Most important, he needed money to plan for future contingencies and to train a cadre which would stand ready to run another draft. Hershey had confidence that, like the phoenix, the system would soon rise from the ashes.[9]

The state of world affairs in 1947 made Hershey confident that he would continue to play an active role on the national scene. Hardly a week after informing Congress of his intention to end the draft, President Truman sent a message requesting military aid for Greece and Turkey, both allegedly threatened by communists. "I believe," Truman informed Congress, "that it must be the policy of the United States to support free peoples who are resisting attempted subjugation by armed minorities or by outside pressures." He pointed specifically at Soviet actions in Poland, Rumania, and Bulgaria, besides the threat to Greece and Turkey. The Cold War was now officially launched. Within weeks Secretary of State George Marshall was offering a massive program of economic aid to Western Europe, indirectly aimed at helping Italy, France, and Great Britain to resist Communist pressure.[10]

Truman had stressed the preservation of records as the primary justification for creating the Office of Selective Service Records. Hershey made the same pitch when appearing before the Senate Armed Services Committee, but he also suggested that there was "an outside possibility" that the draft might be needed again within the fiscal year. Several senators, including Millard Tydings, wondered whether the records were really needed. Hershey insisted that "the only way you can judge the future is to intelligently use your past." He made it clear, however, that the principal reasons for passing the bill were to provide some skeleton in case UMT passed, to plan and train for over-all mobilization of manpower, and to preserve records.[11]

In fact, the president and Hershey had totally different ideas about the role of the new office. Hershey spoke of the importance of his records, but it was a cover for other purposes. Indeed, on 6 May 1946 he had told his state directors, "I can't think of anything I have less of an opinion about than what ought to be done with the records." Keeping records was just an excuse to create an office which could maintain a training program for Selective Service cadre. As Hershey read the bill creating OSSR, the key charge was "to perform such other duties relating to preservation of records, knowledge and methods of Selective Service, not inconsistent with law." This section provided a loophole through which Hershey proceeded to march.[12]

Hershey wanted to maintain his state connections, especially his relations with the governors. He also wanted to assume responsibility for manpower planning. Although this job had been given to other offices by President Truman, Hershey was not satisfied with what had been done. The National Security Resources Board was a fine idea but had not really started work. Given the current state of uncertainty and the president's remarks on Greece and Turkey, Hershey felt it essential to keep alive the organization which could handle mobilization. Although local boards were killed by the new bill, Hershey was better equipped for planning and training a cadre than he had been in the 1930's. He began reverting to the old system of having earmarked officers in each state attend two-week conferences held across the country. Old state directors of Selective Service now became state directors of the OSSR. Hershey traveled to these training conferences, and extension courses were again drawn up by national headquarters.[13]

These ambitious plans did not fit in with Truman's program. The president, counting on passage of the UMT program, had given manpower planning responsibility to the National Security Resources Board. On 1 June 1947 the special Compton advisory committee on UMT issued its favorable report. A bill was sent to Congress. Already the voluntary recruitment program was proving inadequate, except for the air force. The UMT bill did provide for a selective training system to handle procurement of men. Local boards would be created and would function much like the old draft boards. Yet, as Hershey wrote the president on 30 July, while UMT was a definite advance, "the manpower lesson of World War II is a simple one, namely, that nothing less than universal mobilization will save the Nation in the event of a third world war." Compulsory service, rather than mere training, would have to be adopted.[14]

Truman nevertheless expected Hershey to fight for passage of UMT. Hershey fell into line with enthusiasm, even as he continued to train his cadre for a renewal of the draft. On 17 June he appeared on the "American Forum of the Air" broadcast to debate the question "Do we need UMT?" Other members of the panel included Congressman F. Edward Hebert of Louisiana, Dr. Ralph McDonald of the National Education Association, and Congressman Dewey Short of Missouri. To Short's contention that the plan was un-American and that volunteers would suffice, Hershey argued, "I don't know what in a democracy you can do if you do not require each citizen to take all of his responsibility." McDonald pointed out that for $2 billion the nation "could put every one of the boys you want to put in camps through Harvard or Yale." Hershey charged McDonald with wanting to use the poor and ignorant to "save the country so a few can become Ph.D.'s." "I have seen," Hershey insisted, "a great deal of instruction in colleges that didn't add up to very much." Educators such as McDonald wanted a few rich kids to go to school and avoid responsibility while we "let the poor go out and die."[15]

Despite this fiery rhetoric, the Towe bill (UMT) remained stuck in Congress, opposed by labor unions, pacifist organizations, and others. The army lagged further and further behind in its recruitment schedule; by October it was more than 100,000 men short of its authorized strength. Hershey continued his campaign with a growing sense of fatalism. He informed the Union League Club of New York that UMT was needed because "for the last two years we've been at war without any fighting." On the "American Forum of the Air" in November he insisted that UMT must be passed to fulfill "our moral responsibilities, among and for, the freedom-aspiring peoples of the earth." UMT was an inescapable "extension of the accepted civil principle of compulsory education." It provided for democracy of service.[16]

As 1947 drew to a close, Truman had succeeded in unifying the armed forces but had not found a satisfactory replacement for the draft. UMT remained stalled. To make matters worse, in January 1948 a special presidential commission appointed to study the problem of air power in the atomic age issued a report which called into question the need for UMT, let alone for the draft.[17] The White House asked Hershey for recommendations. If UMT failed, Hershey suggested that the president reestablish Selective Service and proceed with the registration of all citizens between the ages eighteen and forty-five. He assured Truman that OSSR already had several bills drafted and was busy training a draft cadre.[18]

Congress, however, had different ideas. To the amazement of several congressmen, Hershey requested $3,195,000 for fiscal year 1948–49 from the House Committee on Appropriations. When Hershey sensed that his recordkeeping function did not impress the committee, he turned to what he felt was his primary mission—training and planning. "I would guarantee," he argued, "if we ever have to mobilize, that it (OSSR) will save anywhere from 30 to 90 days." The House committee, however, was shocked rather than gratified to learn of the extensive training program that Hershey was operating under the guise of record management. Congressman Albert Thomas insisted that the law did not mention this training mission and that Hershey was stretching his mandate. Hershey replied "that in the training and planning the contribution that I can make to the survival of the United States is more clearly set out than anything else I do." He began to portray himself as the only man in Washington concerned with planning manpower mobilization for war, despite the work of the Department of Defense and the National Security Resources Board. The House Committee on Appropriations refused to accept this self-image and cut the funds for training.[19]

The Senate Committee on Appropriations was equally hostile. The House had cut Hershey's budget by $718,000, of which he asked the Senate to restore $500,000. Without these funds he could not continue to plan as Congress wanted. Senator Leverett Saltonstall immediately insisted that Hershey was mistaken about his mission. OSSR was for liquidating records, not for training. Hershey replied that the law also provided that OSSR preserve the knowledge and methods of the system, and he kept insisting that "preserving methods" implied training. Nevertheless, the committee insisted that he needed additional legislation if he wanted to train. Hershey seemed on the verge of losing his one remaining tie to national defense policy. Once again, however, international events came to his rescue.[20]

American defense policy in 1947 reflected a Janus-like perspective. One face, looking outward at the world, spoke of the Truman Doctrine, the Marshall Plan, and obligations under the United Nations. The other face, peering inward toward the domestic scene, spoke more realistically of balanced budgets and reductions of force levels. The United States had a monopoly on the atomic bomb, and the Finletter report promised world power through air power, but the armed forces were merely an empty shell. On 18 February 1948 Major General Alfred M. Gruenther told a White House audience that the ground force alone was some 100,000 men under authorization. The voluntary recruitment plan, together with reenlistments, had been contributing an average of 14,000 men each month, but gross monthly losses totaled 29,000. Gruenther warned that he had only two and a half divisions to spare for any emergency conflict. His assessment raised the serious prospect that the United States might have to use atomic bombs as a first option in any crisis.[21]

Earlier, at a meeting of the National Security Council, Secretary of Defense James Forrestal had raised the idea of reestablishing the Selective Service System. He felt that the draft might be needed if the United States was called upon to act under the United Nations' mandate in Palestine, where Jews and Arabs were fighting. Secretary of State George Marshall was sympathetic; he was tired of talking tough while having little military power to defend such postures.[22]

Dramatizing the danger of ignoring military manpower needs during the Cold War, the Communist party of Czechoslovakia launched a successful coup on 24 February 1948. Sending planes to drop atomic bombs on Prague seemed rather an inappropriate response. But was this the first step in a more grandiose Soviet move in Western Europe? General Lucius Clay, the American commander in Berlin, telegrammed on 5 March that he "felt subtle change in Soviet attitude which . . . now give me feeling that it [war] may come with drastic suddenness." On 8 March the American embassy in Nationalist China reported that Chiang Kai-shek was about to lose his civil war with Mao Tse-tung. As for UMT, it remained stalled in Congress.[23]

President Truman reluctantly concluded that a renewal of the draft was needed. He still hoped for the passage of UMT and the success of voluntary recruitment, but he knew the country could not rely upon such vague hopes in the face of ominous Soviet moves. On 17 March 1948 he went to Congress and named the Soviet Union as the chief threat to world peace, accused her of planning the subjugation of Europe and of masterminding a worldwide Communist plot. To make clear America's firmness in resisting this threat, he called for "temporary" reenactment of Selective Service. Out in Salem, Oregon, Lewis Hershey heard the call and announced that the draft could begin taking men within forty-five days after passage of a new law. A Gallup poll on 24 March reported 63 percent favorable to a new draft law, with only 23 percent opposed.[24]

When hearings on the draft bill began in April 1948, Hershey had several goals. He hoped, first of all, to separate the Selective Service from the politically unpopular UMT. He also argued for a permanent restoration of the draft, rather than the temporary return that Truman desired. At the very least, he hoped to convince Congress to permit the OSSR to continue in existence even while the draft was being conducted. During the subsequent debate Hershey won a few points and lost a few. The UMT idea was removed from the bill and replaced with vague encouragement for recruitment. Hershey had to be satisfied with a two-year time limit for the draft. The OSSR was killed.[25]

On 24 June 1948 Truman signed a law that largely re-created the system Hershey had watched die only a year earlier. Congress did insist upon shortening the draftee's term to twenty-one months and placing a two year limit on the life of the draft. No provisions for alternate service were included, but the status of conscientious objectors was recognized. The law did extend a reserve obligation of up to five years for anyone drafted or enlisted under it. All males eighteen to twenty-six were required to register, but induction liability was limited to those between nineteen and twenty-six. Deferment provisions remained similar to those in the earlier draft.[26]

As the bill moved through Congress, several threats to the independence of Hershey's agency appeared. The National Security Resources Board sought policy control over Selective Service. The departments of labor and commerce, the Federal Security Agency, and others criticized the bill for giving Hershey too much power. Hershey stood firm against these raids, having planned carefully for his return. Weeks before the bill passed Congress his planning group had arranged area conferences to study operation under a new law. Furthermore, Hershey had some 60 percent of his old local board personnel ready to serve again.[27] Eventually President Truman made it clear that Hershey would report directly to him, rather than through the National Security Resources Board.[28]

Hershey approached his new task with most of his old concepts intact. On 21 April 1948 he recommended to the secretary of defense that the same physical and mental standards for induction be adopted by all services. More important, he urged that all draft calls be consolidated by the secretary of defense before being sent to Selective Service. Decentralization was again emphasized. Local boards should make their own mistakes because, he insisted, "I have infinite faith in the ordinary

American." He informed state directors, "When you are stopped from doing what you think you ought to do because you do not have authority—write in, and I promise to grant that authority."[29] As expected, President Truman appointed Hershey to head the new Selective Service System. Congresswoman Clare Boothe Luce wrote to wish Hershey well in his "new old assignment." "I know you will do the same great job you did before," she added.[30]

The draft began in June 1948 as a temporary solution to manpower shortages, yet within weeks Soviet actions convinced many Americans of the wisdom of renewing conscription. On 24 July Soviet forces in East Germany stopped all rail and road traffic into Berlin. Although the USSR had begun interfering with the traffic as early as 1 April, suddenly American, British, and French garrisons were isolated in the former German capital. The United States stood on the brink of war. President Truman decided to use air power to resupply the garrison. American public opinion endorsed his actions and became more sympathetic to the draft.[31]

Public support, however, could not solve all of Hershey's operational problems. One issue, as old as the nation and as controversial as any, involved the rights of black Americans. The new law again prohibited racial discrimination in the draft. President Truman was on record as opposing segregation in the nation, and both the advisory committee on civil rights and the committee on UMT had recommended an end to it in the armed forces. The black community had made its feeling clear during hearings on the draft bill: A. Philip Randolph, who had led the March on Washington movement for equal job opportunities during the war, testified that he would organize blacks against serving if segregation continued. Hershey had fought the notion of racial calls, not because he favored integration but because the practice created administrative headaches. He now advised the secretary of defense and the department of the army that he planned to select men without regard to race or color under the new law. President Truman made this action official on 26 July, issuing Executive Order 9981 and calling for "equality of treatment and opportunity for all persons in the armed services without regard to race, color, religion or national origin."[32]

A much more troublesome problem, one which would continue to plague Hershey for the rest of his career, involved the essentially negative purpose of the new Cold War draft. Truman and the military chiefs preferred UMT and the recruitment of volunteers. The draft had been proposed as a temporary device, aimed first at encouraging young men to enlist and only secondarily at drafting them. While Hershey never agreed with the idea, he lived with it. His new mission meant that draft calls would be consistently low and that deferments would multiply. To make matters even worse, from his perspective, the number of young men in the eligible age brackets would increase because of birth patterns, and he would be able to use only a small fraction of them. The problem became manifest almost immediately. The army needed an additional 250,000 men by 1949, but, what with recruitment and reenlistments, Hershey did not expect the draft to furnish many. No one was to be drafted until after 1 October 1948.[33]

Under Roosevelt, Hershey had been free to run Selective Service with little interference. Under Truman, things had changed. All regulations on the draft had to be scrutinized by the various branches of government, in particular by the Department of Defense. These staffings slowed the process by which Hershey could control his agency and also placed limits on his actions. Truman also insisted that Hershey and other military figures stay out of the appeal system. Through an Executive Order (9988) issued on 20 August 1948, Truman created a National Selective Service Appeal Board staffed by civilian appointees. The order specifically stated that the board would be totally independent of the director of Selective Service.[34]

Hershey disliked both of these requirements and consistently worked to regain his lost power. Nevertheless, he found himself in 1948 with less power and a limited mission. With few men to call in an ever-expanding pool of eligibles, he devoted more and more of his time to the vexing problem of deferments. He had a pool of over 5 million males between ages eighteen and twenty-six, of whom he expected to draft a modest 60,000. How was he to decide who the lucky few would be? The law once again provided deferments for men who were needed in industry and science or who were training to enter those fields. Hershey established special advisory committees in virtually every academic discipline to help him decide on student deferments. But he did not expect to draw heavily from any segment of society. He described his predicament in the following lament: the law "says you have to be fair and just, which means you have to play around, and then it says you have to share it generally, which means you have to pass it around, and then it gives you so few to pass around that you couldn't possibly pass them around." Without quite realizing it, Hershey had shifted from being a procurer of manpower to being a manager of surplus manpower.[35]

The next two years saw increased international tension. Soviet control over central Europe proceeded inexorably, and the Berlin blockade remained in force until May 1949. Recognizing the Soviet threat, Britain and France created the Brussels defense pact, which, when joined by the United States in April 1949, evolved into the North Atlantic Treaty Organization. In China the Communist forces of Mao

Tse-tung continued to advance; by October Chiang Kai-shek had fled
the mainland. Perhaps most ominous, in September 1949 the White
House announced that the Soviet Union had successfully exploded a
nuclear device. America's atomic monopoly had ended.

In this tense environment the Selective Service was relegated to the
inglorious task of frightening men into volunteering for military service. The plan worked very well. Hershey did not begin inductions until November 1948; by February 1949 all inductions ended. He had
drafted a modest 35,000 men in three months before the services reported a surplus of recruits. The secretary of the army announced that
the draft had "acted as a spur to thousands of otherwise undecided
youngsters and that the prompt enlistments following its passage raised
our recruiting quotas dramatically." Soldiers were volunteering at a
rate of 35,000 a month by January 1949. In the same month the army
upped the minimum tour for volunteers from two to three years—a
move which resulted in no need for draftees from February 1949 to August 1950.[36]

Hershey witnessed this triumph with mixed emotions. He disagreed
with the rather limited strength authorizations for the armed forces,
and he worried about the effect of a negative role upon his own organization. With 3,775 local boards sitting on their hands, morale was bound
to decline. With no one being called, everyone would begin to assume
that he should be deferred. Some 9 million men had registered for the
draft, but Hershey had taken only 35,000. "We have the machinery
whirling at top speed," he explained, "but we are not taking anyone."
This approach would convince the public that the nation could have a
draft without drafting anyone. "People are creatures of habit," he argued. "When you get people into the spirit of not taking certain individuals, you almost have to shoot three or four before you will get
them to drop the standards at a time when you must have people."[37]

The Truman administration perceived the Selective Service as a
quick and cheap fix for the armed forces manpower shortages. The
United States would become an international rival to the USSR, even
as Congress refused to spend huge sums for the military. It was only
through pleading monetary efficiency, among other things, that Truman had pushed through the National Security Act in 1947; this law
began the process of creating a new Department of Defense, although
this was not made final until 10 August 1949. Henceforth the army,
navy and air force would have subcabinet status, and the secretary of
defense would oversee budgets for all.

With a budget-conscious Congress agreeing with Truman, Hershey
found his own agency being starved for funds. During fiscal year 1948–
49 Congress authorized a Selective Service budget of $27 million; for

1949–50, however, Truman recommended a budget of only $16.7 million. Such a reduction seemed consistent with the reduced mission of Selective Service. True, Hershey still had to register all young men when they reached age eighteen, and he had to keep records on the 9 million already registered—but he was not drafting anyone. In April 1949 a House committee recommended a cut to $9 million, but the House itself cut the sum to half as much, a paltry $4.5 million. Hershey remarked: "I feel like the hounddog that was shot after it caught a rabbit."[38]

Hershey began to economize. He was required by law to maintain one local board for each county, but he soon had these boards operating only once a week. Records were moved to a central location. Yet, even with 37,000 volunteers, the system could not continue under the new budget. On 9 September 1949 he wrote the president that he would have to stop functioning by 1 January unless he received a supplemental appropriation of $4.5 million.[39]

Despite his apparently desperate financial plight, Hershey continued to operate his training program, and he attempted to make his agency responsible for manpower planning. The new 1948 law was hardly on the books when Hershey informed Secretary of Defense Forrestal that it gave him authority to conduct training and planning for mobilization. Hershey was committed to building an organization similar to the old JANSSC. Throughout 1949 and early 1950 he traveled across the country to attend training conferences at each army corps area. In San Antonio, San Diego, Fort Meade, and elsewhere, he continued his program of training while local boards sat idle.[40]

Even with the training mission Hershey's frustration grew. He now had a draft law but could not draft anyone. Because of budget economies and confidence in the atomic bomb, Congress had placed a strict ceiling on military manpower. Hershey could not understand the confidence in the bomb as a guarantor of peace; he thought it dangerous to assume that the next war would be fought by a few scientists pushing a few buttons. "In another war," he wrote, "we undoubtedly will have the same trouble we have had in the past wars—finding men young and courageous enough to go out and meet the enemy." The country hoped that through the Marshall Plan, the Atlantic Pact, and other devices that it could avoid fighting. Hershey warned: "I don't think we can escape living ourselves, and I don't think we can escape dying ourselves if we get around where dying is going on."[41]

Not only were Hershey's words ignored by the administration, but his own limited program of training and planning also came under attack in early 1950. When he appeared before the House Committee on Appropriations on 10 January 1950, he faced a difficult prospect. Of-

ficially he had to present a budget for the liquidation of the draft and
the reinstitution of the OSSR. Chairman Albert Thomas immediately
launched into an attack of Hershey's elaborate training program. The
same argument which had emerged in 1947 was replayed, as the two
men began to quibble over the meaning of the phrase "preserving of
knowledge and methods." Hershey was quite willing to play loose with
words to save his training mission. Thomas, however, insisted that
when Hershey reverted back to the OSSR or Public Law 26, he had
only two duties: to preserve and service records, and to perform other
duties directly related to such records.[42]

During this time of travail, of having a draft without drafting men,
of operating a training program which some congressmen thought illegal, of being so strapped for funds that local boards could only meet
once a week, Hershey again began to think of retirement. He was fifty-
six years old, with thirty-three years of service. If he retired he would
be entitled to monthly pay of $744.70. His health was still excellent,
except for a mild case of hypertension and a growing cataract on his
remaining eye. In December 1948 Raymond E. Willis, the retiring
president of Tri-State College, wrote to request Hershey to succeed
him. Hershey was tempted but eventually refused. During his various
travels across the country he scouted retirement sites. While his old
friends proclaimed that they enjoyed their retirements, Hershey wondered whether he could be happy playing bingo and canasta all day.[43]

Perhaps the biggest reason for staying on active duty was his conviction that he still had a job to do. Despite all his frustrations, he still had
hopes of convincing the president and Congress of the need for a permanent Selective Service System. He had another chance when the
1948 draft act was due to expire in 1950.

President Truman and Secretary of Defense Louis Johnson could
take little comfort from the state of international affairs in late 1949
and early 1950. The Russians had the bomb, tension over Berlin remained high, China had gone Red, and the American armed forces
were now under strength. Despite the lack of inductions and the shortage of funds, Hershey had no trouble convincing Johnson that Selective Service should be extended beyond the June 1950 deadline.[44]

In his state of the union address in January the president insisted
that an extension of the draft was needed because of the unsettled condition of the world and the need to maintain a strong armed force. This
call for an extension was not unpopular, for Truman had done a good
job of selling the American people on the dangers of Communist expansion. A Gallup poll on 11 February found 57 percent approving a
continuation of the draft and only 33 percent opposed. Several newspapers carried editorials supporting extension and echoing Hershey's

arguments that an existing draft would save six months of mobilization time, which might mean the difference between national survival and annihilation.[45]

In late January Hershey appeared before the House Armed Services Committee to make his case for HR 6826, which called for a three-year extension. Hershey supported passage by insisting that the draft helped preserve the peace. Such a commitment would provide confidence to "our UN brothers" and would be a statement of the nation's resolve. Hershey admitted that some critics felt an extension was not needed because the existing draft had not been used; he pointed out, however, that the draft had forced over 250,000 men to volunteer. The Selective Service performed its mission without drafting men, much as a fireman or a policeman sometimes performs his duty without direct action.[46]

Yet, even as Hershey testified, the administration began to water down its proposal. Congressman Carl Vinson kept insisting that a draft extension include a proviso that no inductions would occur without congressional approval. Secretary of Defense Johnson, with the approval of the joint chiefs of staff, decided to take this half-loaf. Even this compromise failed to satisfy the members of the National Security Resources Board. John R. Steelman explained to the president that, while the NSRB accepted the idea of putting the draft on a standby basis, other changes were also needed. Steelman argued for inducting men on the basis of age groups and occupations, something Hershey had resisted.[47]

Hershey was appalled at the administration's willingness to compromise before the first week of hearings had concluded. Unlike Johnson, Hershey had confidence that a three-year extension of the current system could pass. His optimism grew when the chairman of the joint chiefs, General Omar N. Bradley, testified vigorously in favor of the original bill, and chastised the House committee for its failure to act. As the hearings dragged on, Bradley pointed out, "There has been no let up in the pressure that the Soviet Union has exerted wherever there has been an opportunity for disagreement. . . . There has been no let up in the aggressive extension of communism toward its goal of world domination." He urged an immediate approval of Selective Service extension which would buy the nation six months time in a crisis.[48]

By late May the full House had adopted a revised version of the original bill, extending the draft for two years on a purely standby basis. Before inductions could begin, Congress had to authorize them. Hershey resented this so-called trigger amendment and hastened to testify against it before the Senate Armed Services Committee. He tore into the argument that the draft was not needed because no one was being drafted, insisting that the existence of the draft had kept the Cold War from becoming hot. He concluded by recommending that the Senate extend the 1948 act, without amendments, for three years. Yet the standby draft idea remained popular. Something more convincing than Hershey's rhetoric would be needed to save his organization.[49]

Even as the Senate and House conferees discussed the bill on 22 June 1950, events on the other side of the world upset all draft plans. Korea had been a satellite of Japan for years; after World War II the peninsula was occupied by the United States and the Soviet Union, with the 38th parallel established as a dividing line between the two forces. Developing postwar tensions between the United States and Russia helped to legitimize the temporary division. The United Nations considered the problem in 1947 but could not resolve it. By the summer of 1950 two different states existed on opposite sides of the parallel. To the north, a People's Democratic Republic under the presidency of Kim Il Sung benefited from Russian support. To the south, the Republic of Korea under the American-sponsored Syngman Rhee was created. Both Rhee and Sung claimed sovereignty over the entire peninsula and filled the air with threats of war. Though many Asian experts predicted that a conflict would soon occur, the Truman administration was caught by surprise when, on 25 June, North Korean troops poured across the 38th parallel.

President Truman responded quickly, authorizing American troops in Japan to intervene and calling on the United Nations to establish an immediate ceasefire. In the absence of the Soviet delegate, the United States succeeded in having the United Nations declare North Korea the aggressor. By 8 July President Truman had appointed Douglas MacArthur as commander of the United Nations forces in the area. The president swept the United Nations along in his enthusiasm to throw back what he saw as a deliberate testing of the West by the forces of communism.

As this sea of events flooded Washington, Congress followed in Truman's wake. The conference committee on draft extension gave full support to his decision. On 26 June Hershey appeared before the House Armed Services Committee to answer questions on a draft extension. The same representatives who had earlier spoken of a standby draft now wanted to know how long it would take Hershey to begin his first draft. The conference committee recommended a simple one-year extension of the 1948 law. Congressman Edward de Graffenried, unintimidated by the Korean emergency, accused Hershey of plotting to make the draft permanent. "I have to frankly say," Hershey confessed, "I have not received from year to year the encouragement that I would ever live long enough to see a time when we shouldn't have a selective service system ready to move at any time in this country." On 27 June Congress passed the one-year extension without changes. President Truman signed it on 30 June. Hershey was back in business, and news from Korea indicated that it would be a brisk business.[50]

The Truman administration deserved little credit for anticipating the need to begin drafting thousands of men in the summer of 1950. The brave rhetoric of the Cold War and the increasing commitments under NATO had failed to generate an appreciation, on the part of Congress or the American public, of what was involved in assuming the role Truman had outlined in his March 1947 address. Now, almost overnight, the United States was fighting a real war in Korea, a place most Americans had trouble locating on their maps. Truman portrayed the conflict as part of a global struggle with communism. This interpretation led some to wonder whether World War III was about to begin. Might Russian planes appear over Washington, D.C.? Hershey had no special insight into what Korea meant. As for the Russians bombing Washington, he joked: "I have always thought that any wise enemy would think a long time, before they interfered with the madness normally going on on the banks of the Potomac."[51]

Selective Service headquarters, not far from the Potomac, was as unprepared for Korea as was the rest of Washington. Since the passage of the 1948 law the draft had become moribund. Some 40 percent of all local boards operated only once a week. Money was so scarce that many important officials had been released. But Hershey did have earmarked officers serving in the National Guard and in reserve units across the country. The system was decentralized and would operate even if Washington disappeared, so, despite his problems, Hershey approached the war with optimism. His state directors assured him that they would have no trouble finding 300,000 men within ninety days.[52]

The armed forces needed these men. The army currently had 592,000 men but was authorized 835,000. The entire armed forces lacked a half-million of the 2 million authorized. Draft calls started to come in rapidly. The army acted cautiously at first, asking for a modest 10,000 for delivery in September. General Lawton Collins, the chief of staff, soon had second thoughts about this figure and asked for an additional 40,000. To Hershey's gratification, the system worked smoothly; by the end of 1950 he had delivered 220,000 men. By then Congress had authorized an increase in total strength to 3 million by January 1953. So successful was the draft that the army began to complain that induction stations could not handle the backlog of draftees. The chief of staff ordered Hershey to cut back on the drafting.[53]

From near oblivion Hershey now returned to the public limelight and political controversy. Once again he was in demand to explain a draft which touched an increasing number of Americans. In a press interview in September 1950 he argued that the draft should exhaust the supply of men under twenty-six before seeking older eligibles. Faced with calling 170,000 men by the end of November and developing an armed force of 3 million by the end of 1953, Hershey hoped that the military would relax induction standards; otherwise the law would have to be amended to allow drafting of fathers and of veterans under twenty-six. By October the White House became concerned about how his statements were affecting the congressional election campaigns. The Democratic National Committee wired the White House asking that Hershey be muzzled because he was providing the opposition with "political advantage."[54]

Rather than a muzzle, Hershey had a bullhorn. He accused the armed forces of being like the Bourbons, "learning nothing and forgetting nothing." Induction standards remained high and led to a rejection rate of over 35 percent on the 1,555,198 men examined from July 1950 to June 1951.[55] Hershey fought to reduce standards and to protect local boards from restrictions on their classification powers, complaining that "we are missing some fine fighters by these tests." Above all, he called for an end to the "inventory method" of accepting men and for the adoption of a functional examination. Men should be taken on the basis of what they could do, not rejected because they failed to meet an ideal standard.[56]

While General MacArthur surprised the North Koreans with an amphibious assault at Inchon and developed a deadly case of hubris, Hershey complained at the "business as usual" attitude in America. The nation had become physically and psychologically soft since World War II. Local boards spent much of their time listening to special pleading from industrialists and others. No one seemed to realize that the nation needed "killers." The rush for deferments had reduced the draft pool of men between nineteen and twenty-five by some 80 percent. Appearing before a House subcommittee, Hershey admitted that Truman's goal of 3 million by 1953 was unrealistic unless some serious changes occurred. Induction standards had to be lowered, eighteen-year-olds had to be drafted, deferments for collateral dependents had to end, and veterans might have to be drafted. Hershey complained, "Everyone has the idea no one can make a contribution unless the country can use him in his own peculiar profession, trade, or specialty." Unfortunately, he continued, "I haven't seen a draft questionnaire yet in which the guy said he shot people for a living."[57]

Hershey found it necessary to recommend an amendment providing for a special draft of physicians. The bill (S 4029) was designed to coerce physicians to volunteer in return for a commission and extra pay.

If they failed to volunteer, they would be subject to the draft as enlisted personnel. The American Medical Association and several senators opposed the bill because there was already a nationwide shortage of physicians. Hershey insisted that the draft had not reduced and would not reduce the number of physicians in the country, noting that during World War II, when medical students were given deferments, there were more candidates than at any other time in history. A majority of congressmen agreed with Hershey, and the bill was approved by President Truman on 9 September 1950. By 16 October Hershey had begun registering health specialists under the age of fifty.[58]

Despite these problems, the Selective Service System had provided more men than the army could use during the initial Korean buildup. As American and South Korean troops marched north of the 38th parallel and approached the Yalu River in early November, Hershey argued for a broader mandate from Congress. He requested that Truman ask for an indefinite extension of Selective Service in his 1951 state of the union address. The president had projected an armed force of 3 million men, and a still secret National Security Council paper (NSC 68) recommended a massive commitment of American arms to stem the worldwide tide of communist aggression. Hershey warned that these policies could not be implemented without a permanent draft system. He also called for more rigid deferment standards for dependency and occupations and for a removal of the restriction on drafting veterans. Finally, he requested a thirty-month tour of duty for draftees.[59]

Even as Hershey wrote, hundreds of thousands of Chinese troops, hidden in the mountains of North Korea, fell upon MacArthur's divided forces. With sobering suddenness the Korean police action took on a new complexion. United Nation forces fell back south in defeat. MacArthur began to talk of the need to bomb China, unleash Chiang Kaishek, and perhaps retreat to Japan. Back in the States, the draft board of Roosevelt County, Montana, wired Hershey that no additional boys would be drafted until the president used atomic bombs in Korea. The army informed Hershey that 160,000 recruits would be needed in January and February 1951, an increase of 70,000 over the prior call. General Eisenhower warned that the nation might have to put everyone in uniform.[60]

The war had entered a new phase. President Truman requested that members of the administration clear all statements on foreign policy with the White House. (Neither General MacArthur in Korea nor General Hershey in the United States paid much attention to this request.) Hershey had been worried even before the Chinese attacked; now he faced a mid-December presidential announcement that the armed forces should reach a ceiling of 3.5 million, even though there were only

2.5 million men in the draft pool. By the first of the year George C. Marshall, the new secretary of defense, was agreeing with Hershey about the need to revise draft restrictions.[61]

Marshall and Truman agreed on the need for a new mobilization bill which would include the long-term solution of UMT. On 3 January 1951 Truman went before Congress to call for a universal military training and service law, a combination of UMT and the draft. The bill was needed to combat the Russian attempt at world conquest. Truman warned: "We will fight, if fight we must, to keep our freedom and to prevent justice from being destroyed." The Truman Doctrine was guiding American policy, and Hershey considered himself a loyal soldier. His main concern centered on obtaining a permanent and flexible draft system. He offered two proposals: extend liability to cover eighteen-year-olds, and extend the tour from twenty-one to twenty-four months. He also wanted a stricter limit on deferments and approval for the drafting of some veterans. Without such revisions, Hershey warned, he would not be able to furnish the armed force called for by Truman. "What I have to do," he complained, "is to figure out how to raise an armed force of 3,500,000 without taking anybody."[62]

To a surprising degree, the public accepted Truman's interpretation of the Cold War and supported the need for draft expansion. Even as Congress began hearings on the new bill, Gallup polls reported that 74 percent of the public supported a tour of twenty-four months or longer. When asked about Hershey's idea of drafting World War II veterans who had one year or less of service, some 41 percent approved, while 40 percent said no. On the question of liability, the public by a 62 percent margin supported eighteen and one-half or eighteen years; only 17 percent of those polled preferred an older age. Hershey's recommendations seemed fairly close to the opinions of most Americans, according to Mr. Gallup.[63]

On 18 January, Hershey appeared before a subcommittee of the Senate Armed Services Committee to defend the new universal military training and service bill he had helped draft. The senators received him with enthusiasm. Lyndon B. Johnson, who introduced the bill, had great respect for Hershey. He asked if Hershey endorsed the bill and if he had any amendments to suggest. Hershey explained that he preferred an even stronger measure because of his assumption that the country faced the immediate prospect of "all-out war." The current bill had the virtues of being long range (4 years), flexible, democratic in obligation, and simple to administer and understand. But Hershey also urged that the Selective Service be extended indefinitely, that the age of liability be reduced to eighteen, and that the period of service be extended to at least twenty-seven months. With calls running at

80,000 a month, he would really prefer to extend the tour to thirty months and make eighteen-year-olds liable for immediate calls.[64]

The Senate hearing also provided Hershey with an opportunity to speak out strongly against excessive deferments. He had spent the past few months arguing with physicians, engineers, and other specialists over the supposed need for protection from the draft. Hershey emphasized to Senator John C. Stennis of Mississippi that local boards should make their own decisions based on national guidelines. During World War II local boards had to read over 2,000 occupational bulletins, which only confused them. "I am very much opposed," he stressed, "to starting here as a bureaucrat telling the people in those communities of yours down in Mississippi how they ought to operate their business." To this blatant appeal to his states' rights mentality, Senator Stennis could only mutter: "I think that is entirely sound." By 14 February the Senate Armed Services Committee had approved the bill authorizing a twenty-six-month draft for eighteen- to twenty-five-year-olds.[65]

Unfortunately for Hershey's argument, the army began cutting back on calls while the House hearings continued. On 23 March the April call was slashed from 80,000 to 40,000. President Truman made things worse by easing the regulations on college deferments. Hershey considered these steps politically inept and warned against them, but Truman was too busy trying to drag General MacArthur back from the brink of all-out war with China. Peace feelers were extended to the Chinese after the United Nations force had stabilized the front. Such events did little to help Hershey sell his manpower crisis to the House. Chairman Carl Vinson sent warnings that the committee was pro-draft but not pro-UMT.[66]

The House committee enjoyed questioning Hershey, who had by now become as familiar a figure as the Lincoln Memorial. Several members of the committee had heard him for over ten years. Although Hershey enjoyed their respect for his expertness on the draft and for his Will Rogers personality, committee members nevertheless had several reservations about the current bill, especially about the drafting of eighteen-year-olds and UMT. Congressman Overton Brooks and Chairman Vinson began the interrogation by asking Hershey why he was not drafting men from inactive reserve status, as provided for in the 1948 law. Hershey lamely replied, "Well, I didn't refuse to draft them. I merely postponed the action of the law." Here was another example of Hershey interpreting the intent of Congress according to his own lights.[67]

Drafting reservists and members of the National Guard raised as many political problems as did drafting eighteen-year-olds. Many reservists were veterans with families, and Hershey felt that a better means of finding men involved reducing armed forces induction standards. The rejection rate was now running about 34 percent, of whom over 60 percent were being turned down because of mental problems—failure to pass the armed forces qualification test, or because of a nervous disorder. Congressman L. Mendel Rivers of South Carolina agreed with Hershey that the tests were based on unreasonable standards: "Korea has taught us one thing if it has taught anything. You don't need a Ph.D. degree to fight those Chinks." Rivers and others worried about a disproportionate number of the healthiest and brightest Americans suffering casualties while the weakest and least intelligent stayed home to procreate.[68]

Hershey sympathized with such fears and felt that eighteen-year-olds should be drafted. When Congressman Clyde G. Doyle accused him of robbing the cradle, Hershey exploded in indignation. "I think one of the things that we have done is tried to live our youngster's lives," he argued, "just as long as we could to the detriment of the youngsters." Now the country was being told that a seventeen-year-old, about to graduate from high school, was a baby. Congressman Rivers tried to explain that times had changed from when Hershey was a boy, but Hershey argued that, if the nation hoped to survive, those old ideas of expecting youth to accept responsibility had better be reinstituted. Congressman Edward de Graffenried asked whether nineteen years old was not young enough to die—a question to which Hershey replied: "I don't believe there is any age that a man ought to die for his country." But an eighteen-year-old would fight better than an older man.[69]

From February to June, as the debate continued, events in Korea affected its urgency. The Truman administration was now seeking an armed truce in Korea. This policy had been defined by Truman's decision to relieve MacArthur of command on 11 April. The army also began cutting back draft calls; the April call had been reduced from 80,000 to 40,000. The May call was cut from 60,000 to 40,000, and a call of only 15,000 was projected for July. This retrenchment took place as House and Senate conferees drafted the final form of the bill. Passed by huge majorities and signed on 19 June, this law, which would define manpower procurement with few revisions until 1967, represented more of a triumph for General Hershey than for President Truman. The UMT principle, which Truman and Marshall had pushed, was endorsed, but no provisions for implementation were included. In contrast, the Selective Service System was established on a permanent basis, although induction authority was limited to four years. The law lowered the draft age to eighteen and one-half and provided for a twenty-four-month tour of active duty, plus six years in the reserve.[70]

Hershey derived great satisfaction from the recognition that Selective Service should be a permanent agency. True, he would have to return in four years to fight for a renewal of induction authority, but at least his organization would have some security. The reduction of age liability represented an acceptable short-term compromise. Just as satisfying was the bill's instruction that the armed forces reduce induction standards. Finally, decentralization, with its virtue of sensitivity to local conditions and its defect of lack of uniformity, was now enshrined in the law.[71]

With his agency now permanent and the draft guaranteed for another four years, Hershey should have felt comfortable. But he still worried over lack of preparedness. The very definitions of "peace" and "war" had changed. Maintaining troop strength was now a much more troublesome proposition than it had been during World War II. Americans did not understand the notion of limited war, and Asia was far away. Replacements would have to be found for the regular rotation of troops and to replace casualties. The birthrate during the Depression had declined in such a precipitous manner than only 87,000 males would reach eighteen each month during 1952. Of this total, only about half would be eligible for military service. Even as truce talks continued in Korea, Hershey warned against complacency. Given his commitment to Truman's globalism and the projected manpower figures, Hershey still had much to worry him.[72]

Truman demonstrated part of his globalism when the United States signed the North Atlantic Treaty on 4 April 1949. By 1951 Congress had endorsed the stationing of additional American troops in Europe. General MacArthur's plea for an Asia-first policy was rejected. Hershey himself had an interest in Europe. In 1951 he and Ellen toured the continent. Although he studied the problem of registering Americans living abroad, he was also interested in visiting his youngest daughter, who lived in Germany with her soldier husband. In Germany Hershey visited Nuremberg and Göring's prison cell, Bastogne and Patton's grave. He was well satisfied with how his "graduates" were performing in the occupation units. After a brief excursion to Switzerland to root out some of his ancestors, the Hersheys shipped home in early October, laden with Hummel bookends, German tailored suits, beer steins, and expensive china.[73]

The trip confirmed Hershey's view of America's responsibilities in the world. Even during the retreat of the 1920's and 1930's he had argued for a broader interpretation of America's role. After World War II the survival of Selective Service seemed tied to the nation assuming a global responsibility. His internationalism and his paternalism toward Selective Service became hopelessly intermingled; self-interest in the perpetuation of his agency became hard to distinguish from the new national interest. Without a second thought, Hershey gave full support to President Truman's policy of globalism. Indeed, he pushed for permanent conscription and military training, even while Truman hesitated over massive defense spending. The Korean war pushed everyone along the path of increased defense spending, but Hershey still feared that neither Truman nor the nation understood the full implications of the new road. To maintain the armed forces at a 3.5 million level Hershey needed to induct 750,000 men each year, but if a peace treaty were signed in Korea, Hershey predicted that "everybody will think that we won it." Interest in the draft and UMT would then disappear.[74]

The current rejection rate and the deferment system made nonsense of the claim that the country had surplus manpower. There were 8 million men under twenty-six, but 2 million had already been drafted or enlisted; another 2 million were veterans, and 1 million were rejectees. Very soon, Hershey predicted, he would be limited to the 75,000 new eighteen-year-olds each month. Fewer than 50,000 of these young men would be qualified for service. These figures pointed clearly to a shortage for military calls through 1953.[75]

By 1952 the fighting in Korea had settled down to occasional forays, interrupted by a provisional ceasefire as armistice talks continued. The negotiators at Panmunjom could not resolve the problem of a prisoner exchange. Truman, having announced his intention not to run for reelection, concentrated on maintaining a strong global military commitment. To achieve this objective he still hoped to induce Congress to pass UMT, but even the passage of such a measure (highly unlikely during an election year) would not provide a solution to the short-range need for men. Selective Service still had to draft soldiers and indirectly drive others into enlisting. Hershey again confronted several old problems: an uncontrolled recruitment policy, a high rejection rate, and the misuse of reserve status.[76]

The Department of Defense contributed to Hershey's problems. All of the services, even the army, continued to look upon the draft in different ways from him. While he saw the draft as an essential and permanent arrangement for maintaining military manpower levels, officials in the Department of Defense saw inductions as disagreeable but necessary. They had hopes of establishing a sizable volunteer force through long-term enlistments. Kept in existence as a means of inducing volunteers and as a symbol of America's Cold War commitments, the draft became an institution functioning in a vacuum. The habits and policies cultivated during such a period would create problems, thought Hershey, should the draft ever revert to its original mission of universal conscription.

The mad race for volunteers began creating havoc for Hershey as early as 1951. Zealous army, navy, and air force recruiters set up offices near the sites of pre-induction physicals to discover who had passed the exam. The draftee was then approached by recruiters and offered an opportunity to volunteer for another service.[77] In early 1952, when Hershey brought up this problem to the president, Truman responded by suggesting to Anna Rosenberg, special assistant for manpower under General Marshall, that voluntary recruitment be ended and Selective Service used for all procurement. The Pentagon opposed this idea. Rosenberg sent Truman a memorandum which listed reasons why recruitment should continue; she argued that recruitment provided top quality at minimum cost, that an enlistee served for three to four years, that many volunteers came from outside the draft-eligible pool, that cost would increase because of the increased turnover rate (draftees served only two years), that effectiveness would be reduced, and that ending recruitment would deny a young man the right to enlist in the service of his choice at the time of his choice.[78]

These arguments were filled with unproven assumptions and errors. Rosenberg made much of the 220,000 out of 700,000 enlistees in fiscal year 1951 who were outside the age range for draft liability; however, the vast majority of these were *under* eighteen and a half. These young men would merely have moved into the draft pool if they had not enlisted. While Rosenberg claimed that ending the volunteer system would increase costs to the armed services, her figures ignored the high cost of running a recruitment service. No source of manpower was as cheap as the draft. Nowhere in their arguments did the armed forces admit that the real reason for maintaining recruitment was the desire to skim off the cream of the manpower supply before it became diluted in the vat of draftees.

Despite his strong case, Hershey also failed to convince the Office of Defense Mobilization Manpower Committee, which recommended unanimously to Truman that volunteering be continued. The committee felt that the problems affected only a small number of men and could be solved by administrative action, whereas the termination of enlistments would have a disastrous effect on training time and combat effectiveness for the navy and air force. The armed forces carried the committee and President Truman, despite Hershey's protest.[79]

When Hershey failed to end recruitment, he again began attacking selection standards. During the doldrums between 1948 and June 1950, the rejection rate had reached 72 percent of the few men delivered by the draft. After the Korean invasion, however, rejection rates declined. When the Chinese intervened, rejection rates declined still further, to a low of 27 percent for February 1951. After fighting stabilized in the summer and armistice talks began, the rejection rate again climbed; by July the armed forces were rejecting 50 percent of the men delivered by the draft. Faced with a shrinking pool, Hershey began to complain bitterly to the Department of Defense.[80]

Testifying before a House committee, Hershey blamed the rejections on what he called "the philosophy of abundance in this country." The same attitude that had led to the rapid depletion of material resources was now wasting military manpower. Taking October 1951 as an example, he pointed out that 88,034 men had been forwarded by local boards for examination. Of 39,300 rejected, 17,269 (44.5 percent) failed the mental test. Reverting to the homespun style so beloved by the committee, Hershey explained that when you are sent to the store to get a dozen tomatoes, you pick the best ones you can find, but you pick a dozen. "If we are to survive," he insisted, "we must get the last ounce of sweat out of the bad as well as the good."[81]

When, a few days later, the Senate Armed Services Committee opened hearings on military manpower utilization, Hershey continued his campaign. The only solution was a centralized procurement agency—namely, Selective Service. The law insisted that military service be shared universally; yet, with deferments and the high rejection rate, this ideal was not being realized. Neither the slightly inferior nor the very superior man would serve. Hershey feared that the nation was moving toward the kind of draft used by the Nationalist Chinese government during the mid-1940's. "I don't know exactly how it works," one of his advisors had written, "but the ones who get inducted are always coolies."[82]

This concern over the rejection rate should have made Hershey an advocate of a better national health system. Early in his second administration Truman had recommended a national health insurance program; Hershey had not endorsed the program, although he admitted that "there is a real youth-health problem in this country which we cannot afford to ignore." At the American Medical Association convention in June 1952 physicians insisted that Hershey was exaggerating the problem, and a few accused him of pushing socialized medicine.[83] Hershey had no desire to promote socialized medicine (or socialized anything), yet he knew his manpower pool would soon dry up unless some solution was found.[84]

Hershey's ranting over the rejection rate was, in part, an expression of frustration because his organization was playing only a supporting role in defense mobilization. Instead of becoming the central procurement agency, Selective Service continued as a backup service to induce men to volunteer and to provide a quick fix in the event of a drop in enlistments. Such a role was disappointing for a man who had assumed a much larger task during World War II. But Korea, as Hershey well knew, was not World War II.[85]

The fall of 1952 was not a propitious time to change the draft system. A presidential election campaign was in full swing. In July the Democrats at Chicago turned to Governor Adlai E. Stevenson of Illinois; after a bitter fight the Republicans nominated Dwight David Eisenhower, war hero, former president of Columbia University, and recently commander of Allied forces in Europe. Eisenhower had been courted by both parties since the end of World War II; his decision to seek the Republican nomination sprang in part from a desire to shut out Robert A. Taft, an Ohio senator and an opponent of NATO. With Stevenson and Eisenhower crisscrossing the country and outbidding each other in their stated commitments to the Truman Doctrine, but simultaneously promising cuts in federal spending, there seemed little hope of attending to draft problems.

Hershey refused to accept the political adage which insisted that unpopular prospects be downplayed during election years. He announced in August 1952 that he might have to draft fathers and men under age nineteen. Surprisingly, the public seemed sympathetic: Gallup polls in June reported 60 percent favoring the draft of young men working in defense industries, and over 55 percent endorsed the draft of eighteen-year-old high school graduates. Only in his threat to fathers did Hershey run counter to the polls. On the question of drafting young married fathers, 43 percent approved while 48 percent disapproved.[86] Hershey had no expectation of an imminent change in draft regulations. On 3 November 1952 Eisenhower swamped Stevenson at the polls. For the first time in his career, Hershey faced the intriguing prospect of working with a president who was a Republican and an ex-military officer.[87]

An election provides an opportunity for a modest national reassessment, which in this case produced Eisenhower. Hershey also spent time in 1952 reassessing his own state, the state of the nation, and the role of Selective Service. Personally, he had much for which to be thankful. His health, with the exception of his eyesight, continued excellent. With undiminished energy he continued to roam the country visiting the offices of his agency. His children were all departed, married and working across the globe. The only discordant note in this domestic opera erupted in September 1952, when word arrived from

Korea that Captain Gilbert Hershey had been wounded in combat. Although close to death from a severe stomach wound, Gilbert managed to pull through with the constant encouragement of his father.[88]

Hershey had every confidence in his son's full recovery. He had less confidence in the state of the nation. He worried in particular about the growing indulgence in creature comforts. Reverting to a theme he had developed while awaiting the call for World War I, Hershey decried the love of physical ease which was encouraging young men to become escapists. He felt parents were prolonging their children's adolescence. This trend threatened national survival.[89]

In an earlier day the lack of national preparedness had been only an inconvenience, but in 1952 it was dangerous. Hershey's views emerged in an exchange of letters with Arthur Hays Sulzberger. The publisher of the *New York Times* admitted a reluctance to see a Korean truce signed; he saw the Korea action "as a containment of Soviet aggression" and worried that the nation might have to deploy military forces elsewhere at a greater cost. Hershey replied that the nation was "approaching an adulthood which may very well compel us to count as victory the retention of that which we have." In the past the nation had demanded military victories in the field. Perhaps those victories were no longer feasible, but he worried that Americans might interpret the truce in Korea as grounds for demobilization. The nation had elaborate plans for fighting total war with the Soviet Union, but people refused to face the prospect of perpetual limited war. Complacency and the search for an easy, comfortable life were even infecting Selective Service.[90]

In many ways Hershey viewed the Selective Service System as a means of preserving traditional values—patriotism, individual responsibility, decentralization of government. The system would not only provide manpower but also serve as an example of traditional virtues. As the system reflected Hershey's own philosophy, he believed it could be an educational tool. He was constantly teaching his values to the members of the Selective Service, and he expected them to teach the nation.

Hershey reiterated several themes. Decentralization was his ideal, but it would not work unless the local board members assumed responsibility. He warned that the threat to America's freedom existed not merely from abroad, or from a fifth column, but from within each individual. Whenever a citizen lacked the courage or energy to act on his own, freedom suffered a setback. Examples of such loss of freedom appeared when local board members refused to exercise the authority delegated to them. The local board was the foundation of the system. Individuals, rather than laws, would save the system and the nation.

As for charges that the system lacked uniformity or that management was sloppy, Hershey dismissed such notions as irrelevant.[91]

Repeatedly he explained to the members of the system that he deplored excessive legalism: "I do not want you to ignore the laws of this country or the Executive orders or the directions of the Budget, but for goodness sake, if we can, let us be practical about it." He urged them not to become slaves to paper and to exercise their own initiative. If they were caught doing something illegal, he would back them up. With a wink he said, "I do not advise you to leave a lot of memoirs on what you did. If you make decisions, you will not have time to justify them."[92]

Because he viewed the system as a family and himself as the godfather, Hershey viewed any threat to the integrity of the group as a personal affront. When a case arose in 1952 over some board members taking fees for advising registrants on regulations, he reacted angrily. Although the culprits might not be legally guilty, he considered them ethically depraved. "Our code must be higher than mere law," he argued. When the American Legion accused him of exerting undue political pressure to override a local board decision, Hershey vigorously denied the charge and invited Congress to investigate the entire affair. He admitted, however, that perfect equity was impossible, especially when draft calls were low. Problems arose during the twilight time when the draft continued but drafted only a few. Hershey was about to enter a long period of such service; the next ten years would sorely test the integrity of the family he had so carefully nurtured since 1940.[93]

VIII. Ike and Deferments

As he was leaving office, Truman wrote to commend Hershey on the manner in which he had restructured the system since World War II. In particular, the president noted the expeditious way in which Hershey had met the challenge of Korea. From a standing start the system had inducted nearly 1,500,000 men to frustrate the communist threat. While General Hershey appreciated the accolades and personally liked Truman, he was a life-long Republican who had served for twelve years under Democratic administrations. Like many Republicans, he supported the Democrats in their foreign policy, but not in their domestic programs. Now, at the age of fifty-nine, with thirty-six years of active military duty behind him, he finally had a chance to serve under a Republican president— one who had the added advantages of being an ex-army officer and an advocate of decentralized government.[1]

It took only a few days for disenchantment to set in. Rumors began circulating that Eisenhower planned to appoint a new Selective Service director. Congressman Wayne L. Hays of Ohio urged Ike to replace Hershey with someone who talked less about the uncertainty of the draft. Hershey became concerned when the president invited General Franklin McLain, an old friend and former National Guard officer, to Washington to discuss Selective Service, but it turned out that McLain had no desire to direct the draft, and he informed Eisenhower that Hershey was the best man to handle that tricky assignment. Although the "dump Hershey" movement died stillborn, the episode undoubtedly influenced Hershey's view of Eisenhower. Soon Hershey was reminding his friends that Ike had never backed up his men in Europe, and that he was indecisive.[2]

The early days of the Eisenhower administration represented the high-water mark of the anti-communist crusade begun under Truman. Thanks to the revelations of atomic spy rings and Truman's warnings of a Soviet threat to peace, Americans became increasingly edgy about internal conspiracies. By 22 March 1947 Truman had established a Loyalty Review Board to check on the political integrity of government workers. Truman's board and his heated rhetoric about the Communist threat served to keep the issue alive, and the Alger Hiss case of 1948 fed public fears.

By February 1950 the junior senator from Wisconsin, Joseph R. Mc-Carthy, had tested the water and found it inviting. A stormy career in invective, calumny, and character assassination soon followed. With the aid of the press, McCarthy became a national celebrity. With the blessings of Republican leadership, he became a thorn in the side of the Democrats. His charge that the Democrats were soft on communism became part of the Republican rhetoric in 1950 and 1952. After Eisenhower's election, McCarthy was appointed to head the Senate Permanent Investigations Subcommittee, where he launched a new offensive against internal subversion. On 27 April 1953 President Eisenhower issued an executive order providing for a new check of loyalty of government workers.[3]

Hershey worried about the state of the nation, but he never accepted the notion that traitors were running government. For Hershey, the major threat came from the Soviet Union. He had been indifferent to the Truman loyalty program and had managed to keep his own protected; but under Eisenhower, Hershey had to institute a security program by the end of May 1953. Hershey considered the idea of security boards "baloney." Since he would be held responsible if one of his top aides turned out to be a Soviet spy, he wanted to assume responsibility for investigations, rather than have the FBI or any other agency snooping around his office.[4]

Above all, he tried to keep snoopers away from his local boards, assuming that local board members were loyal because governors recommended them. Only for a very few sensitive positions in the Selective Service headquarters did Hershey require FBI investigations. He insisted upon making the final decision on whether or not a man should be dismissed. As he wrote in an editorial in July 1953, "I have faith that the present members of the S.S.S. are good security risks. I am also anxious to preserve maximum individual personal liberty, consistent with the security of the group." This approach proved successful in keeping Hershey away from McCarthy's tar bucket. Only seven loyalty cases were raised in the next two years. Undoubtedly, because he used elite groups, volunteers, who were nominated by governors, he had a high loyalty rating.[5]

Besides promising to root out communists at home during the presidential campaign, Eisenhower had promised to "go to Korea" if elected. On a hurried trip to the battlefront he observed, pondered, visited his son, muttered a few platitudes, and then returned home to prepare for his inauguration. Once in office he took several steps designed to break the deadlock of negotiations. On 3 February 1953 he "unleashed" Chiang Kai-shek, who proved once again that his only weapon was rhetoric. The State Department began sending warnings that the administration would use atomic weapons in any renewal of the Korean fighting. Stalin died on 5 March. The Eisenhower administration succeeded in controlling Syngman Rhee, who wanted to continue the war for unification, and on 16 July 1953 an armistice was finally signed.[6]

The end of the fighting in Korea meant changes for Hershey and his agency. From inactivity in the spring of 1950 the draft had moved into high gear for thirty-four months. The calls had averaged 42,373 per month, ranging from a high of 80,000 to a low of 10,000; some 1,605,173 men had been delivered for induction.[7] This movement of men had been accomplished with speed and efficiency. A Gallup poll in February 1953 reported that 70 percent of respondents thought the draft was being handled fairly, while only 11 percent disagreed. The largest approval rating came from men twenty-one to twenty-nine, with 64 percent agreeing that the draft operation was fair. Despite this success, Hershey knew that with the armistice in Korea he would now be hardpressed to keep the system alive.[8]

Even as the fighting in Korea wound down in early 1953 and induction calls dwindled, Hershey told his state directors that they should concentrate on trying "to live and keep our organization hanging together." With a pointed reference to Indochina, he mentioned that "some people are coming down into Southeast Asia—down into areas that they have not been in before." Ike was again sponsoring the UMT idea, but Hershey warned that such an approach could not replace the draft. Rather, he urged an expansion of draft power to take men for short tours, followed by assignments to ready reserve units.[9]

While most of the country rejoiced at Eisenhower's announcement of a truce, Hershey assumed the role of Cassandra, warning that draft calls would become larger, not smaller. With men serving only two-year terms, replacement needs would be massive and constant. He hoped the country would take a long-range view of military manpower needs. "If I were 17," he explained, "I would say that this truce thing might make two or three months difference in my plans, but I'd go on figuring on spending two years in the armed forces." Twice in his lifetime wars had ended and rapid demobilization had followed. Such demobilization had simply helped prepare the ground for future conflicts. He hoped the public would not be so optimistic about the Korean truce.[10]

Hershey was casting bread on the water. He would soon find himself spending most of his time figuring out ways of deferring men from service and channeling them into vocations of national interest. Instead of calls increasing, as Hershey predicted, they declined drastically and continued to fall throughout Eisenhower's two terms. From July 1953 to June 1954 calls averaged 20,916 per month; six years later they were averaging 7,458. While this decline stood as evidence of Eisenhower's success in avoiding military adventures, it also reflected the continued reluctance of the armed forces to rely on the draft as a primary means of manpower procurement and the refusal of Congress and the public to back up Cold War rhetoric with military personnel. With the availability of nuclear weapons and air power, the draft seemed increasingly obsolete.[11]

During the 1950's the integrity of the Selective Service System was tested more than ever. Its very character continued to change, as Hershey ceased being primarily a procurer of men and instead became a manager of manpower. But managing surplus personnel was a much more difficult proposition than drafting huge numbers to fight a war. The system was bombarded by the pleas of special interest groups seeking to protect their engineers, physicians, dentists, or whatever. This pressure threatened to replace local board autonomy with group exemptions based on nationally imposed standards. Faced with the impossibility of drafting all young men and with some potential draftees pyramiding deferments into exemptions, many local boards became demoralized. Yet Hershey tried to make the best of the situation. The law mentioned "universal" training, but he realized that he now lived in an age where the emphasis would have to be on selectivity.

Providing deferments had always been part of Hershey's job. He had lived with deferments for farmers and specialists during World War II. The student deferment program, which would prove to be the most troublesome aspect of the system in the 1960's, also had its origins in World War II. When Hershey began his career as director of Selective Service in early 1941, he had little use for the idea of a college deferment: "I do not believe," he told a National Committee on Education and Defense, "that the colleges can afford to be accused of demanding privileges which appear to be for the benefit of the individuals concerned." Hershey expected colleges to revamp their entire programs—entrance rules, vacation periods, and graduation requirements—to reflect the needs of national defense.[12]

After the attack on Pearl Harbor and the bill to extend draft liability, Hershey felt less pressure from the education lobby. On 13 December 1941 Stephen Early, presidential secretary, wrote Hershey that Roosevelt now felt that "everybody in college should consider himself available for his country's defense in any capacity for which he is called at any time; that the only exception to this rule might be in the case of those boys who are well along toward completion of their training for relatively small numbers of professions, such as medicine and certain kinds of engineering and chemistry." Above all, the president assured Hershey that all decisions on student deferments would be left up to the Selective Service.[13]

During World War II Hershey had established a college deferment program. At his urging, college officials aided local boards in deciding which students in specialized courses should be deferred. While accepting the need for some deferments, Hershey never became an enthusiastic defender of the program. Above all, he fought against allowing the colleges to become havens for men avoiding military service. He worried because a few educators he met "were willing to use questionable means in order to maintain their enrollments."[14]

When the administration began efforts to renew the draft act in 1948, the issue of student deferments caused much concern. Because the draft was justified as a safety precaution and there were no current plans for large calls, the administration could hardly resist those who wanted to insure protection for students. The 1948 law authorized the president to provide special deferments to men "whose activity in study, research, or medical, scientific or other endeavors is found to be necessary to the maintenance of the national health, safety, or interest." High school seniors and college students were granted postponements in reporting for induction.[15] Although deferments were still supposed to be granted on an individual basis, the wording of the law implied clearly that the president could authorize group deferments. Student protection was also needed to insure that the armed services could later obtain men with special training.[16]

The deferment for scientists was merely the other side of the same coin. The significant contribution of science to World War II had not been ignored by the War Department. After the war Secretary Patterson explained to Hershey that the deferment of scientists and students should continue. Patterson urged that "we do not relax the concerted effort which was made during the war to concentrate the best of our scientific brains on the development of weapons." Several congressmen wanted Hershey to provide deferments for high school students who showed scientific potential. In July 1946 Hershey and John R. Steelman, director of the Office of War Mobilization and Reconversion, agreed to a deferment policy which would provide protection to certain scientific researchers after certification. The total number, however, would be limited to 5,000.[17]

As the Cold War developed, more and more people accepted the need to protect America's scientific manpower. College presidents liked the idea of deferments for their students. Even the American public accepted the need for such deferments in 1948. Pressure groups, such as the American Chemical Society, warned against destroying the nation's scientific potential by indiscriminate drafting of young scientists. The 1948 draft law declared "that adequate provision for national security requires maximum effort in the fields of scientific research and development, and the fullest possible utilization of the Nation's technological, scientific, and other critical manpower resources."[18]

With the draft designed merely as an inducement for enlistments, and as calls remained low, Hershey anticipated few problems. He personally thought the uproar over scientists and students was exaggerated, but he knew the value of placating critics. Above all, he wanted to insure that any student deferment program was administered by Selective Service, rather than by outside lobbyists. At the recommendation of Colonel Renfrow, Hershey appointed a national advisory group to provide suggestions for a college deferment program. The National Security Resources Board endorsed the idea. Hershey explained to President Truman that, during World War II, "we felt keenly the absence of uncolored, factual data on manpower needs of essential activities, especially in the fields of science and research." Hershey proposed to appoint five advisory committees composed of nationally recognized specialists in the fields of engineering sciences, agriculture and biological sciences, physical sciences, social sciences, and humanities.[19]

Committing what one staff officer later described as "one of the biggest mistakes we made," Hershey now became enmeshed in student deferments. After soliciting advice from the National Security Resources Board, the Social Science Research Council, the American Council of Learned Societies, and other professional organizations, Hershey appointed five special committees, plus an additional committee to deal with medical, dental, and other health sciences. To Dr. Charles E. Odegaard of the ACLS, Hershey explained that he wished to "classify each individual that he may be left or placed where he may best serve the national interest." This objective seemed so laudable that the American Council on Education endorsed it. Without such an advisory group, many educators feared that local boards would conduct indiscriminate raids on students and faculty in the event of a major call-up.[20]

Hershey assembled an impressive collection of academicians to serve on his six advisory committees.[21] Under the chairmanship of Dr. M. H. Trytten of the National Research Council, a committee of the whole met in November 1948. Hershey explained at the first meeting that he sought advice on the following questions: How essential were the different scientific activities? What percentage of men could be replaced by women? How many of these scientists were males over eighteen and under twenty-six, single, and not veterans? How many college students were preparing to enter each field? How could the draft earmark those scientists best left in their jobs? How could Hershey earmark students so as to insure a sufficient supply of scientists to support national defense? Hershey urged the committees to remember that the Selective Service's primary role was to provide men for the armed forces. If the nation lost a war because of inadequate manpower, there would be little solace in having preserved the national economy.[22]

The special committees met in November and December 1948 and submitted a list of recommendations to Hershey. As Trytten explained, the committees agreed that there should be established within the draft a classification for any registrant whose educational aptitude suggests he is of potential special value, and that this educational aptitude should be defined as a minimum score on a general classification test and as a record of previous educational accomplishment. Trytten's group also recommended that special advisory boards be assigned to each local board to provide guidance. With unusual accord, these professionals agreed that engineering, physical sciences, biological sciences, social sciences, and the humanities had all contributed to victory in World War II. They concluded, "We cannot permit any of these areas of knowledge to be seriously crippled." The committees chose to protect the brightest students, no matter what their fields.[23]

Hershey agreed with most of the committees' recommendations. While it had been recommended that test scores and class ranking be used to determine who deserved deferments, Hershey soon realized that such an approach might cause problems. The more elite schools, whose student bodies could be expected to score higher on general tests, would still have students ranked in the bottom of each class; in contrast, small schools, such as Tri-State, might have fewer students who scored high on the test. Hershey preferred to use either test scores or class ranking, rather than both.[24]

In view of the continued reduction in draft calls during 1949, the entire question of student deferments seemed academic in more ways than one. Hershey was bombarded by those who wanted all men deferred, and by those who wanted none deferred. The Association of American Universities adopted a resolution at its 4 December 1948 meeting, opposing all educational and occupational deferments for men under age twenty-two. Hershey sympathized with those who argued that machinists were just as deserving of deferments as college boys. Theoretically, he insisted, "there is no question but that we should not leave people behind so that they may go to school." Low calls and strong pressure from the scientific community and the Department of Defense had forced him to erect an elaborate system of student deferments. With an end of all draft calls in early 1949, however, the plan lay unused.[25]

With the outbreak of the Korean war in June 1950, Hershey again began to study scientific and student deferments. He invited representatives from the departments of defense, labor, agriculture, and others to send representatives to an interagency committee on deferments. As he explained at the first meeting on 14 July 1950, the group should attempt to take a large view of manpower needs and should consider whose deferment would be in the national interest. Hershey had several large calls to meet, and he was sure that claims for deferments would rise. "There is no such thing as deferment," he explained, "it's merely a term used to denote when one man goes in another man's place." He wanted the group to provide him with additional ideas on how to establish specialized deferments.[26]

At the very first meeting of the interagency committee it became clear that Hershey was unsympathetic to the entire idea of special deferments. He raised the problem of distinguishing scientists from other kinds of specialists. He agreed that the country needed to defer scientists but, from past experience, he knew how hard it was to define these men. He recalled that during World War II he had offered 10,000 deferments to Vannevar Bush if he could pick out future scientists from among college students; Bush had admitted that he could not pick them even after they had their doctorates. Reacting to Hershey's tone, J. F. Victory, the executive secretary of the National Advisory Committee for Aeronautics, accused him of being indifferent to the defense contributions of young scientists. Losing his patience, Hershey denied indifference but, to end Victory's complaints, he said he was willing to admit "any damn thing you want." He finally closed the first meeting by emphasizing that he wanted two things: 1) a means of scientific deferment which would be so simple that the average citizen could understand it and believe in it; 2) a system which would insure that deferments were not made available merely because some boys were rich enough to go to college. For twelve months he did not expect to take men from vital positions.[27]

Trytten's plan for student deferments had lain unused for a year and a half, but now Hershey sought to resurrect the idea. He invited the advisors to return to Washington to consider the need for updating or revising the original plan for a nationwide test. He wanted to have something in operation before the new school year began. On 30 July 1950 the advisory committee gathered in Washington and polished the plan. In reviewing the committee's work, Hershey agreed to allow all students, rather than just those in scientific and technical fields, to take the test. He rejected, however, a suggested format which requested considerable personal information of the testee. He did not wish to conduct a massive experiment on students through the Selective Service. Furthermore, the format of the test suggested that if the student did well he would be exempted. Such a tone was unsuitable because the decision would still be made by the local board. Even someone who failed the test could still be deferred.[28]

Hershey got his way on the test format, but he was unable to launch the program in 1950. Time was needed for putting out a bid on manufacturing the test itself; in addition, there was the more serious problem of convincing state officials, Congress, and the public of the value of this new system. At a meeting of state directors in November 1950, he made his case for the advisory committee's plan. Hershey, himself a product of a nontechnical education, explained that world progress also depended upon nonscientific fields. "I still happen to believe," he argued, "that I will bet on the future of this country with its smart people rather than its technicians."[29]

Hershey also had to sell the public on the student deferment plan. He explained the plan at a meeting of the American Council on Education, stressing that it provided a deferment, not an exemption, for students. As for charges that the plan would be unjust, he explained that such inequity was inevitable. "There is no justice," he explained, "in taking boys between eighteen and twenty-five to save the nation. That is just necessity." As for charges that the system would allow the rich to escape service, Hershey insisted that many students worked their way through college.[30]

When public opinion approved the deferring of college students until graduation, Hershey arranged for the Educational Testing Service of Princeton, New Jersey, to create the exam.[31] But Congress still had to be convinced. In testimony before the Senate Armed Services Committee on 18 January 1951, Hershey explained the recommendations of the Trytten group. He stressed that the program rested on the assumption that Congress wished to restrict itself to a general directive on protecting the nation's technical manpower while leaving the details to the administration. As for the decision to use test results or class standing, Hershey explained, "I do not have as much hope and faith in grades as some people." He anticipated that only 75,000 students would be deferred under the plan, less than the number deferred under ROTC programs.[32]

Despite the explanation, congressmen harbored reservations. Hershey harmed his own case by issuing a special order in January which allowed graduating college students a four-month grace period during which to find a job deferment before having their draft numbers called.

This scheme looked to some congressmen as though Hershey approved of parlaying deferments into exemptions. Hershey explained that Congress had told him to insure that scientific and technical people were available in the job market. The student had been deferred because he was being trained, so why not use his training? As for the fairness of allowing 75,000 bright kids to continue in school, Hershey admitted it was hard to accept. But if the country wanted trained manpower, it seemed logical to defer those who were bright enough to take the training. Slower students could always return to school after their service.[33]

Some congressmen still thought the plan too elitist. To obviate the charge that the plan protected only the rich, Senator Homer Capehart offered an amendment to the draft law which provided a government subsidy for college students. Hershey objected to this proposal because it would "so swell enrollment that the colleges and universities would be unable to carry the freshman load." More to the point, he feared every college might become a refuge from the draft. Others challenged the commitment of Selective Service to protecting scientists and engineers. Fed up with the adoration of science, Hershey charged that these complaints were "a lot of baloney." He explained that the country needed people who knew about something other than physical science; perhaps it would be wise to start promoting "the science of living with each other and governing each other and getting along with each other." During the World War II draft the country had tripled the rate at which it produced engineers, but many young engineers merely read gauges.[34]

While Congress continued to debate the new draft law and college deferments, Hershey became desperate to implement some plan. The old law provided for a mere postponement to the end of the academic year. If he was to protect specialized manpower, he had to begin a plan by mid-March. It would take considerable lead time to prepare and schedule the tests. Rather than wait until all congressional objections had been settled, Hershey convinced President Truman to issue an executive order on 31 March implementing the Trytten plan. Hershey felt reasonably confident in taking this step, largely because Congressman Carl Vinson, chairman of the House Military Affairs Committee, had urged him to act.[35]

The plan was no sooner promulgated, however, than several leading educators attacked it. Henry M. Wriston, James B. Conant, Harold W. Dodds, and A. Whitney Griswold, presidents of Brown, Harvard, Princeton, and Yale universities, all complained that the plan was too elitist. Conant went on the radio to denounce the plan because it violated the democratic principle of equal sacrifice. At first these criticisms, voiced by the leaders of elite institutions, sounded refreshing. The leaders of more typical schools did not denounce the plan, for they knew that using either a test score or class standing insured draft protection for a certain percentage of their students. The best schools, already oversubscribed, could afford to be critical of a plan which insured inferior schools the same percentage of deferments as the elite institutions. General Renfrow explained to the president of Brown that without such a plan most of the small schools would have to close their doors. Dr. Wriston replied that this would be a good idea.[36]

Convincing everyone that the college deferment program was a good idea taxed Hershey's talents. To his later regret, he oversold the program. Only a few months earlier he had publicly announced that the American people had been "sold a bunch of baloney" on the need to defer scientific students; now he had to defend the baloney. When the United Auto Workers passed a resolution calling for an end to the system because it discriminated against the poor,[37] Hershey responded that the Trytten plan was the best idea to emerge in a hundred years. As for discriminating against the poor, he explained that a study by the Federal Security Administration reported that over 65 percent of all men enrolled in college had either earned money or had scholarships. "I went to college without money," he explained.[38]

To the charge that the plan discriminated against the slower students Hershey pleaded guilty. He admitted that, while all bright boys did not go to college, the schools did produce the doctors, lawyers, and scientists. "Until the nation believes it needs to subsidize college education for all" (something Hershey had opposed), he argued, "we must find our professionals from those who find the means to go." Any testing system would be discriminatory, but using grades and tests would insure that the best students were protected. Above all, he reminded the public that the draft system was based on the principle of selectivity. Deferments had been granted on such a basis for years. Some complained that the plan did not discriminate enough because it provided protection to students studying music as well as those studying physics. He answered: "There never was a piece of music that moved our people like, for instance, the French National Air that was written in the revolution, moved France."[39]

During an interview on NBC, Hershey admitted that members of a few local boards had resigned in protest against the new college plan. He felt that they had quit because they misunderstood its operation. Congress had insisted, and Hershey had agreed, that the college deferment plan was strictly advisory. Students volunteered to take the test and submitted the results to their local boards. The boards could still draft students. If local board members knew of other facts which went beyond academics and which convinced them that a student should be drafted, they were still free to do so. The public misunderstood if it believed that the college plan provided an automatic special classification for the student.[40]

When Truman approved the program, Hershey arranged for the Selective Service College Qualification Test (SSCQT) to be held on three dates during 1951. Before the first test, Hershey sought to explain the program on a special radio program called "Youth and the Draft." He emphasized that one virtue of the plan was its flexibility; scores could be raised or lowered, depending upon whether the government thought fewer or more students should be deferred. A score of 70 had been established as the minimum for deferment consideration by the board. Hershey explained carefully that each student was merely being deferred to allow him to acquire valuable training; after the young man had become more valuable, he would be asked to serve his country. Indeed, Congress passed an amendment to the new draft law providing that anyone who received a deferment was to remain eligible for the draft until age thirty-five.[41] Hershey announced to the students at Montana State University, "I do not intend to draft you all," but he warned that deferments were only temporary and were not offered merely because a student was a "good football prospect."[42]

The program moved forward to the big day. Students obtained applications from their local draft boards. Applications were sent to the Educational Testing Service. Testing centers were established all over the country, to operate on 26 May and 16 and 30 June.[43]

Of 335,837 students who took the test (out of a male student population of 1,259,000), over 63 percent scored at least 70. By the end of the first year some 891,000 students from ages eighteen to twenty-six were either exempted or deferred. From 1951 through 1960 a total of 606,883 students took the test, and 64.4 percent scored at least 70. In 1960 only 3,316 students bothered to take the exam. With the truce in Korea and the reduced calls by the armed forces, the draft had almost no impact on college students, regardless of their class standings or test scores. At no time during the program were as many students deferred because of the test as because of ROTC, 4-F status, or married status. The program continued largely because it provided a rather sophisticated rationale for deferring young men who were not needed.[44]

The first series of exams had no sooner been administered than complaints poured into national headquarters. Students wrote in when they failed, arguing that the test was unfair. Senator Lyndon B. Johnson suspected the test discriminated against Southerners. Hershey tried to explain that the exam was designed to test general intelligence, and that the test was only one of many factors considered by local boards. Students majoring in the humanities complained about questions in the sciences; students in the sciences complained about questions requiring broad reading.[45]

Even more disturbing than individual complaints was the growing reluctance of some colleges to cooperate with the program. State directors reported that, because the regulations varied so much from school to school, it was difficult to establish a definition of a full-time student. Some schools claimed it was impossible to establish class standings. A few schools just could not be bothered with reporting to local boards. Hershey was furious and felt betrayed. If the colleges refused to cooperate, they should be told: "Go ahead, but we are not going to send other mothers' sons to Korea ahead of your students." As for not being able to tell local boards whether the student was in good standing, Hershey denounced this as "nonsense." "I'll be damned," he shouted, "if I buy that we will let an institution have the custody of a man that somebody else goes out and dies for, and that institution be permitted to so laxly handle its problem that they don't know from day-to-day who is going to their institution." If the schools refused to cooperate, Hershey had the solution: "I would presume that the way to discipline the school that didn't want to let you know is to take their students."[46]

By June 1952 the American people gave evidence of accepting Hershey's plan. A Gallup poll asked whether "students now getting good marks in college should be allowed to graduate before they are drafted." Some 69 percent of respondents agreed that such students should be deferred.[47]

Thus, when President Eisenhower assumed office, the Selective Service System was already committed to the deferment of specialists. During the next eight years this commitment grew, aided immeasurably by Eisenhower's success in reducing world tensions and by national demographic changes. In fiscal 1954 the draft inducted 265,000 men; by fiscal year 1961 the number had declined to a mere 60,000. In mid-1953 over 9.5 million men were registered with the draft; by mid-1957 this pool had grown to over 11 million in the age group from eighteen to twenty-six, and by mid-1961 to 14.4 million. The average age of an inductee in 1953 was between nineteen and twenty; by mid-1961 it had risen to between twenty-five and twenty-six. The system was suffering from a surplus of candidates.[48]

Even before this pattern became well established, Hershey was concerned and disillusioned. He worried about the campaign of professional organizations to obtain veto power over classification procedures of local boards. "You can't teach democracy and practice oligarchy of any intellectual sort," he warned. In particular, he despaired over engineers and physicians. When a student entered engineering school, it was "almost an act of treason to even think of taking him out, whether he makes grades or not." The public bowed "to the doctor that kills most of the patients and an engineer whose million-dollar bridges fall down." If the country collapsed, Hershey warned, it would not be because of a shortage of scientists but "because we didn't know enough to own our own souls." Most of the engineers he knew were busy working on automobiles and other luxuries—"the butter of our civilization and not for the guns."[49]

Hershey found that it was much easier to begin such a program than to change or curtail its operation. When he called for tightening up the program in 1953, he met with opposition from the American Council on Education and others. Cary H. Brown, chairman of the Engineering Manpower Commission of the Engineer Joint Council, warned against such a reform. According to Brown, the country was already critically short of engineers. Dr. Farrington Daniels, chairman of the chemistry department at the University of Wisconsin, explained to Hershey that the supply of trained scientists was at a dangerously low ebb. Hershey's own scientific advisory committee echoed these sentiments.[50]

To end one embarrassment in the program, Hershey called for removing dependency deferments for those who claimed student status. This would eliminate the pyramiding which the public criticized. He also wished to raise test scores in general and those of graduate students in particular. Trytten and the committee opposed any changes, arguing that only a small number of students were affected—one out of every ten male students, or a mere 3 percent of the total college-aged group. As for specialist deferments, there were only 31,000 total occupational deferments in existence. Trytten argued that the student program should be seen "from the point of view of the relative strength of the Russian bloc and the Western world in the field of technology." Reducing the program would be against the national interest, he argued. After all, the ROTC program was offering twice as many student deferments as was the 2-S program.[51]

For Hershey, the race in technology was of secondary concern. More worrisome was that the student program was creating political problems that threatened the integrity of his organization. On 9 February 1953 a group of congressmen led by Charles Halleck and Leverett Saltonstall took their complaints to President Eisenhower. The congressmen wanted the student deferments tightened up, and Ike agreed to study the problem.[52]

Hershey responded enthusiastically to the president's request for a review. He announced publicly that he expected everyone from ages eighteen and one-half to twenty-six to be drafted. The deferment system would be tightened up, despite the activities of various lobbies that "are making a virtue out of escapism." Despite increasing evidence to the contrary, Hershey continued to claim that armed service was certain and universal. To students at Northwestern University he preached the virtues of duty to one's nation as comparable to the duty to family and home. Students had to stop engaging in "self pity" and complaints about inequity.[53]

In response to Ike's request, Hershey drafted a reform of the program for review by Arthur S. Fleming, director of the Office of Defense Mobilization. The reform called for an end to pyramiding of deferments and recommended that the passing score for graduate students be raised to 80. Those entering professional school would have to score 75 or be in the upper half of their preceding class. Seniors and juniors were also required to score 75 or stand in the upper two-thirds and one-half of their respective previous classes. Sophomores had to score 75 or be in the upper one-third of their freshman class. High school students would be allowed to take the exam and would be eligible for deferments if they scored 75. While these changes were really quite modest, Hershey predicted that they would cut student deferments by 50 percent. He expected that by 1955 the reforms would lead most young men to military duty before school. These changes were needed because local boards were raising hell about the program, in particular about the problem of students obtaining permanent exemptions by marrying.[54]

Fleming agreed with most of Hershey's recommendations. The problem of a student who obtained an additional deferment by becoming a father received priority. The question was, How to close the loophole? Hershey had little liking for an executive order which prevented anyone in 2-S (student deferred) status from claiming a dependency deferment from the date the order was signed, preferring instead to make the effective date retroactive to the beginning of the Korean war. The public identified the earlier date with the expansion of the draft, and it was public unrest which had "brought the college deferment program into jeopardy." Fleming, however, refused to make the order retroactive. When President Eisenhower issued his order on 11 July, he discontinued draft deferments based on attaining fatherhood after 25 August 1953.[55]

Most of Hershey's reform efforts remained stuck in White House channels. Local boards continued to resist the existing program. At a meeting of the state directors in May 1953, Hershey made clear his distaste for the entire operation: "a very foul thing that we wished on the public." His reform suggestions had still not been cleared by the president, but he recommended that if local boards want to "wipe it [college deferment] out, let them wipe it out." Unfortunately, he had to admit that in the future the agency would be plagued not with the need to find men but with the "purgatory of special registrants." The ROTC program and the recruitment operations would continue to create problems. The ready reserve was a mere shell, and in an emergency the country had but one option: general mobilization. Like Cato in the days of Carthage, Hershey continued to remind the public of the need for universal service through a single procurement agency.[56]

Although he regretted the student program, Hershey had learned several lessons from the experience. He was disillusioned with the lack of cooperation by colleges and dismayed at the narrowness of specialist lobbies. In 1948 he had thought it a good idea to appoint special committees as part of the system, hoping to control the lobbies this way, but by September 1953 he had had enough. "I cannot escape the conviction," Hershey wrote to Trytten, "that the Committee's interest has turned largely to those phases of policy which may generally be considered as national rather than agency responsibilities." This remark was a euphemism for Hershey's belief that the tail was wagging the dog. The educators and scientists took their dismissal with good grace. Trytten, Dr. Stockton Kimball, Dean Ralph E. Cleland, and others all agreed that Hershey had shown remarkable breadth of vision in establishing the system and great willingness to accept the committee's ideas.[57]

Hershey, to his chagrin, now faced the problem of dealing with the deferment system he had helped create. By the end of 1953 American college enrollment stood at record heights. Draft calls, down to 23,000 a month, would be reduced to 18,000 in January 1954, making it foolish to speak of the universality of military duty. Yet, with President Eisenhower calling for universal military training and Secretary of State John Foster Dulles raving about the worldwide communist threat, Hershey seemed in step. Oddly enough, although the draft was having minimal effect on American youth, the lobbying for special deferments was becoming more intense. While addressing the American Association for the Advancement of Science on 23 December 1953, Hershey explained that he favored better training and utilization of specialized personnel. The rub, however, came in defining who was specialized. He warned the scientists to avoid promoting the idea that any civilian activity should provide an exemption from military service.[58]

Hershey misjudged his audience. He was soon attacked by scientists for being indifferent to the nation's brainpower. Howard A. Meyerhoff, executive director of the Scientific Manpower Commission, complained long and loud about Hershey's seeming unconcern over the plight of graduate students in the sciences. Hershey had established a policy of allowing such students only four years of full-time graduate work from their bachelor's degree to their doctorate; Meyerhoff complained that local boards were ignoring this rule when dealing with students who took positions as part-time instructors. Many were being deferred for only two years. He was also disturbed at Hershey's charge that the scientific community demanded special treatment. Meyerhoff believed that a scientist could serve his country better by working on weapons technology than by becoming an infantryman. Alden H. Emery, the executive secretary of the American Chemical Society, made the same complaints.[59]

Hershey rejected such criticisms. Although he admitted that fewer graduate students entered programs in 1951 and 1952, there was no shortage. As for charges that Selective Service had stripped the enrollments of such prestigious schools as Cal Tech, MIT, and Harvard, Hershey found that none of these schools reported a shortage of students. A 1 percent sample inventory of graduate students revealed that those in the basic sciences who had requested deferments had all been granted them. In the cases of chemists and other scientists who moved into jobs, Hershey explained to Emery that Congress said such men were to remain eligible until thirty-five if they had taken student deferments. Most of the men were in jobs more related to consumerism than to defense and would not be missed, Hershey insisted. He applauded on 20 September 1954, when President Eisenhower finally signed the executive order raising the requirements for graduate-student deferments. Effective 1 January 1955, the student had to be in the upper one-fourth of his senior class or had to score a minimum of 80 on the SSCQT.[60]

The entire deferment scene was becoming slightly ridiculous. Draft calls were going down; deferments, going up. Hershey continued to insist that the draft obligation was universal, all the while approving deferments for students and scientists. Congress continued to cut the budget for the Armed Forces, and the army continued to reduce its calls. Hershey knew that such a trend would insure more deferments, yet he was worried about public attitudes toward defense. As he explained to the members of the Industrial College of the Armed Forces on 21 September 1954, if the nation got into the habit of easy deferments, it would be hard to mobilize for war. His system was becoming soft.[61]

Perhaps—but Congress and the administration continued to seek ways to cut defense spending and balance the budget. One way to achieve these goals was to rely more on "massive retaliation," rather than on a large standing army. The president in particular was interested in striking a balance between defense spending and the health of the domestic economy. Given this attitude, it made sense simply to end the draft and rely instead upon volunteers. Yet Eisenhower insisted that the nation still needed the draft, and he called for an extension in 1955.

The president and Congress were interested in cutting military expenditures, but no one seemed interested in reducing the level of American involvement in foreign affairs. During 1955 several new adventures began. Congress authorized the president to provide military support to Chiang Kai-shek, who was yearning to return to mainland China. Eisenhower wrote the new leader of South Vietnam, Ngo Dinh Diem, that he could count on American aid in his efforts to contain the communists in the north. Secretary of State Dulles succeeded in creating the Baghdad Pact as part of his overall policy of containing the Soviet Union's influence in the Middle East. In Europe, a divided Berlin continued to vex relations between the United States and Russia, following a fruitless summit meeting in Geneva. No wonder Eisenhower, in his state of the union address of 6 January 1955, asked for an extension of the draft and the adoption of a military reserve plan. The nation could hardly continue this high level of global involvement without some commitment to compulsory military service. Draft calls would continue to remain low, but the administration required some symbolic commitment to its adventurous foreign policy.[62]

Hershey accepted political reality. He considered it essential to preserve the draft system, even if the armed forces refused to call many men. The major criticism facing the system in early 1955, as Congress began considering a draft extension, was the problem of graduate student and science deferments. Some wit had published a poem in the agency newsletter of March 1955 which probably reflected the feeling of most agency members, including the director:

"On The Student's Lament"
by G. J. Furey

Today in college
To gain more knowledge
More and more I strive.

A student deferment
Is my preferment
'Til I reach thirty-five.

But Selective Service
Has me nervous
They grant but one degree.

Despite my plea
for a Ph.D.
They offer me a P.F.C.

To the surprise of many, as congressional hearings began on the draft bill, Hershey spoke of the value of the deferment system. He was trimming his sails in order to obtain speedy approval of the bill.[63]

Few members of the administration, especially Hershey, expected trouble with renewal of the draft. When hearings on the renewal bill began in February 1955, Secretary of Defense Charles Wilson explained to the House Armed Services Committee that the armed forces could not maintain their strength of 2,850,000 men through volunteers. Hershey went even further, explaining that one-third of the men who had entered the armed forces in the last year had been drafted. As for the so-called volunteers, most of them were forced to join by the threat of the draft as an alternative.[64]

Although draft renewal had strong support in both houses of Congress, criticism emerged over Hershey's handling of scientific deferments. Meyerhoff, Philip Powers of the Monsanto Chemical Corporation, and others challenged Hershey's insistence that the draft was supposed to be universal. These men gained support from Senator Stuart Symington and Congressman Carl Hinshaw, who worried about the growing shortage of scientists. Hinshaw introduced an amendment which would channel scientific students directly into defense laboratories, rather than into the armed forces. Others recommended establishing an advisory board to direct the deferment program.[65]

Displaying his usual dexterity, Hershey refused to challenge the claim that America needed more scientists. Instead, he appeared to sympathize while insisting upon complete independence for his agency in classifications. He explained that he already had scientific advisory committees operating in some twenty-six states. He also supported a Department of Defense proposal which would allow certain specialists to enlist for only six months of active duty and then to transfer into a defense industry. But he refused to accept responsibility for the shortage of scientists. The problem, he argued, was larger than the draft. Students were graduating without having studied mathematics and other tough subjects. Although he disliked regimentation, Hershey admitted: "I think Selective Service can do something to encourage men to enter these fields." As for the suggestion that a special national committee be established, Hershey refused to clear his decisions with a dozen people who were not in government. Regarding the prospect of ending the draft, a solution which would solve all of the problems raised by critics, Hershey dismissed this idea: "I don't believe personally that I am going to live long enough to see the daily threat we live under removed." Congress agreed and passed the extension by overwhelming majorities in both houses. President Eisenhower signed the bill on 30 June 1955.[66]

Hershey had won his extension. From this point on, he began promoting the deferment system as a virtue rather than a mere necessity, seeing it as a means of keeping his organization alive in a period of low draft calls. Within weeks he had reestablished a National Scientific Advisory Committee to advise him on deferments. More important, he began speaking in a positive vein of how the Selective Service had a new major task—that of channeling young men into nationally needed careers. What he had earlier called a vice, and then a necessity, now became a virtue. The change required a drastic shift in Hershey's thinking. True, the very act of classification implied a channeling of manpower, and in World War II men had been channeled more into agriculture than into scientific positions. But now there was no war. In 1955 Hershey embraced channeling, although he admitted privately, "I have had many reservations on increasing any profession by using means which were too highly flavored with escapism."[67] But at least the draft would continue.

The very concept of "selective" service implied deferments, and deferments led to channeling. At no time did Hershey believe that his sole function was to procure men for the armed forces. Now, with draft calls down and the population growing, he exhibited bureaucratic resilience by realistically accepting the importance of other functions. As he explained in July 1956, Selective Service had "become . . . the storekeeper for the manpower supply that can be conceivably needed for survival." He had no objection to deferments, provided that each individual eventually performed some function promoting the national purpose. He did worry about deferments which turned into exemptions. The public was unconcerned, however, as long as very few men were being drafted and those who were taken were not asked to die in combat.[68]

In 1955 Hershey could foresee few of the problems that would arise in the 1960's and lead to scathing criticism. What he did foresee was the danger that fewer and fewer young Americans were obtaining any military training. UMT was now dead. Draft calls were at their lowest ebb since Korea. True, Eisenhower had signed a Reserve Act which required men leaving active duty to join a reserve force, but the percentage of American men with no military training was growing. To cope with this problem Hershey received Eisenhower's approval to revise the order of call. After January 1956 the Selective Service began calling the oldest men first. This sequence was intended to prevent too many men from totally avoiding what Hershey still characterized as a universal obligation to serve.[69]

On 26 January 1956 Hershey traveled to the Hotel Statler in New York City to meet with the Engineer Joint Council. In this cool environment, he made jokes about their past difficulties, but he denied that Selective Service was responsible for the depressed wage scale in their profession. If they wanted better treatment, he recommended that they adopt the guild mentality of physicians. When Meyerhoff and others raised questions about the drafting of young workers just out of school, Hershey reassured them that employers had a good chance of persuading local boards that such men should be deferred. The entire system had entered upon a liberal phase. In contrast to his tough talk a year earlier, he now admitted that his deferment rules were too restrictive for the current demands. He promised to be generous in interpreting the rules for people with technological knowledge.[70]

Hershey and the system settled into the doldrums for the next few years. With calls running lower than ever, the director of the Selective Service System faded from the public eye. In August 1957 he announced that there would be only one SSCQT held in 1958. So few young men were being drafted that students did not bother to take the test. The administration continued to cut back on the armed forces. On 19 September Secretary of Defense Charles Wilson ordered a reduction of 100,000 men to bring strength down to 2.6 million by 1959. But even with low calls Hershey had to stay on his toes. On 4 October 1957 the Soviet Union surprised the world by launching the first earth satellite. Sputnik I was soon followed by Sputnik II as Americans stood earthbound, gawking at their loss of technological superiority. Hershey immediately instructed the system to offer more deferments to teachers in scientific fields. With many blaming the American school system for the setback in space, Hershey wanted to be sure that the draft did not provide an easy scapegoat.[71]

By 1958 Hershey had forgotten his demand that the draft be universal. Instead he was busy assuring everyone that Selective Service was cooperating in protecting the nation's scientists. In January he admitted that there was a shortage of engineers and specialists, but he denied that the draft was responsible. The Selective Service was now protecting teachers as well as working scientists. Since Sputnik, Hershey explained to Congress, he had promoted the channeling of men into science teaching by offering deferments. With calls running only 10,000 a month, he could not exert much pressure.[72]

The scientific community no longer complained at Hershey's lack of sensitivity. Instead, professional organizations began to applaud him.

The Engineering Manpower Commission and the Scientific Manpower Commission, both of which had been highly critical of Hershey, now spoke of his admirable leadership. "It is especially reassuring at this time," the SMC newsletter wrote, "to know that . . . the Selective Service System will not be hidebound by the anachronistic letter of the law," and that Hershey will administer the law "in the light of the changes that have occurred since it was placed on the books." Hershey, the commission reminded its readers, had the power to channel men into civilian careers as well as in the military. The commission pledged full support for his efforts.[73]

Hershey had reestablished a national advisory committee while Congress was debating extension of the draft in 1955, but it seldom met and was merely window dressing. Members had little knowledge of the manpower scene. When the committee met for only the third time on 18 December 1958, Hershey explained that the draft was up for renewal in 1959 and the concept of service was changing. Prospects for extension were not enhanced by Secretary of Defense Neil H. McElroy's announcement that he was cutting strength to 2,525,000 men by June 1959. Monthly draft calls were running only 11,000. Yet if the draft was not extended, Hershey warned, there would be no vehicle for channeling manpower and no pressure on volunteers. He now enlisted his former critics to preserve his system.[74]

World tensions aided Hershey in his efforts. In 1958 President Eisenhower sent troops to Lebanon to insure the stability of a pro-Western government. By early 1959 Berlin again became a source of friction, with the Soviets stopping U.S. convoys and Nikita Khrushchev threatening to sign a separate peace treaty with East Germany. Not surprisingly, most Americans began to consider the draft a permanent government agency, much like the Internal Revenue Service. Very few men were being drafted, with only 7,000 being called in the midst of the Berlin crisis. All undergraduate students were being deferred. The Gallup poll had inquired about the draft in October 1956 and found that some 77 percent of those questioned felt conscription should be continued. This endorsement was consistent in both sexes, in all age groups, and in both political parties. Indeed, 81 percent of men twenty-one to twenty-nine endorsed a continuation. In contrast to earlier extension battles, Hershey now felt virtually invulnerable.[75]

By the autumn of 1958 the campaign for renewal was well under way. Assistant Secretary of Defense Charles Finucane supported Hershey's recommendation that the administration seek a simple extension of the current law. The American Legion, Veterans of Foreign Wars, Disabled American Veterans, Jewish War Veterans, National

Guard Association, Adjutants General Association, Reserve Officers' Association, and other such groups publicly endorsed extension.[76] Within days, however, this consensus fell apart.

J. Roy Price of the Office of Civilian Defense Mobilization and representatives from the Department of Labor began hearing from critics who charged that the draft was a sieve that filtered out the rich. Articles critical of the draft appeared in national magazines. Given these objections, Price suggested a comprehensive study of the draft's effect on manpower before the administration approached Congress. When the Bureau of the Budget supported this call for a study, Hershey and Finucane were furious. They understood that a decision had been made, and that the president had agreed to a simple extension. The charge of mass escape from the draft was nonsense. Some 70 percent of all men reaching twenty-six in 1958 had been in military service; between 33 and 40 percent had entered the service by the time they were twenty. Adding a political gloss to his defense, Hershey insisted: "We are not willing to become a party to lessening the President's authority."[77]

In January 1959 the administration sent Congress a request for a simple extension of the draft law. In his testimony Hershey met with universal sympathy for the last time in his career. Justifying the extension, Hershey explained that the draft imposed upon young men one of the few remaining obligations which conveyed a sense of citizenship, of being a part of the nation. Yet he was also willing to claim merit for his deferment program, which now took up almost 85 percent of his time. Without the channeling effect of such deferments, he argued, the nation's professional schools would suffer. Though this was a challengeable statement, the bottom line was national defense. Hershey explained (and was supported by Department of Defense evidence) that the nation could not maintain an armed force of 2.5 million without a draft. For every man drafted, three or four were frightened into volunteering. Rejecting the draft, he argued, would "encourage not only the Russians, satellite countries, but . . . make the neutrals move a little bit toward the fellow with the big club."[78]

Hershey, showing political flexibility, now became a champion of the deferment program he had once cursed. Meyerhoff appeared to recommend an amendment allowing scientists to fulfill their military obligation in a specialized civilian capacity. Hershey had considered introducing a broader concept of "service" in the law but decided it was the wrong time, instead; he praised the fine deferment system which was keeping young men "channeled into scientific schools, into engineering schools, into medical schools, into teaching."[79]

The other major challenge revolved around the suspicion of some congressmen that the law allowed too much delegation of authority.

Hershey thought such delegation was a virtue. "This bill," he candidly explained, "has so many more things in it than we even implemented—that is why I want to keep it. But most of the things that everybody has ever asked for we have been able to do with this bill." At one point he even suggested that he did not need an extension in order to continue drafting, because the 1951 law allowed him to keep drafting men who had taken deferments. Congressman Albert Thomas of Texas would have none of this interpretation. Such disagreements were rare, however, and the bill flew through the House by a vote of 381–10; in the Senate it passed 90–1. Draft protesters and objectors hardly disturbed the administration steamroller. On 23 March Eisenhower signed a four-year extension of the draft.[80]

As the end of the Eisenhower administration drew near, Hershey became increasingly reconciled to the deferment program. In the summer of 1959 the President's Science Advisory Committee reported on a continued national shortage of engineers, scientists, and teachers. Hershey took the occasion to praise the system for anticipating such shortages and for providing deferments. He admitted there were problems but explained that "only an emergency will change the present indefinite deferments some enjoy." Writing in the August 1959 issue of the *Army Times*, he explained, "I suspect that the channeling of manpower into the several professions and skills is not well understood by our public, but I believe it should be ranked first in the success achieved by the Selective Service System since the end of the Korean War."[81]

A realist, Hershey had accommodated the drive for deferments to a point that by the end of the decade no students were being drafted, but the experience had soured him on higher education. As he saw it, the colleges were filled with faculty members teaching pacifism and other forms of escapism. Instead of teaching democracy and patriotism, schools were teaching snobbery and "softening the moral fiber of the college man." Instead of stressing learning, the college presidents were promoting buildings and winning football teams. In his work as a trustee at Tri-State College he fought such tendencies. Above all, he feared that too many students were going to college because higher education provided an escape and because it cost them nothing. Such young men were delaying their acceptance of responsibility.[82]

Not all of Hershey's time in the 1950's was devoted to preserving the system and erecting a deferment program. In 1957 he arranged another extensive tour of Europe so he could study the conscription methods used by America's NATO allies. Incidentally he hoped to obtain information on how America's drafted soldiers were performing in the field. He visited West Germany and was much impressed with its military preparedness. The same could not be said of Italy. England was another disappointment; the British were giving up conscription and accepting what Hershey termed a "second team status" in world affairs. His trip took him all over NATO, from Turkey to Sweden. Tours with attachés from the American embassies were supplemented by visits to the Blue Grotto in Capri, the Follies in Paris, and the Abbey Playhouse in Dublin. The side trip to Ireland could have proved fatal—Hershey's plane crashed on takeoff, but no one was seriously injured. [83]

This trip proved several things to Hershey. For one, American draftees seemed to be performing very well. In comparison with European conscription systems, the American scheme seemed superior because of less regimentation. European nations had many of the same problems that the draft faced in this country, with high rejection rates and specialist deferments. Yet, while the draft there might be inferior to America's, Hershey returned convinced that Europe was psychologically much better prepared for war than was the United States. Europeans were healthier because of a more rugged lifestyle. [84]

The trip also reinforced Hershey's Cold War mentality, adopted under President Truman. The crisis events of the 1950's, such as the invasion of Hungary and the Suez crisis in 1956, only confirmed his belief that the world remained a dangerous place. Wars, to Hershey, were as natural as earthquakes. Perhaps total war was not around the corner. For this potential respite he was thankful, because the current operations of his system were not suitable for all-out war. [85]

The trip also convinced Hershey that the United States was showing signs of moral decay. Even before the youth revolt of the 1960's raised the issue, Hershey had concluded that the American character needed reforming. "I probably believe," he explained, "that with the disappearance of the frontier, with the possibilities of behavior becoming more standardized, that there is something in the more primitive person that is lost as it becomes exposed to softer physical living more involved in intellectual practices, and more shades of gray rather than white and black in moral practices." With unintended irony, while speaking to the Honolulu Chamber of Commerce, Hershey wished there were some way to "make clear to these kids that they are the custodians and guardians of a civilization for which Anglo-Saxons have given blood for hundreds of years." [86]

On a personal level the 1950's had been less trying. The family was now scattered. Gilbert had recovered fully from his Korean war wound after a series of operations. Ellen was kept busy traveling to help with the arrival of grandchildren around the country. As a trustee at Tri-State College, Lewis drove back to Angola several times a year; in

Washington he spent much of his spare time working with the local Boy Scouts and the Red Cross. Despite the growing weakness of his eye, he continued to enjoy good health. His annual physicals at Walter Reed Hospital found only minor problems.[87]

By the time John F. Kennedy won the presidency in 1960, Hershey was sixty-seven years old and had served as director of the Selective Service System for almost twenty years. His work in the 1950's had met with recognition at all levels. The state of Texas had made him an honorary citizen, and veterans' organizations had honored him in many ways. The Freedom Foundation of Valley Forge had presented him with a special George Washington Honor Medal. In 1956 President Eisenhower had nominated Hershey for promotion to the permanent rank of lieutenant general. The Senate confirmed the appointment on 22 June.[88] This promotion did not come easily for Hershey. The general staff had no desire to promote someone who had never been involved in combat; they felt that Hershey worked for the president, and that he should make the promotion. Hershey had now served since 1942 as a major general. But when Ike decided to let the army make its decision, the chief of staff turned down the idea of a promotion.[89]

Hershey's friends in Congress soon reversed this decision. In the spring of 1956 Paul G. Armstrong, the state Selective Service director for Indiana, approached Senator Everett M. Dirksen with the promotion idea. In Washington, state director Chester J. Chastek did the same with Senator Warren G. Magnuson. When the senator attached the promotion as a rider to an appropriations bill, the White House and the secretary of the army began complaining. Eisenhower wanted the rider killed. Magnuson agreed to withdraw the proposal if Ike would send up the promotion. On 6 June the nomination went from the White House to the Senate.[90]

With awards and a rank that only a few men achieved, Hershey was in a perfect position to step down with dignity. As he was leaving office, President Eisenhower wrote Hershey that he had served his country faithfully and well. Yet Hershey decided to stay on and work with the young Massachusetts Democrat. Had the general been blessed with clairvoyance, he would have decided otherwise. If the 1950's presented a few problems for Hershey, the 1960's would bring disaster.[91]

IX. The Turbulent Sixties

When John Fitzgerald Kennedy stood in the cold Washington air to take the oath of office on 20 January 1961, his thoughts were on more pressing issues than the draft. For President Kennedy, and for most Americans, the draft system resembled the local fire department—apparently essential, but not worth much reflection. Eisenhower had made a reputation for keeping the peace, but the peace that Kennedy inherited was rather precarious. Gary Powers's U-2 spy plane had recently been shot down over the Soviet Union. Fidel Castro had assumed dictatorial powers in Cuba and was making overtures to Moscow. Communist guerrillas roamed Laos and South Vietnam. In Europe, tensions rose as Premier Nikita Khrushchev sought to push the Allies out of Berlin by threatening a separate peace treaty with East Germany. How would the young American president respond to these threats? In his inaugural address and in his cabinet appointments Kennedy made it clear that he would continue the containment policy created by Truman and endorsed by Eisenhower, but that he would do it with a new style.[1]

The Kennedy people boasted that they represented a new generation of leadership, the junior officers of World War II come to command responsibility. Given the emphasis upon youth and vigor, a sixty-seven-year-old one-eyed lieutenant general seemed somewhat out of step. The Kennedy transition team, led by Clark Clifford and Larry O'Brien, had already begun rooting out Republicans. Yet Hershey had no intention of offering his resignation. To insure the general's survival, Bernard Franck, the political liaison man for Selective Service, and others began a campaign to impress the new administration about Hershey's indispensability. Vice-President Lyndon B. Johnson agreed. State directors wrote their congressmen, who in turn wrote to the president. Carl Vinson and John Sparkman both threw their weight behind Hershey. While such endorsements were important, perhaps more important was Kennedy's need for the draft. Directing conscription in the United States was not a job for which men lined up. Given U.S. foreign policy commitments and the army's inability to find volunteers, conscription would continue. If the draft remained, Hershey would remain, no matter how incongruous he appeared next to New Frontiersmen.[2]

As he had done with other presidents, Hershey tried to convince Kennedy that the Selective Service was a vibrant example of federalism at work, and that it deserved more attention. The president, however, never seemed very interested in the draft. He managed to pass on congratulations when Hershey passed a particular milestone in his career, but the two men met only once. Hershey succeeded in having Kennedy greet the state directors on 23 May 1962. At an informal White House gathering Kennedy praised the directors for their fine work in registering some 75 million Americans since 1940. "The pressures upon them [Selective Service officials] are tremendous," Kennedy announced, "yet I cannot think of any branch of our Government in the last two decades where there have been so few complaints about inequity." Kennedy admitted that if the public lost confidence in the equity of the system, it would be destructive of the general welfare. These were ironic words in light of what was soon to come. The administration seemed perfectly satisfied with the system and willing to continue Hershey's leadership without any serious reexamination. Yet the confidence which Kennedy called essential to the draft would soon be eroded.[3]

Hershey had been operating an anomaly since 1953. The draft, which was supposed to procure men for the armed forces, had drifted into managing men who could not be drafted because of reduced calls. Serving an indirect function (to frighten men into enlisting) presented problems. The Kennedy years did little to relieve Hershey's predicament. Average monthly calls totaled only 9,400 in 1961, 6,330 in 1962, and 9,900 in 1963. These reduced calls occurred as the number of draft-eligible young men increased because of birth patterns in the 1940's. During Kennedy's first year in office calls dropped to 1,500 in April, then to zero in May and June.[4]

The closest Hershey came to resuming his primary mission was in July 1961. During a meeting with Kennedy in Vienna, Khrushchev had made clear his intention to solve unilaterally the Berlin problem. On 8 July 1961 the Soviet Union announced a 25 percent increase in defense expenditures. Kennedy responded to this threat with alacrity. Convinced that Khrushchev understood only force, and needing a boost after the collapse of the Bay of Pigs invasion of Cuba, Kennedy declared a state of national emergency. On 25 July he announced that draft calls would be doubled and reserve units called to active duty. The original call for July was only 6,000 men; calls were increased to 13,000 for August, 25,000 for September, 20,000 for October and November, and 16,000 for December.[5]

The Berlin crisis hardly disturbed Hershey or Selective Service. When reporters besieged him about the effect of the emergency on draft calls, Hershey reassured them that the system was more than adequate to the task. With a pool of 100,000 men classified as 1-A and ready to go on short notice, he would have little trouble filling the new calls. Indeed, the average age of inductees would probably remain at twenty-three. What worried Hershey was not the new calls but the nation's general decline in military strength. He was concerned that over 5 million men out of 9 million between eighteen and twenty-six had had no military training. As for Kennedy's declaration of an emergency, Hershey referred to it as a mere "flurry." The nation seemed to prefer crash programs, rather than long-range mobilization. Though he admitted that the communist threat in Berlin presented dangers, more dangerous was the increasing lethargy of the nation's commitment to defense.[6]

Ironically, during the Berlin crisis Hershey worried less about filling calls than about preventing local boards from destroying the elaborate deferment program built up during the 1950's. Some local boards reacted to the crisis by cancelling college deferments, an action that Hershey soon ended. The current supply of 1-A men would be more than adequate without revoking existing deferment patterns. His major problem, he explained to the press, was "to kind of throttle them [local boards] back." He informed them that there would be no changes in rules and regulations on deferments.[7] By February 1962 calls had dropped to 8,000, and they continued down from there. In retrospect, Hershey concluded, "the untrained potential military manpower resources of the nation was only very lightly invaded by withdrawals through induction and enlistment during the Berlin buildup."[8]

Hershey now presided over a draft agency that did more deferring than drafting. He explained to one college audience, "We deferred practically everybody. If they had a reason, we preferred it. But if they didn't, we made them hunt one." By January 1962 some 350,000 students, 1,300,000 fathers, 60,000 industrial workers, and 20,000 farmers were deferred. Even these figures were distorted, for by claiming a deferment an individual had his liability extended to age thirty-five. With calls running so low, many preferred not to apply for deferments, instead gambling that their numbers would not come up. Hershey informed Congress in 1962 that out of the 26 million existing registrants, nearly 15 million had served or would serve by age twenty-six. He optimistically anticipated getting some service from six out of every ten young men who were physically qualified. "I do believe," he informed the House Armed Services Committee, "that for the last twenty years the SSS has been what we call a channeler." Drafting men now took only 15 percent of his time. To maintain the draft, he had to spend more time satisfying strong interest groups representing scientists, students, and farmers. When Congressman Albert Thomas wondered why he needed $38,000 for advisory boards, Hershey was candid: "I think what you are paying it for is to placate them and keep them quiet." Hershey had more men than he needed.[9]

Yet even the elaborate deferment system erected in the 1950's proved inadequate to cope with the surplus. In 1963 another method of reducing the pool was considered. State directors had recommended that married nonfathers be put into a "less liable" category than single men. By August this idea had infiltrated the White House. Kennedy asked Hershey to explain why unmarried men were being treated the same as married nonfathers. Hershey explained that the law currently provided that married nonfathers could be deferred only for hardship. He admitted, however, that the husbands, who numbered some 340,000 in the pool, might well be made less liable than single men, and he recommended that the president issue an executive order providing that no married men would be selected until after all single men had been called.[10]

The order that Kennedy signed on 10 September 1963 put only "a very small dent in the pool," according to Hershey. Many people nevertheless complained at this special treatment. Hershey had to defend it by pointing out that the married nonfathers had not been deferred but had been put further down in the call sequence. He also explained that the decision was based on the desire of the Department of Defense to draft single men who had fewer distractions and cost the government less than men with dependents.[11]

With calls running low and the pool expanding, Hershey had little influence on national defense. The Department of Defense seemed indifferent to Selective Service's future. In early 1962 DOD informed him that he would have to cut the number of paid drills for his Selective Service reserve units from forty-eight to twenty-four. As these reserve units provided the trained manpower for staffing his organization, Hershey was furious at the decision. DOD had earlier agreed that such training was essential for the system's continuation. Now, to save a few dollars, Hershey's organization was being starved. Rather than accept the decision, he launched a political counterattack. Members of the reserve units, many of whom had political influence in their states, began a letter-writing campaign to DOD and Congress. On 28 September 1962 DOD informed Hershey that, effective 1 October, Selective Service reservists would be restored to the old status of forty-eight paid drills.[12]

In contrast to this success, Hershey's dealings with Kennedy were less fruitful. Early in the new administration Hershey attempted to repossess the power of appeal that he had held during World War II.

He had never accepted the National Selective Service Appeal Board (NSSAB), a Truman creation. The board was staffed by civilians who were totally independent of Selective Service but who received pay from Hershey's budget. On several occasions Hershey found the board reversing decisions made by his staff; such reversals detracted from Hershey's policymaking power (something he was supposed to have lost). Kennedy had no sooner moved into the White House than Hershey dashed off a memorandum with a proposed executive order to allow the director to issue regulations without clearing them with the White House, to revise the student deferment program, and to put the NSSAB under Hershey's control. Hershey justified this power grab by arguing that it would save the president's time and make for more consistent operation of the draft.[13]

David Bell, the director of the budget, circulated this proposed executive order to other branches and asked for comments. The response was almost universally negative. DOD argued that draft regulations involved major policy on manpower procurement and should be staffed and issued by the president. Not surprisingly, the NSSAB resented the attempt to emasculate its power, something Hershey had been seeking since 1950. Hershey also wanted to delete the rules prescribing class standing and test scores for student deferments. Since no one was taking the test, Hershey considered these rules superfluous; yet the secretary of labor wanted a chance to comment on any change in standards for students. In the face of this opposition from so many corners, Hershey retreated. When Kennedy issued EO 10984 on 5 January 1962, he merely created a new 1-Y classification (physically deficient but trainable) and eliminated the existing criteria for class standing and test scores. The National Selective Service Appeal Board remained independent, and Hershey still had to obtain presidential orders for changes in regulations.[14]

Given this setback, the low calls, and the inaccessibility of the White House, Hershey had little reason to be optimistic about the future. Nevertheless, he continued to believe that the draft was essential for national security, even if in a merely negative way, as part of America's strategic deterrent. He also hoped that, given the correct circumstances, the system might evolve into the exclusive means of procuring military manpower. While he was not invited to the White House, he still enjoyed enormous respect in Congress—respect that he needed during his annual pleas for funds to support a draft that was drafting hardly anyone.

In his appearances before budget committees Hershey displayed all of the political savvy he had accumulated over twenty-five years in Washington. While admitting that calls were low, he consistently asked for more money from 1961 to 1963. His success was a tribute to his skills and to longtime friendships on the Hill. Congressman Albert Thomas always welcomed Hershey with open arms and asked him to share his refreshing philosophy. This philosophy included a worship of states' rights and a warning against central government. Hershey always explained that he needed money for his state headquarters and local boards. He also played up the uncertainty of foreign affairs and mentioned the need to retain a conventional war capability. "Our problem," he explained, "is to stay small enough to remain alive and potent enough to do the job." He emphasized that most of his workers were volunteers, something unique in a federal agency. As for his own military status, he dismissed his rank by assuring congressmen that no one took it seriously. "When I talk to civilians," he joked, "I wear a uniform and tell them what we must do. When I talk to the military I wear civilian clothes." [15]

In addition to seeking funding, Hershey also had to worry about an extension of induction authority. With the Chinese shelling the offshore islands of Quemoy and Matsu, the possessions of America's ally Chiang Kai-shek, and the Soviet Union planting missiles in Cuba, renewal of the draft seemed assured. Kennedy's blockade of Cuba in October 1962 served to remind most Americans of the precariousness of peace, but it had little effect on draft calls. Not one to merely wait upon events, Hershey began campaigning for renewal several months before hearings began. In testimony before the House Committee on Appropriations in January 1963 he took a moment to remind the congressmen that his induction authority would expire in a few months. When Joseph Evins asked if Hershey considered Selective Service a permanent government agency, Hershey replied candidly. He felt the agency was permanent because it would always be impossible for the United States to rely upon a professional army. [16]

Hershey need not have worried about an extension. DOD realized that, for all the talk about professionals and volunteers, fully one-third of all enlistees and 41 percent of officers would not have entered except for the draft. Assistant Secretary of Defense Norman S. Paul testified in March that the draft was "one of the most vital elements in our defense." Congressman Carl Vinson welcomed Hershey to the hearings before the House Armed Services Committee by announcing, "In all my experience with executive administrators, I know of none who have made a record surpassing that of General Hershey." Hershey read a prepared statement which emphasized that the draft sent a message, to friends and enemies, of America's commitment. Congressman Clarence Long raised the issue of increasing military pay and moving to an all-volunteer force. Hershey would have none of this idea. "Any person that I get in the armed forces," he explained, "that comes for pay alone, I don't want." On 5 March 1963 the committee voted 37–0 to report the bill intact; on 11 March it passed the House by a vote of 387–3. In the Senate the bill moved even faster. A voice vote approved it on 15 March, and Kennedy signed it into law on 28 March 1963.[17]

The Hershey who now assumed responsibility for another four years of the draft had changed very little from the officer who had testified in 1940.* Of course he had aged, but his health remained good, despite a cataract, an enlarged prostate, and a mild case of hypertension. His blood pressure stood at 159/96, and his sitting pulse was a modest 72. Many of the men who had launched the system with him were dying off, but Hershey continued to travel around the country visiting state units. With forty-three years of military service behind him and twenty-three years running the Selective Service, he had no trouble garnering recognition. The awards came in from Indiana and North Dakota, from the National Guard and the American Legion. Yet, to a surprising degree, Hershey maintained the same personal style. In his travels around the country he frequently washed his underclothes in a motel basin. At home, where he and Ellen were spending their fourth decade together, he worked at his usual chores of cutting the lawn and doing the dishes.[18]

America had changed more than Hershey had. His philosophy continued to emphasize the same virtues: patriotism; duty to community, family, and church; the virtues of decentralization; the blessings of stability in the social order. Despite the remarkable material progress he had witnessed, Hershey felt uneasy at the pace of change. Too much time was spent on identifying the new, rather than contemplating what remained the same. Yet "the key to human relations are in these things that do not change."[19]

All around him he saw dangerous trends. Even in his work with the local chapter of the Red Cross he observed a push toward uniformity and centralization. Centralization of power he considered a serious error; on the other hand, he had no faith in excessive individualism. The nation rested upon the concept of community, with everyone cooperating for the common good. His experience with college deferments had caused him apprehension over American youth. Kids were too soft, too selfish, and too long immature. He warned about prolonging adolescence. An increasing percentage of youngsters seemed to reject any responsibility for national survival.[20] As a member of a special investigating committee to study the causes of a race riot at a high school football game in Washington on Thanksgiving 1962, Hershey observed at first hand the dangers of inadequate discipline in local high schools.

The next few years would bring more riots, but the draft, rather than race or football, would be at their center. The sign that this new age had begun appeared on 22 November 1963. To Hershey and the world's dismay, Lee Oswald assassinated President Kennedy in Dallas, Texas.[21]

Lyndon Baines Johnson's assumption of the presidency represented the culmination of a remarkable political career. Johnson had entered Texas politics in the 1930's as a stalwart supporter of Franklin D. Roosevelt and the New Deal. Although grown more conservative after the war, Johnson remained an important figure in Washington. As the Senate majority leader during the Eisenhower administration, he had demonstrated considerable legislative skill. More important for his future relations with Hershey, Johnson accepted the major tenets of America's Cold War strategy. As vice-president, Johnson had carried the torch of American containment to such hot spots as Berlin and Southeast Asia. Now, as president, he faced direct responsibility for maintaining continuity in this foreign policy. In dealing with these problems he would have to deal with Hershey and the draft.

Hershey had known Johnson for years. Like most congressmen, Johnson respected and admired Hershey as a capable administrator and an excellent politician. The two men had much in common. Both sprang from the soil, rather than from the asphalt jungle; both gloried in their homespun qualities. They shared values on the virtues of home and patriotism. In the 1960's many Americans came to feel obsolete, but none more than Johnson and Hershey. General Hershey had grown up in an America of small towns, limited mobility, stable marriages and stable institutions. In 1900 the U.S. population density per square mile had been 25.6; by the 1960's it was over 50. Population had increased from 75,994,572 in 1900 to 179,323,175 in 1960. The divorce rate nationwide, a modest 0.7 percent in 1900, was approaching 3.0 percent by the 1960's.

More than population figures had changed. An ungainly offspring of the civil rights movement, the beatniks, and the California drug culture, the youth culture of the 1960's offered a new view of America. All institutions were called into question, all values challenged, and all people over thirty distrusted. Much would soon be made of youth as a virtue, rather than as an inevitable chronological fact of nature. Oddly enough, the America which produced Hershey was even younger than the America of the 1960's. In 1900 32.3 percent of the population was from five to nineteen years old; another 37.8 percent was twenty to forty-four. By the 1960's only 29.4 percent of Americans were five to nineteen and only 31.7 percent twenty to forty-four. It was not the number of young people which began causing problems for Hershey, but the values that they espoused—especially the challenges to Cold War doctrines which had been accepted by four consecutive presidents and the majority of Americans. Because the draft represented a major tool in conducting this Cold War foreign policy, and because Hershey symbolized the draft, he would soon have problems unlike any he had confronted during his twenty-three years in office.[22]

In contrast to his distant relationship with Kennedy, Hershey was closer to Johnson. When the newly elevated president assumed office, Hershey immediately sent over a message offering his resignation, because "I believe that it is essential for you to be free to select your top advisors." Hershey had never offered to resign when prior changes had occurred at the White House, and he felt confident that his offer would be refused. Johnson was pleading with Kennedy people to remain in office. Desperately needing to stress continuity in the aftermath of the assassination, Johnson had little inclination to clean house. Hershey was no Kennedy man, but he was a sacred cow to many congressmen. Johnson kept him in office.[23]

Hershey remained secure because President Johnson was convinced that the Selective Service System was working well. He frequently met with Hershey's officials and complimented them on their good work. Within a short period Hershey established close ties with the White House, the best since Truman. Joseph Califano, Marvin Watson, and Walter Jenkins proved valuable sources of information. As the draft became a larger political issue, Califano became the major liaison agent. Despite all the difficulties which were soon to come for Hershey and the draft, Johnson never changed his mind about the general. As late as November 1967 Johnson wrote Hershey, "What pride must fill your heart as grateful Americans everywhere admire your rewarding career in public service."[24]

In late 1963 the subject of the draft hardly surfaced, as President Johnson was too busy stretching the presidential chair to fit his more than ample talents. He stressed the theme of carrying on the programs of the fallen hero. Such continuity applied not merely to domestic programs but also to foreign policy. Kennedy had become embroiled in Southeast Asia. Laos had been neutralized in 1962, but the situation in South Vietnam was more troublesome. After conceding to Laos a coalition government which contained communist elements, the administration, given its belief in containment, could ill afford the loss of South Vietnam to Marxist guerrillas.

Ngo Dinh Diem, who had come to power in 1954 with American aid, represented the Eisenhower administration's nationalist alternative to a communist takeover. Supported consistently with arms and advisers since that time, Diem had failed to solve the problems of his new state.

In October 1963 Kennedy had sent Secretary of Defense Robert McNamara and General Maxwell Taylor to discover why guerrilla activity had been so successful. McNamara and Taylor, underestimating Diem's vulnerability, sounded out alternatives to his leadership. With American foreknowledge, several generals launched a coup on 1 November 1963, killed Diem, and began playing musical chairs in the government. As President Johnson took office, Ambassador Henry Cabot Lodge informed him that South Vietnam, which had enjoyed American support for ten years, was verging on collapse and on a communist takeover. Johnson had few alternatives. In the next two years, according to one scholar, "Johnson transformed a limited commitment to assist the South Vietnamese in putting down an insurgency into an open-ended commitment to use American military power to maintain an independent, non-Communist South Vietnam." One of the instruments for this transformation of policy was the Selective Service System.[25]

Weeks before Johnson assumed the presidency, the Wisconsin headquarters of Selective Service was firebombed and some records were destroyed. Even before Johnson's Vietnam buildup, the draft had serious critics.[26] The student deferment plan was now providing reasons for congressional criticism. Hershey admitted that such deferments created problems, but he reminded the Senate Committee on Appropriations that "the reason why we can afford to defer people is because we can't use them all." Time and time again he insisted that "equity is unattainable." Such statements failed to satisfy the press or manpower analysts.[27]

Throughout 1963 and 1964 editorials rang with arguments that the draft was no longer needed. More men were being deferred than conscripted. People began to complain that local boards displayed wide discrepancies in applying draft rules. The anthropologist Margaret Mead complained because women were ignored by the draft apparatus. Morris Janowitz, a sociologist at the University of Chicago, accused boards in ghetto areas of failing to recognize local values.[28]

With criticism growing and draft calls dwindling, President Kennedy had begun a review of the draft system in September 1963. He had made it clear that he believed the system "is administered as fairly as it can be but falls far short of being perfect." In particular, he worried about the growing pool of eligible men; he also wanted to minimize the uncertainty facing young men about their future status in the draft. Despite the problems, however, Kennedy firmly believed that Selective Service "must be kept operable" in case of war. Universal military training provided a theoretical alternative but was politically impossible. Kennedy preferred an all-volunteer system, but DOD assured him that it was impracticable. As a substitute, the president hoped to reform the draft. He established a Task Force on Manpower Conservation on 30 September, long before draft riots over Vietnam.[29]

As the task force began its work, the Senate Committee on Labor and Public Welfare called Hershey to testify about the prospects of moving to an all-volunteer system. Hershey explained again that such a system would never work as long as the armed forces needed over 1 million men. As for criticism about the deferment program, he justified the protection of students and specialists by reminding the committee of England's experience in World War I. Using volunteers, she had seen her brightest young men killed. England would be better off today, he insisted, if she "had her deaths scattered over a little wider area of their population." He admitted that 85 percent of his work involved channeling, but with a world filled with Berlins and Cubas, he had no expectation that the draft would end soon.[30]

Kennedy did not live to see any change in the draft. His task force made its report on 1 January 1964, calling for an early classification of registrants and for efforts at rehabilitation of rejectees. Though the draft law called for early classification, Hershey had convinced many states that such an exercise was ill advised, given the low calls. In August 1963 2,384,295 registrants remained unclassified. On 10 January 1964, reacting to the report, Hershey reversed himself and ordered all boards to expedite the classification of registrants. By 30 June the backlog had been reduced to 699,262. These steps were hardly a major revision of the system. An opinion poll indicated that over 62 percent of the public preferred to draft men under age twenty. Several resolutions to revise the system were introduced in Congress. President Johnson felt the initiative slipping out of his hands. With an election coming up soon and his likely opponent, Senator Barry Goldwater, urging an end to the draft, Johnson sought an administrative alternative.[31]

On 18 April President Johnson announced to the press that he had approved plans for a comprehensive study of the draft system. Although the study would take one year and no changes in the draft were currently contemplated, Johnson wanted his group to study alternatives to the present system, including an all-volunteer approach. The study group was led by Secretary of Defense McNamara. To reassure America's allies in Europe, the State Department informed all ambassadors that they should stress the long-range character of the study. At home, Congress was reassured that the president was looking into the problem. Several bills calling for draft reform died in committees.[32]

When Johnson made his announcement, Hershey was busy trying to extract a supplemental appropriation from Congress. Congressman Joseph Evins wondered why Hershey needed more money when Johnson wanted to implement an all-volunteer system. Hershey pointed out that the volunteer system had been tried earlier; furthermore, the president had not promised an early change. Hershey recalled that, while in Congress, Johnson had voted for each renewal of Selective Service. The director of Selective Service fully expected to have an opportunity to comment on any study produced by DOD on the future of the draft.[33]

Johnson had launched the study of the draft in hopes of defusing the issue in the coming election. With the hope that the system might be ended, political opponents would be hard pressed to blame him for current inequities. Hershey understood political reality better than most men, and he exhibited little concern over the McNamara study. As for inequities in the system, he explained to Ralph A. Dungan, a special assistant to Johnson, that by "equity" we mean "the ones selected have been taken by rules made in the national interest, not in the interest of particular individuals." More worrisome to Hershey than political charades was the increasing role he was being asked to play in the Great Society. A conservative Republican, he was uncomfortable serving as an agent of social reform.[34]

The idea of using military training as a means of uplifting American youth had been around for years; during World War I General Leonard Wood had pushed it with his Plattsburg Movement. Hershey himself agreed that military service provided something essential to a young man's character. During World War II he had emphasized how Selective Service could cooperate with other agencies in identifying young men needing physical rehabilitation. In the 1960's, with so few men being called, some Americans began to ask whether the massive records accumulated in the registration and classification process might not be used for purposes of social rehabilitation. Already the system was helping to insure college enrollments; perhaps less advantaged youths might also be helped.

One idea which kept popping up involved converting military service into national service. John F. Kennedy had sparked considerable idealism among American youth with his Peace Corps. This program of using volunteers to perform social, educational, and technical tasks in the Third World had considerable support. Hershey had no great enthusiasm for the program, and he dismissed any suggestion that such work might be used as a substitute for military duty. But he was willing to work with R. Sargent Shriver, the new director of the Peace Corps. After a conference Hershey announced that, like others working in the national interest, young volunteers for the Peace Corps would be offered temporary deferments. When they returned they would be eligible for additional deferments, but such would not be automatically granted. This scheme seemed to work fairly well, until a bill was introduced in Congress to give members of the Peace Corps and Volunteers in Service to America exemption from the draft. Hershey immediately insisted than the current arrangement seemed adequate, and that it would be unwise to allow such duty to provide a haven for draft dodgers.[35]

Of greater concern than these few idealists entering the Peace Corps were the millions who failed to pass the induction examination. Long concerned about the deplorable physical and mental condition of American youth, Hershey found a sympathetic leader in Kennedy with his cult of fitness. Hershey argued that there was a direct connection between the state of national health and fitness and defense preparedness. The rejection rate of draftees had averaged 38.1 percent from 1948 through 1956; by December 1958 it had climbed to 49.1 percent, and by June 1961 it stood at 52.7 percent.[36]

These figures were deceptive. Because Hershey was now sending forward for examination only a very select group, the percentage of rejectees hardly indicated nationwide decay. This pool had been screened to eliminate all men deferred for school, marriage, and jobs. Yet Hershey felt the rate of rejection did reflect something about the state of the manpower which would have to be called in an emergency, and he was only too happy to accentuate the dire implications of these statistics to both Congress and the White House.

Responding to a presidential request for information on rejectees, Hershey wrote on 4 August 1961 that one man of every four was found physically disqualified for military service. The rejection rate was higher in 1961 than it had been during World War II. Hershey felt this rejection represented a "tremendous waste of human resources" which could be avoided. Within weeks President Kennedy began informing the country that, since October 1948, one million of the six million men examined for the military had been rejected for physical reasons alone. Such a situation called for a national program of fitness.[37]

Even before President Johnson appeared with his Great Society program, Lewis Hershey was up to his crewcut in social reconstruction work. On 30 September 1963 he became a member of the President's Task Force on Manpower Conservation. Along with the heads of the labor, HEW, and defense departments he was to study the relationship between unemployment and lack of schooling in rejection for the draft. Hershey immediately launched a limited review in certain key states and cities, with local boards providing information and reviewing the files of those rejected in the previous year. Special attention was paid to Atlanta, Baltimore, Detroit, Newark, New Orleans, Philadelphia, and Washington, all cities with high percentages of minorities and high rejection rates. By the end of the year, to no one's surprise, the task force had presented a report showing a clear relationship between unemployment, lack of schooling, and rejection.[38]

President Johnson reacted to the report with his usual vigor. Denouncing the conditions which led to one-third of potential draftees being unqualified, he identified the major cause as poverty. Waging war against poverty was one of Johnson's major ambitions, and he now enlisted Hershey in this crusade.[39]

Under Johnson's oral instructions, Hershey began expediting the classification of each eighteen-year-old so that problems could be identified. Johnson promised to bring to bear all of the agencies of the government to provide for rehabilitation. Hershey, as a member of a new ad hoc committee on manpower conservation, met with the other agencies to decide how the program would work. His actions reflected his belief in the armed forces as a rehabilitating agency. He proposed that all men classified in the new 1-Y category be drafted and rehabilitated in the army, asserting that this experience would teach them teamwork and citizenship. The ad hoc committee, however, preferred to move more deliberately. Hershey was urged to initiate a program of identification and referral to other social agencies. Soon local boards began alerting other federal agencies of likely candidates for aid. Selective Service also sent each rejectee a letter explaining that free help was available from the Department of Labor and elsewhere. Selective Service represented a key element in Johnson's plan for national rehabilitation because it was the one agency capable of screening and identifying literally all of the nation's young males.[40]

On 3 February 1964 Johnson informed Hershey that the recommendations of the Kennedy task force were to be put into effect. Hershey was now responsible for referring all rejectees to the Manpower Conservation Program. He would have preferred to induct those with minimum defects and have the armed forces conduct the rehabilitation,[41] finding such a program more consistent with his primary mission of procuring men for the armed forces. This approach was not adopted, however, because the Department of Defense continued to resist assuming responsibility for social reform. Also, Hershey's approach resembled a universal military training program in disguise—something that Congress had repeatedly rejected. He reassured his state directors that, since colonial days, the draft had always been associated with some rehabilitation and conservation of manpower, and he strongly urged all members of the system to cooperate fully. "The battle against poverty," he explained, "can be furthered by improving the effectiveness of our less capable citizens."[42]

Being a soldier in the War on Poverty entailed certain political risks for Hershey. National defense was a bipartisan issue; social reform was not. When Hershey appeared before the Senate Committee on Appropriations to request a $5 million increase over the preceding fiscal year, he pointed in justification to the referral program. This subject provoked Senators Gordon Allott and Warren Magnuson to ask how Selective Service had become involved in social reform. What authority did Hershey have for such a deviation from his primary role? Hershey, hinting that he was acting under presidential orders, admitted that in a narrow sense the program might not be authorized by the draft law, but said he felt that there was sufficient authority. "It is difficult to argue with people that make the law," he admitted, but the work was implicit in the law's call for military service to be shared generally.[43]

Hershey's use of the draft apparatus for the War on Poverty continued until the fighting in Vietnam led to increased calls. By 1965 the system was engaged in a variety of civilian tasks: referring some 80,000 eighteen-year-olds for counseling by the Department of Labor, supporting HEW pilot projects to explore the efficacy of counseling, referring another 250,000 non-eighteen-year-olds for counseling, distributing information for the Jobs Corps at local boards, supplying estimates of rejectees to Community Action Programs, and working with VISTA representatives in obtaining deferments for volunteers. Hershey obtained over $11 million in additional appropriations for the classification procedure. When President Johnson established the Economic Opportunity Council, Hershey became a member. Despite this work, he continued to prefer to draft and to permit the armed forces to engage in rehabilitation.[44]

Hershey was convinced that rehabilitation could not be accomplished on a voluntary basis. Only by forcing the young man to improve under military discipline would any substantial progress be made. As early as 1964 Secretary McNamara proposed a Special Training and Enlistment Program (STEP) which would allow the army to induct some 20,000 men from the 1-Y class for rehabilitation. The plan was revived in 1966, but with the army expanding due to the conflict in Vietnam, such a proposal presented problems. Members of the black community argued that McNamara's plan was merely a device to call more blacks so that white college students would be protected. Hershey, however, had no trouble supporting the plan. In public and private testimony he argued that STEP would help to deal with a rejection rate now reaching 50 percent. As he explained to the House Armed Services Committee, the program would provide education and physical training for misfits. In addition, military duty would help control juvenile delinquency by teaching discipline and patriotism. The War on Poverty was fine, said Hershey, but "I think a fellow should be compelled to become better and not let him use his discretion whether he wants to get smarter, more healthy or more honest." People had to be forced to improve.[45]

Reforming American society was no substitute for procuring military manpower, and under President Johnson an opportunity also arose for Hershey to return to his original role. The political chaos in Vietnam continued in 1964, despite Johnson's attempt to stabilize the problem until after the election. Viet Cong control of the countryside continued to grow. Then, on 18 September 1964, the North Vietnamese attacked two U.S. destroyers in the Gulf of Tonkin. Although there was much confusion and deception about why the destroyers were in the gulf, and about whether a second attack really occurred, Johnson used the event to obtain a Congressional resolution providing him carte blanche for use of military force in the area. In November Johnson won a massive victory over Barry Goldwater. The president had campaigned as a moderate, attempting to take advantage of Goldwater's aggressiveness. Part of this moderation involved the study of the draft, with the hint that it might be abolished.

Hershey was worried and complained during the election that the public misunderstood the new role of Selective Service. Monthly calls for September dropped to 4,900, and they remained below 10,000 a month until April 1965. True, the draft still served as an inducement to volunteer, but Hershey began to worry that McNamara's study might end up recommending an all-volunteer system or using a lottery system for selection. Anticipating such ideas, Hershey began a public and private campaign against reforms. The lottery scheme had failed repeatedly during World War II because no one could devise an equitable manner in which to integrate separate lottery priorities. The lottery also replaced human judgment with chance. As for an all-volunteer system, history had shown that, without the draft, not enough men would volunteer.[46]

Rather than merely offering criticism, Hershey proposed his own reform. Arguing that the country needed some clarification on the future of the draft, an end to uncertainty, Hershey suggested that a reformed system could provide for the national defense and for the "realization of the Great Society." Appealing to Johnson's domestic bias, Hershey pointed out that the system existed in every community. The system's "distribution and its relationship to manpower has been actively engaged with other Governmental agencies in early efforts to abolish poverty and ignorance." Hershey, a conservative Republican, was willing to speak as a social reformer if it would preserve the draft. On the military side, where Hershey felt more comfortable, he recommended that the Selective Service System be used as the sole procurement device for staffing the armed forces. He urged that all available and qualified men be inducted for six months of training, following which they would be offered the option of either enlisting or being drafted for two years of active duty. Here, once again, was the old scheme of universal military training.[47]

Johnson and McNamara were not interested in such a radical departure. The Department of Defense argued that Hershey's plan would be too expensive. The armed forces expected to need a mere 600,000 new personnel per year; the Hershey plan would increase training costs and would reverse a trend established early in Eisenhower's administration. The country now expected military needs to be serviced primarily by volunteers, with only a modest draft to cover temporary shortfalls in recruitment goals. This reasoning made considerable sense in the political and foreign policy climate of late 1964, but within months a new environment was created.[48]

In January 1965 Maxwell Taylor, the new American ambassador to South Vietnam, wired President Johnson: "We are presently on a losing track and must risk a change."[49] On 6 February the Viet Cong attacked an American supply base. The president ordered an air attack on the North, and American involvement in Vietnam took a new turn. When Johnson took office there were already 16,000 American soldiers in Vietnam acting as advisors. He had added only 7,000 to this total in 1964. Now, with reports arriving of the imminent collapse of South Vietnam, Johnson responded in the tradition of a Texas gunfighter. By 8 March he had authorized two marine divisions for Vietnam; in late April he approved another 40,000 army troops, as requested by General William Westmoreland. In the same month 12,000 students in Washington, D.C., demonstrated against the war. On 4 May the president went to Congress to request a special appropriation of $700 million for Vietnam. As he signed the bill he said, "America keeps her promises. And we will back up those promises with all the resources we need."[50]

The major resource needed was men. By July 1965 Secretary McNamara had returned from a visit to Vietnam with the recommendation that Johnson call up 235,000 reservists and expand the regular forces by 375,000 through the draft and recruitment. For the next few days Johnson deliberated on this expansion. Although the action was to have a revolutionary effect on Selective Service, Hershey was not consulted. By 28 July President Johnson acted. The system, which had grown rusty since Korea and which had become involved in ventures only tangentially related to military manpower procurement, was now being asked to resume its primary task.[51]

Johnson did not ask Hershey whether expanding American involvement in Vietnam was a good idea—but then, neither did he ask Congress or the American public about the war. The commitment, which had begun as part of the containment policy of three previous presidents, seemed to enjoy public support. Hershey shared this belief in the basic ideas of containment and the fears of communist expansion. If he worried about the expansion, it was because he knew from the Korean experience that the American people had trouble understanding limited war and that they soon grew tired of battles in Asia. He also worried about the idealistic terms in which Johnson justified the involvement. In a private letter Hershey wrote, "I want to make no charges against our idealists but certainly our entanglement on 22,000 miles of front has been partially brought about by people who wanted to do good in the world and to share what perhaps we do not have with people who are in need of many things, but perhaps not the things that we have to give."[52]

Hershey was a member of the administration and a general on active duty. Whatever his slight doubts about Johnson's decision, he played the role of the good soldier. He had preached loyalty throughout his career, and he would remain loyal. As an administrator, he would argue that he had nothing to do with policy. When critics raised objections because there had been no official declaration of war, Hershey dismissed this as a poor excuse for not serving. "I'm not so sure," he remarked, "in the future we're going to declare any war. We've been able to be flexible enough to kill people very handily without war." Everyone wanted a popular war, but Hershey knew that soldiers had to fight even if the war was unpopular. He found it hard to accept that the public could be so naive as to believe that the huge American military establishment was designed only for peaceful purposes. Everyone wanted security without killing, but the entire training of a soldier pointed to the end result of combat.[53]

Such candor had little role as President Johnson went about expanding American involvement in Vietnam. The joint chiefs of staff urged the president to declare a state of national emergency and call up the reserves as an answer to increased pressure by the Viet Cong in the summer of 1965. By July, however, Johnson decided that such action would only frighten both the Soviets and the Chinese. More important, he worried that such a mobilization would have a disastrous impact on his domestic reform program. Instead of calling for mobilization, Johnson decided to expand his commitment very gradually and to rely primarily upon the draft. Selective Service was a tried and true organization; the public had come to accept it and support it. Opinion polls at this time revealed that 63 percent were in favor of the draft and only 13 percent opposed. Even among college students the draft drew a 60 percent approval rating. Using the draft, Johnson felt, would create less criticism than would a reserve callup which would upset families and the middle class.[54]

On 28 July 1965 Johnson announced that draft calls would be doubled, from 17,000 to 35,000 a month. He planned to add 330,000 men to the armed forces. From 1965 to 1967 the armed forces would jump from 2,650,000 men to 3,380,000. This expansion entailed an increase of 24 percent for the army in one year. Although the growth looked significant on paper, the draft system had managed much greater demands in the past. Indeed, the inductions from July 1965 to June 1966 averaged only 28,623 a month, hardly an unreasonable burden for an apparatus which had taken 200,000 a month during World War II and 80,000 a month during the Korean war.[55] Hershey had every confidence in the system. He had a pool of 1,965,000 1-A men to draw upon. When the press asked him about the projections, he replied that he had been expecting the increases. On 26 August, when Johnson ended the special status of married men, the job became even easier.[56]

Unfortunately, both Johnson and Hershey had neglected to consider that the draft system had been dormant for over twelve years. An elaborate deferment system had developed and had been defended as channeling; that deferment system was now accepted as an integral part of the draft. Deferments had been translated into exemptions in the minds of many. To now revive the draft in order to fight a limited war in Southeast Asia might prove troublesome.

The troubles were made greater by Johnson's insistence upon a very gradual escalation. Between September 1965 and 31 January 1966, the draft was responsible for 170,000 inductions; another 180,000 men enlisted after being classified 1-A. Although on the surface the draft seemed to work smoothly, Hershey soon realized that he had problems. DOD calls began to fluctuate greatly from month to month, jumping from 40,000 to 15,000 and back again as enlistments went up and down. Many 1-A members of Hershey's pool began to emerge as fathers or in other deferred classes. Many had not bothered to inform local boards of their student status when calls were low; others were in reserve units. With some 150,000 young men turning nineteen each month, he still had a surplus, but by the end of 1965 Hershey was emphasizing the need to tighten up on deferments. College deferments now totaled almost 2 million men. In 1966 he reinstituted the Selective Service College Qualification Test, at the urging of educators.[57]

To make his job even more difficult, Hershey now found a new, more powerful antidraft movement emerging. The draft became a symbol of America's adventure in Vietnam. As the war became more unpopular, the antidraft movement gained momentum. Ironically, the protest erupted independently of draft calls. All of the major deferments remained in place throughout 1965, and draft calls were very low (17,000 in July) when protests began. The movement had begun early in the 1960's as part of the civil rights movement. In California youths developed a movement of cultural revolt. As American involvement in Vietnam seemed to exemplify the corruption of the entire system, such organizations as the Students for a Democratic Society added war to their catalog of issues. The draft system was easily available as a target of protest. Most of the young men carrying on the protest were also carrying draft cards, albeit with student deferments. Draft boards were located within almost every community. On 1 March 1965 a full-page ad against Vietnam involvement appeared in the *New York Times*. On 23 March the son of a University of California professor tore up his draft card at Sproul Plaza in Berkeley. Teach-ins against the war began on college campuses across the nation. Thus, in the summer of 1965, an old American tradition reappeared—protest against conscription.[58]

By early August so many protesters were burning draft cards (or reasonable facsimiles) that Congress reacted. Mendel Rivers, chairman of the House Armed Services Committee, introduced a bill making it a felony to "forge, alter, knowingly destroy, mutilate, or change a draft card." The maximum penalty for conviction would be five years in jail and a $10,000 fine. As Rivers explained, "These bums that are going around the country burning draft cards while people are dying in South Vietnam have brought about this type of action." Although one or two colleagues urged greater deliberation, Rivers had no trouble rushing the bill through for Johnson's signature by 26 August. David Miller, a Roman Catholic pacifist from New York City, had the distinction of being the first man convicted under the new law.[59]

Rivers had checked with Hershey before drafting the bill, and Hershey had accepted the idea, although with reluctance. His reaction to the card-burning was surprisingly moderate—he considered it a mere fad which would soon peter out. Refusing to get excited about a few exhibitionists (as he called them) Hershey would have preferred to handle such cases himself. Since the existing draft law required that all registrants carry their draft cards, and since the punishment for failure to do so was reclassification as a delinquent, Hershey felt that he had adequate power to handle the protest. One of the penalties for being a delinquent was to be pushed to the front of the draft line, losing all deferment status. Throughout the protest movement Hershey consistently argued that the proper remedy was not a jail sentence but an early induction.[60]

This philosophy had its first test in October 1965, when the antiwar movement sponsored a Stop the Draft Week from the 16th to the 21st. In forty major cities across the country young men and women picketed and protested. In Ann Arbor a group of thirty-nine demonstrators approached the offices of Local Board 85. After entering, the protesters engaged in the familiar practice of a sit-in, making it impossible for the board to conduct business. Several hours later the police arrived and removed them. The group consisted of several young professors and many students from the University of Michigan. Within hours Colonel Arthur Holmes, the cigar-smoking state director for Michigan, had talked to Hershey and called for the files of all draft-eligible protesters. After a cursory examination, Holmes returned the files to the appropriate local board with the strong suggestion that each deferment be reviewed. Within weeks, draft boards began reclassifying twelve protesters into 1-A as delinquents. In addition, twenty-eight of the protesters were convicted of illegal trespass and given jail sentences and fines.[61]

Although Hershey had given no direct orders, he approved Holmes's action and saw nothing unusual about the procedure. The law provided for advancing the induction of delinquents. During World War II Hershey had engaged in massive reclassification actions to serve the national interest. At the request of the War Department, strikers in vital war plants had been threatened; the same approach had been used against agricultural workers, and Congressman Lyndon B. Johnson had called for such action against industrial workers who had deferments but were guilty of absenteeism. But the United States was no longer fighting World War II, and the Vietnam war had to be handled in a different manner by both Hershey and Johnson. Hershey seemed to miss this point. In an interview with the University of Michigan campus paper he announced, "I'm one of those old-fashioned fathers who never let pity interfere with a spanking." To others he declared that the threat of induction would stop sit-ins faster than a criminal indictment.[62]

When draft protests began in 1965, then, Hershey was worried about rhetoric which indicated that individualism had become exaggerated and which emphasized civil disobedience, but he saw no major threat to his operation. In fact, he felt that such radical protests might make his job easier. "I guarantee you," he explained, "if the casualty rate continues as it is now, the courts will be less and less tolerant of them." But the attempt to organize a draft evasion movement in 1965 appeared a flop. Hershey predicted that a patriotic counterreaction would make it easier to expand the armed forces.[63]

By taking this position, Hershey insured himself more publicity and attention than he had received in years. From this point until his retirement in 1970 he remained a controversial public figure, identified by some as a perfect representative of the old system which had to be replaced. His statements about drafting protesters provoked criticism from the editors of the *New York Times* and the *Washington Post*. The *Christian Century* and the American Jewish Congress denounced the attempt to use the draft to stifle free speech and the right to demonstrate. One writer feared that Hershey was debasing the Selective Service System by turning it into a thought-control agency. Over one hundred law professors from such schools as Harvard, Yale, and Wisconsin sent a letter to both Johnson and Hershey rejecting such a use of the draft.[64]

Reclassification of protesters continued, but the complaints caused concern in the White House. President Johnson disliked this publicity surrounding the draft, for his plan had called for a low-key expansion of the armed forces. But he also sympathized with Hershey's approach. Although Johnson refused to criticize Hershey, something had to be done. Presidential aide George E. Reedy explained to Johnson that Hershey's policy presented legal problems. The students at Ann Arbor had been guilty of trespassing, something unrelated to their draft status. If their original student deferments were justified, Reedy did not think they should be revoked as punishment. Such an action would stigmatize military service as a form of punishment and would open the door for use of the draft as revenge. Public acceptance of the draft, Reedy argued, depended upon the belief that it operated fairly and efficiently.[65]

The administration responded by having the Justice Department toss a crumb of solace to critics. Senator Philip Hart had written the department to inquire about Hershey's argument that the law justified reclassification of delinquents. Assistant Attorney General Fred M. Vinson, Jr., responded with a public letter stating, "I am satisfied as a matter of both law and policy that sanctions of the Universal Military Training and Service Act cannot be used to stifle constitutionally protected expressions of views." Vinson insisted that his department would follow this principle in any court challenges. Presidential aide Bill Moyers endorsed Vinson's views at a White House press briefing. But, as the American Jewish Congress pointed out, no endorsement had come from Hershey.[66]

No endorsement would come. Throughout the remainder of his career Hershey defended this reclassification action, basing his decision upon precedent and his experience. He had little fear at this time of the few protesters he encountered. The system had become accustomed to reclassifications for delinquency. In dozens of congressional appearances, politicians told him that malingerers should be drafted rather than merely imprisoned, so his reaction to new critics was perfectly predictable.

In his defense, Hershey made several distinctions about the law. He insisted that reclassification was not a response to legal protest. He lived with pickets around his office and home, but he would not tolerate illegal actions which interfered with the administration of the draft law. According to Hershey, protesters were reclassified not for trespassing but for interfering with the draft. He also denied that reclassification and induction amounted to punishment, or that service in the armed forces was comparable to a jail sentence. He explained that the entire process was merely an administrative action and not comparable to passing a law. He defended reclassification of any man who had been deferred to contribute to the national interest. If the man ceased to perform in a manner which had earned him the original deferment, the local board might properly revoke it. Congress had insisted that the board retain independence in deferment decisions regardless of class standing or test scores. As for charges that he was personally responsible for these reclassifications, Hershey insisted that local boards were totally independent of the national director in classification decisions.[67]

Hershey remained steadfast in this interpretation because he was convinced that he had the support of the public, the president, and Congress. In testimony before the House Committee on Appropriations on 1 February 1966, he spoke clearly about his intention to put men into the armed forces rather than into jail: "If I err, Congress can do something about it." He was convinced that Congress wanted him to enforce the law in this manner. As he explained to Dr. Meyerhoff, "I have felt that the course that we were pursuing was either one in which they [congressmen] would approve by ignoring us" or, lacking an attractive alternative, they would do nothing.[68]

A few, however, did more than ignore Hershey. Congressman Emanuel Celler of New York complained about the Ann Arbor action. Senator Gordon Allott of Colorado called the draft a fiasco. Senator Philip Hart rejected Hershey's interpretation of the law. Several members of the House, including Edith Green of Oregon, John Brademas of Indiana, and Philip Burton of California, challenged Hershey's interpretation of the Ann Arbor incident. Hershey refused to back down, announcing that it was the clear intent of Congress to have violators drafted rather than jailed. Such comments finally provoked thirty Republican congressmen to sign a petition calling for a thorough investigation of the draft. Richard S. Schweiker and others felt the draft was inefficient and using outmoded methods. After so many years of isolation, Hershey and the draft became issues of partisan politics.[69]

X. Vietnam Protest and Reaction

Draft protests began before Hershey recommended restricting student deferments. At first Hershey considered such protests insignificant, the uproar of a few "misguided kids." He felt confident that they would still make good soldiers, given six weeks of training. He thought that the majority of such youths were sound but confused, and that they misunderstood the conflict in Vietnam. With these ideas in mind, he sought in vain to distinguish protesting the war from interfering with the draft.[1]

Given his conviction that the protesters represented only a small minority, Hershey traveled without fear to college campuses. Demonstrators appeared wherever he was scheduled to speak, but he gave them a dose of his Will Rogers charm which had won friends in Congress. When he appeared for the first time before his youthful constituency in the 1960's, Hershey demolished their stereotypes. Expecting a ramrod martinet with a chest full of ribbons, spouting Marine Corps slogans, the students instead saw a gray-haired, generally disheveled grandfather in civilian clothes who sounded like a Chautauqua comedian.

Appearing before 700 students at a Columbia University political forum in March 1966, Hershey disarmed his listeners by appearing to be an ally. Marching through signs reading "Put Hershey behind bars" and accusations that he was a fascist, Hershey told his audience that he sympathized with their conscientious objection to this particular war. Unfortunately, Congress had made no provision for rejecting individual wars. As for the loss of deferments, he explained that the original deferment was a gift; now the country wanted a return, in the form of military service. At American University he faced the same gauntlet of protesters. Answering a question about the all-volunteer concept, he explained that he was a volunteer. "If you think it was fair for others to stay home and let me do service . . . you've never been a volunteer." The audience rewarded his wit with applause which drowned out the few hecklers. These halcyon days were shortlived. Soon Hershey faced so many threats that the Federal Bureau of Investigation provided him with protection.[2]

The student protests grew uglier because of the constant expansion of America's commitment in Vietnam. Initially the expansion had not meant an expansion in draft calls,[3] but by January 1966 Hershey had to fill a call for 37,280 men. Up to this time he had indicated that the available pool would be adequate without having to tap students; now things began to change. There were over 1,600,000 men with college deferments, and Hershey announced that this group would have to be used. Despite the considerable unrest on college campuses, Hershey had no hesitation in beginning the draft of students. He still considered the protests the work of a very small minority. Public opinion polls in 1965 had indicated strong support for the draft and for drafting those who destroyed their cards.[4] Hershey now resurrected the Selective Service College Qualification Test. When the test had last been given, in 1963, only 2,145 students had bothered to take it, but in the spring of 1966 767,935 worried students rushed to the testing centers. Antiwar protesters found their ranks being augmented.[5]

In summer 1966 Hershey found himself besieged from several sides. On some campuses students and faculty called him a fascist and demanded his resignation. Several congressmen demanded an investigation of the draft. By July 1966 a Gallup Poll reported that only 43 percent of those questioned thought the draft was fair, while 38 percent thought it was unfair. But public opinion continued to endorse the need for a draft, by a 69 percent to 24 percent margin.[6] With increased calls the issue became not the idea of a draft, but its operation. Here there were problems—the same problems that had been raised in the past. The system lacked central control. Local boards operated arbitrarily and promoted inequities. College deferments discriminated against the poor, minorities had no role in the system, and channeling through deferments was illegal.

President Johnson, committed to a gradual escalation of the Vietnam war and a continued emphasis on domestic programs, could ill afford turmoil over the draft. A study of Hershey's organization seemed overdue. Hershey considered such scrutiny perfectly normal, and when thirty Republican congressmen called for an investigation, he welcomed the idea. He explained to reporters that "everybody on the hill is up for reelection in the House, and some in the Senate." The congressmen were worried about public reaction to the war. "Hell," he admitted, "they've got to attack somebody." Hershey's equanimity flowed from his conviction that both the president and a substantial majority in Congress supported the current method of operating the draft. His conviction proved true, at least for another two years.[7]

Lyndon B. Johnson had observed Hershey running the draft for some twenty-five years. After becoming president he had repeatedly expressed confidence in the operation of Selective Service and praised Hershey's leadership, which "had provided inspiration and guidance for your patriotic programs."[8] Yet Johnson also knew how to trim his sails to the political wind. In 1964 he had asked Secretary of Defense McNamara to study the draft, hoping that such a step would remove the issue from the presidential campaign. Now, in 1966, criticism was mounting and nothing had yet been heard from McNamara. The study had been finished, but Johnson had no desire to focus attention on a problem he had sought to defuse rather than to solve. The McNamara report endorsed a continuation of the draft but criticized the existing college deferment program, called for alternate service, and recommended more centralization of the system through the use of computers. Joseph Califano reported to the president that such information was "bound to put you on the spot." The draft was due for extension in 1967, and both Senator Richard Russell and Congressman Mendel Rivers had indicated strong preferences for a simple renewal. As a means of avoiding political problems, Califano recommended and Johnson accepted the tactic of yet another study of the draft, this time conducted by a civilian blue-ribbon panel.[9]

The new study commission was another attempt to forestall public criticism. Califano went about selecting members of the commission from across the entire political spectrum, although there was difficulty in obtaining a representative Polish member. From the black community John Johnson of *Ebony-Jet* was recruited. From the college campuses came Kingman Brewster, president of Yale, who had publicly complained about the current system. All of the appointments were cleared with Hershey and with the chairmen of the House and Senate armed services committees. Burke Marshall, former head of the civil rights division in the Justice Department, was made chairman.[10]

The Executive Order of 2 July 1966, establishing the National Advisory Commission on Selective Service, offered an impressive mandate. The twenty-five-member commission was instructed to review Selective Service by considering such issues as fairness to registrants, military manpower requirements, uncertainty and interference with careers and education, and other factors. The commission was expected to make recommendations on the methods of classification and selection, the qualifications for duty, the grounds for deferment and exemption, the appeal system, and the administration of the Selective Service System at all levels. Califano, who attended the first meeting, assured the group that the president was not seeking an endorsement of the present system and that they should seek the fairest method of obtaining draftees. The president endorsed this mandate in an address to 14,000 students in Washington for summer internships with the government. He called the draft "a crazy quilt" system in need of change and assured the students that he was not bound to the old approach.[11]

Hershey calmly accepted this review. He predicted that people would continue to criticize the decentralization of classification authority, as they had in the past, but he hoped that the reviewers would also determine whether the system had fulfilled its primary mission of furnishing men for the armed forces. The system, he felt, could withstand questions on whether the draft had been conducted without upsetting the national economy, without misusing technical and scientific personnel, and with compassion for individual rights. Hershey cooperated fully with the Marshall committee. All local boards and appeal boards furnished information for such questions as the following: "Did you consult with State Headquarters about classifications of any cases last fiscal year? If Vietnam continues for another year will the local board have to reclassify men now deferred into 1-A or will men becoming nineteen fill the quotas? If reclassification is needed, which sources should be considered first? What are the major problems facing the board? Do you need more or less direction from National Headquarters to do the job?"[12]

To Hershey's advantage, Congress had no intention of allowing Johnson to assume exclusive responsibility for draft reform. Legislators were much less sensitive to criticism of the draft than was the White House staff. Hershey was sure of a warm welcome from both armed services committees. Senator Edward M. Kennedy, a newcomer, paid homage to Hershey by writing, "I have long been an admirer of yours and of the tremendous contributions you have made to this country in your long career of public service." Scanning the political horizon, Hershey saw few problems for either his tenure or the system.[13]

Pressure for a 1966 congressional review of the draft came from several directions. Mendel Rivers was worried about men evading the draft. Robert F. Ellsworth and twenty-nine other Republicans still requested a hearing on the student deferment program, which seemed to discriminate against the poor. Others had questions about the inconsistency of local boards in granting deferments and about the drafting of protesters. The House hearings opened on 22 June 1966. To speed the process, Rivers decided to restrict testimony to government officials.[14]

As though to confirm Hershey's reading of the political signs, the House Armed Services Committee applauded him when he entered the hearing room. The scene was set for a love feast of extraordinary proportions. Rivers opened the hearings by announcing that the committee "has a very high, warm respect for you and a great regard for what you have done." As for drafting the protesters, Rivers announced: "God bless you, you did right." Hershey's "wisdom," Rivers explained, "has been the guiding light by which the Congress has approached this unpalatable thing [the draft]." Charles S. Gubser announced that, in fourteen years in Congress, he had never seen another witness "who can say so exactly what he means and be sure that everyone who is listening knows what he means as you do." This was a remarkable statement, considering Hershey's wandering syntax. In the Senate Jacob K. Javits of New York remarked, "I believe we must defer to the wisdom and experience of General Hershey in his historic administration of our draft laws for the past 26 years." [15]

Hershey had achieved this remarkable rapport through years of careful cultivating of congressional allies. Now, faced with the strongest recent challenge to his leadership, he again displayed all of the ideas and characteristics which made him such a favorite. Once again he stressed that he was merely an administrator who carried out the policy established by Congress and the president. Although anyone familiar with his influence over Selective Service personnel could have challenged this assertion, congressmen merely nodded in agreement. Again Hershey stressed his philosophical sympathy for the states' rights idea so beloved by the senior members of the committee. When asked about instituting a centralized draft using computers, Hershey waxed eloquent about preferring a decentralized system based on citizens of the states. "I have more confidence in the people down in Charleston, of course, they have proved that several times, I guess by the fact that we have seniority from some of the people who come from there." The people in Michigan and Texas were both wise, and he loved both states. To this blatant blarney Rivers could only reply: "You sure know how to get along before this committee all right." [16]

For the next several days Hershey performed like a virtuoso in repelling all attacks on the draft. Perhaps the most fundamental challenge to the existing system was the charge that there were no national standards and that local boards varied greatly in how they applied the rules. The criticism amounted to a recommendation that the organization become more centralized and that local board independence be ended. As Hershey considered decentralization the lodestar of his creation, he reacted vigorously. He did not understand the term "national standards." It sounded nice but fell apart when one attempted to apply it to individuals. "I happen to believe," he insisted, "that the strength of America starts with probable affection within the families and it goes very early to communities, and I do not think I like to see too much centralization." On the absence of uniformity, he reminded his audience that the Supreme Court frequently split 5–4 on decisions. When Congressman Otis G. Pike inquired about the qualifications for membership on a board, Hershey admitted that one had only to be male, over thirty, and a resident of the county, but, he sallied, "this is not the only occupation we have in Government for which people are chosen that do not have to be educated." The audience roared in laughter.[17]

Hershey had even less trouble with the problem of student deferments. Critics charged that the current system of taking the oldest registrant first created uncertainty for students moving into professional careers. Others insisted that the college deferment program allowed the rich to escape and forced the poor to serve. On the uncertainty of the draft Hershey quoted President John Kennedy, observing that "life was unfair." "In life," Hershey answered, "we will never remove uncertainty, and it would ruin the human race if we did." As for taking the oldest first, this approach encouraged volunteer enlistments over a longer span of time. It also provided an incentive to keep a man working longer in the national interest. On the charge that the rich were avoiding the draft, something they had done throughout recorded history, Hershey sputtered in frustration at this perennial allegation. There were more rich college students serving in the army in 1966 than at any time in history. When he had been a battery commander, he seldom saw a high school graduate. The draft might not get all the rich sons, but it got "the ones colleges won't tolerate."[18]

The few opponents of the draft on the House committee were frustrated in questioning Hershey. Alvin O'Konski finally announced that the entire system was riddled with prejudice against the poor and "nauseates me." As a substitute, he recommended a lottery system. Hershey had enough experience with the lottery during World War II to reject the idea out of hand. A lottery presented many problems, including the difficulty of integrating the results of one lottery with the next. Repeated lotteries only increased uncertainty for the draftee. Hershey objected to the lottery primarily because it called for substituting blind chance for the decisions of local boards. He admitted that without a national system, such as a lottery, he would never be able to computerize his agency (as some wished, including the secretary of defense), but he still opposed any change. "I personally am still sticking with people," he announced. On the idea of an all-volunteer army, Hershey explained that all the army recruiters had assured him that, without the draft, their enlistees would disappear.[19]

The hearings achieved little. For the majority, who favored Hershey's approach, there was confirmation; for the minority, frustration. But the draft remained under scrutiny. President Johnson had just announced the creation of the Marshall committee to review the system. Not to be outdone (and suspicious of Johnson), Mendel Rivers created his own private review committee under the leadership of General Mark Clark. The law was not due for reconsideration until 1967. Draft calls for June 1966 dropped to a mere 18,500; McNamara launched a program of drafting and rehabilitating some 40,000 men in the 1-Y category; Hershey won a Distinguished Service Award from the Military Order of the World Wars; draft protest continued. With Congress unwilling to act and Johnson conducting another study, debate moved outside the government.[20]

In November and December a series of conferences were sponsored by various universities. Participants included a wide array of academicians and members of the Selective Service. Hershey himself attended a gathering in Washington and was met with boos. He decided to pass up another at the University of Chicago in December.[21]

In many ways, the Chicago meeting was the most important. With academicians such as Bruce Chapman, Geoffrey C. Hazard, Jr., and others, the critics of the draft had a field day. Many took their key from the earlier remarks of Kingman Brewster, president of Yale and now a member of the Marshall committee. Brewster had denounced the current draft as a mockery of the duty to serve. The Hershey system merely encouraged "cynical avoidance of service, a corruption of the aims of education, and a tarnishing of the national spirit." With the administration floundering rather than reforming, these critics called for an all-volunteer system. If not volunteers, than at least a lottery system should be used. A lottery would have some predictability, while the current system seemed to have none.[22]

Hershey sent a written statement to the Chicago conference. He welcomed a study of the draft and insisted that he was always open to constructive criticism, but he reminded the conferees that the system had three basic responsibilities: to provide men for the armed forces, to cause no disturbance to the civilian economy, and to guide deferments into areas of national interest. If the conferees ignored these duties, they would miss the point of the draft. Dee Ingold, Hershey's representative, spoke out strongly in defense of current operations in the face of a hostile audience. When the dust settled, Hershey merely yawned. He explained that he thought "it was a favorable meeting, not for what they did but rather for what they didn't do." A few "fanciful solutions" were offered, but Hershey was unimpressed. He would go his own way, confident in the support of Congress.[23]

Despite mounting criticism, Hershey welcomed the arrival of 1967. Reports from Vietnam indicated that Johnson's policy was working. The Department of Defense informed Hershey that the draft call for March would be only 11,900. The Supreme Court had refused to review the conviction of David Miller for burning his draft card, thereby upholding the new law. With these promising signs appearing, Hershey had no trouble tolerating the antiwar protesters he encountered around the country and the picketing of his headquarters. More worrisome than the few picketers was the scrutiny of the system by the Marshall committee. In addition, the draft act would come up for extension in the spring. With both the White House and Congress reviewing his operations, Hershey was to have a busy year.

Burke Marshall and his committee members had been avidly collecting information on the draft, using questionnaires and interviews. The commission finally determined that there were several problems with the existing system. The deferment and exemption apparatus had the effect of limiting service opportunities for the poor and disadvantaged, on one level, and for the brightest student and specialist on another level. The commission members also found great variations from board to board in how the rules were applied. Indeed, over 40 percent of local board members expressed a desire for more specific guidance from national headquarters. These local boards, which Hershey had always referred to as "neighbors," were not representative of urban America. Board members were all white and mostly veterans; the median age was fifty-eight, with 20 percent over seventy. The members were mostly white-collar workers and representatives of local elites. The commission found no evidence of overt bias against blacks or the poor, but it recommended an increase in minority membership and a more uniform system of rule enforcement. Given the 2 million men reaching draft age each year, the commission also felt the government could move to a system of random selection through a lottery.[24]

As soon as these findings became apparent to the White House, efforts were made to reconcile Hershey to some reform. Both Marshall and Cyrus Vance approached him. Although he privately thought the findings were misguided and, in the case of national standards, totally wrongheaded, Hershey explained that he was "a good soldier" and would support whatever program the president sent to Congress. He did indicate that he had serious reservations about the call for a uniform national policy.[25]

Califano knew that some of the recommendations would cause problems. The local board system had strong support from many governors and congressmen. Furthermore, Hershey's support would be "essential" to pushing reforms through Congress and implementing them. "We will need him," Califano explained, "and it will be important for him to continue in his current job." Califano wanted to tell Hershey that President Johnson supported the three major changes: an end to college deferments, a centralized administration, and adoption of random selection (a lottery). Johnson, however, refused. To Califano he wrote, "Don't quote me or imply. Better get his best judgment."[26]

The president knew that making a fundamental change in Selective Service would create political problems. Rivers and Russell had made their position clear. Clark's report, sponsored by Rivers, was issued on 28 February and endorsed the fundamental structure of the system, calling for only modest changes. Hershey also personally lobbied Johnson against the Marshall recommendations. At the White House one night, Hershey told his old story. If responsibility for drafting remained in the community, it would create a greater sense of national involvement. Furthermore, such an approach insured that criticism of the draft would always be defused and decentralized. The president found this last argument particularly appealing.[27]

On 6 March 1967 President Johnson finally sent his draft message to Congress. He used an approach which had served him well in the past, offering something for everyone. To the friends of the system he announced that Selective Service had done a good job and had implemented the basic concept of citizen service. All of the studies he had seen, including McNamara's, Clark's, and Marshall's, agreed on the need for a draft. He therefore called upon Congress to pass a four-year extension. For critics of the system Johnson offered several plums. He recommended that induction take place at age nineteen under a system of random selection. He also called for tightening up on undergraduate deferments and an end to graduate deferments except in the health sciences. He recommended an improved system of counseling, with more information to the registrant, and more time for appeals. He also promised to work at making local boards more representative of the community. As for the centralization of the system, Johnson hedged. Using what was now his accustomed method, he decided to appoint yet another study group to study Marshall's study, which had followed fast upon the heels of McNamara's study. This new study group consisted of McNamara, Director of the Budget Charles L. Schultze, and Lewis Hershey.[28]

Since most of Johnson's "reforms" were cosmetics and could be implemented without new legislation, Hershey wasted no time. On the problem of uniformity, he appointed a committee of his senior staff members to study and report. Each state director was asked to do the same. As for increasing information on how the draft worked, he sent out copies of the various studies to each state, revised several pamphlets explaining the draft, and scheduled several personal appearances on radio and television. On a substantive level, he drafted an executive order for Johnson's signature which extended from ten days to thirty days the time in which a registrant could appeal his classification. Hershey also sent out a bulletin instructing local boards to inform each registrant, after classification, that an appeal agent was available to help with any challenge.[29]

Hershey had every reason to stall before implementing any fundamental changes. He was reasonably confident that, when Congress began hearings on a draft extension, there would be little interest in abolishing the local boards. As a member of the Marshall committee admitted, "General Hershey is an institution in himself. He personifies the system, the local draft boards and the whole process." The institution was still popular in Congress. Already Congressman F. Edward Hebert and Senator John C. Stennis had indicated a willingness to draft a law to protect local boards. Hershey knew he had a strong argument in favor of the local boards. "If you can get the people to participate in their mobilization," he explained, "then you've got something." To use regional centers would make the system remote from the people when critics were already complaining that it was too remote in New York City. Having run the system without major scandal for twenty-seven years, Hershey planned no important changes until Congress had spoken.[30]

Congress could speak with many voices. Hershey expected hearings to begin in the armed services committees, filled with his supporters. To his surprise, he found himself on 20 March speaking to a subcommittee of the Senate Committee on Labor and Public Welfare. Edward M. Kennedy had assumed temporary chairmanship of this subcommittee and planned to push upon Hershey a national classification scheme, random selection, and an end to all student deferments. Despite the forceful questioning of Senators Kennedy and Joseph S. Clark, Hershey remained unconvinced of the need for substantial reform. He admitted that he was now in favor of taking the youngest men first and probably would implement some form of random choice; he was a team player and the president had called these signals. He warned, however, that random choice would not end criticism of the draft. He could give no precise date when these limited changes would take place. As for the idea of a more centralized system, he made clear his firm opposition. "I suppose one can be proud of very little in this life," he preached, but he was proud that he had persuaded American citizens "to participate . . . without pay in one of the most thankless jobs we can imagine."[31]

The Kennedy hearings provided Hershey with a warmup for the big show—the draft extension sessions of April and May 1967, as civil disobedience and demonstrations increased.[32] Hershey learned at first hand that the protest movement had become more violent. On 21 March he appeared for a talk at Howard University in Washington. Before he could speak, a group of protesters began shouting and disrupting the meeting. Hershey left without speaking. The *New York*

Times complained that the incident resembled "ugly censorship," and officials at the university moved to punish the demonstrators. In Congress, Rivers again called for the drafting of protesters.[33]

Hershey still remained undisturbed about the protest. (He refused to accept a friend's suggestion that the protesters were part of a communist conspiracy. The communist, Hershey insisted, had too much sense to engage in such frolics.) Protesters represented only a small minority of the student population. He explained, "They have some queers just the same as any place, except in Congress." He dismissed some of the protest as mere youthful exuberance: "The college kids in Ann Arbor have always been playful." He remembered that during his childhood the circus refused to stop in Ann Arbor because "the college students would always tear the tent down." A few of the students had, he felt, gone to school "longer than they should for the amount of storage space they had for ideas," but he remained undismayed by the criticism he received.[34] The public was less serene; a CBS poll in early 1967 indicated that only 46 percent of the public favored the current draft operations. Public opinion notwithstanding, Congress preferred to rely again, as it had for many years, on the testimony of General Hershey.[35]

Appearing before the Senate committee in April and the House committee in May, Hershey provided a colorful contrast to witnesses from the Department of Defense who, like one of McNamara's computers, regurgitated endless statistics. With all of his warts, his white hair still in a crewcut, his vision so poor that he dared not attempt to read a statement, Hershey was full of life and strong opinions about his system. He was in a unique position—he simply knew so much more than the committee members that he had little difficulty in answering, avoiding, or obfuscating whenever he chose. The legislators welcomed him with open arms. Richard Russell, chairman of the Senate Armed Services Committee, deliberately scheduled Hershey as the final witness so that he could "clear up some of the confusion and misconceptions that have been created regarding the draft law and its administration." Hershey was to have the last word. Senator Stennis lauded him as the greatest bureaucrat in Washington. A similar welcome awaited him in the House, where Charles A. Halleck recommended that the general be awarded a Purple Heart for the abuse he had been receiving on college campuses.[36]

Before launching into a general defense of his organization, Hershey admitted that "I think the Congress has been, throughout the years, the best friend I ever had." So Congress would remain. After explaining how Selective Service had done its job in filling calls, Hershey listed the current reforms he had adopted at President Johnson's urging. Throughout his testimony in both the Senate and the House hearings he discussed similar topics. Although wide ranging in his speech, he provided his listeners with several strong opinions. The law as currently drafted was good because of its flexibility. He had no use for any attempt to do away with the autonomy of local boards by substituting some centralized system.[37]

Hershey made it clear to Congress that he preferred to stand by the status quo. He admitted that he much preferred the Clark to the Marshall report. As an administrator, Hershey was willing to work with whatever law Congress passed, but he had received clear signals from the president that he was free to speak out. He pointed to Johnson's appointment of a special taskforce to study the Marshall recommendations as evidence that debate was still open.[38]

Johnson had called for a system of random selection in his message to Congress. Hershey admitted that he was a very recent convert to this idea; further questioning revealed that he was an even more recent apostate. He admitted that the entire operation was designed to provide a better image for the draft. Personally, he wondered at this strategy. The argument seemed to be that a lottery could be handled by machines, and that removing individual decisions would remove inequity. Yet Hershey pointed out that inequity was built into the system because not everyone would be in the pool for random selection. All men with deferments, defects, and key jobs would remain outside the pool. Still, as a presidential loyalist, he would work up a random selection scheme.[39]

Congressmen also raised the issue of student deferments. Several, including Senators Howard Cannon and John Stennis, sympathized with the drafting of protesters.[40] Since President Johnson was already preparing an executive order ending all graduate-student deferments, Hershey explained that he had decided to stop the SSCQT; yet he had not lost faith in the undergraduate deferment program. Since he did not need to draft everyone who became eligible, he defended the flexibility of the current law. Such a policy allowed the country to ensure the proper training of its manpower. If college graduates were worthless, then he recommended an investigation of colleges.[41]

The general saved his strongest statement for challenges to decentralization. When Chairman Rivers in the House committee announced, "We need uniformity," Hershey quickly replied, "No we don't." When Congressman Richard Schweiker urged him to become the commander-in-chief of the system and bring order to local boards, Hershey used an old analogy about battles being lost because platoon commanders would not take the initiative. "Uniformity," he explained, "is something that everybody talks about and nobody knows what they are talking about when they say it." Having thus called several committee members fools, albeit indirectly, Hershey went on to explain that he had examined thousands of files and never found two exactly alike. If Congress decided to adopt the recommendation of General Clark, limiting local board tours to ten years, Hershey would certainly go along, but he would prefer to acquiesce without a law. He urged the committees to retain the fine flexibility which existed in the current law.[42]

Even before the hearings concluded Hershey was confident that he had won another big battle. In some cases the victory came because he had simply outlasted and frustrated his questioners. His only worry was that Congress, in an anti-reform mood, might attempt to write a more restrictive law than he would prefer. "I personally opposed any encroachment on Executive authority," he told his state directors, "even though the Executive at the moment may be under the influences that I regret." But he was quite confident that in 1968 he would be operating with a law identical to the old one, "despite all the talk." He predicted—correctly, as it turned out—that Congress might just make it harder to revise the old system.[43]

While Congress debated the bill, President Johnson appeared before a conference of Hershey's state directors. On 3 May 1967 he called for a system of induction which would be fairer to all. He wanted to make local boards more representative of the communities. Yet, on the fundamental issue of local control, he again announced that the idea of centralization "needed further study." He was confident that the state directors would be pleased with the results.[44]

The final bill, which Johnson signed on 30 June 1967, did include some of the recommendations put forth by reformers. In contrast to several early drafts, the final law allowed the president to call the youngest draftees first. Local board members were limited to a twenty-five-year tenure and had to retire at seventy-five. Sexual discrimination in membership was specifically prohibited. The law even made a slight bow toward national uniformity of standards by stating that the president "may . . . recommend criteria for the classification of persons subject to induction." If he decided such action was required in the national interest, he could "recommend that such criteria be administered uniformly throughout the United States whenever practicable."[45]

But Congress still had faith in Hershey's decentralized system, the Marshall report notwithstanding. The law clearly specified that no local or appeal board or other agency of Selective Service was forced to defer any person because he was engaged in any study or activity in the national interest. While Congress was willing to expand membership on the boards to include women, it had no intention of diluting the local board's power to classify. As for the related idea of a random selection procedure, the law prohibited the president from adopting any such idea without new congressional authorization. The definition of a conscientious objector excluded specifically as grounds for deferment any political, sociological, or philosophical views and "merely personal moral codes." Congress prohibited judicial review of any classification, unless it involved a criminal prosecution, until after a registrant had accepted or rejected an order to report for induction. Sending a direct message to the attorney general, the law warned that, at Hershey's request, the Justice Department "shall proceed as expeditiously as possible with a prosecution under this section." If his department refused to act, the attorney general "shall advise the House . . . and the Senate in writing the reasons for its failure to do so."[46]

Despite the unreconstructed tenor of the bill, Califano urged President Johnson to sign it. The bill had passed by huge majorities: 377–29 in the House and 72–23 in the Senate. Hershey had indicated a willingness to work with Attorney General Ramsey Clark to "resolve any problems."[47] The president himself had serious reservations about radical revisions; indeed, his hesitancy was revealed in the way he piled one study group upon another. Johnson signed the bill on 30 June 1967. Clearly Hershey's approach to the draft remained overwhelmingly popular in Congress.[48]

Johnson tried to ease the defeat of the Marshall committee by using the cosmetic device of another study. By appointing Hershey to the new committee the president must have expected little change, yet when the special task force first met both McNamara and Schultze stated that Selective Service "was an archaic system that needed to be completely restructured." Hershey and General Carter Magruder, the committee's secretary, disagreed with any call for drastic revision. The committee seemed headed for a stalemate. Magruder nonetheless asked the departments of defense, budget, and Selective Service to share in investigating all charges. Representatives from defense and budget presented the objections to existing arrangements; Selective Service presented a defense.[49]

After nine months of study at all levels, the report went to the president on 9 January 1968. It provided additional vindication for Hershey. The present system should be kept. The local and state structure, the report concluded, "exemplifies the best in our democratic tradition of local citizenry participation in, responsibility for, and support of a necessary governmental activity." Reading much like a Hershey speech, the report continued that the local boards were able to make better judgments on social and economic facts than could a distant board.

Gubernatorial participation was considered a "noteworthy strength." Most damaging to the reformers was the task force study of alleged lack of uniformity. Such charges of inequity rested on "statistical findings relating to procedure and policy" but were unsupported by the final actions of local and appeal boards, which "showed a high degree of uniformity, in spite of widely varying procedural practices."[50]

The task force did make several recommendations involving modest administrative reforms. These included having Hershey intensify his efforts to develop additional criteria for local boards' guidance, standardizing operating procedures so boards could "avoid the appearance of lack of uniformity," and expanding field supervision and review of the system. With these actions, the task force concluded, "we think the system will meet the objective of equity you [Johnson] established." McNamara still desperately wanted a random selection scheme, but he could not overrule a study his own staff had helped prepare. He sought to save face by calling for a review of the results of the new program after one year. "If current inequities in the system have not been eliminated," he warned, "further action will be required."[51]

Califano sent a copy of the report to Hershey with the note that the president wanted action. Since the report amounted to an endorsement of Hershey's original position, what Johnson wanted remained unclear. Hershey sought publicity for the report because it refuted much of the Marshall study. When the press finally learned of it, reporters poured into Hershey's office for questions. Seated behind his huge desk and circled by fifty state flags, Hershey smiled like a contented cat with a mousetail hanging from his lips. Dressed in a black suit with a beaver scout tieclasp shining from his tie, he admitted that he was "very favorably impressed" with the report. He had always been disinclined to change a working system. As for the Marshall report and its recommendations, he acknowledged that he had good friends on that committee but could not help wondering "what they were eating" when they made their recommendations. When one reporter asked Hershey whether he would continue operating the draft as he had in the past, he replied, "I'll go along with you on that."[52]

Hershey had survived yet another attack on his "family," but he had to accept some changes. Congress had indicated clearly that women were eligible for board duty. When it came to women, Hershey was decidedly conventional. He had helped draft the original law prohibiting women from serving on local boards because he feared they would be embarrassed when a physical question emerged. By 1966 he admitted that he had a plan to draft women should the need arise. "Whenever we need women," he insisted, "I think we ought to draft them." But he did not think women should be drafted to support any abstract notion of equality of sexes, because he found them "not alike in several very commendable respects."[53]

The issue he confronted in 1967 was not drafting women, but using them as part of the draft system. He had always used them in some capacities. Women worked as clerks for almost every local board. He had a few women in civil service grades at national headquarters and in clerical positions, but this tokenism failed to satisfy critics and President Johnson. Now, with the 1967 law lifting the prohibition against women serving on local boards, Hershey sought to convince governors that they should seek out female appointees. With great fanfare he announced the appointment of the first woman to a local board in September 1967. (Mrs. Emma Tibbets of Rapid City, South Dakota, was also a member of the Santee tribe of Sioux.) He traveled to Fort Lauderdale in May 1968 to recognize the appointment of Mrs. Janet C. Heinrich, the first female appointee in Florida. Mrs. Heinrich announced to the press, "I'm inspired by this man, General Hershey." Mrs. Pearl B. Wollins, the first woman appointed in New York, announced that she hoped to bring compassion to the draft. By July 1968 there were fifty-four women among the 17,000 local board members. Almost all of them were white and middle class.[54]

White was another problem. The race of local board members was a part of a long-standing system of segregation. Harry S Truman had ordered an end to segregated units in the armed forces and had stopped racial calls in 1948; Hershey had then acted swiftly to remove all references to race from his records. His attitude toward the entire race question evolved over the years and kept pace with that of most middle-class Americans. Raised in an area where the race question seldom emerged because there were few blacks, Hershey unconsciously adopted traditional racism. Yet during World War II he began to understand that racism created serious problems for mobilizing society in national defense. For this reason, rather than because of any sudden enlightenment, he became a foe of Jim Crow.

By the 1950's the Supreme Court had ruled against segregation, and civil rights became a major domestic problem. In April 1956 Hershey responded to a request from the Institute for Religious and Social Studies of New York City by penning an essay on "human equality." In his one and only foray into the theoretical aspects of racism, he bemoaned the lack of progress in understanding human relations. "I do believe," he wrote, "that race and color are rationalizations for both to justify possession by the haves and to furnish excuses for the have-nots." He added that ending separate calls and removing the race category on Selective Service records "seems to me to constitute an advance in improving human relationships." But he had certain reservations about more radical calls for equality. He would not support any program of compensatory aid but preferred allowing minorities to compete equally. He also rejected the simplistic theory that inequality would disappear with the end of racial, religious, or language discrimination.[55]

Hershey's interest in the race question was more than merely theoretical. In 1956 he found himself embroiled in a case which went to the heart of black efforts to desegregate the South. That year a black boycott of buses in Montgomery, Alabama, became a cause célèbre. Fred D. Gray, a local minister and attorney, filed suit in federal court to end segregation on city buses. Gray, as a minister, had a draft exemption. His actions in the bus boycott led his local board to reclassify him into 1-A status. Since it was clear to many that the reclassification was a punitive action, Hershey was besieged with calls from the National Association for the Advancement of Colored People and other groups. After examining the Gray file and receiving additional evidence, Hershey halted all action on Gray's induction and requested that the local board reopen his case. Gray had held a ministerial exemption for five years.[56]

In Alabama, Johnny Rebs rose up. George Wallace (an appeal agent) and a dozen other members of the system submitted their resignations and denounced Hershey's political interference. The protest had little effect. As Hershey explained to his critics, Gray enjoyed a ministerial *exemption*, not a deferment. Such exemptions were based on a national belief in the importance of maintaining religious life during war and peace. As for charges that Gray had been engaged in secular activities, Hershey insisted that determination of his status should depend only on his ministerial activities. "Let us not forget," he wrote, "that the greatest of them all worked as a carpenter, and that his ministry at times was on a part-time basis."[57]

This controversy soon disappeared, but Hershey could not escape the problem of race. In the 1960's, with the expansion of civil rights agitation, the growth of an independent youth protest movement, and the anti-Vietnam activity, the issue of racial discrimination in the draft reemerged. Black leaders charged that the draft was discriminating against black Americans in induction calls. Statistics showed that blacks made up 31 percent of all combat troops at the start of the Vietnam war and, in 1965, accounted for 24 percent of all combat deaths. While it was true that blacks constituted a large percentage of the armed forces, this had come about because the army, in particular, had proved to be one of the few havens of opportunity and advancement for blacks. As for the charge that blacks were being drafted in a discriminatory fashion, this accusation had little to do with Hershey. The armed forces decided who would be accepted for induction. The president and Congress had helped create a deferment system which provided maximum protection to middle-class whites. Racism in National Guard units blocked this avenue of escape from the draft for blacks. But when all men in the eligible age group were counted, it was clear that blacks were drafted in a smaller proportion than were whites. The draft system, in fact, enjoyed a higher favorable opinion among black draftees than it did among whites.[58]

Although black men might regard the draft as more equitable, since World War II very few of them had been appointed to local boards. Since the job drew no pay and one's selection for it depended upon status, middle-class white professionals predominated. But with the rise of black consciousness in the 1960's and the disenchantment over Vietnam, the all-white character of the boards proved embarrassing for Johnson and Hershey. In May 1966 Hershey found it necessary to fire Jack Helm, the chairman of the largest draft board in Louisiana, who was also the grand dragon of the state's Ku Klux Klan. In the Bedford-Stuyvesant area of New York, some 300,000 blacks found that their "little group of neighbors" was all white. Hershey tried to defend this situation by explaining that Nelson Rockefeller and other governors were responsible for local boards. Of course, the boards *were* representative, in a sense—if the community itself was controlled by a white oligarchy, as was frequently the case. But the boards did not mirror the racial makeup of many communities.[59]

When President Johnson signed the new Selective Service law in 1967 he was well aware of the lack of black membership on local boards. Of over 17,000 members less than 1.5 percent were black. Unfortunately, unlike other purely federal programs, Selective Service was not easily amenable to an executive order. Congress had just reaffirmed the role of the governors, and one of these roles was to appoint local board members. Attorney General Ramsey Clark and others nevertheless began pressing Johnson to end discrimination. In Alabama and Mississippi no blacks were serving on boards, and a few black draftees refused to accept induction by all-white boards. Hershey, when approached about the problem, warned that usurping governors' prerogatives would create other political problems. He believed that, given time, he could bring about reform by talking with governors. Because he had no other option, Johnson decided to give Hershey an opportunity.[60]

Hershey faced a formidable task in the South. In Texas he managed to obtain an agreement for the appointment of one black and one Mexican-American. In Florida he obtained the appointment of fourteen blacks, but only five on local boards. During telephone conversations and private meetings with Governor George Wallace, a former appeal agent, Hershey received a promise of cooperation, but by July 1968 only three blacks had been appointed to local boards in Alabama. Mississippi was impossible: one year after Hershey began his effort, there were still no blacks on local boards. Hershey was convinced that his failure was due to the violent racism which had emerged during primary elections. More changes occurred in Arkansas (from 0 to 35), Louisiana (0 to 40), Missouri (1 to 28), South Carolina (1 to 12), Texas (8 to 26), and Georgia (2 to 17).[61]

Hershey made some progress. From a modest total of only 278 blacks on local boards in January 1967 the figure rose steadily until by January 1970 there were 1,188. Although this was only a little over 5 percent of the 18,749 total board members, the figures had climbed steadily. During 1968 and 1969 thirty to forty blacks were joining local boards each month, despite the absence of pay and the criticism by others that they were Uncle Toms. The system in January 1970 was quite different from what it had been in 1967, not merely because of the blacks but also because of some 190 women and 575 Mexican-Americans. In May 1970 Hershey visited a small town in South Carolina. A reception was arranged at the home of a white physician. To Hershey's surprise, the sole black member of the local board was invited to the reception and to the dinner which followed at a local Kiwanis club. Hershey admitted, "I realize this is a pretty small start but at least it was some beginning."[62]

The campaign to appoint minorities did little to deflate the growing protest movement against the war and the draft. The war in Vietnam continued to prove intractable, and local draft boards continued to send their unpopular messages. Draft calls during the last six months of 1967 were lower than usual, averaging only 21,850 a month, but with President Johnson deeply committed to victory everyone knew they would have to rise. By January 1968 calls were at 34,000 per month; the Department of Defense recommended 48,000 for April. Hershey soon found himself surrounded by antiwar and antidraft picketers at his headquarters, at his home, and on the road. Their signs said, "The draft equals slavery."[63]

The resistance was only beginning. "Draft Protest Day," 16 October 1967, was proclaimed across the nation. Thousands of young and old turned out to demonstrate in major cities. In Boston hundreds of draft cards, or reasonable facsimiles, were destroyed. Protesters poured blood on draft records. Joan Baez was arrested in Oakland, where demonstrators attempted to burn down an induction station. At Selective Service headquarters a group of protesters demanded to see Hershey. He was out of town but his assistant, Daniel Omer, had ten of the group in for a talk. After the meeting Omer told reporters he thought the young men were simply mad at the war and were basically decent chaps. Such an attitude was not shared by the White House. President Johnson was fed up with the demonstrations. To cap a dismal month for Johnson, on 21 October thousands of protesters, including the author Norman Mailer, marched on the Pentagon. After an unsuccessful attempt to levitate this center of the war machine, the crowd dispersed, scattering flowers on the way. When a few demonstrators sought to force entry, they were promptly beaten and arrested by the police and National Guard.[64]

President Johnson reacted to these protests in a manner that Hershey was soon to regret. Frustrated over the failure in Vietnam, over the stubbornness of Ho Chi Minh and the Viet Cong, and disappointed over the derailing of his Great Society programs, Johnson was in no mood to coddle protesters. He wished to strike out at his domestic critics. He found the perfect instrument in the draft, and a willing subordinate in General Hershey.

When Hershey had approved the drafting of protesters at Ann Arbor in 1965, Johnson had said nothing. In the discussions over the draft the president had indicated his sympathy for Hershey's interpretation of the law. In early 1967 Johnson issued an executive order which allowed men convicted of violating the draft law to be paroled for active duty in the armed forces. During the debate on the 1967 law Rivers, Hebert, and other legislators had complained that the Justice Department was not moving fast enough on prosecuting draft violators. Johnson agreed. On 20 October 1967, during the national draft protest, Johnson wrote a stinging letter to Attorney General Ramsey Clark, requesting prompt reports on the "progress of investigations . . . of any violations of law involved." Johnson explained to Clark, "It is important that violations of law be dealt with firmly, promptly and fairly." The next day Mailer and the protesters marched on the Pentagon and Johnson decided to use another instrument of pressure. He called Hershey and asked what could be done. Hershey mentioned that the law provided for drafting those who became delinquent; illegally protesting the war seemed an obvious case of delinquency. Johnson immediately approved the idea and instructed Hershey to send out the orders.[65]

Within the next three days Hershey sent out a series of instructions to his system which eventually erased his aura of political invulnerability. On 24 October Local Board Memorandum No. 85 was issued to cover the burning of draft cards. Hershey informed all board members that, when a draftee destroyed or returned his card, the board should immediately declare him delinquent and reclassify him as 1-A. The next day a letter went to state directors informing them that any person counseling evasion of the draft or interfering with its administration should be reported to the U.S. attorney and to national headquarters.[66]

Hershey saved his most potent broadside for 26 October. In a letter to all members of the system, he explained that the purpose of the draft was to insure the survival of the nation. Since the obligation to serve was universal in the liable age group, and since deferments were given only in the national interest, he called on all local boards to begin reclassifying protesters. "It is obvious," he wrote, "that any action that violates the Military Selective Service Act or the Regulations, or the related processes, cannot be in the National interest." Logically, violators "should be denied deferment." In addition, he insisted that any activity which frustrated recruiting or caused men to refuse to serve was against the national interest. Participation in illegal demonstrations should influence the board's classification decisions. Unlike the earlier Ann Arbor case, Hershey now wanted local boards to consider reclassifying *all* protesters who were upsetting President Johnson. Trying to play both sides, Hershey did ask the boards to consider reporting information to U.S. attorneys for prosecution; the board members, however, had years of experience with the problem and knew the director preferred a draft action to a prison term.[67]

Not satisfied with enlisting the system in the suppression of protest, Hershey also acted to turn his agency into an auxiliary police force. He wrote to all government appeal agents (lawyers assigned to each board to provide counseling to draftees) with a request that they inform the local board if a registrant had violated the draft law. If the appeal agent had new information on noneligible men, that information should be reported to the state director. Hershey wanted the information so that local boards could quickly process as delinquents the liable men and report to the Justice Department those not liable. Several members of Hershey's own staff worried over this attempt to turn appeal agents into stool pigeons, but the president had ordered action, and Hershey delivered. His own inclinations closely paralleled those of the commander-in-chief.[68]

This assault on the domestic front was no sooner launched than Hershey found himself standing alone. He had expected President Johnson to back up the letters. Remembering the uproar over the University of Michigan incident, Hershey now sought an executive order from Johnson. On 27 October Hershey sent Charles Schultze a draft of an executive order which gave presidential legitimacy to the letters already released. As Hershey explained to Schultze, the EO would change the regulations so that delinquency could be defined on the basis of positive actions against the draft, rather than the existing provisions which required a failure to act on the part of the registrant. Hershey assured Schultze that the order was clearly covered in the law and that "there appears to me no possible reason why all registrants who are violators of the . . . law should not be considered as delinquents." Hershey urged that the order "be processed without delay in order to assist me in prompt compliance with the President's directive."[69]

To Hershey's surprise, President Johnson decided to stay in the background. As the executive order moved through the labyrinth of the White House staff, more and more reservations emerged about the wisdom of having Johnson sign it. The Bureau of the Budget complained that the order did not provide clear criteria for determining which positive acts were prohibited by law. Some argued that the entire matter was essentially a judicial rather than an administrative responsibility. Larry Levinson, a White House aide, made the problems clear in a memo to Califano. The order gave the impression of punishing protesters, which would bring down the "wrath of liberals on us." Levinson was not sure the order could survive a court test. Surprisingly, Attorney General Clark responded to the order in a more positive manner. He felt Hershey could get away with his order if inductions were limited to those who committed an offense involving their own personal draft status, rather than merely violating the law.[70]

The most convincing argument against any executive order involved political reality rather than legal niceties. Johnson was already feeling the pressure from his former liberal followers, who were deserting him over the war. He could ill afford any more gratuitous insults by approving Hershey's action. Califano put it bluntly: "I believe it is important that you stay out of this controversy." When Hershey learned of this attitude, he bore up bravely and informed Califano that the executive order would not be needed. Both Califano and Johnson breathed easier.[71]

Hershey's instructions had hardly reached local boards before a cry of protest arose. The reaction came from some surprising quarters. Without mentioning Hershey by name, W. Willard Wirtz, the secretary of labor, condemned the idea of drafting protesters. Israel Margolies of the People's Temple of New York City called the letter a "disgrace to our democracy." While speaking at Colgate University, Abe Fortas, a Supreme Court justice and a close friend of President Johnson, denounced Hershey. Fortas assured his audience that the letter did not have White House approval. Even Richard Nixon, planning his political resurrection, now endorsed a volunteer army to replace the draft. One editor commented, "When Nixon prepares to abandon a ship it must truly be sinking."[72]

The response from the academic community was just as heated. Grayson Kirk, the chancellor at Columbia, announced that the letter was a disgrace and ordered a ban on all campus military recruiting until it was revoked. Deans and chancellors at Brown, Cornell, Stanford, and other institutions shared in the protest. Meanwhile, the American Civil Liberties Union joined with the National Student Association and the Students for a Democratic Society to challenge this punitive reclassification. This strategy had little effect at first, because a federal district judge ruled that Hershey's letter was merely a personal opinion and had no legal standing.[73]

The press was also critical. Richard Harwood of the *San Francisco Chronicle* wrote a lengthy article presenting a biographical sketch of Hershey, the enduring bureaucrat. Harwood compared Hershey to J. Edgar Hoover of the FBI, observing that Hershey, too, "has grown immune to the shifting tides of both politics and public opinion." Russell Baker of the *New York Times* took a more sardonic view, complaining that Hershey was going soft. The general had insisted that military service was a privilege, but now he seemed willing to pass the reward to campus loafers and troublemakers. "General Hershey's attitude reflects a weakness of will, a disturbing tendency to permissiveness." Instead of such rewards as military service, Baker recommended four years in a chemistry lab. Not many younger men could afford to take such a jocular view of Hershey's actions.[74]

Although Congressman Rivers thought Hershey's action only fitting "for these buzzards," others disagreed. In the Senate, Edward Kennedy, Philip Hart, Mark Hatfield, Jacob Javits, and others cosponsored a bill to prohibit the drafting of protesters. In the House, eight congressmen called for Hershey's immediate retirement. John E. Moss, chairman of the subcommittee on government operations, began a series of letters to Hershey, demanding that he cite the authority for such an order.[75]

Hershey did have a defense of his action, but his correspondence with Moss did little to clear the air. Moss released his initial letter to the press before Hershey received it; this prompted Hershey to suggest that Moss wanted not an answer, but only publicity. Hershey recommended that Moss talk with Rivers because "I know of no more accurate reflection of the intent of Congress than the statement of the chairman of the committee with jurisdiction over Selective Service." The dialogue went downhill from here. Moss replied by accusing Hershey of ignorance and being no longer fit to serve as director. The problem, Hershey countered, was Moss's attitude that acts which interfered with the draft should be considered solely as criminal actions and should not serve as a basis for local board classification. As for the 26

October letter, Hershey informed Moss, "I subscribe to it in its entirety and my . . . letter remains in effect without modification." Rivers publicly warned Moss that if he summoned Hershey before "the subcommittee to horsewhip him . . . if necessary I'll appeal to the leadership to stop him." Hershey did not appear before Moss's subcommittee.[76]

Many Americans disliked protesters waving enemy flags and breaking the law. The letters which poured into Selective Service headquarters were overwhelmingly favorable to Hershey. The American Legion and twenty other veterans' organizations telegraphed the president in support of Hershey's action. Ironically, Hershey was on safe legal ground because he had issued no directives; only the president could officially change the regulations. Hershey's "advice," however, had the impact of a marching order to the members of his administrative family. While the courts might eventually challenge his statements, local boards were already acting.[77]

Hershey's defense of his action appealed to many Americans. He pointed out that military service should not be considered punishment. Deferment, according to Hershey, was not justified if it did not promote the national interest. Congress had recognized the power of local boards in the recent draft law, which had restricted the jurisdictions of the court. Privately, Hershey also defended his letter because he believed that the current wave of protest threatened the survival of the nation and the morale of troops. The soldiers in Vietnam, he explained to Bruce Comly French, could not understand how college students, a privileged class, could get away with such actions. His letter would reassure the boys in Vietnam that the nation would not succumb to lawlessness. He was disappointed that some political leaders seemed more interested in short-range popularity.[78]

Defending himself against the protests of a few congressmen and college presidents was relatively easy. Hershey, however, soon found himself at odds with the Justice Department,[79] where, under the law, the responsibility for prosecuting violators of the draft law rested. As protests increased, so did prosecutions. In fiscal 1966 652 prosecutions resulted in 366 convictions. In the first nine months of fiscal 1967 939 prosecutions resulted in 510 convictions. These statistics satisfied neither members of Congress nor President Johnson. Resentment boiled over at the antidraft statements of such men as Stokely Carmichael, Cassius Clay, and Martin Luther King. During the debate on draft renewal in 1967 Chairman Rivers called for increased prosecution. When representatives from the Justice Department argued that the protest was legitimate under the First Amendment, F. Edward Hebert recommended that the Justice Department "forget the First Amendment," or let the courts worry with it. After Hershey issued his October letter, lawyers in the Justice Department expressed serious reservations about its legality.[80]

Hershey had expected trouble with the department even before he issued the letter. He explained to the White House that "the lack of reasonable enforcement of the law" and the lack of funds were the major problems facing the Selective Service System, and he insisted that the lack of prosecution was "contrary to the desire of the President." As a partial remedy he recommended reinterpreting registration as induction and putting the men under the jurisdiction of military courts. In other words, he wanted to take Selective Service out from under the civil courts. Attorney General Clark explained to the president that his department was acting vigorously. The number of draft prosecutions in 1967 set a record. In 1953 twice as many men had been called as in 1967, whereas the number of men who failed to report in 1967 was only one-third of the comparable total in 1953. Many delinquencies resulted merely from procedural problems, not from willful violations. The Justice Department, with Hershey's approval, always allowed such men to fulfill their induction commitment rather than suffer prosecution. Hershey's new letter, however, presented many problems. Several government attorneys thought Hershey's recommendations were unconstitutional.[81]

Hershey could ignore such comments because he felt he had the silent support of President Johnson. Hershey knew there would be a dispute over what constituted a violation of the draft law, but he made it clear that his recommendations stood, even if the Department of Justice objected. He would pull back only if ordered to do so by the president. He also knew he had strong support from Mendel Rivers, who applauded the October letter and suggested that the attorney general make clear what additional authority Hershey needed. Rivers was sure Congress would provide that authority.[82]

Within weeks, however, Hershey realized that the president was apprehensive about the protests the letter had provoked. The proposed executive order died in the White House. Hershey decided to trim his sails by explaining to the press that his letter was "only an opinion because I don't have any power to direct local boards." As Hershey's opinion within the system resembled the opinion of Wilt Chamberlain at a midgets' convention, something more substantive was needed to defuse the issue. Under White House guidance, Hershey and Ramsey Clark drew up a joint statement to provide reassurance to such men as Kingman Brewster. The letter was released on 9 December and made several points: Legal protesters should have no fear of their deferments being cancelled, but those registrants who violated some duty which affected their own status as draftees might be declared delinquent and be advanced for induction. Acts which violated federal law would be handled according to the nature of the conduct. In addition, the Justice Department would establish a special unit to coordinate prompt prosecution of draft offenders, including those who counseled evasion of the draft.[83]

The joint statement did little to end the controversy. Clark felt vindicated because he had insisted that lawful protest, even against the draft system, should not lead to accelerated induction. Nevertheless, Hershey made it clear to Neil Sheehan of the *New York Times* that the joint statement had not invalidated the October letter. Although emphasizing that he and Clark were "not at war," Hershey explained, "I'll continue to act according to my lights and he'll continue to act according to his lights, and if we have a case to discuss then we'll talk about it." The basic disagreement centered on the definition of delinquency. According to the original definition, a delinquent obtained that status by failing to do something. Hershey had broadened the definition to include positive acts against the system. "When a fellow goes into a draft board and pours ink on his own file," Hershey explained, "then there's no disagreement—he's affecting his own status. But when he goes in and pours ink on his brother's file—there's the disagreement." Later Hershey insisted that the differences between his October letter and the joint statement only amounted to "verbiage, a hollow exercise in semantics."[84]

President Johnson, besides his other headaches, was now confronted with the embarrassing public spectacle of Clark and Hershey arguing over the law. Califano explained to Johnson that the Justice Department planned to insist that only a direct illegal action against one's own draft status merited acceleration. Hershey was just as adamant in his own views. Califano complained that Hershey "keeps citing you [Johnson] to Ramsey and me as authority for his earlier memorandum." While Califano agreed with Clark, he admitted that, if Johnson rejected Hershey, the congressional armed services committees would raise hell. Johnson preferred to remain above the battle, but he did authorize Califano to write to eight Ivy League presidents, telling them that the system "is not an instrument to repress and punish unpopular views." Nor did the law vest the system or the local boards with "the judicial role in determining the legality of individual conduct." Undeterred, Hershey continued on his path and refused comment on Califano's letter.[85]

The squabble finally had to be settled in the courts, rather than in the White House. Hershey's letter had no sooner been issued than dozens of court challenges emerged. As these cases slowly worked their way through the appeal system, Hershey had reason for concern. He had always worried about how the courts would treat the administrative regulations of his system. During the Korean war, as rapid draft expansion led to increases in delinquency, the courts, by granting delays, had proved a thorn in his side. He warned that, when the nation lost respect for its courts, it would be because the courts had brought it on themselves. He told his aides to seek all nonjudicial means of resolving problems. They should go to court only if many men refused to serve, rather than because of some individual technicality. When Earl Warren had taken his seat as chief justice, Hershey had warned him that the future of the country would depend "on the manner in which the Supreme Court . . . meets its challenges." [86]

By 1968 Hershey's judicial position seemed very vulnerable. Several lower courts declared his October letter ill advised. At first the courts refused to rule for the plaintiff because the letter constituted merely Hershey's private opinion, rather than a regulation, but when local boards continued to operate on the basis of a habit formed over twenty-seven years in carrying out Hershey's opinion, the courts began intervening. Hershey became increasingly angry and frustrated over the problem. He kept arguing that the Selective Service was an administrative rather than a judicial agency, and that the courts were trying to assume the power of classification. Of course, he admitted, "we fool around with the law, lots of agencies in Washington fool with the law without going to court." But he refused to rescind his letter as court cases continued. [87]

The Justice Department was to have the last word after all. The issue came to a head over the case of James J. Oestereich, a twenty-four-year old ministry student who had turned in his draft card in protest against the war. His local board had immediately reclassified him 1-A. Oestereich brought suit not merely against the reclassification but against the provision of the draft law which precluded judicial review until he had refused induction. To Hershey's surprise and dismay, Erwin N. Griswold, the solicitor general of the United States, used the case to attack Hershey's October letter. Oestereich had lost his case in a lower court because of the congressional restriction on court review. In 1968, however, he appealed to the Supreme Court, and Griswold submitted a lengthy brief recommending that the court hear the case. [88]

Hershey attempted to prevent the review by writing his own brief and submitting it directly to Chief Justice Warren. Unfortunately, the law required that all government briefs to the Supreme Court be submitted by the solicitor general. Hershey was indignant at what he considered a betrayal by the Justice Department. He was confronted with a brief by Griswold which admitted that the Hershey letter had "invited local boards to utilize delinquent reclassification in a punitive fashion." Were local boards acting at Hershey's behest? Griswold called it a "serious question." Griswold also defended the restriction of judicial review as written in the law, but in this case he admitted that the local boards had been in error in their reclassification.[89]

The court finally ruled that Oestereich had been illegally reclassified, stating, in a 6–3 decision, that a local board could not take away a man's lawful exemption because he turned in his draft card in protest. Justice William O. Douglas insisted, "There is no suggestion in the current draft law that the Selective Service has free-wheeling authority to ride herd on registrants, using immediate induction as a disciplinary or vindictive measure." The court did sustain the congressional restriction on judicial review, with the exception of suits involving punitive reclassification. This was small solace to Hershey.[90]

Yet, even after the court decision, local boards could continue to accelerate their calls and force draftees to sue. The courts had not issued any injunctions because of what was called "the obvious impracticality" of enforcing such a decree against over 4,000 local boards. Though Hershey had been repudiated by the courts, his action undoubtedly had the short-range effect of both stimulating increased protest against the draft and probably dissuading a few from invading draft boards if they held deferments. Altogether, the October letter represented a Pyrrhic victory for both Hershey and Johnson. For the president it was merely another disappointment in a general disaster called Vietnam.

By January 1968 the administration had come to rely upon General Westmoreland's generally optimistic reports about the course of the war. Then, early in the morning on 30 January, on the Tet holiday, the Viet Cong launched an attack. To the surprise and consternation of Americans, the offensive included the American embassy in Saigon and objectives in several other major cities. Although short lived (and, from a military standpoint, a defeat for the Viet Cong), the attack helped convince a growing number of Americans that the conflict was not worth the cost. One of those converted was Lyndon Johnson. General Westmoreland immediately requested 200,000 more troops; General Earle G. Wheeler, chairman of the joint chiefs, wanted a mobilization of the reserves. Before adopting such a policy Johnson polled a group of old Washington hands, including Dean Acheson, Omar Bradley, and Matthew Ridgway. A majority of this group recommended withdrawal. Johnson also found protest accelerating at home. The press and television networks turned against the war, and there was a falling away of support from economic elites. The president's political base was crumbling.[91]

In November 1967 Eugene McCarthy, a senator from Minnesota, declared his intention of contesting the Democratic presidential nomination. The gesture was considered quixotic by many, including Senator Robert F. Kennedy of New York. McCarthy had to rely upon hundreds of young idealists who poured in from college campuses to help in the New Hampshire primary. To the surprise of all, including McCarthy himself, he managed to poll 42 percent of the vote compared to 48 percent for the president. Robert Kennedy now decided to become a candidate as well, and Lyndon Johnson decided to address the nation. On 31 March, with the presidential campaign looming on the home front, he announced that he would now institute a bombing pause and a peace offensive. To insure that he would not be distracted from his search for peace, he announced: "I shall not seek, and I will not accept, the nomination of my party for another term as your President."[92] The man who had pressed Hershey into vigorous action in support of Vietnam was retiring. Hershey, who had no intention of retiring, pressed on and immediately became involved in the 1968 presidential campaign.

XI. Working with Nixon

The last year of Johnson's administration was hard for Hershey, and for most Americans. Despite constant presidential reassurances about the war, the fighting continued. Draft calls for fiscal 1968, originally estimated at only 85,000 men, finally took some 345,000. Johnson always underestimated draft calls to placate critics of the war. This practice led to constant budget problems for Hershey, who repeatedly turned to Congress for supplemental appropriations. Insuring the induction of 345,000 draftees required that Selective Service deliver for pre-induction examinations over 1,186,473 men. Although the Department of Defense projected that draft calls for fiscal 1969 would be only 240,000, Hershey warned that the actual figure might reach 340,000. He planned for the worst, "because the best I can always live with." In March 1968 DOD wanted Hershey to deliver some 39,000 men, the highest call since 1966.[1]

With this increase in draft calls and a presidential election campaign under way, Hershey expected more protests. He was not disappointed. Early in the year he continued to visit college campuses. His appearances, not surprisingly, generated considerable unrest. At Vermont, Wisconsin, Pittsburgh, Tennessee, Rensselaer Polytechnic Institute, and even tiny Washburn University of Topeka, Kansas, students jeered him. Picketers appeared shouting, "Hell no, we won't go." One student at the University of Tennessee tried, unsuccessfully, to burn a Hershey candy bar. Eggs flew in Hershey's direction, and students pounded on his car. Soon he needed special FBI protection and began using back doors to avoid protesters. Eventually even these measures proved inadequate. He had to cancel a scheduled talk at Florida Atlantic University.[2]

Hershey reacted to this attention with aplomb. On several occasions he spoke with protesters and even joked over the wording of their signs, but as the protest became meaner in character, he stopped joking. When a reporter asked him if he feared assassination while on the road, he replied that he never flattered himself into believing he was that important. By the summer, however, he decided that the protests had become dangerous to the nation. "The First Amendment," he wrote, "should not be allowed to furnish cover for movements to overthrow the Government of the United States." As for college campuses sponsoring such protests, Hershey warned that such actions would surely lead to a backlash and the cutting off of funds for these institutions. He would be sorry if schools were closed. A certain amount of protest was inevitable, like the sawdust which accumulated when sawing. If you stopped sawing it ended the sawdust problem—but it also ended the supply of lumber.[3]

Despite the protests, the Supreme Court, and constant badgering from Congressman Moss and Senator Ted Kennedy, Hershey remained committed to the ideas expressed in his October letter. He continued to reject any need for national standards and denied that deferments were sacred. He could afford to stand firm, for the draft continued to fulfill its mission by filling all calls, even with the demonstrations. President Johnson and Congress remained behind the war, and the draft was needed to allow its continuation. As for the increasing number of judicial decisions that were going against Hershey, the courts could not effectively reverse his leadership or replace an institution as decentralized as the draft. Judges might decide against Hershey, but local boards continued to move men along the pipeline toward the armed forces. Hershey compared his situation favorably to the draft protest of the Civil War. "We will have some law suits," he admitted, "but if we have only one for every ten we get in we will be doing well."[4]

Hershey still believed, with good reason, that the majority of Americans supported his tough stand. After his October letter Selective Service headquarters had received an unusual volume of mail, with criticism accounting for only 25 percent of the letters. A January 1968 Lou Harris poll in the *Washington Post* revealed that 53 percent of respondents agreed with Hershey's position of drafting students who obstructed recruiting efforts. Only 30 percent argued against such a draft. Hershey was outlasting his critics. At a special meeting of members of the American Political Science Association in Washington, Professor Morris Janowitz of the University of Chicago threatened to "drop dead of apoplexy" over Hershey's attitude. The general kindly extended his arms in a mock gesture of rescue.[5]

If Hershey had chosen to maintain a low profile, merely allowing the system to function despite protests, his future might have been more secure and his bureaucracy might have survived. Unfortunately, through the October letter and subsequent statements, he became a major spokesman in defense of the war. He need not have assumed this role, but he could not resist answering his critics, and during 1968 his rhetoric became increasingly provocative. Upset at the refusal of the press to provide equal time for supporters of the war, he suggested that newspapers should not be controlled by the irresponsible. Hershey also argued that protesters were aiding the enemy. When Dr.

Benjamin Spock, a leading protester, was arrested, Hershey commented: "If I were a Viet Cong, I would certainly be all for him." Protesters were, according to Hershey, misguided young men who needed their hair cut and their ears cleaned. Draft card burners were phonies who were merely burning blank cards. On the issue of free speech he announced, "The individual citizen of a Nation has no right to ask his Nation to commit suicide to satiate the individual desire to destroy." As for those who gave aid and comfort to the enemy, he wondered if they could "wash from their hands the blood of their fellow citizens who are bleeding for them."[6]

Such rhetoric, given the continued stalemate in Vietnam and the inexorable operation of the draft, insured that Hershey would become an arch symbol of a national policy being debated in the presidential election. With President Johnson out of the race, the campaign turned into a free-for-all. Eugene McCarthy, Robert F. Kennedy, and Vice-President Hubert H. Humphrey all made strong bids for the Democratic nomination. Former Vice-President Richard M. Nixon had an easier time in the Republican contest. The political scene was scarred by the unrest over Vietnam and the civil rights struggle at home. Robert Kennedy was shot down in California just as he claimed victory in that state's primary. George Wallace of Alabama led a third-party movement which appealed to a white backlash. Riots occurred at the Democratic convention in Chicago when Humphrey was nominated. The continued fighting in Vietnam proved to be one of the most important issues in the campaign. Nixon, taking a cue from Eisenhower and Korea, explained that he had a secret plan to end the war. Humphrey, as vice-president, felt compelled to follow the administration's line until very late in the campaign.

Hershey viewed the campaign with resignation. Approaching seventy-five years of age and with twenty-eight years of Washington duty under his belt, he had seen many campaigners come and go. Yet there had never been a campaign in which his own name was such a popular item of political rhetoric. Senator McCarthy, representing the peace wing of the Democratic party, told his audiences that one of his first steps as president would be to remove Hershey. The Americans for Democratic Action, while endorsing McCarthy, passed a resolution calling for Hershey's immediate discharge. Governor Nelson Rockefeller of New York, who was making a weak attempt to derail the Nixon express, blamed the system rather than Hershey, but he, too, had plans to revise the system and would probably make Hershey's retirement inevitable. Nixon refused to comment on Hershey but did commit himself to an all-volunteer system which would make the draft obsolete. Humphrey, who had praised Hershey only two years before the campaign, remained silent until he heard that the general had endorsed Wallace for election.[7]

In fact, that story was inaccurate. The general was on a first-name basis with the Alabama governor, had worked with him on integrating local boards, and admired his administrative ability. But Hershey had too much sense to become a political partisan at this stage of his career. The wire services carried the story of Hershey's endorsement of Wallace based on a press conference held in Cheyenne, Wyoming, on 31 July 1968. Only one reporter, a first-year journalism student at the University of Wyoming, who was covering the conference as a stringer for UPI, interpreted Hershey's remarks as an endorsement for Wallace. Once again, Hershey's wandering syntax had created the problem. "Question: of all the political candidates now who do you think you could work with best? Answer: Oh, I haven't the slightest idea. There has been some rumor about some that I wouldn't necessarily have to plan on it. But I don't get into political campaigns. You might be surprised if I told you some that I have worked with very, very—to me, and I think to him—very, very successfully. And that isn't why because I'm for him. . . . Question: Who? Answer: George Wallace. Well, he is the Governor—anybody who had been Governor of a state—and of course you said Rockefeller. . . . Well, I don't have any quarrel with Rockefeller." When the UPI ran the endorsement story, Humphrey reacted by announcing that, while General Hershey had a preference for president, "I have my own preference for director of Selective Service." Humphrey promised to make "the needed change."[8]

After the story appeared and Humphrey reacted, Hershey explained that he had been misunderstood. With his syntax, he could not claim to have been misquoted. Asked if he had made an endorsement, he replied: "Oh heavens. I've been around thirty years. Obviously not." He held no grudge against Humphrey. As a seasoned veteran of Washington political wars, Hershey understood the need for candidates to take certain stands at certain times. If there were votes to be had by attacking him, he expected no better treatment.[9]

As the campaign intensified, so did the draft. Both Nixon and Humphrey attempted to win votes by solving Selective Service problems. Nixon argued that the draft could end when the war in Vietnam ended; he was sure that the United States could rely on an all-volunteer force. Humphrey responded to this idea by advocating the reforms enumerated in the Marshall report. He denounced Nixon's proposal for an all-volunteer force as prohibitively expensive. Rather than ending the draft, Humphrey promised to reform it by replacing Hershey, making men liable for the draft for only one year (at age nineteen), using a lottery for selection purposes, and establishing uniform nationwide rules and procedures. Ironically, such a program would soon be established—but the man who would put it into effect would be Nixon, not Humphrey. In November the voters elected Richard M. Nixon by the slimmest of margins, 31,785,480 votes to 31,275,166 for Humphrey and 9,906,473 for Wallace. The electoral vote went Republican, 301–191. Wallace's American Independent party received 46 electoral votes.[10]

For the sixth time Hershey prepared to work under a new president. He liked Nixon. They had met during the Eisenhower administration and had worked together on a Fitness of American Youth conference in 1955 and 1956. Hershey felt Nixon was a talented individual who could handle difficult jobs. Now, in the wake of the 1968 election, an immediate and difficult job was the question of Hershey's reappointment.[11]

Hershey had indicated to the press that he had no intention of stepping down voluntarily. Although no one from the Nixon administration approached him about continuing, he was unworried. "I've gone through eight of these [inaugurations] and no one has talked to me before any of them. But I've always stayed on." Indeed, Daniel Omer of Selective Service informed the White House that Hershey would continue "until notified otherwise." As for his age, Hershey dismissed charges that seventy-five was too old for the job. He felt fine and was in good health, except for his eyesight. More important than his health was his deep feeling of duty. His own son was now fighting in Vietnam. Hershey had helped in the escalation of the conflict. Unlike Johnson, Hershey did not feel he could retire while so many draftees continued to fight.[12]

President Nixon had other ideas. He was convinced that an all-volunteer force would end the protest over the draft. Nixon had no plans for a unilateral withdrawal, but he was committed to winding down the conflict in Vietnam. He needed time to work his will and could not afford to allow domestic protest to get out of hand. Hershey seemed a liability to the new administration. As the conservative *National Review* wrote, "Through his public pronouncements, he has given a distinctively Hershey tinge to an agency that requires a bureaucrat of the most colorless sort at its head." Unfortunately, Nixon could not immediately replace him without additional political problems. Hershey still had strong support in Congress and with the public. A Gallup poll of 26 January 1969 indicated that, even if the Vietnam war ended, some 62 percent of the public thought the draft should be continued. Only 32 percent preferred an all-volunteer force. Nixon needed time to extricate the United States from Vietnam and to con-

vince the public of the wisdom of an all-volunteer force. In the meantime Hershey remained, but the new president took steps to change
the image of the draft.[13]

Nixon immediately moved to increase White House control over the
system's operations. Peter Flanigan, a White House aide, kept close
tabs on what was happening at Selective Service. Through such men
as Jonathan Rose, a Flanigan aide, David Klineberger of the budget
office and Herbert Klein in press relations, Nixon soon had a much better idea of how the system functioned and the problems that existed.
These new organization men were stunned at Hershey's horse-and-
buggy approach. Although willing to settle for cosmetic changes at
first, Nixon made it clear that he was serious about moving to an all-
volunteer armed force. On 31 January 1969 he instructed Secretary of
Defense Melvin Laird to prepare a plan for this transition.[14]

While the all-volunteer plan was being prepared, Nixon implemented
a transitional draft reform. The Department of Defense had been
ready to begin a lottery system for several months. President Johnson
had attempted to institute such a program in 1967, only to be rebuffed
by Congress. Now, in April 1969, the lottery or random selection plan
reemerged with the endorsement of Nixon and Laird. Hershey had
earlier made clear his own skepticism about the lottery. Surprisingly,
public opinion also rejected the idea for nineteen-year-olds. A Harris
poll of 3 March indicated that the public preferred the present system
to an all-volunteer force by 51 to 38 percent and the present system to
a lottery by 60 to 27 percent. Yet, when asked if they thought the
present system was working fairly, only 50 percent said it was. Despite the division of opinion, on 13 May the president asked Congress
to amend the draft law.[15]

President Nixon explained to Congress that he was committed to
ending the "disruptive impact of the draft." Although he hoped to
move to an all-volunteer force, Nixon admitted that the draft was currently needed. As a temporary expedient, he wanted some procedural
modifications. He called for three specific changes: reversing the order
of call from oldest first to youngest first; reducing the period of prime
draft vulnerability to one year, at age nineteen; and using a lottery or
random system of selection. This plan did not go as far as the reforms
being pushed by Ted Kennedy and others in Congress, but it did undercut the growing opposition to the draft. Nixon would keep college
deferments, but he had resurrected many of the suggestions made by
the Marshall committee. While these ideas had gone nowhere in 1967,
prospects looked better now. Despite his dislike for these reforms,
Hershey helped the president draft his message. Reverting to his
"good soldier" image, Hershey urged Congress to act quickly and fa-

vorably on Nixon's request. Without some reform, he feared that congressional radicals would move too quickly to end the draft.[16]

Having cut the ground out from under Ted Kennedy and others who had been drafting a radical bill, Nixon now procrastinated. Congress delayed hearings on his request, and public opinion polls revealed little interest in the changes. Both the Harris and Gallup polls found approximately 54 percent of respondents opposed to a lottery. A Harris survey showed Americans now favoring the existing system by 53 to 36 percent. Realizing that his program of withdrawing American troops from combat and introducing Vietnamization was going to take more time than he had anticipated, Nixon did not press draft reform. Instead, he settled for a public relations program which Hershey had originated.[17]

In an attempt to defuse some of the protest in 1968 Hershey had begun a five-state pilot program of appointing seven to fifteen young people, male and female, with an emphasis on minority representation, to youth advisory committees. These committees were to meet every two weeks and provide information to the state director. Although the youngsters had no policymaking responsibility, Hershey hoped that an exposure to the regulations and operations of the system might lead to less destructive criticism. The pilot program was evaluated at the May 1969 meeting of the state directors in Washington. Hershey still had some reservations; he expected radicals to infiltrate the committees, and he had no sympathy for those who violated the law. "I know you can't shoot people for moral treason," he told the directors, "but probably in this beautiful day when we let everybody be a conscientious objector that wants to, I think then we will probably have to start shooting people who at the present time we tolerate." Despite these misgivings, he informed the press that he was thinking of adopting the youth advisory system on a national level.[18]

Before Hershey could act, the White House became involved. Nixon learned of the program through Peter Flanigan and Bryce Harlow. The idea seemed conveniently designed to improve the image of both the draft and the president. On 6 June 1969 President Nixon announced the new program from San Clemente, California. Nixon explained that the committees were designed to provide "a better informed and more responsible" draft system. Ten youthful members of the existing committees flew to California to visit him. In a press release Nixon explained, "We believe that those who administer our draft laws should systematically seek advice from young people about young people." The president assumed credit for the Hershey program, but the two men had different expectations.[19]

Privately Hershey had little sympathy for the president's draft reforms. He pointed out that such a system would hardly eliminate inequity because the lottery would deal with only those who were not deferred. Of that select pool, over half would be rejected by the armed forces. Those selected by the lottery and inducted would be just as upset as those selected under the current system. Using a lottery only for nineteen-year-olds insured that men not taken would be lost forever for national defense. Most of all, Hershey disliked the idea because it seemed a slap at the local board system. A lottery substituted the chance of a drawing for the thoughtful decisions of local boards. Some critics had suggested using a computer for the drawing, but Hershey felt that such a mechanical approach would lack the credibility of his old system—a credibility already fast disappearing without Nixon's help.[20]

During the 1968 campaign Nixon had gotten political mileage out of his promise to move toward an all-volunteer armed force. Although he admitted the cost would be high, he felt it could be offset by reductions in the heavy turnover rate among draftees. (This rate was running 93 percent after one tour.) Furthermore, he felt the current draft selection process violated "our whole concept of liberty, justice and equality under the law." This rhetoric pleased many people in the Pentagon who had always preferred a highly paid volunteer force. Polls indicated that the public strongly favored making military pay equal to civilian minimum wage rates (80 percent in favor), but over half of those polled did not think higher pay would attract enough volunteers to render the draft unnecessary.[21] With this background, Hershey was not surprised when Nixon appointed a study group on 27 March 1969. The group, headed by former Secretary of Defense Thomas Gates, would study the feasibility of moving to an all-volunteer force. Nixon stressed that the idea was a long-range goal to be implemented after the Vietnam affair had been settled.[22]

Hershey was neither surprised nor convinced by the president's argument in establishing the Gates committee. The general had long been on record as opposing the all-volunteer concept. When pressed in the late 1960's, he reiterated his major arguments. These included a philosophical disinclination to put national security in the hands of mercenaries. At the same time, he believed (ironically, in light of recent criticism) that the draft was more democratic and just. An all-volunteer system would bring in the poor and perhaps a mostly black population. Hershey explained that the draft insured service from more of a cross-section of American youth. "In thirty years in the Army," he insisted, "I never saw a college student and few high school students except during a war and compulsion." With all volunteers, he warned, the military would become totally alien to civilian society.[23]

On a more practical level, Hershey insisted that a volunteer system would not produce enough men. If the nation wanted a large force, it had to use compulsion. He estimated a cost of an additional $17 billion a year to replace the draft with higher-paid volunteers. Other feeder systems for the armed services might also suffer. The officer recruitment program under ROTC would dry up; a similar fate awaited the reserves and the National Guard, since 71 percent of those who joined did so for fear of the draft. Hershey felt confident that Nixon could not do away with the draft as long as the fight in Vietnam continued. But what of the future?[24]

Even with these misgivings, Hershey had to support the new president. As the general explained to Congress, in a football metaphor so beloved by Nixon, he was a team player, and the quarterback had called new signals. When asked about Nixon's draft ideas, Hershey announced that the reforms were "workable and in the best interest of the country." Yet on the issue of an all-volunteer force he refused to budge from his earlier skepticism. Of course, he explained, if the nation reduced its armed force to less than 2 million men, rather than the current 3.6 million, anything was possible. But when a reporter asked him if young men would have to live with the draft for a long time, Hershey candidly replied that they would. Such words grated on nerves at the White House. Hershey's doubts about the all-volunteer concept and his growing image as the symbol of an unfair draft and an unpopular war insured that his tenure under Nixon was to be short.[25]

Nixon's early hopes of avoiding the albatross of Vietnam were rapidly fading. He wanted out of the war; unfortunately, he also wanted the continued existence, at least for a decent interval, of a non-Communist South Vietnam. These goals proved elusive, as did "peace with honor." He tried some of the tricks he had learned at the knee of President Eisenhower, including the threat of massive retaliation. When that threat proved inadequate, he authorized bombings of North Vietnam and Cambodia. To prove that this escalation did not contradict his desire for peace, he ordered the withdrawal of 25,000 American troops in June 1969 and a speeding up of Vietnamization.

The war and the killing continued, and by the summer of 1969 the protest movement was again in full bloom. A number of universities decided to drop ROTC programs. A national moratorium day was held in March. Local draft boards became convenient targets for those seeking to halt the war, as protesters broke in and attempted to destroy records. When Hershey traveled around the country he was consistently plagued by picketers and hecklers who interrupted his remarks and threw eggs. Burning draft cards again became fashionable.

Hershey's reaction to this protest hardly helped defuse the problem for the White House. To his state directors Hershey explained, "We've got some lousy little cusses" who do not belong in school. He began publicly to suggest that the demonstrators were being partially subsidized by "foreign subversives." How else could the same protesters follow him around the country and engage in so many lawsuits?[26] The colleges seemed to be centers of radicalism, and Hershey warned against professors who made careers out of debunking the United States. "It is past time that our citizens should know whether they are for the United States or whether they are enemies of the United States." College presidents, faculty, and students should realize that the country had no intention of continuing to subsidize rebellion. Cutting off public funds might teach these academics a valuable lesson, he felt.[27]

Hershey believed that protest was popular because of the support of several key institutions: the colleges, the courts, and the press. He was particularly disappointed in the failure of the courts to punish protesters after a slumbering Justice Department started prosecution. "I am disturbed by the usurpation by the judiciary of the legislative and executive functions," he explained. Appeals courts were destroying the power of the draft system by refusing to punish protesters and delinquents. The press and television were also to blame because they paid too much attention to protesters and ignored the success of the system. Despite these attitudes, Hershey vowed as late as May 1969 to continue to use the delinquency clause to reclassify and draft men "whose behavior is not in the national interest." Protest was particularly galling to Hershey because he was utterly convinced that it represented only a minority opinion. He believed, as President Nixon would later insist, that there was a "silent majority" who still believed in the old virtues. As for the draft apparatus, Hershey was impressed with the "oneness" of the system and the strength of the real America.[28]

Whatever the strength of the real America, President Nixon had to deal with the Americans pouring into Washington for antiwar protests. The National Movement against the War called Vietnam Moratorium Day for 15 October 1969. With Congress still stalling on the draft lottery proposal, Nixon tried to undermine the protest movement by showing his sincerity about draft reform. In September he announced a reduction of draft calls for October and a cancellation of calls for November and December. Rumors began circulating that several university presidents had urged Nixon to save their campuses from the expected disturbances in October by reforming the draft.[29]

Seeking to prove that his policies had the support of youth, Nixon inveigled some 500 student leaders to the White House on 20 September for a conference on the draft. Hershey came over to address them in his folksy fashion. For ninety minutes he answered questions. One of the first was, "When will you resign?" He announced, to the dismay of the Nixon officials, that he had no intention of resigning in the immediate future. As for student problems with uncertainty and the draft, he explained that life and college were full of uncertainty. "You don't want everything beer and skittles because nothing will degenerate life faster than that." On the idea of a lottery, Hershey assured them that he would be quite happy to have one, if a majority of the people wanted it. The student leaders chuckled at Hershey's performance. As one radical explained, the removal of Hershey would be unfortunate: "Everytime he opens his mouth, he gets hundreds of draft cards." Columnists admitted that Hershey was a disarming enemy because he came across as a "teddy bear," an administrator with loads of crackerbarrel humor who was merely trying to do a thankless task.[30]

The days of his task were numbered. Even the youth advisory committees turned against him. The New York committee announced that Hershey should be replaced because "he no longer reflects the attitudes and feelings of the nation concerning the draft."[31] At age seventy-six, with calls for his resignation filling the air, Hershey refused to retire. He remained as mentally alert as ever, although his failing sight created problems when in strange surroundings. He had a son, a son-in-law, and a grandson in Vietnam and he felt committed to his role on the home front. He continued to enjoy the support of many influential congressmen. Despite the current hostile atmosphere, he still believed he could weather the storm. Retirement held no appeal because he had devoted his entire career to the draft system. When he heard in early October that the president wished to reassign him, Hershey was disappointed.[32]

There should have been no surprise, for Nixon had several reasons for replacing Hershey. Most important, the president had been committed to an all-volunteer army even before his election. As a stopgap measure he had called for a lottery to replace the existing draft. If Nixon wished to reform the draft, he had to begin at the top. In addition, Nixon faced the problem of Hershey's image. As an old man with the job of drafting young men, Hershey symbolized to many the failure of the establishment. Even the Department of Defense considered Hershey a political liability. If Nixon wished to create support for his reform program, he could not retain Hershey to direct the new effort. By removing Hershey only five days before a scheduled national demonstration against the war, Nixon also hoped to defuse some of the impending protest.[33]

Hershey's removal was effected with the indirection which was a hallmark of the Nixon administration. Many members of the White House team, including Bryce Harlow, Peter Flanigan, and Secretary of Defense Laird, hoped that Hershey would voluntarily retire after several strong hints. Hershey had no intention of making things easy. The job was his life, and he felt a responsibility to his descendants in Vietnam. As he wrote to his granddaughter, "I do not intend to offer a resignation for no other reason perhaps than a feeling that these are not the times that citizens of the United States ask to be relieved of difficult assignments."[34]

Faced with this attitude, Flanigan and Harlow finally visited Hershey and explained that the president wished him to assume a new assignment. Hershey agreed to abide by the president's wishes. On 10 October he slipped into a side entrance at the White House, avoiding the press, and spent fifty minutes chatting with Nixon. True to form, not once did the president raise the distasteful topic of removal. Instead, the two men spoke of the general condition of the nation. With the interview over, Hershey again disappeared without confronting the press. He learned the details of his removal from a news release issued a few hours later by presidential press secretary Ron Ziegler. Nixon lauded Hershey for serving "with distinction" for thirty-three years with the Selective Service. Nixon looked forward to having Hershey's "advice and counsel" in his new role as presidential advisor on manpower mobilization policies. Hershey would remain at Selective Service until 16 February 1970, the fifty-ninth anniversary of his enlistment in the National Guard. In addition, he would be promoted to the rank of full general before assuming his role as presidential advisor.[35]

Hershey accepted the reassignment with the same sense of realism and resignation which had always marked his career until Vietnam. As reporters flocked over to interview him and as letters of support poured in, he adopted a stoic pose. "People don't let me down much," he explained, "because I don't expect much." Yet he was disappointed, especially about the way the courts were confusing the operations of the system. To his friends he put on a brave face: "It looks as though I have received something and there were touches of martyrdom around it so all in all it was rather an ideal exit." He held no bitterness toward Nixon and continued to admire him. Hershey reassured his colleagues and friends that his departure did not mean the end of the system. "The unit has been built well," he insisted. "It will run no matter who drives it," but, "if it hasn't been built well, probably the sooner that it falls apart the better." Even as Hershey wrote, the president was in the process of reforming the draft in a way which Hershey had rejected innumerable times. Ironically, his last important task as director of the Selective Service System was to provide loyal support to Nixon in pushing a draft lottery through Congress.[36]

For the last time in his career Hershey plodded the now worn promenade to Capitol Hill to testify. Nixon's May 1969 call for draft reform had gone largely ignored by Congress, but with protest rising he began to threaten to institute his own lottery. The 1967 law specifically prohibited the president from taking such action, but many in Congress, especially the chairmen of the armed services committees, were reluctant to open debate on the draft for fear that the reform movement would get out of hand. F. Edward Hebert of the House resented Nixon's request for a "blank check."[37]

By 1 October, however, the House Armed Services Committee had begun hearings. At the outset several members indicated their dislike of the lottery idea. Hershey, despite his own skepticism, acted as a loyal member of the Nixon team. To the surprise of several congressmen, Hershey announced that he favored a rapid implementation of the president's scheme. In explaining this about-face, Hershey pointed out that he followed orders from his team captain, and he insisted that a majority of the American people now wanted such a system. With a growing surplus of young men (2 million now reached eighteen each year), he was willing to give random selection a try. He admitted, however, that the lottery would not end the protest, since some men would still be drafted.[38]

When Hershey tried to explain how the lottery would work, Hebert and a few others became hopelessly confused. The plan involved placing men at age nineteen in a pool for twelve months. A drawing would be held based on date of birth. Hebert still could not follow the process, and the hearings concluded without a clear vote to endorse the reform. Hershey would have been just as happy had no endorsement been made, but, to the surprise of many, on 16 October the committee voted 31–0 to approve the Nixon lottery. Hebert explained that he was willing to give Nixon what he required as commander-in-chief.[39]

On 23 October Hershey revealed more of his feelings before a subcommittee of the Senate committee on the judiciary. Edward M. Kennedy, as chairman, had decided to hold hearings on the draft. Kennedy hoped to demonstrate by his hearings that Nixon could reform the draft without Congress. Ignoring a tradition which gave draft responsibility to the Senate Armed Services Committee, Kennedy called Hershey as the first witness. During his testimony Hershey made it clear that his recent removal and the protests had done little to change his mind, whatever the captain's signals. When asked about drafting protesters, he stood by his October 1967 letter. Those who broke the law were delinquents and were subject to early calls. Kennedy asked about allowing the draftee the right of counsel before his local board. Hershey rejected the idea and insisted that the draft was drowning in too much legalism, rather than too little. As for the college deferment program, Hershey surprised many by continuing to favor the idea, despite being harassed on college campuses. When Kennedy raised the perennial problem of inequity due to the absence of national standards, Hershey offered up a quote from his questioner's brother, John F. Kennedy, that "Life is unfair." The Kennedy hearings led to little of consequence, but they did prompt the Senate Armed Services Committee to begin hearings on Nixon's random selection system.[40]

Hershey made a final appearance before the committee members with whom he had grown old. On 14 November the sixty-eight-year-old chairman John Stennis, welcomed seventy-six-year-old General Hershey in an affectionate manner. The committee approved of his new assignment and of the promotion. Senator Harry Byrd, hardly a sentimental type, offered an accolade: "I submit that any man who can serve under six Presidents must be a man of superior qualifications." Repeating his pro forma performance before the House, Hershey endorsed the random selection system. He explained that it would reduce the registrant's vulnerability from seven years to one year. When asked about the effect of such a system on voluntary enlistments, he assured the committee that the impact would be minor. In reality, Hershey did not expect the proposal to obtain approval, but with protesters gathering in Washington for a November "March against Death," senators agreed that Nixon deserved his reform. By late November the amendment had passed both houses.[41]

Nixon had his reform, but the protests continued. When over a quarter million people gathered around the Washington Monument for a peace rally on 15 November, they had an unexpected visitor. Slipping on a black beret and an overcoat, Hershey accompanied his granddaughter, Joan Hershey, to the scene. He roamed around the area without any trouble; indeed, he was recognized only twice. When reporters heard of this foray, they asked Hershey for his impressions. With his reassignment now confirmed, Hershey could afford to be generous. He explained that he saw no evidence of lawbreaking and that he was treated courteously. "I don't agree with their reasons for demonstrating, but they had every right to do what they did."[42]

When Nixon signed the reform amendment on 26 November he explained to the audience, which included members of the youth advisory committees, that the change would end the "agony of suspense." Although inequities would remain, Nixon insisted that the bill was merely one step toward his real objective, "a system of completely volunteer armed forces." [43]

With the preliminaries over, Hershey began to organize the public relations extravaganza which would be the Nixon lottery. The drawing was Hershey's last major duty as director. In keeping with his insistence that the lottery should be simple and understandable to small-town America, Hershey rejected all plans to use a computer. Once again the old World War II fishbowls were taken out of storage and dusted off. The scheme called for 366 capsules to be drawn from one bowl. The sequence of dates drawn would establish the order of induction, based on birthdates for eligible men in their prime year of liability. Another fishbowl was filled with letters of the alphabet, to establish a random sequence for distinguishing among last names of men born on the same day. [44]

On 1 December 1969, cameras and microphones cluttered the scene as the first drawing was held. Seeking to dramatize the significance of the reform, Hershey arranged for members of the youth advisory committees to draw the capsules. The first date drawn was 14 September; the final was 8 June. Across the country thousands of young men received the news in different circumstances. At Brandeis University a recording of machine gun fire provided background for the drawing. At the University of California the sound of taps and then a chorus of "Happy Birthday" sounded. Howie Vogel, a senior at the University of Florida, found himself with the enviable date of 8 June. As he explained to a reporter, "Like, I don't want a recount." [45]

Hershey announced that he was pleased with the drawing, despite the defection of a few capsule pickers. As a public relations extravaganza, it was a success—afterward a Harris poll revealed that 73 percent of the sample approved of the new plan, while only 16 percent disapproved. Much more important for the White House, the polls showed that 60 percent now rated Nixon's handling of the draft as "good to excellent." Dumping Hershey and instituting the lottery had paid handsome political dividends. [46]

Hershey seemed to underestimate the political motive for reforming the system. As power slipped from his grasp he tried to convince the president that the draft should be kept on standby status (with continued registrations but no inductions), even if an all-volunteer system was adopted. But Nixon was no longer listening, if he ever had, to words from Hershey. The random selection system had no sooner been introduced than the administration began delaying calls. Hershey was indignant at the effect of these actions on his system. In a blistering note to Peter Flanigan on 6 February 1970, only a few days before stepping down, Hershey complained that White House meddling had achieved what all the protest and sabotage had attempted but failed to do—caused the system to fail in its mission of delivering men. He informed Flanigan, "The Director of Selective Service is placing the call for March in accordance with the provisions of the law."[47]

The White House was less concerned about the system failing than with evidence that the public now approved the president's program. By the summer of 1970 polls indicated that some 71 percent of the public approved Nixon's plan to replace the Selective Service System. With such support building, Nixon began dismantling the system. After searching among and receiving rejections from several college football coaches, Nixon finally turned to Charles J. DiBona, an expert weapons-system analyst, as a replacement for Hershey. Unfortunately, DiBona was too candid in his testimony before the Senate Armed Services Committee; he explained that his task would be to liquidate the draft and prepare the way for an all-volunteer system. After several senior members of the committee came out in opposition, DiBona withdrew from consideration. Unable to find a replacement in time for Hershey's 16 February departure, Nixon turned to Dee Ingold, Hershey's deputy, as interim director.[48]

On 16 February, his last day of work, Hershey arrived at headquarters at the usual time, 8:30, to be greeted by the press and by a huge Valentine in the lobby. A Hershey profile had been mounted on the Valentine, signed by hundreds of employees. Dee Ingold had few illusions about his own role, muttering to the press, "A funny thing happened to me on the way to the guillotine." The Hershey system was dying.[49]

In a few weeks, Nixon finally found his own man—Curtis W. Tarr, a former air force official. Tarr was a young man and a former president of a small college. Within weeks of his appointment he had made it clear that older men were expected to retire. He explained in a form letter of 14 April 1970, "It shall be my policy, in keeping with the desires of the President, to establish a more youthful image for the Selective Service System." Hershey offered assistance, but Tarr went his own way. The Hershey mystique was ruthlessly erased.[50] Within weeks draft officials were issuing fake Selective Service cards, to be used by FBI undercover agents and members of other law enforcement agencies who sought to infiltrate the peace movement. With all of his fear of dissent, Hershey had never taken such a step.[51]

Hershey faded from the scene but found some consolation in his promotion to full general, confirmed by a voice vote in the Senate on 3 November. He also read with pleasure the many letters which poured into headquarters, offering congratulations for a job well done. John J. McCloy, a former official in the State Department and high commissioner in Germany, asserted that no other official had such a long span of service in a position relating to the security of the United States, and no other official "deserves better of his country for the devotion, loyalty and skills which you have devoted to it." Lawrence Spivak, long noted as the acerbic host of the television show "Meet the Press," was equally laudatory: "I can say with conviction that I know of no one, in or out of government service, who has demonstrated greater ability, integrity and dedication. . . . Any summation of your twenty-eight years in office will place you right at the top of the list of those who have rendered extraordinary service to the country."[52]

Nixon also offered Hershey a parting gesture. On 17 February 1970 the president hosted a White House dinner in Hershey's honor. Some one hundred guests were invited—a small affair, by White House standards. The guest list included friends from Washington and around the country. Congress was represented by John Stennis, Leslie C. Arends, F. Edward Hebert, L. Mendel Rivers and Gerald R. Ford. The armed forces sent Stanley R. Resor, secretary of the army, and John H. Chafee of the navy. General William C. Westmoreland, General Lauris Norstad, and Admiral Arleigh A. Burke came as well. From the White House Peter Flanigan and Bryce N. Harlow took seats. The guest list included other dignitaries who supported the defense policy which had created confusion for Johnson and Nixon. The president took the occasion to utter a few words of praise. Expressing gratitude for the general's staunch service, Nixon, with a straight face, expressed regret that Hershey was leaving office. The president was reassured, however, that Hershey would continue to make his wisdom available to the administration as presidential advisor. At 11:00 P.M. Lewis and Ellen returned to their home and a new role.[53]

Beginning a new career at age seventy-six presented certain problems. Mentally Hershey remained as alert as ever, but physically he was slowing down. His functioning eye was developing a cataract, and his hearing was fading. Despite these problems, he continued to keep busy. Sitting in the rose-colored chair in his living room, surrounded by Persian rugs, carved tables, oriental vases, silk prints, and other reminders of his travels, he forced himself to read. He and Ellen were at home alone now in their ranch-style house in Bethesda; even the picketers had left. Two generations of Hersheys were fighting in Vietnam. Kathryn (or Kitty, as she was known) was the only child still living in the Washington area, having married Aaron A. Layne, a local attorney.

On some nights the Hersheys dined with the Laynes. Hershey enjoyed these entertainments, partly because he and Kitty usually argued over politics. Kitty was the liberal Democrat of the family and detested President Nixon, while Hershey continued to defend him. The Hersheys usually left early because Ellen was in ill health, still suffering from a variety of heart and lung ailments, but the couple's relationship had never wavered over the years. In 1967 they had celebrated their fiftieth wedding anniversary with 400 guests at Fort Myer in Arlington, with the army chorus for entertainment.[54]

Despite his age and experience, Hershey's outlook on life had changed little over the years. He had been bullish on youth as a young man and he remained optimistic now, despite his experiences with protesters. "I don't think fundamentally that kids have changed much," he explained. What had changed was the environment. The material wealth of the nation, the weakening of the family unit, and the lapses of responsibility by elders (in particular professors, who ignored the classroom in favor of research) were more to blame for the current unrest. He was disturbed at the tendency to prolong adolescence, but he thought this was a natural side effect of material progress.[55]

The affluence of the nation worried Hershey, not merely because it had a bad effect on youth, but because all citizens were becoming apathetic. He reminded his audiences that great nations generally had an average life span of two hundred years and that they fell because of internal weaknesses. Was the United States to follow this path? As for himself, he remained committed to that folk patriotism embodied in his favorite quote from Stephen Decatur: "Our country, in her intercourse with foreign nations, may she always be in the right; but our country, right or wrong." Chesterton had written that this was the equivalent of "my mother drunk or sober." But Hershey never read Chesterton. In Hershey's opinion those who expected survival to be easy were whistling Dixie. "I don't say total war is inevitable, but total peace is a long way from inevitable too." Yet if America refused to demand sacrifice from her citizens, perhaps the nation was doomed. Americans refused to be realistic about conflict and war. Hershey always favored full information on casualties in war, even though his insistence that the draft sought "killers" got him into trouble with those who wished to use a soft sell. He worried about a country in which euphemisms replaced candor.[56]

Although his critics in the 1960's had their suspicions, Hershey insisted: "I haven't got a God complex." Despite clinging to such traditional values as patriotism and the family, he was quite willing to admit that "the world of today, in a material sense, is greatly different" from the world in which he had grown up. But he insisted that the changes had occurred only in superficial areas. The times were always going to the dogs, but men continued to find answers. As for new ideas, he did not reject them out of hand: "I'm not so old that I believe that things that never have been done can't be done." Yet, as his record showed, he had little interest in change for its own sake. His local board system had worked, and he refused to consider replacing it with something untried.[57]

Hershey still kept busy. He roamed the country collecting awards from such organizations as the Masons, the Association of the United States Army, and the Reserve Officers Association. He kept in touch with his family by traveling to such outposts as Hawaii, and at home he continued his work with the Boy Scouts. He remained a trustee of Tri-State College. His alma mater had sought to capitalize on his notoriety by using his name for a new physical education building and inviting all of his friends to send in donations, but little money had appeared. His returns to Angola became depressing; his old home had been displaced by a new superhighway, and most of his old school chums had died. In Washington, Hershey had his job as presidential advisor. He soon discovered, however, that the White House did not expect to keep him busy.[58]

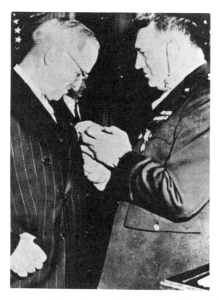

*President Truman and Hershey exchange awards, 21 January 1946
(courtesy of Hershey family)*

*Secretary of the Navy Forrestal awards the Navy Distinguished Service
Medal to Hershey, 3 May 1946 (courtesy of Hershey family)*

Hershey awards Selective Service medal to J. Edgar Hoover, 1946
(courtesy of Hershey family)

The draft again; President Truman signs draft law, 31 March 1947
(courtesy of Hershey family)

Hershey appears on "Meet the Press," 14 July 1950
(courtesy of Hershey family)

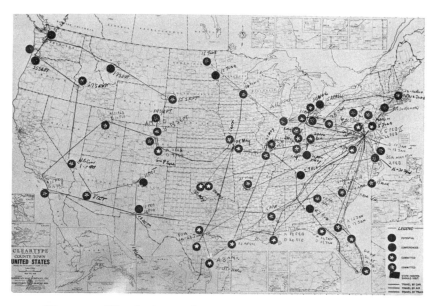

Itinerary of Hershey's travels, 1961 (courtesy of Hershey family)

President Kennedy signs EO deferring married men, 12 September 1963
(courtesy of Hershey family)

Hershey briefs President Johnson as McNamara and Califano listen, 27
February 1967 (courtesy of Hershey family)

"The Untouchables," cartoon by Lou Grant, ca. 1967 (reprinted with permission of the Oakland Tribune, *Oakland, California)*

Next challenger.

Cassius Clay and Hershey, cartoon by Crockett, 8 February 1967 (permission of Gib Crockett and the Washington Evening Star)

Hershey briefs President Nixon, 1969 (courtesy of Hershey family)

President Nixon's farewell party for Hershey, 17 February 1970
(courtesy of Hershey family)

'Now, General—permit me to help you upstairs!'

President Nixon promotes Hershey, cartoon by Crockett, 14 October 1969 (permission of Gib Crockett and Washington Evening Star*)*

'My first advice, Mr. President—is to draft somebody!'

Cartoon on replacing Hershey, 18 February 1970 (permission of Gib Crockett and the Washington Evening Star*)*

*President Nixon and his unused advisor on manpower, 2 June 1971
(courtesy of Hershey family)*

*Retirement ceremony at the Pentagon with Secretary of Defense Elliot
Richardson, 27 March 1973 (courtesy of Hershey family)*

XII. Taps and an Assessment

After finding space in the Executive Office Building, Hershey began the last phase of his career. Rather than leading a staff of hundreds, he had one secretary and a driver. As the presidential advisor on manpower, Hershey's official task included reviewing information and legislation and attending briefings. This job description had little relation to reality. He entered the job with few illusions and was not disappointed. With self-mocking humor, he explained to reporters that he had little to do, "but then I haven't had many people to help me." Most of the time he sat in his office visiting with old friends and providing interviews for young scholars seeking an understanding of the history of the draft. Whenever he could, he took to the road to address various organizations. As he explained to one friend, "Somehow, I create the impression of being busy. But I have no illusions. . . . When asked what I do, I usually take the Fifth Amendment."[1]

Hershey whiled away his time in isolation as President Nixon moved to dismantle the draft apparatus. The lottery was already being used to reduce the influence of local boards, much to Hershey's dismay. In February 1970 the special committee under Thomas Gates finally reported favorably on the prospect of an all-volunteer army. Nixon immediately endorsed that recommendation. To Congress Nixon explained that he planned to move as quickly as possible, given considerations of national security, to end the draft. His first objective was to reduce calls to zero.[2]

From out in the cold Hershey fought a last battle to save the system from what he considered a stupid policy. As Nixon planned his draft message, Hershey urged him to delay any discussion of reform until 1971, when the law would come up for renewal. Hershey feared that attempts to change the law during an election year would invite critics to take radical steps. He also sent several memos to the White House elaborating his reservations about the new direction of Selective Service, where Curtis Tarr was removing all the old hands and defusing bombs which arrived in the mail. But Hershey was more worried about the lottery being used as a fixed national selection sequence, rather than as a guide to local boards. He warned Nixon about the dangers of centralizing the system.[3]

Hershey found the Gates plan very dubious. The expense of an all-volunteer system was unreasonably high. Without a big appropriation approved by Congress, debate would be a waste of time. Antidraft sentiment remained intense and would insure a dearth of volunteers. Opposition existed toward the entire military idea, not just the draft. Hershey felt that the Gates target date of 1 July 1971 for starting an all-volunteer system was unrealistic. With Congress preaching a tight budget, there was little prospect of finding the additional pay for early enlistees and junior officers. Nixon had also suggested that the draft go on standby status, to be reactivated by congressional initiative. Hershey felt this delegation of presidential power was a mistake. When his warnings were ignored in the White House, he began taking his case to the public.[4]

Hershey had always enjoyed appearing in public, treating audiences to his midwestern humor, but by 1970 those audiences were becoming more and more raucous. Although no longer in charge of the draft system, he was still considered by many college students to serve as a symbol of a mistaken policy in Vietnam. Now, at the age of seventy-seven, he made one last foray. In the fall of 1970 he received an invitation to address students at UCLA. This school had invited him on two earlier occasions, but his aides had successfully prevented his appearance because of the fear of violence. Having lost authority and guardians, Hershey finally decided to make an appearance. Appropriately, he entitled his speech "Age Talks with Youth." On 9 October 1970 Hershey left his hotel room at the Statler Hilton for the UCLA campus. An hour later he was booed off the stage.[5]

He returned to Washington, where Congress once again began considering a renewal of the draft authority to induct, due to expire in July 1971. For the first time since the original law passed in 1940, Hershey did not appear before Congress. He watched from the sidelines as President Nixon accepted a bill providing for a two-year extension. (Nixon hoped to end the draft even earlier.) In a memo of 19 August Hershey pointed to several weaknesses in the bill. He was upset at two amendments from the pen of Senator Kennedy; one allowed the draftee to bring witnesses with him when he appealed a classification before a local board. Hershey considered such a step merely another move toward the "judicialization" of the draft process. Second, Kennedy obtained approval of a requirement that all draft regulations be published thirty days before going into effect. Hershey considered this requirement totally impractical, and he warned the president that the system would be less able to respond in an emergency. But Nixon knew that, without the Kennedy amendments, there would be no draft bill. Despite Hershey's advice, the president signed the bill and moved to end all calls.[6]

With the authority to induct due to expire in 1973, Hershey made one last attempt to convince Nixon that he should save the system. He emphasized that the draft should be extended to 1977, and he urged the president to end efforts to centralize the draft through a misuse of the lottery. "To use the lottery system to establish a national priority," he explained, "violates the fairness it seeks to establish. In seeking fairness for the individual registrant, the principle of equality among the states and communities has been violated." Once again Hershey gave evidence of his dedication to the concept of localism, of community, of a nineteenth-century vision of America. Nixon, however, was more concerned with the political reality of 1972. When, in January 1973 Melvin Laird announced the end of all inductions, most of Hershey's concerns became largely moot. The system he had nurtured from birth was now moribund, or, to use a military phrase, "in deep standby."[7]

This last episode was especially irritating to Hershey because he was convinced that Congress would have extended induction authority if Nixon had only asked for such power. But the president refused to save the system. No one in the White House cared what Hershey thought about manpower or the draft. When he first became a presidential advisor, his memos usually elicited some response from the staff, even if it took several weeks. But in a short time he was simply ignored.[8]

With inductions ended, the time had come to clear Hershey out of his office. He had received his fourth star and been given a two-year grace period. With the press now concerned with other problems, including the Watergate scandals, Hershey's retirement was expected to receive little notice. On 25 January 1973, after the second Nixon inauguration and on the night of Lyndon Johnson's funeral, a White House staff member called Hershey and told him his job was ended. General Creighton Abrams, the chief of staff, assumed the responsibility for pushing Hershey into retirement. Undersecretary of the Army Kenneth E. Belieu arranged for an exchange of formal letters between Hershey and the president. Hershey spoke of the "high privilege" he had in serving Nixon. "I am proud," Hershey wrote with unintended irony, "to have been on your team when you took giant strides toward peace." He concluded the note with one final plea for the retention of decentralization. Nixon replied in the same spirit of hyperbole: "Millions of Americans have been called to the colors, reassured by your uncompromising fairness that their calling was not only necessary but eminently right and just." The president insisted that few Americans had so distinguished themselves in the onerous duty of citizen-soldier.[9]

Almost a month passed before Hershey formally retired. He took a physical at Walter Reed Hospital which concluded that he was suffering from 90 percent disability and was unfit for further duty. A special bill was introduced in the Senate to insure that he would retire with the rank and pay of a full general. Finally, on 26 March 1973, a reception was held at Fort McNair so that he could bid farewell to his many friends in and out of Congress. The next morning he appeared in full-dress uniform for a ceremony on the steps of the Pentagon. After the army band played "Ruffles and Flourishes" and troops fired a seventeen-gun salute, Secretary of Defense Elliot L. Richardson awarded Hershey the Department of Defense Distinguished Service Medal and spoke of his marshaling two generations of Americans for war. The ceremony over, Hershey retired to an obscure office in the Pentagon to await Senate approval of the special bill. The official date of his retirement was 10 April 1973. He had concluded sixty-two years of active military duty.[10]

At the age of seventy-nine Hershey packed away his uniform for the last time. The thought of retirement hardly excited him. His last physical exam had noted that he was "well nourished and in no acute distress," yet he had enough physical problems to satisfy most men. He had lost virtually all his vision. While his pulse was a steady 82 beats, he was suffering from high blood pressure (172/92) and from pernicious anemia. Considering these problems, and a few other minor deficiencies, he was reassured to learn that his peristalsis was normal.[11]

When someone had broached the idea of retirement to him several years earlier, Hershey had dismissed the prospect of bingo five nights a week. He need not have worried about inactivity. Soon he was being called upon by the Boy Scouts, for whom he helped finance a new camp at Goshen, Maryland. The Red Cross used him to help restore the Clara Barton House. His alma mater, Tri-State, continued to hope that he could help finance a physical education building in his name. Attempting to make the prospect more attractive, the school created a Hershey museum in part of the building, and Hershey sent his official papers to Tri-State as part of the project. But the school had neither the staff nor the interest to make use of such a collection. After learning that the papers remained unpacked, Hershey transferred them to the Army Military History Institute at Carlisle Barracks, Pennsylvania. He also spent time traveling, going to Hawaii for a conference on one occasion. His birthdays were celebrated by the Washington chapter of the Reserve Officers Association.[12]

Life at home also proved full of work. Ellen's chronic illnesses were becoming more severe. Many days she remained in bed while Lewis fixed and served the meals. He handled the other chores around the house because Ellen could not abide the several domestic servants who were hired. He also made frequent trips to Walter Reed Hospital and was amazed that he could consume up to seventeen different pills in one day without any discomfort. On a few occasions a physician raised the prospect of removing the cataract from his remaining eye, but opinion was divided on how much improvement such a procedure would produce, and Hershey dreaded the prospect of total blindness because of Ellen's needs. Some afternoons he spent in his office. A young scholar seeking information on the draft might arrive for a garrulous interview.[13]

When he reflected upon his career during such hours, Hershey expressed the attitudes he had formed many years earlier. He continued to emphasize the virtues of patriotism and to warn about illegal protests. The nation could not expect to survive if no one was willing to sacrifice. He admitted that Vietnam, or rather the way the country fought the Vietnam war, created special problems. Even after developing second thoughts about American intervention, however, he had little sympathy for those who had dodged their duty. When amnesty for those who had fled to Canada to avoid the draft was suggested in 1975, he lost his temper: "If you let all these bastards come back, if you ever have another war, who do you think is going to fight it?" He consistently opposed amnesty, although he was willing to have a special committee consider each case on its individual merits. He suggested that the maximum punishment for those found guilty should be only two years in jail or three years in the army.[14]

Hershey was disappointed with Nixon's dismantling of the system. He considered the Watergate scandals much overblown by the press and worried more about Nixon's attitude toward national defense than about such goings on. Hershey refused to adopt the neo-isolationist position of many critics of Vietnam. He felt that isolationism had become obsolete in the modern world, and that if America was to remain strong she needed a strong armed force. The all-volunteer system could not provide such strength. He hoped that the nation would see the dangers of disarmament before it was too late. In one of his last public appearances, during his birthday celebration on 11 September 1976, he insisted that his optimism remained constant: "If you trust the people they will do the job."[15]

The job had to be done without Hershey. On 20 February 1977 he suffered a stroke. Rushed to Walter Reed Hospital, he underwent neurosurgery for the removal of a blood clot. Although on the critical list for a few days, he soon rallied and began a slow recovery. President Carter sent a note of good wishes, adding, "You have encouraged and inspired so many of us over the years." The stroke had crippled Hershey and affected his speech. As he began a laborious program of rehabilitation, another blow fell. Ellen, as though reacting to the loss of her constant aide, suffered cardiac arrest on 3 April 1977. The loss undoubtedly affected Hershey's outlook, but he refused to give up. At Ellen's funeral he walked out of the chapel with someone holding his arm. For the next few weeks he worked diligently at his exercises, both verbal and physical, with aid from Gilbert and Kathryn. His temper became short as he felt the frustration of one who can still think clearly but cannot express his thoughts in an understandable fashion, but he made progress.[16]

Looking forward to resuming some activities, he accepted an invitation to attend the annual trustees' meeting at Tri-State in May. On 19 May he and Gilbert boarded a private plane for the flight to Bryan, Ohio. After a short ride to Angola and a visit to the Hershey museum, they checked into the local Holiday Inn, which sat almost on the top of the old Hershey farm. After dinner, Hershey visited his sister-in-law, Ruby, who was now confined to a rest home. Returning in good spirits to the motel around 9:30, he retired for the night, surrounded by pseudo-Spanish decor. At six the next morning he became ill; an hour later he was dead. With the cooperation of the military commander at Fort Benjamin Harrison in Indianapolis, the body was removed and an autopsy performed. The cause of death was established as cardiac arrest and general arteriosclerosis. His body was flown to Washington for interment at Arlington National Cemetery in a gravesite which had recently welcomed Ellen.[17]

The weather was overcast with light rain, a day for a funeral. But not even the rain could detract from the noble vista of the Memorial Bridge, the Lincoln Memorial, the Mall, and the dome of the Capitol spread out below Arlington National Cemetery. Visitors strolled through the immaculate grounds with grave markers stretching like neat white tablets from one horizon to the other. Tourists on their way to visit the Kennedy grave noticed activity at the Memorial Chapel, a modernistic building on the grounds of Fort Myer. Someone important was receiving a full-dress funeral from the army. The strains of "The General's March" drifted over the grounds as a casket entered the chapel.

Inside some three hundred people heard Chaplain David W. Kent read the appropriate passages: "I am the Resurrection and the Life . . . ; for everything there is a season . . . ; the Lord is my shepherd . . . ; let not your heart be troubled." After a brief eulogy by Colonel Arthur Holmes of Michigan, the casket left the chapel to "Ruffles and Flourishes" and "O God, Our Help in Ages Past." The caisson was loaded and 175 men representing the five branches of the armed forces, including the young men of the Old Guard, began the slow march of escort. Memories of the Kennedy funeral stirred as the six black horses pulled the caisson, followed by Midnight, the riderless horse with boots reversed in the stirrups. The procession wound its slow way toward a section of the cemetery distinguished by the graves of General George C. Marshall and General Walter Bedell Smith. The army band, known as "Pershing's Own" by the soldiers of the 3rd Infantry, played "Onward, Christian Soldiers" as the procession stopped before an open grave marked with a black marble headstone.

Suddenly the visitors were shocked by the roar of cannons firing a seventeen-gun salute. After a brief benediction at the gravesite, a squad of infantrymen fired three volleys of musketry. From a small knoll overlooking the scene a solitary bugler played "Taps." General Lewis Blaine Hershey, after over sixty years of active duty, took his rest. His grave overlooked the halls of Congress where, on this twenty-fifth day of May, 1977, politicians debated the future of the Selective Service System that he had created and shaped for thirty years. The controversy over the draft remained visible in graffiti scribbled by youthful protesters on the monuments of Washington. Hershey had left the scene of combat, but the problems of military manpower remained.

Lewis Hershey had died only a few yards away from the site of his boyhood home, but he had traveled a mighty distance during his career. As the man in charge of conscription for over thirty years he had touched the lives of millions of Americans. In the last stage of his career he had become a public figure on the order of J. Edgar Hoover, a symbol to many of either virtue or evil. Hershey's career had taken him around the world; the farmboy from Hell's Corner had rubbed elbows with presidents and princes. In a material sense, however, he had not been greatly enriched. When he died his estate totaled less than $400,000 and included two shares in the Dusenberg Motor Company, dated 1922.[18]

Biographers face the danger that, thinking they know all, they may justify all. It is also difficult to assess a personality who has so recently made his mark. Hershey himself pointed to this problem: "I suppose if one listens to a historian we will have to wait fifty years or so to find out if a mistake was made and even then I am sure it will be debatable." Debate in history is partially the result of shifting perspectives, different points of view. Even during his career Hershey's behavior was subject to evaluations from different points of view. What appeared virtues to some seemed clearly vices to others.[19]

In a narrow context, Hershey did succeed in his primary task as director of Selective Service. Under his leadership the system delivered manpower to the armed forces in adequate numbers. Not until Nixon began his campaign to dismantle the system in 1970 was there any serious failure to meet calls. During Hershey's directorship the Selective Service System inducted over 14,555,000 men into the armed forces. Remarkably, this system received a high degree of public endorsement in a nation not accustomed to conscription. Even as late as 1965 over 64 percent of those polled approved of the draft; a 1966 poll of students revealed that 90 percent favored it. The draft had many problems, but it was emphatically not unpopular; nor was it an agent of social Darwinism, as some critics have charged, grinding up society's losers. After a short experience with the all-volunteer army, some wondered whether the Selective Service did a better job of distributing the burden of military service among all social classes.[20]

One scholar has called Hershey a classic institutional leader, a man who led by virtue of his mastery of the bureaucracy rather than because of his charisma. Yet Hershey himself, when asked to describe his techniques of leadership, offered the acronym WALK: work, adaptability, loyalty, and knowledge. Clearly his success as a leader came from informal techniques, rather than formal structures. In a sense Hershey could be considered a godfather to the Selective Service System. He stressed the idea that the system was a family; all across the country local officials looked upon him as the pater familias who presided benignly. As two of his staff officers recalled: "We were his family. When you hurt, he hurt."[21]

Hershey achieved this paternal status primarily through the force of his own personality. He was a man of physical and intellectual vigor, to which he added a remarkable integrity which stood the test of journalistic scrutiny for almost thirty years. Given the sorry records of many of his political contemporaries, this was a remarkable achievement. He put people at ease with his self-effacing posture. Despite his rank, he never posed as a prima donna; he went out of his way to become familiar with everyone in the system, from elevator operators to state directors. Above all, he maintained a human touch and always reminded everyone that their work concerned individuals rather than numbers. His loyalty to subordinates was legendary and frequently led to problems. Although frugal in his personal expenses, he freely subsidized friends in need. His tolerance ranged from homosexuals to religious dissenters. Congressmen applauded him because he seemed to embody what was called the "common touch."[22]

Hershey also succeeded in his leadership role because he reflected and supported several enduring myths. The system was built upon the myth of rural America, of small towns where everyone knew everyone else and where defense was the responsibility of the citizen-soldier. Hershey believed in the patriotic community, where loyalty was a paramount virtue and where the most honored citizen was the veteran. He was committed to an egalitarian community, where class and race tensions did not exist and everyone worked for the general good. This philosophy stirred strong feelings of support among his "family," whose members responded with enthusiasm to his leadership. Hershey did not need statutory authority to influence his system. As one staff officer wrote, "For twenty-five years I have tried to do successfully a job in which the impetus and the inspiration came 80 percent directly from you as an individual. I have found myself unconsciously sounding like you and telling your stories because your own personality has influenced mine so greatly over these years." Time and time again his state directors spoke of the "genuine affection we hold for you, our greatest chief." Local boards tried to do what Hershey wanted without being asked. No godfather could have asked for more.[23]

As a national bureaucrat Hershey showed remarkable political talents. He took a very flexible approach to his power under the law, admitting that he frequently had to act on his own interpretation of congressional intent. To his staff he insisted, "It is quite a bit easier to have the righteousness of being legally right rather than to have the character to be sensibly illegal." Even when Congress authorized him to act, he felt no compulsion to use his potential power. Such an attitude did little to hinder his reputation in Washington.[24]

Hershey's experience with the Selective Service System enhances our understanding of the growth of modern bureaucracy. If nothing else, the Hershey story shows the caution with which students should approach "the emerging organizational synthesis" in recent American history, to borrow a phrase from Louis Galambos.[25] For all the literature about the twentieth-century United States experiencing changes leading to the managerial, the positive, the regulator state (call it what you will), the Hershey experience provides little support for such trends. The Selective Service System seems an anachronism in the face of such developments, which move with what some call "an irresistible historical logic."[26]

A recent study has emphasized that the public wants its federal bureaucracy to be both efficient and responsive—occasionally incompatible goals. Two models for bureaucracy exist. One goes back to the interest group theory of James Madison, where broad access to government by a variety of interest groups generated safety in countervailing forces. The other revolves around the efficiency and rationalistic notions of one side of the Progressive movement, with emphasis upon experts making objective decisions free from politics. Hershey seemed to favor the Madisonian approach, despite his claims to be apolitical. On more than one occasion he emphasized his hope that democracy might be preserved through finding voluntary rather than compulsory ways to have citizens do their duty.[27]

Hershey was a permanent bureaucrat who saw presidents come and go. As such, his career should be filled with information on organizational trends. Instead, we find that the draft system resembled a dry goods store of the nineteenth century, rather than a modern supermarket. It was this character which shocked the young organization men sent over by Nixon in 1970. On several occasions the system faced challenges from within the federal government. After World War II the National Security Resources Board tried and failed to bring Hershey under its wing. The Hoover commission's attempt to place Hershey and the draft under the Department of Labor was likewise frustrated by the director's political astuteness.

Clearly, as the most recent study has shown, there was no overall manpower planning in the post–World War II period.[28] Yet, ironically, Hershey should not be blamed for this failure. While he ran a decentralized organization, he personally advocated manpower planning as indicated by his constant calls for centralization of military manpower sources. Above all, his notion of using the draft for channeling young men into useful occupations and college courses exemplifies his sympathy for planning. Yet, while such a plan might look attractive to efficiency experts, historical circumstances insured that such channeling would be one of the most condemned aspects of the draft in the 1960's. Here is another reminder that general societal and organizational trends can be evaluated only within their historical context. Of course, Hershey should not be taken for a committed national planner. He had ideas which promoted planning, but his philosophical commitment to the decentralized system of local boards made him a rather exceptional national bureaucrat.

In many ways Hershey was sui generis in the federal government. As a general officer he was tied to the military establishment, but he was first and foremost a civilian bureaucrat who understood how politics worked at the state and national levels. He was a member of each new administration but frequently found himself opposed to such ideas as the volunteer system and the lottery. When testifying in public he supported the administration's line, but in private he conveyed his own views—views which became known to draft officials and to congressmen.

The knowledge Hershey accumulated over decades in the same role insured that he would have little trouble answering questions. He was well aware of the importance of congressional committees and went out of his way to cultivate important leaders by uttering phrases they would enjoy. He was always fond of praising the particular states represented by the committee members. By the 1960's he had become a legend on Capitol Hill. Hebert and other congressmen might shake their heads at Hershey's wandering syntax, but they always enjoyed his appearances. By running a system which depended upon the cooperation of governors and local elites, he had developed a broad base of sympathetic political factions across the country. In his headquarters he assigned one man responsibility for liaison with all veterans' organizations, another source of political muscle. Although some were embarrassed by the idea, all of his associates had to admit that their director was a magnificent political animal.[29]

Hershey never took time to write his autobiography, but there is little question about what he would have stressed as his most significant achievement. He was always convinced that he had made a valuable contribution to the preservation of democracy by demonstrating that decentralization of responsibility could work, even in modern America. As a life-long Jeffersonian, Hershey believed deeply in the ideal of community and of the common man, in making decisions at the local level, in assuming responsibility for his own welfare without awaiting direction from Washington.[30] Ironically, Hershey, who played a major role in preserving and expanding a bureaucracy which directly expressed the conscription power of the federal government, always retained an anticentralist point of view. Once, when discussing the dangers of a nuclear attack, he offered his state directors what would be his last words if the bomb fell on Washington: "Carry on, boys. All authority is vested in you."[31]

From the vantage point of those outside the system, Hershey, like all godfathers, had many failings. His rather flexible attitude toward administering the law could be seen as bordering on irresponsibility. By the 1960's he seemed to have lost his political touch and his flexibility. In refusing to accept any revision of the system, he invited critics to launch additional attacks. Although he probably could not have avoided becoming a symbol for an unpopular war, his adamant rejection of reform proposals and his frequent public statements deriding protesters did not help his cause. When he did begin to compromise, under Nixon, it was too late.

Although many in government admired his administrative talents, Hershey was not without faults. His management of the draft apparatus was a classic example of rule through elites. In this case the elites resided on the local and state level. What bound these men together was not so much wealth as worldview. The draft system united individuals with a similar outlook on foreign affairs. The boards were male, white, and middle class. Members came from veterans', patriotic, and business groups; such men uniformly favored a strong defense system and supported the anti-communist programs of various presidents. Hershey also had access to political elites at the state and national levels. The system made participants out of governors, adjutants general, and congressmen. Many of the congressmen who questioned Hershey had previously served in the system on the state and local levels. Perhaps such elite leadership was to be expected; certainly, when one thinks of alternatives, such as the Pentagon elite or a federal bureaucratic elite, these local elites seem more democratic. Local men with influence were needed to mobilize the community.

Because he viewed the system as a family, Hershey fell into cronyism. Rather than maintaining a vibrant staff, constantly welcoming new blood with new ideas, Hershey remained satisfied with his old hands, many of whom were either too old or too indoctrinated to provide the type of criticism he needed. He consistently refused to train his own replacement. This same attitude created problems in the local boards, where the lack of turnover insured an aging staff. Hershey could never accept the criticism that local boards were not functioning according to his community myth. To admit that an urban, restless America had made the local boards inefficient or inappropriate was to admit that the old America and its traditional values no longer existed.

Perhaps Hershey's major failing was the narrowness of his vision. He represented a conservative tradition not merely in his view of society but also in his view of national defense. In his commitment to the draft he carried on the nineteenth-century tradition of relying upon the citizen soldier, a militia rising to arms. The army, however, had rejected this concept as outmoded. In the twentieth century the armed forces, like civilian associations, began a drive toward total professionalism. To make this new organizational concept work it was necessary to insure long-term service by volunteers. While the crises of World War I, World War II, Korea, and Vietnam might force the army to swallow the bitter pill of the draft, officials were never reconverted to the older concept of the citizen soldier as represented by Hershey's draft. Unfortunately, new global responsibilities assumed after World War II required that any professional force be of significant size, but the United States never accepted the implications of such a commitment in its military spending. Hence Hershey became tied in a paradox: the army wanted a professional force; the administration wanted worldwide commitments on a lean defense budget. The draft was cheap, but only Hershey thought it the best solution. When an opportunity arose in the early 1970's to move away from conscription toward a better-paid professional force of volunteers, the draft died.[32]

Hershey, however, believed that a professional army was inimical to the concepts of democracy and America. He failed to anticipate problems that would arise both from within the administration and from opponents of the Vietnam war. He reacted to these new problems in an uncompromising way, elevating the preservation of the unchanged draft system into an end in itself. The system was his life, and it embodied his deepest beliefs about the nation. A threat to its destruction was a personal threat. Hershey had built the system and his career upon powerful national myths, myths eventually made insecure by an urban, pluralistic America fighting an undeclared war in Asia. But for Hershey the myths also functioned as normative guides, as signposts of how Americans should travel, and he committed much of his career to enhancing their reality. The draft system should be retained, he felt, because it was a school teaching these values.

Hershey worshipped his own vision of community. This vision stayed with him when he left his own small town and took a role on a much larger national stage. In the Selective Service System he found a perfect instrument for the preservation of his concept. Soon signs appeared, however, indicating that the older village and community must be replaced by modernization, urbanization, anomie. The weakening of patriotism, loyalty, and duty during the Vietnam war seemed dangerous trends to Hershey; hence it became, in his mind, all the more essential to preserve one institution which represented the older concept of community. In fact, local community or village systems continued to thrive in modern urban America. Much of the youth revolt of the 1960's stressed the communal life style. In big cities neighborhood villages existed. Hershey saw only the signs of attack on his cherished folk vision of community as institutionalized in the Selective Service System. These attacks made him even more committed to preserving unchanged his community of local boards.

Over thirty years he had developed a system in which the draft apparatus appeared to him as an extended family rather than a federal bureaucracy. At the end of his career this community was threatened by modernizers who wished to streamline, centralize, nationalize. Small wonder, then, that Hershey should fight such trends. They threatened not merely his job, but also his very hope for America. Hershey made many mistakes in his last few years, but, in a sense, he was no different from other leaders who sought to mold their environments to fit their own conceptions of the good society.

Notes

ABBREVIATIONS

ARC	Army Record Center, St. Louis, Mo.
DF	Elizabeth Denny File, Vienna, Va. (private).
EP	Dwight D. Eisenhower Papers, Eisenhower Library, Abilene, Kans.
FDR	Franklin D. Roosevelt Papers, Roosevelt Library, Hyde Park, N.Y.
GF	Gilbert Hershey Files, Jacksonville, N.C.
GMP	George C. Marshall Papers, Lexington, Va.
HD	Lewis Hershey Diary, in Gilbert Hershey Files.
HHP	Harry Hopkins Papers, Roosevelt Library, Hyde Park, N.Y.
HP	Lewis Hershey Papers, Military History Institute, Carlisle Barracks, Pa.
HST	Harry S Truman Papers, Truman Library, Independence, Mo.
JFK	John F. Kennedy Papers, Kennedy Library, Boston, Mass.
JH	Joan Hershey Notes, Gilbert Hershey File, Jacksonville, N.C. (private).
KLF	Kathryn Hershey Layne Files, Washington, D.C. (private).
KP	Frank V. Keesling Papers, San Francisco, Calif. (private).
LBJ	Lyndon B. Johnson Papers, Johnson Library, Austin, Tex.
LC	Library of Congress, Washington, D.C.
MHI	Military History Institute, Carlisle Barracks, Pa.
MD	Henry Morgenthau Diaries, Roosevelt Library, Hyde Park, N.Y.
NA	National Archives, Washington, D.C.
NYT	*New York Times*.
OF	Official Files.
OHC	Oral History Collection, Military History Institute, Carlisle Barracks, Pa.
OP	Official Papers.
PMP	Paul McNutt Papers, Lilly Library, Indiana University, Bloomington, Ind.
RG	Record Group
RPP	Robert Patterson Papers, Library of Congress, Washington, D.C.
SD	Henry Stimson Diary, Sterling Library, Yale University, New Haven, Conn.
SP	Henry Stimson Papers, Sterling Library, Yale University, New Haven, Conn.
SRP	Samuel Rosenman Papers, Roosevelt Library, Hyde Park, N.Y
SS	*Selective Service*, monthly newspaper, 4 pp.
WP	James Wadsworth Papers, Library of Congress, Washington, D.C.
WP	*Washington Post*.

PROLOGUE

1. Transcript of UCLA talk, 9 Oct. 1970, Lewis Hershey Papers, Military History Institute, Carlisle Barracks, Pa. (hereafter cited as HP).

CHAPTER I

1. Joan Hershey notes, 19 June 1977, in Gilbert Hershey file, Jacksonville, N.C. (hereafter cited as JH).

2. Ibid. For the elaborate Hershey genealogy, see Henry Hershey, comp., *Hershey Family History* (Scottdale, Pa.: Mennonite Publishing House, 1929), and Scott F. Hershey, *History and Records of the Hershey Family from the Year 1600* (New Castle, Pa.: Petite Book Co., n.d.).

3. JH, 19 June 1977; Hershey to Mrs. Peggy Bush, 12 Jan. 1971, ibid.

4. JH, 19 June 1977; Hershey to Joan Hershey, 3 Aug. 1969, JH.

5. JH, 19 June 1977; Ruby Hershey interview.

6. Ruby Hershey interview; Hershey to Joan Hershey, 10 Aug. 1969, Gilbert Hershey file, Jacksonville, N.C. (hereafter cited as GF); JH, 19 June 1977; Hershey to Mrs. Grace V. Welsh, 3 Feb. 1942, HP; Gary L. Wamsley, *Selective Service and a Changing America* (Columbus: Charles Merrill, 1969), p. 185; Kathryn Hershey Layne interview; Latta Hershey, obituary, *Steuben Republican*, n.d., Kathryn Hershey Layne files, Washington, D.C. (hereafter cited as KLF); Lewis Hershey Diary (hereafter cited as HD), 17 July 1917, GF.

7. Lynn W. Elston interview; John W. McClellan interview; JH, 19 June 1977; Lewis to Mr. Powell, 20 Nov. 1967, alpha file, HP; Viola (Blackman) to Hershey, 6 May 1913, GF; Aunt Alma to Lewis, 20 Nov. 1917, ibid.; Ruby Hershey interview.

8. Ellen Dygert Diary, 20 Feb. 1911, GF; Ruby Hershey interview; JH, 19 June 1977; HD, 22 July 1917, ibid.

9. Documentation of sexual activity is difficult, but the correspondence of these young men and women is filled with allusions to the subject. See Paul Shelley to Lewis Hershey correspondence, 1910–15; Hazel I. Shirly to Hershey, 2 Dec. 1913; Ellen to Lewis, 24 Sept. 1908; Floyd Eckert to Lewis, 4 Mar. 1912; Ellen Dygert Diary, 4 July 1910, all GF.

10. JH, 19 June 1977; Hershey to Joan Hershey, 10 Aug. 1969, JH; Indiana State Series, 3rd and 4th Readers, all ibid.

11. Hershey report cards, 6 Oct. 1905, 2, 31 Mar. 1906; Hershey to Joan Hershey, 10 Aug. 1969, JH; Hershey essay, "Success," 2 June 1906, all ibid.

12. JH, 19 June 1977; Hershey to Barbara Burkanzer, 29 Jan. 1963, alpha file, HP; Bruce R. Corey to Hershey, 25 Apr. 1910, GF; Hershey report cards, 1908–9, 1909–10, ibid.; Lynn W. Elston interview.

13. JH, 19 June 1977; Gilbert Hershey interview, 8–15 Aug. 1977; Kathryn Hershey Layne interview; Teresa Kundred interview.

14. Ruby Hershey interview; Lynn W. Elston interview; Ellen to Lewis, 28 July, 9 Nov. 1916, GF.

15. Several hundred letters are in GF.

16. Ellen to Lewis, 13 June, 5 Nov. 1908, 11 Oct 1909; Ellen Dygert Diary, 19 Nov., 20 Dec. 1909; JH, 19 June 1977, all ibid.

17. Ellen Dygert Diary, 16 Feb., 13 Apr., 4 May 1910, ibid.

18. Ellen Dygert Diary, 27, 28 May 1910; Ellen to Lewis, 1 June 1910, both ibid.

19. Ellen Dygert Diary, 1911, 1912, ibid.

20. Ellen to Lewis, 1913–14, Manila letters, ibid.

21. See Lewis Hershey correspondence, 1913–14, ibid.

22. Paul Shelley to Hershey, 16 Feb., 16 Mar., 22 Apr. 1914, ibid.

23. Tri-State College catalog, 1910, Tri-State Archives, Angola, Ind.

24. Faculty handbook and catalogs, 1913–14, Tri-State Archives; Lynn W. Elston interview.

25. JH, 19 June 1977; Peggy Bush interview of Hershey, 28 May 1971, HP.

26. Bush interview of Hershey, 28 May 1971, HP; JH, 19 June 1977.

27. Hershey's teacher's certificate, State of Indiana, 25 Mar. 1911, GF; Hershey to Joan Hershey, 23 June 1968, ibid.; Lynn W. Elston interview.

28. Hershey to Joan Hershey, 23 June 1968, GF; Lynn W. Elston interview; Hershey to Doc Elston, 26 Feb. 1970, alpha file, HP; Ruby Hershey interview; O'Sullivan questionnaire, 13 Sept. 1974, GF.

29. Lewis Hershey report card, 23 Feb. 1912, GF; teacher's certificate, 25 Mar. 1911, ibid.; Bush interview of Hershey, 28 May 1971, HP; JH, 19 June 1977.

30. Bush interview of Hershey, 28 May 1971, HP.

31. Class grade books, 1910–13, Tri-State Archives; Lynn W. Elston interview.

32. Lynn W. Elston interview; Ellen Dygert Diary, 6 Dec. 1911, 17 Jan., 20 Feb. 1912, GF.

33. Copy of debate, n.d., GF; Bush interview of Hershey, 28 May 1971, HP; Gertrude to Lewis, 21 Aug. 1914, GF; Ellen Dygert Diary, 29 Mar. 1912, ibid.

34. Lynn W. Elston interview; Mugs to Hershey, 19 Sept. 1914, GF; Bush interview of Hershey, 28 May 1971, HP.

35. JH, 19 June 1977; Kathryn Hershey Layne interview; John W. McClellan interview; Harry S. New to Hershey, 7 Apr. 1916, GF; Ellen to Lewis, 21 Nov. 1916, ibid.; HD, 23 Sept. 1916, ibid.; County Board of Education, 1916, ibid.

36. "Rules and Regulations of the Steuben County Board of Education," 1916, GF.

37. JH, 19 June 1977; William Ayres to Hershey, 7 Oct. 1916; sundry letters to Hershey, Oct., 1916; Opal L. Bowerman to Hershey, 1 Oct. 1916; Lora to Hershey, 2 Aug. 1916; Shank to Hershey, 27 June 1916, all ibid.

38. Elsie Hoopingarner to Hershey, 2 Feb. 1913, ibid.

39. Martha Derthick, *The National Guard in Politics* (Cambridge: Harvard University Press, 1965), pp. 14–28.

40. Ruby Hershey interview; Ellen Dygert Diary, 9 Feb. 1911, GF.

41. Teresa Kundred interview; JH, 19 June 1977.

42. Sewerd Pipe to Hershey, 15 Dec. 1913, GF; Lewis to folks, 7 Nov. 1913, ibid.

43. JH, 19 June 1977; O'Sullivan questionnaire, 13 Sept. 1974; HD, 17 June 1920; Roy Kauffman to Hershey, 22 Feb. 1913; Harris Garrett to Hershey, 13 May 1913; Fred Godlove to Hershey, 20 June 1913, all GF; John W. McClellan interview.

44. Jesse Covell to Hershey, 8 Aug. 1913; Willis Leming to Hershey, 21 Aug. 1913; Foster Hanck to Hershey, 5 June 1915; N. Rewling to Hershey, 26 July 1915, all GF.

45. Faye Bangs to Hershey, 19 June 1916; HD, 19 June 1916, both ibid.

46. HD, 7–13 July 1916; Lewis to folks, 8 July 1916; Ellen to Lewis, 13 July 1916, all ibid.

47. HD, 12 July 1916; Lewis to Latta, 20, 27 July, 6 Aug. 1916, all ibid.

48. *Steuben Republican*, 26 July 1916.

49. HD, 11, 17 July 1916; Lewis to Dad, 13 July, 6 Aug. 1916, GF.

50. HD, 21, 29 July, 23 Oct., 11, 17 Nov. 1916, ibid.

51. HD, 29 July, 12 Aug. 1916, ibid.

52. Mrs. Georgia Ickes to Hershey, 24 July 1916; HD, 29 July, 7 Aug. 1916, ibid.

53. HD, 19 Aug., 14, 16 Sept. 1916, ibid.

54. HD, 25 Aug. 1916; Hershey to folks, 3 Oct. 1916; Jesse Covell to Hershey, 10 Sept. 1916, all ibid.; Hershey interview, Sept. 1974, HP.

55. HD, 2, 5, 16, 23 Sept. 1916, GF.

56. Ellen to Lewis, 11 Oct. 1916; HD, Oct. 1916; Lewis to Dad, 31 Oct. 1916, all ibid.

57. HD, 4, 13, 18, 25 Nov. 1916; Lewis to Latta, 12 Nov. 1916; Ellen to Lewis, 18 Nov. 1916, all ibid.

58. HD, 11 Dec. 1916, ibid.

59. HD, 29 Dec. 1916, ibid.

60. HD, 2 Jan. 1914, 9 Sept. 1916, ibid.

61. HD, 23 Sept. 1916; Ellen to Lewis, 26 Sept. 1916; W. O. Bailey to Hershey, 29 Sept., 16 Oct. 1916, ibid.

62. HD, 29, 31 Jan. 1917; 9, 12 Feb. 1917, ibid.

63. Lewis to Dad, 13 Feb. 1917; HD, 2, 3, 5 Feb. 1917, ibid.

64. HD, 2, 8, 21 Feb., 2 Mar. 1917, ibid.

65. Hershey lesson plan, 1917, ibid.

66. IU transcript, Lewis Hershey 201 file, Army Record Center, St. Louis (hereafter cited as ARC).

67. Dean H. L. Smith to Hershey, 6 June 1917; HD, 3 Feb., 5, 12 Mar. 1917; Jesse Covell to Hershey, 10 Feb. 1917, all GF.

CHAPTER II

1. Ellen to Lewis, 30 Mar. 1917; Lewis to folks, 27 Mar. 1917; Jesse Covell to Hershey, 7 Mar. 1917, GF.

2. Jesse Covell to Hershey, 3 Apr. 1917; HD, 4 Apr. 1917, ibid.

3. HD, Apr.-June 1917; draft letter to Dean William A. Rawles, 21 May 1917; Hershey to Commander J. B. Koch, 7 July 1917, ibid.

4. HD, 7 June 1917, ibid.

5. HD, May and June 1917, ibid.

6. HD, 27 July, 5, 12, 29 Aug. 1917, ibid.

7. HD, 9, 10 Sept. 1917; Lewis to Latta, 18 Sept. 1917, all ibid.; *Steuben Republican*, 12 Sept. 1917.

8. Lewis to Dad, 2, 18, 22 Oct. 1917; Latta to Lewis, 23 Oct. 1917, all GF; quote in HD, 15 Oct. 1917, ibid.

9. Rigelmann to Hershey, 6 Nov. 1917, GF.

10. Ellen to Lewis, 27 June, 5, 7, 19 Aug. 1916, 22 Feb., 8 Mar. 1917, ibid.; Joan Hershey interview, 27 Aug. 1977.

11. Ellen to Lewis, 8, 10, 22 Sept. 1917, GF.

12. Lewis to Ellen, 30 Oct. 1917, ibid.

13. Ellen to Lewis, 1 Nov. 1917; Lewis to Ellen, 6 Nov. 1917; Ellen to Lewis, 12, 21 Nov. 1917; HD, Nov.-Dec. 1917, all ibid.

14. Lewis to Russ, 10 Dec. 1917; HD, 13 Dec. 1917, 25, 28 Jan., 11 Mar. 1918, ibid.

15. HD, 28 Sept. 1917; Edgar Williams to Hershey, 22 Aug. 1918; Jesse Covell to Hershey, 7 Mar. 1918, ibid.

16. HD, Mar.-Apr. 1918, ibid.

17. HD, 4, 6 Apr. 1918; Ellen to Lewis, 3 Apr. 1918, ibid. His father, meanwhile, had a different opinion and raced down to Fort Wayne to buy a suitcase full of booze at a closing sale.

18. HD, 30 Apr. 1918, ibid.

19. HD, 27 May-8 June 1918, ibid.

20. HD, June-Aug. 1918; Lewis to Dad, 11 Sept. 1918; Ellen to Latta, 12 Aug. 1918; report of physical, 29 June 1918, all ibid.

21. Ellen to Lewis, 12 Sept. 1918; HD, 12–19 Sept. 1918; Lewis to Dad, 13 Sept. 1918, ibid.

22. HD, 12, 17, 19 Sept. 1918, ibid.

23. HD, 13, 16 Nov. 1917, 25, 26 Sept. 1918, ibid.; editorial, *Selective Service* (hereafter cited as *SS*), Nov. 1966.

24. HD, 28 Sept., 7 Oct. 1918, GF; Ellen to Lewis, 17 Nov. 1918, ibid.; Hershey to Raymond W. Miller, 31 Oct. 1969, alpha file, HP.

25. HD, Oct. 1918, GF.

26. HD, 30 Oct., 6, 9, 11, 17 Nov. 1918, ibid.

27. HD, 29 Nov.-5 Dec. 1918, ibid.

28. HD, 29 Nov., 10 Dec. 1918, 6 Jan. 1919; Lewis to Ellen, 26 Dec. 1918; Lewis to Dad, 20, 25 Dec. 1918, all ibid.; Lt. Col. F. F. Jewett to Hershey, 23 Aug. 1919, Hershey 201 file, ARC.

29. Lewis to Dad, 20 Dec. 1918; HD, 24–31 Dec. 1918, GF.

30. Lewis to Ellen, 13 Jan. 1919; HD, 21 Dec. 1918, 29 Jan. 1919, ibid.

31. HD, 31 Dec. 1918; Lewis to Ellen, 24 Dec. 1918, 1 Jan. 1919; Ellen to Lewis, 7, 10 Jan. 1919, ibid.

32. HD, 15, 18 Jan. 1919; Lewis to Bess, 15 Jan. 1919, ibid.

33. O'Sullivan questionnaire, 13 Sept. 1974; HD, 18, 26 Feb. 1919; Lewis to Dad, 8 Mar. 1919, all ibid.

34. O'Sullivan questionnaire, 13 Sept. 1974; Lewis to Dad, 8 Mar. 1919, ibid.

35. HD, 26 Mar., 22 June 1919; Lewis to Dad, 21 Apr. 1919, ibid.

36. HD, 3 Apr., 27 July, 1, 4, 11 Aug. 1919, ibid.

37. HD, 1 May, 18 Sept. 1919, ibid.

38. HD, 14–15 May 1919, ibid.

39. HD, 16–31 May 1919; Lewis to Aunt Alma, 31 May 1919; HD, 15 June 1919, ibid.

40. HD, 28 Aug., 6 Sept. 1919, ibid.

41. Lewis to Dad, 12 Dec. 1918; HD, 5 Nov. 1918; Lewis to Aunt Alma, 24 Nov. 1918, ibid.

42. HD, 13, 25 Apr., 9 May, 6, 25 June 1919, ibid.

43. HD, 28 Nov. 1918; Hershey to *Steuben Republican*, 11 Feb., 6 Apr., 30 May 1919; Lewis to Dad, 16 Aug. 1919; Ellen to Lewis, 21 Apr. 1919, ibid.

44. Lewis to Dad, 12 Dec. 1918; Ellen to Lewis, 26 Nov. 1918; Lewis to Dad, 12 July 1919, ibid.

45. F. F. Jewett to Hershey, 23 Aug. 1919, ibid.; Hershey efficiency report, Feb.-Aug. 1919, Hershey 201 file, ARC.

46. HD, 14–29 Sept. 1919, GF.

47. HD, 29 Sept.-8 Oct., 18 Nov. 1919, ibid.

48. Ellen to Lewis, 28 Apr. 1919; HD, 28 Oct., 3, 5, 6, 7 Nov. 1919; 19, 30 Apr. 1920, ibid.

49. HD, 9 Jan., 21, 25 Feb. 1921, ibid.

50. HD, 28 Jan., 18 Feb., 4 Mar., 4 June, quotes in 8 June, 7 July 1920, ibid.

51. HD, 2, 21 Sept., 6 Oct., 2 Nov. 1920, 10 Mar. 1921, quote in 26 Mar. 1921, ibid.

52. HD, 16 Oct. 1919, May 1920, 15 Jan. 1921, ibid.; efficiency reports, 1921, and educational certificates, 1919–20, Camp Pike, both in Hershey 201 file, ARC.

53. HD, Mar., May 1920, Apr. 1921, GF.

54. HD, 18 Mar., 20 May 1920, quotes in 24 June, 8 July 1920, ibid.; applications and recommendations, 1920, Hershey 201 file, ARC. The effective date of his commission was 1 July 1920, but he officially accepted it on 2 Sept.

55. HD, 13, 29 Nov. 1920, GF.

56. HD, Jan.-Apr. 1921, ibid.

57. HD, Sept. 1921, ibid.

58. HD, Sept.-Oct. 1921, quote from 17 Dec. 1921; Lewis to Dad, 16 Sept. 1921, ibid.

59. HD, Nov.-Dec. 1921, Jan.-Apr. 1922, ibid.

60. HD, Oct.-Nov. 1921, ibid.

61. Hershey to Lee Williams, n.d., alpha file, HP; HD, Dec. 1921, Jan.-June 1922, GF.

62. HD, 1 Nov. 1921, quotes from 4 Mar., 2 May 1922, ibid.

63. HD, 6 Apr., 8 July, 4 Aug. 1922, ibid.

64. HD, 6 Feb. 1922, ibid.

65. HD, July-Sept. 1922, ibid.

66. HD, Sept.-Dec. 1922, Jan. 1923, ibid; student report, Field Artillery School, 15 June 1923, Hershey 201 file, ARC.

67. HD, 23 Aug., 6, 7, 9 Nov., 31 Dec. 1922, 29 Jan. 1923, GF.

68. Quotes in HD, 31 Dec. 1922, 23 Jan. 1923; see also 26 Jan. 1923, ibid.

69. HD, 31 Dec. 1922, 11, 21 Jan., 19 Feb., 4 Mar., 6 Apr. 1923, ibid.

70. HD, 27 Feb., May-June 1923, ibid.

71. HD, 12 May, 20–21 June 1923, ibid.

72. Ellen to Lewis, 30 July, 1 Aug. 1923, 13 June, 1 July 1924; Lewis to Ellen, 20, 27 Dec. 1924; 13 July 1925, ibid.

73. Quote in HD, 17 Aug. 1923, ibid; Peggy Bush interview of Hershey, 28 May 1971, HP; Hershey memo to Director of Intramural Athletics, n.d., GF; Major B. E. Brewer to Col. Arthur M. Shipp, 26 May 1927, ibid.; Hershey to Laurel E. Leonard, 14 Apr. 1970, alpha file, HP.

74. Ruby Hershey interview; Lewis to Ellen, 29 Sept. 1927, GF; Kathryn Hershey Layne interview.

75. HD, Sept.-Oct. 1927; Lewis to Ellen, 11, 22 Sept., 2 Oct. 1927, GF.

76. HD, Apr.-May 1929; quote in Lewis to Dad, 21 Apr. 1929, ibid.

77. Certificate by Captain Milton W. Hall, MC, 23 Nov. 1927, Hershey 201 file, ARC; board of inquiry report, 29 Nov. 1927, Fort Bliss, ibid.

78. Efficiency reports, 28 July 1927–30 June 1928; 1 July 1928–30 June 1929; July 1929–June 1930; quote from report of July 1930-June 1931, ibid.

79. Captain B. M. Sawbridge to Hershey, 27 Feb. 1931, GF; Gilbert Hershey interview, 8–15 Aug. 1977; *Steuben Republican*, n.d., KLF.

80. Efficiency reports, Aug. 1931–June 1933, Hershey 201 file, ARC; Col. E. K. Sterling to Hershey, 1 Feb., 6, 24, 27 May 1933, GF; Bush interview of Hershey, 28 May 1971, HP; Gilbert Hershey interview, 8–15 Aug. 1977.

81. Quotes from Lewis to Ellen, 26, 30 July 1933, GF; see also Hershey to George, 2 July 1933, and Hershey to Kathy, 27 June 1933, both ibid.; Gilbert Hershey interview, 14 Nov. 1977.

82. Special Orders 34, 6 June 1933, Camp Pike, GF; Special Orders 39, 12 June 1933, Camp Pike, ibid.

83. Lewis to Ellen, 8, 13, 16, 18, 23 June, 5, 23, 26 July 1933, ibid.; efficiency report, June-July 1933, Hershey 201 file, ARC.

84. Lt. Col. T. D. Osborne to Hershey, 10 Mar. 1933; General Simonds to Hershey, 18 Apr. 1933, GF.

85. O'Sullivan questionnaire, 13 Nov. 1974, ibid.; Gilbert Hershey interview, 8–15 Aug. 1977.

86. Lewis B. Hershey, "Fear as a Factor in Leadership Problems," 22 Apr. 1933, GF. This study was later published in the *Signal Corps Bulletin* and drew approval from Professor L. W. Keeler, an educational psychologist at the University of Michigan. See Keeler to editor, *Signal Corps Bulletin*, 29 Oct. 1934, GF; Hershey to assistant commandant, 5 May 1934, ibid.

87. Hershey memo for Assistant Commandant, 22 June 1934, GF.

88. Hershey efficiency report, MG George S. Simonds, 2 July 1934, Hershey 201 file, ARC.

89. Hershey to Dr. James Iams, 13 Mar. 1973, Hershey 201 file, ARC; Col. C. B. Elliot

to Hershey, 4 May 1936, GF; Gilbert Hershey interview, 8–15 Aug. 1977; Hershey notebook, 5 Nov. 1935, GF.

90. Kathryn Hershey Layne interview; HD, July 1936, GF.

91. HD, June 1936, GF.

92. HD, July 1936, ibid.

93. HD, July-Aug. 1936, ibid.

94. Ibid.; Gilbert Hershey interview, 8–15 Aug. 1977; Kathryn Hershey Layne interview, 7 Aug. 1977.

CHAPTER III

1. HD, 20 Oct. 1916, GF.

2. Gilbert Hershey interview, 14 Nov. 1977; Hershey to William C. Matthews, 5 Apr. 1971, alpha file, HP. Hershey's gregarious nature was testified to by dozens of his associates: Daniel Omer interview; Juel Peeke and Clark Smith interviews; Gareth N. Brainerd and William S. Iliff interviews; K. D. Pulcipher interview; Hershey to Ethel T. Hobart, 17 Mar. 1942, HP.

3. On his generosity, see I. R. Appleman to Hershey, 11 July 1919, GF; Hershey to Lester L. Boss, 7 Sept. 1918, ibid.; Gilbert Hershey interview, 8–15 Aug. 1977. On frugality, see Hershey to Edward H. Jones and Company, 23 June 1914, GF; Hershey to Chesapeake and Potomac Telephone Co., 5 Dec. 1967, ibid.; William Averill interview.

4. Hershey to Mrs. Ted M. Levine, 20 May 1968, alpha file, HP; Scrapbook 3, GF; Hershey to Roy C. Kent, 18 Mar. 1942, HP; Teresa Kundred interview; William Averill interview; Kathryn Hershey Layne interview; Gilbert Hershey interviews, 8–15 Aug., 14 Nov. 1977.

5. Kathryn Hershey Layne interview; Ruby Hershey interview; Gilbert Hershey interview, 8–15 Aug. 1977.

6. Quote from Hershey to Florence Dygert, 22 Nov. 1942, HP; see also Hershey to Miss Finlkoff, 2 Sept. 1952, alpha file, ibid.; Gilbert Hershey interview, 8–15 Aug. 1977; Kathryn Hershey Layne interview; Ellen Margaret to Dad, 12 Sept. 1937, GF; Men of Achievement questionnaire, 1973, ibid.

7. Quote in HD, 9 July 1917, GF; see also Sam Stavisky, "Who Will Be Drafted This Time?" *Saturday Evening Post*, 20 Jan. 1951, pp. 97–98; Deborah Fader memo, n.d., Elizabeth Denny file, Vienna, Va. (hereafter cited as DF); Frank V. Keesling interview; E. D. Ingold interview; Kathryn Hershey Layne interview; Gilbert Hershey interview, 8–15 Aug. 1977.

8. Stages quote, *SS*, Mar. 1968, p. 3; see also Gilbert Hershey interview, 8–15 Aug. 1977; on lessons of past, Hershey interview, 1974–75, Oral History Collection (OHC), MHI; on material changes, Hershey to Leslie Layne, 2 Aug. 1976, KLF; Hershey to Joan Hershey, 31 Mar. 1969, JH; editorials, *SS*, Jan. 1961; Apr. 1965; Hershey to Joan Teply, 14 May 1959, alpha file, HP.

9. HD, 23 Feb. 1921, GF; editorial, *SS*, Dec. 1963.

10. HD, 8 Nov. 1918; Hershey to Joan Hershey, 25 Mar. 1967; HD, 17 Apr. 1918, all GF; Hershey to Robert Arbuckle, 1 Nov. 1951, alpha file, HP.

11. HD, 20 June 1917, 27 Jan. 1923, GF.

12. Editorial, *SS*, Jan.-Feb. 1943, p. 2; Hershey interview, Sept. 1974, MHI; Kenneth M. Dolbeare and James W. Davis, Jr., *Little Groups of Neighbors: The Selective Service System* (Chicago: Markham, 1968), p. 57n; Hershey to NSA, July-Aug. 1968, newspaper file, HP; Jean Carper, *Bitter Greetings* (New York: Grossman, 1967), p. 106.

13. HD, 17 July, 11 Aug. 1920, GF.

14. Lewis Hershey, "Fear as a Factor in Leadership Problems," Fort Leavenworth,

Kans. 1933, HP; also excerpted in *New York Times* (hereafter cited as *NYT*), 27 Sept. 1942, sec. 7, p. 5.

15. Hershey to Mrs. Enid Kaufman, 15 Apr. 1942, HP; HD, 21 May 1922, GF; Hershey to Rick Layne, 29 Apr. 1968, KLF.

16. Hershey to Dad, 27 Dec. 1935, GF.

17. Robert Liston, *Greetings* (New York: McGraw-Hill, 1970), p. 34; Gary L. Wamsley, *Selective Service and a Changing America* (Columbus: Charles Merrill, 1969), pp. 30, 35.

18. Dolbeare and Davis, *Little Groups of Neighbors*, p. 20; Harry A. Marmion, *Selective Service: Conflict and Compromise* (New York: John Wiley, 1968), p. 12; memo for Chief of Staff from G-1, 16 May 1932, box 116B, Record Group (RG) 147, National Archives (NA), Washington, D.C.

19. Carlton Dargusch interview; Gareth N. Brainerd and William S. Iliff interviews; Frank V. Keesling interview.

20. Hershey interview, May 1975, MHI; Major Jones interview of Hershey, 28 May 1972, HP; Wamsley, *Selective Service*, p. 37; BG H. E. Knight memo for AG, 28 Sept. 1936, and AG to Hershey, 2 Oct. 1936, Hershey 201 file, ARC; Carlton Dargusch interview; K. D. Pulcipher interview; O'Sullivan questionnaire, 13 Nov. 1974, GF.

21. Quote in *Indianapolis Star Magazine*, 23 July 1972; K. D. Pulcipher interview; Bush interview of Hershey, 28 May 1971, MHI; Hershey to Major Paul E. James, 3 May 1972, DF; Hershey interview, May 1975, MHI.

22. E. D. Ingold interview; Gareth N. Brainerd and William S. Iliff interviews; Charles H. Grahl interview.

23. Hershey, "Procurement of Manpower," *The Annals of the American Academy of Political and Social Science* (Sept. 1945), pp. 20–21; Hadley Cantril, *Public Opinion, 1935–1946* (Princeton: Princeton University Press, 1951), p. 458.

24. Gilbert Hershey interview, 8–15 Aug. 1977; Charles H. Grahl interview.

25. BG L. D. Gasser to Chief of Staff, 21 Mar. 1938, JANSSC records, 2C, RG 147, NA; Col. E. B. Colladay to Chief of Staff, 9 Aug. 1938, ibid.; Hershey to Ellen, 7, 12, 15 Feb., 25 Apr., 2 May, 5, 6, 13 Oct. 1938, GF.

26. Hershey to Col. John A. Reddy, 27 July 1938; Hershey to Captain Gareth N. Brainerd, 31 May 1938; Hershey to Major K. D. Pulcipher, 20 Oct. 1938; Hershey to BG Basil F. Marx, 30 Oct. 1938, all in JANSSC file, RG 147, NA.

27. Hershey interview, May 1975, MHI; Jones interview of Hershey, 1972, HP; John W. Chambers, *Draftees or Volunteers* (New York: Garland, 1975), p. 303; George H. Gallup, *The Gallup Poll: Public Opinion, 1935–1971*, 3 vols. (New York: Random House, 1972), I, 147. On 27 Mar. 1939 a Gallup poll reported that 61 percent believed the Constitution should be amended to require a national vote before anyone could be drafted to fight overseas.

28. Quote from Hershey to Major G. H. Schaffer, 27 Nov. 1939, JANSSC file, RG 147, NA. See also Hershey to Major Fred W. Edminton, 25 Apr. 1939, ibid.; Hershey to Major Paul E. James, 3 May 1972, DF. Quote from Hershey to Captain George W. Biggerstaff, 31 Oct. 1939, JANSSC file, RG 147; see also Hershey to BG Maurice Thompson, 13 Jan. 1939; Hershey to Lt. Col. Ralph N. Smith, 1 Nov. 1939; Hershey to General W. G. Robinson, 12 Dec. 1939, all ibid.

29. Hershey to Leo M. Cherne, 28 Oct. 1939, JANSSC file, RG 147, NA; Hershey to Col. John D. Langston, 18 Mar. 1939, ibid.; Chief of Staff to Chairman, National Research Council, 29 Dec. 1939, Hershey 201 file, ARC; Hershey to Lt. Col. Edward A. Fitzpatrick, 26 Aug. 1939, JANSSC file, RG 147, NA.

30. Quote from Hershey to Captain C. G. Banham, 5 Oct. 1939, JANSSC file, RG 147, NA.

31. Lewis to Ellen, 5 Dec. 1939, GF; Hershey to Clarence W. Sorenson, 30 Sept. 1939, JANSSC file, RG 147, NA; clipping of *Washington Herald Times*, 12 Oct. 1939, Scrapbook 3, GF.

32. Hershey to Lt. Col. Neil V. Kimball, 15 Dec. 1938, JANSSC file, RG 147, NA; E. D. Ingold interview; William S. Iliff interview; Lewis to Ellen, 13, 15 May 1940, GF; Gilbert Hershey interview, 8–15 Aug. 1977; Frank V. Keesling interview; Hershey to Major Paul E. James, 3 May 1972, DF.

33. Hershey to Ellen, 17, 18 May 1940, GF; *Gallup Polls*, I, 234.

34. *Gallup Polls*, I, 205, 226, 229, 234.

35. Robert A. Divine, *Roosevelt and World War II* (Baltimore: Johns Hopkins University Press, 1969), ch. 2; J. M. Burns, *Roosevelt: The Lion and the Fox* (New York: Harcourt Brace Jovanovich, 1956), p. 439.

36. Albert A. Blum, *Drafted or Deferred* (Ann Arbor: University of Michigan Press, 1967), pp. 1–3; Grenville Clark to Roosevelt, telegram, 26 May 1940, OF 1413B, box 12, Franklin D. Roosevelt Papers, Roosevelt Library, Hyde Park, N.Y. (hereafter cited as FDR); Hershey memo, 7 Feb. 1976, GF; Hershey interview, 26 May 1975.

37. Hershey efficiency reports, Sept. 1936–June 1937, July 1938–June 1939, July 1939, Oct. 1940, Hershey 201 file, ARC; resolution by JANSSC conference, Fort Sheridan, Ill., 1 Oct. 1937, biog. file, HP; Charles H. Grahl to General Marshall, 27 Mar. 1940, Hershey 201 file, ARC; H. C. Stockham to Secretary of War Harry H. Woodring, 1 Feb. 1940, ibid.

38. Blum, *Drafted or Deferred*, pp. 2–3; Marshall to BG John M. Palmer, 27 May 1940, JANSSC, RG 147, NA; BG William E. Skedd to Marshall, 29 May 1940, ibid.; Hershey to Tompkins McIlvaine, 7 June 1940, ibid.; Major Jones interview of Hershey, 1972, HP.

39. Hershey to Major Paul E. James, 3 May 1972, DF.

40. James W. Wadsworth to Lt. Col. W. G. Robinson, 22 Aug. 1945, box 8A, James Wadsworth Papers, Library of Congress, Washington, D.C. (hereafter cited as WP); Hershey to McIlvaine, 18 June 1940, HP; Major Jones interview of Hershey 1972, ibid.; John O'Sullivan, "From Voluntarism to Conscription: Congress and Selective Service, 1940–1945" (Ph.D. dissertation, Columbia University, 1971), p. 55; Blum, *Drafted or Deferred*, pp. 8–9.

41. *Washington Post*, 15 Sept. 1940 (hereafter cited as *WP*); James Wadsworth to Wendell Willkie, 24 July 1940, box 8A, WP.

42. Hershey to Rep. George W. Gillie, 28 Sept. 1939, JANSSC file, RG 147, NA; Hershey to Col. Morris, 5 Oct. 1939, ibid.

43. For Hershey's testimony, see U.S. Congress, Senate, Military Affairs Committee, *Hearings on Selective Service Bill*, S 4164, 76th Cong., 3rd sess., 12 July 1940, pp. 373–85; House, Military Affairs Committee, *Hearings on Selective Service Bill, HR 10132*, 24 July 1940, pp. 117–25.

44. Hershey interview, 7 May 1975, HP; Roosevelt to Wayne Coy, 15 Aug. 1940, OF 1413, box 1, FDR; FDR to Secretary of War and Secretary of Navy, 27 Aug. 1940, JANSSC file, RG 147, NA; Interim Report, Osborn Committee, 28 Aug. 1940, OF 4122, FDR; Hershey notes on conference with Henry Stimson, 18 Sept. 1940, HP.

45. Hershey to Major Paul E. James, 3 May 1972, DF; Hershey to Col. M. Stephanson, 6 Apr. 1940, JANSSC file, RG 147, NA.

46. Hershey to William S. Mailliard, 19 June 1962, Hershey status file, Frank V. Keesling Papers, San Francisco, Calif. (hereafter cited as KP); Hershey to Colonel J. Nelson, telephone memo, 12 Sept. 1940, Selective Service files, carton 65, RG 147, NA; Charles H. Grahl interview; E. D. Ingold interview.

47. Roosevelt to Governors, 21 Sept.1940, JANSSC file, RG 147, NA; Executive Or-

ders 8553 (28 Sept. 1940) and 8559 (4 Oct. 1940), with attached memo, GF; Hershey to President, 4 Oct. 1940, box 1, OF 1413, FDR.

48. E. D. Ingold interview; James Rowe, Jr., to Roosevelt, 30 Sept. 1940, OF 1413A, box 7, FDR; G.G.T. memo for R.F., 30 Sept. 1940, ibid.; Hershey to Major Victory Kleber, 9 Dec. 1940, HP.

49. Hershey notes on conference with Secretary of War, 23 Sept. 1940, HP; Charles H. Grahl interview; E. D. Ingold interview.

50. Edwin M. Watson to Hershey, 14 Oct. 1940, OF 1413A, box 7, FDR; O'Sullivan questionnaire, 13 Nov.1974, GF; Hershey notes on talk with Mr. Hetzel of UMW, 25 Sept. 1940, HP.

51. Henry Stimson and McGeorge Bundy, *On Active Service in Peace and War* (New York: Harper, 1947), p. 348; O'Sullivan questionnaire, 13 Nov. 1974, GF; John W. Barber interview, 29 Dec. 1978; Hershey notes, 1940, speech file, HP.

52. Hershey speech, 12 Mar. 1941, speech file, HP; O'Sullivan questionnaire, 13 Nov. 1974, GF; Bush interview of Hershey, 28 May 1971, HP.

53. *Gallup Poll*, 30 Aug. 1940, I, 238; Hershey to Major Paul E. James, 3 May 1972, DF.

54. Robert Patterson to Hershey, 20 Sept. 1940, box 173, Robert Patterson Papers (hereafter cited as RPP), LC; Hershey to Fiorello H. LaGuardia, 21 Sept. 1940, HP; Hershey to Dr. Elliott D. Smith, 1 Oct. 1940, ibid.; speech to financiers, Nov. 1940, speech file, ibid.

55. University of Chicago Roundtable, 1940, speech file, HP; *Gallup Poll*, 29 Dec. 1940, I, 255−56.

56. Hershey to Dr. Warner F. Woodring, 25 Nov. 1940, HP.

57. Dee Ingold interview, 20 Feb. 1972, transcript in HP; Hershey to General Metts, telephone conversation, 27 Sept. 1940, carton 65, RG 147, NA.

58. Henry Stimson Diary, 4 Oct. 1940, Sterling Library, Yale University, New Haven, Conn. (hereafter cited as SD); Stimson to President, 27 Sept. 1940, box 2, OF 1413, FDR; Robert Jackson to President, 28 Sept. 1940, ibid.; Hershey to President, 28 Sept. 1940, ibid.

59. Harold Smith Diary, 24 Sept. 1940, FDR; FDR to Smith, 18 Sept. 1940, OF 1413A, box 1, ibid.; Edwin M. Watson to Henry Cabot Lodge, 15 Oct. 1940, box 11, ibid.; Stephen Early to Emanuel Celler, 16 Sept. 1940, ibid.; Morris Sheppard to Henry Stimson, 15 Oct. 1940, GF.

60. Harold Smith Diary, 24 Sept. 1940, FDR; Wayne Coy to Roosevelt, 6 Sept. 1940, OF 1413, box 11, ibid.; Patterson memo to Palmer, 13 Sept. 1940, cont. 173, RPP; Stephen Early to Robert J. Dillion, 1 Oct. 1940, OF 1413, box 11, FDR; clipping of *Washington Times Herald*, 18 Sept. 1940, Scrapbook 1, GF; Fiorello LaGuardia to President, telegram, 20 Sept. 1940, OF 1413, box 11, FDR.

61. Harold Smith Diary, 24 Sept. 1940, FDR; Roosevelt to Clarence Dykstra, 30 June 1939, OF 3689, ibid.; Victor H. Harding to President, 28 Sept. 1940, box 11, OF 1413A, ibid.; HD, 9 Oct. 1940; *Cincinnati Enquirer*, 9 Oct. 1940. Hershey skipped the full colonel rank.

62. *NYT*, 18 Oct. 1940, p. 8; Hershey to Lt. Col. John N. Hauser, 15 Nov. 1940, HP; O'Sullivan questionnaire, 13 Nov. 1974, GF; Colonel Langston interview, n.d., GF; Clarence Dykstra to President, 8 Jan. 1941, Official Papers (OP), HP; Roosevelt to Dyke (Dykstra), 11 Jan. 1941, ibid.

63. O'Sullivan, "Conscription," p. 144; Carlton Dargusch interview; O'Sullivan questionnaire, 13 Nov. 1974, GF; Roosevelt to Clarence Dykstra, 22 Mar. 1941, OF 1413B, box 12, FDR; Jim Rowe to FDR, 16 Jan. 1941, ibid.; Hershey to Dykstra, telegram, 28 Apr. 1941, HP.

64. Carlton Dargusch interview; Hershey to Captain J. M. Pitzer, 22 Apr. 1941, GF;

Major E. W. Shattuck to Hershey, 29 Apr. 1941, ibid.; O'Sullivan questionnaire, 13 Nov. 1974, ibid.; Russell Gore, "Today's Personality," news clipping, n.d., KLF.

65. O'Sullivan, "Conscription," p. 315; O'Sullivan questionnaire, 13 Nov. 1974, GF; news clipping, 25 Mar. 1941, OF 1413A, box 11, FDR; Louis Ludlow to President, 3 Apr. 1941, ibid.; Sam H. Jones to President, 1 Apr. 1941, ibid.; Claude Pepper to President, 7 Apr. 1941, ibid.; Channing H. Tobias to President, 21 Apr. 1941, ibid.; *NYT*, 22 July 1941, p. 18; 1 Aug. 1941, p. 14.

66. Wayne Coy to President, 8 May 1941, OF 1413B, box 12, FDR; Ellen Margaret to folks, 4 Aug. 1941, GF.

67. Loy Warwick, "This Man's Got Your Number," 8 Apr. 1941, MS in Scrapbook 3, GF.

68. Conference of 30 Sept. 1942, Henry Morgenthau Diary, 573: 134, Roosevelt Library, Hyde Park, N.Y. (hereafter cited as MD); Minutes of State Directors' Conference, 10 May 1944, HP.

69. Press conference notes, 15 Jan. 1941, speech file, HP; radio script, 23 June 1941, *Congressional Digest*, 20: 201–4; speech to Commerce and Industry Association of New York, 5 Feb. 1942, misc. L. C. file, HP; U.S. Congress, House, Military Affairs Committee, *Hearings on Lowering Draft Age*, 77th Cong., 2nd sess., 14, 15 Oct. 1942, pp. 79–80.

70. Radio address, 23 June 1941, *Congressional Digest*, 20: 201–4; Blum, *Drafted or Deferred*, p. 21; Minutes of State Directors' Conference, 30 Apr. 1945, HP; *Current Biography*, 1941, p. 380; SS, 15 Dec. 1941, 1 Jan. 1942; quote in U.S. Congress, Senate, Committee on Agriculture, *Hearings on Food Supply*, 79th Cong., 1st sess., 18 Feb. 1943, p. 152.

71. Hershey to Secretary of War, 18 Feb. 1941, HP; Hershey to Conway E. Yockey, 10 Sept. 1942, ibid.; Hershey to Mrs. Peggy Bush, 12 Jan. 1971, GF; Hershey to President, 13 Mar. 1942, HP; Blum, *Drafted or Deferred*, p. 28.

72. Hershey to F. J. Bailey, 26 Aug. 1942, HP; Hershey to Thomas I. Emerson, 23 Mar. 1943, ibid.

73. Hershey to Commissioner of Internal Revenue, 6 Feb. 1943; Hershey to Col. Birely, 25 Mar. 1941; Hershey to Omar B. Ketchum, 21 Jan. 1943; Hershey to General Fleming, 20 Dec. 1944; Hershey to Charles S. Cheston, 3 Feb. 1945, all HP.

74. John W. Barber interview, 6 Aug. 1977; Hershey to Mother, 27 Sept. 1942, HP; Hershey to Gov. Dewey, telephone transcript, 5 Feb. 1943, carton 65, RG 147, NA.

75. Hershey, "Procurement of Manpower," *The Annals* (Sept. 1945), 25; SS, 1 June 1941; Hershey quoted in *NYT*, 1 Dec. 1942, p. 31.

76. U.S. Congress, House, Military Affairs Committee, *Hearings on Government Possession of Plants*, 77th Cong., 1st sess., 16 June 1941, pp. 38, 41; Hershey press conference, 21 Feb. 1942, carton 65, RG 147, NA; U.S. Congress, Senate, Military Affairs Committee, *Hearings on Government Possession of Plants*, 77th Cong., 1st sess., 18 Mar. 1941, p. 138.

77. Hershey to Andrew J. May, 12 Nov. 1941, congressional file, HP; Hershey to Robert R. Reynolds, 2 Mar. 1942, ibid.; U.S. Congress, Senate, Committee on Appropriations, *Hearings on H.J. Res. 82*, 78th Cong., 1st sess., 19 Feb. 1943, p. 3; SS, Mar. 1942.

78. John O'Sullivan questionnaire, 13 Sept. 1974, GF; Minutes of State Directors' Conference, 30 Apr. 1945, HP; U.S. Congress, House, Committee on Appropriations, *Hearings on H.R. 4879*, 78th Cong., 2nd sess., 30 Mar. 1944, p. 373; SS, Aug. 1942.

79. A. A. Hoehling, *Home Front, U.S.A.* (New York: Crowell, 1966), p. 86; SS, Nov. 1944; Chambers, *Draftees or Volunteers*, p. 352.

80. Hershey to Judge Arthur D. Wood, 19 Apr. 1944, box 10, OF 1413–45, FDR; Minutes of State Directors' Conference, 18 Nov. 1944, HP; Hershey to Malvina C. Thompson, 13 Jan. 1944, box 912, Eleanor Roosevelt Papers, Roosevelt Library, Hyde Park, N.Y.

81. U.S. Congress, Senate, Military Affairs Committee, *Hearings on Lowering Draft Age*, 77th Cong., 2nd sess., 14 Oct. 1942, p. 55; Carlton Dargusch interview.

82. Hershey to Milt D. Campbell, 13 Nov. 1942, HP; Hershey to J. Edgar Hoover, 1 Sept. 1942, ibid.; *NYT*, 22 Jan. 1945, p. 19.

83. Hershey to Attorney General, 1 Aug.1941, 30 July 1942, HP.

84. Hershey interviews, transcripts, Sept. 1974, May 1975, HP; quote from F. Edward Hebert interview.

85. Fiorello LaGuardia to Arthur J. May, 11 Mar. 1941, WP, LC; *NYT*, 6 May 1941, p. 4; Hershey to Robert R. Reynolds, 14 May 1941, congressional file, HP; Hershey to Representative Andrew J. May, 12 May 1941, ibid.

86. *Gallup Poll*, I, 280; James Wadsworth to William M. Chadbourne, 26 Feb. 1941, WP; Hershey to Planning Council, 26 Mar. 1941, OP, HP; Hershey to Navy and War, 11 Apr. 1941, deferment file, KP.

87. Henry Stimson to Hershey, 2 May 1941, deferment file, KP; Frank Knox to Hershey, 29 Apr. 1941, ibid.; Hershey to President, 8 May 1941, ibid.; Hershey to Speaker of House, 10 May 1941, ibid.; *NYT*, 13 May 1941, p. 14.

88. *NYT*, 6 June 1941, p. 12; U.S. Congress, Senate, Military Affairs Committee, *Hearings on Age Deferments*, 77th Cong., 1st sess., 6 June 1941, pp. 1–20.

89. Ibid., pp. 21–42; *Selective Service in Peacetime* (Washington: U.S. Government Printing Office, 1942), p. 99. Eventually the registrants in the second lottery were mixed into the older list by placing one new registrant after every ten older registrants.

90. U.S. Congress, House, Military Affairs Committee, *Hearings on Government Possession of Plants*, 77th Cong., 1st sess., 16 June 1941, pp. 32–42, 47, 55; *NYT*, 17 June 1941, p. 14. Public Law 206 (16 Aug. 1941) provided for deferment of men over twenty-eight.

91. Hershey to President, 17 June 1941, White House file, HP; *Selective Service in Peacetime*, pp. 97–99; Hershey speech, 17 July 1941, speech file, HP.

92. Cantrill, *Public Opinion, 1935–1946*, pp. 461–63.

93. U.S. Congress, Senate, Military Affairs Committee, *Hearings on Retention*, 77th Cong., 1st sess., 24 July 1941, pp. 244–52.

94. U.S. Congress, House, Military Affairs Committee, *Hearings on Length of Service*, 77th Cong., 1st sess., 25 July 1941, pp. 99–104.

95. *Gallup Poll*, I, 291–92.

96. *NYT*, 20 Aug. 1941, p. 10; 26 Sept. 1941, p. 8; 17 Oct. 1941, p. 18; Hershey to Gilbert, 20 Oct. 1941, HP.

CHAPTER IV

1. Hershey to David Steinhardt, 30 Apr. 1971, GF; *NYT*, 9 Dec. 1941, p. 26; Hershey to W. M. Jeffers, 19 Dec. 1941, HP.

2. *SS*, 15 Dec. 1941; minutes of meeting, National Committee on Education and Defense, 11 Dec.1941, age extension file, KP.

3. Press conference, 11 Dec. 1941, carton 65, RG 147, NA; *NYT*, 12 Dec. 1941, p. 34.

4. *NYT*, 12 Dec. 1941, p. 34.

5. U.S. Congress, House, Military Affairs Committee, *Hearings on Liability Extension*, 77th Cong., 1st sess., 13 Dec. 1941, pp. 4–22.

6. U.S. Congress, Senate, Military Affairs Committee, *Hearings on Liability Extension*, 77th Cong., 1st sess., 15 Dec. 1941, pp. 3, 23, 28, 33, 35, 42, 86; quotes from pp. 26, 56, 65. The final bill provided for liability for those twenty to forty-four. This was a compromise between the House's lower limit of twenty-one and the Senate's of nineteen. Registration would be held for all males from eighteen to sixty-four.

7. Harold Smith to Roosevelt, 3 Jan. 1942, box 2, OF 1413, FDR; *NYT*, 6 Jan. 1942, p. 1; Hershey to Attorney General, 8 Jan. 1942, HP; *NYT*, 15 Feb. 1942, p. 1.

8. *SS*, Mar. 1942; *NYT*, 18 Mar. 1942, p. 1.

9. Gary L. Wamsley, *Selective Service and a Changing America* (Columbus: Charles Merrill, 1969), p. 39; *NYT*, 28 Apr. 1942, p. 10; *SS*, June 1942.

10. *NYT*, 16 Jan. 1942, p. 42; Hershey to President, 25 June 1942, HP.

11. George Gallup, *The Gallup Poll: Public Opinion, 1935–1971*, 3 vols. (New York: Random House, 1972), I, 278, 529; *NYT*, 27 May 1942, p. 8; quote ibid., 22 Aug. 1942, p. 6.

12. *NYT*, 22 Aug. 1942, p. 6; 16 Sept. 1942, p. 48; 21 Sept. 1942, p. 17.

13. Ibid., 14 Oct. 1942, p. 1; U.S. Congress, Senate, Military Affairs Committee, *Hearings on Lowering Draft Age*, 77th Cong., 2nd sess., 14 Oct. 1942, p. 43; *NYT*, 15 Oct. 1942, p. 1; House, Military Affairs Committee, *Hearings on Lowering Draft Age*, 77th Cong., 2nd sess., 15 Oct. 1942, p. 96.

14. Hershey memo to Gen. White, 21 Oct. 1942, OP file, HP; *NYT*, 15 Oct. 1942, p. 1; 27 Oct. 1942, p. 1; 8 Nov. 1942, p. 31; 14 Nov. 1942, p. 16; 19 Nov. 1942, p. 1.

15. Hershey interview, 7 May 1975, HP; Gilbert Hershey interview, 8–15 Aug. 1977; U.S. Congress, Senate, Military Affairs Committee, *Hearings on Retention*, 77th Cong., 1st sess., 24 July 1941, p. 248. Hershey would exhibit the same loyalty to Lyndon B. Johnson during the 1960's.

16. Carlton Dargusch interview; MHM (Marvin H. McIntyre) memo for Roberta Barrows, 27 May 1942, box 12, OF 1413B, FDR; Stephen Early to Hershey, 4 Apr. 1942, ibid.; Roosevelt to Reverend Endicott Peabody, 9 May 1942, boxes 8–9, ibid.; President to Hershey, 24 July 1942, box 2, ibid.; Roosevelt to Stephen T. Early, 13 Aug. 1943, ibid.

17. Hershey to Clark A. Smith, 15 Sept. 1942, HP; *NYT*, 13 Aug. 1942, p. 13; 29 Aug. 1942, p. 9; Hershey to Edwin Steers, 7 Aug. 1944, HP.

18. Hershey to President, 1 Aug. 1941, and Roosevelt to Forster, 8 Aug. 1941, both boxes 8–9, OF 1413, FDR; MHM for President, 4 Oct. 1943, box 12, ibid.; quote in MHM memo for President, 8 Sept. 1942, ibid.

19. MHM memo to Forster, 6 Mar. 1941, box 13, OF 1413B, FDR; Hershey to President, 6 Mar. 1941, box 2, ibid.; Hershey to Major Wm. J. Rushton, 9 June 1941, HP.

20. Hershey and Olson, telephone minutes, 22 Nov. 1942, carton 65, RG 147, NA.

21. Samuel D. Berger, "Ministry of Labour Opinion on U.S. Manpower Policy," 26 Jan. 1943, box 12, Samuel I. Rosenman Papers (hereafter cited as SRP), Roosevelt Library, Hyde Park, N.Y.

22. News clippings in manpower control file, 1942–45, KP; Hershey to Grenville Clark, 5 Mar. 1942, HP; Roosevelt to Clark, 31 Mar. 1942, Denny file in WP, LC; press conference, 20 Apr. 1942, Paul McNutt Papers, Lilly Library, Bloomington, Ind. (hereafter cited as PMP).

23. Carlton Dargusch interview; War Manpower Commission minutes, 13 May 1942, box 5–100, RG 211, NA; *Monthly Labor Review*, Aug. 1942, p. 225; *NYT*, 20 Sept. 1942, sec. 4, p. 7.

24. U.S. Congress, House, Select Committee Investigating National Defense Migration, *Hearings*, 77th Cong., 2nd sess., Sept. and Oct. 1942; House, Military Affairs Committee, *Hearings on Lowering Draft Age*, 77th Cong., 2nd sess., 15 Oct. 1942, pp. 91, 106, 108, 115, 117; Senate, Military Affairs Committee, *Hearings on Universal Service*, 77th Cong., 2nd sess., 20 May 1942, pp. 68, 74–80.

25. Grenville Clark to President, 3 July 1942, OF 1413D, FDR; *NYT*, 27 Oct. 1942, p. 19; 1 Nov. 1942, sec. 4, p. 7; 24 Nov. 1942, p. 16.

26. *NYT*, 3 Nov. 1942, p. 1; Henry Stimson to Roosevelt, 5 Nov. 1942, OF 4905, FDR; for governors' response, see OF 1413 and OF 4905, ibid.; Walter D. Fuller to Roosevelt, 30 Nov. 1942, misc. 8–9, OF 1413, ibid.

27. *NYT*, 3 Nov. 1942, p. 1; Harold Smith to Roosevelt, 14 Oct. 1942, box 12, OF 1413B, FDR; Isador Lubin to Hopkins, 21 Oct. 1942, cont. 324, Harry Hopkins Papers, Roosevelt Library, Hyde Park, N.Y. (hereafter cited as HHP).

28. George Q. Flynn, *The Mess in Washington: Manpower Mobilization in World War II* (Westport, Conn.: Greenwood, 1979), pp. 197–99; *Monthly Labor Review*, Jan. 1943, p. 2607; McNutt press conference, 4 Dec. 1942, PMP; Administrative Order 26, 5 Dec. 1942, HP; Hershey to all state directors, 7 Dec. 1942, ibid.; *Dallas Times Herald*, 9 Dec. 1942; Lt. Col. Shattuck to Bernard C. Gavit, 9 Dec. 1942, index file, HP.

29. Carlton Dargusch interview; O'Sullivan questionnaire, 13 Nov. 1974, GF; Frank V. Keesling interview; William Averill interview.

30. Minutes of State Directors' Conference, 12 Nov. 1943; Hershey to Executive Director, WMC, 28 Dec. 1942; Hershey to L. A. Appley, 11 Feb. 1943; Hershey interview, 7 May 1975; Minutes of State Directors' Conference, 8 May 1944, all HP; *NYT*, 5 Sept. 1943, p. 1; William Averill interview.

31. *NYT*, 16 Apr. 1943, p. 20, for quote; Frank V. Keesling interview; see also Flynn, *Mess in Washington*, pp. 205–8.

32. Samuel I. Rosenman to President, 27 Nov. 1943, box 12, OF 1413, FDR; Roosevelt to Rosenman, 5 Dec. 1943, ibid.; Hopkins to President, 4 Dec. 1943, ibid.

33. Henry Morgenthau to William H. McReynolds, telephone conversation, 21 Jan. 1942, MD, 489: 29–30; Thompson notes, 30 Jan. 1942, ibid., 490: 152; memo to President from Morgenthau, Stimson, Knox, Hershey, and McReynolds, 5 Feb. 1942, ibid., 492: 328.

34. Henry Morgenthau et al. to Roosevelt, 5 Feb. 1942, MD, 492: 328; President to all heads of departments, 9 Feb. 1942, Roosevelt Press Conferences, vol. 19: 136–37, FDR.

35. U.S. Congress, Senate, Military Affairs Committee, *Hearings on Lowering Draft Age*, 77th Cong., 2nd sess., 14 Oct. 1942, pp. 59–60; House, Military Affairs Committee, ibid., 15 Oct. 1942, p. 92; Hershey to Tydings, 17 Nov. 1942, HP.

36. SD, 40: 120, 2 Oct. 1942; presidential memo, 17 Nov. 1942, box 183, RPP; local board release, 24 Nov. 1942, HP; FDR press conferences, 8 Dec. 1942, 20: 282–83; 18 Dec. 1942, 20: 289–90, FDR.

37. *NYT*, 23 Mar. 1943, p. 20; Forest A. Harness to Hershey, 31 May 1943, HP; Hershey to State Director, District of Columbia, 4 June 1943, ibid.; James F. Byrnes to President, 11 Aug. 1943, box 16, SRP; Hershey to Samuel I. Rosenman, 7 Dec. 1943, box 12, OF 1413B, FDR.

38. U.S. Congress, House, Committee on Appropriations, *National War Agencies Appropriations, 1945*, 78th Cong., 2nd sess., 30 Mar. 1944, p. 262; Hershey to Senator Burnet Maybank, 19 Feb. 1945, in U.S. Congress, Senate, Military Affairs Committee, *Mobilization of Civilian Manpower*, 79th Cong., 1st sess., 8 Feb. 1945, p. 369; Hershey to President, 9 Aug. 1945, HP.

39. Hershey radio transcript, 29 June 1941, speech file, HP; Hershey to Dr. Warner Woodring, 8 May 1942, ibid.; clipping from *Congressional Record*, 26 Nov. 1943, pp. 10112–14, in father draft file, KP.

40. O'Sullivan questionnaire, 13 Nov. 1974, GF; John W. Barber interview; Hershey interview, 7 May 1975, HP; Frank V. Keesling interview; SD, 3 Oct. 1944.

41. Marshall to Hershey, 11 Sept. 1942, Hershey file, George C. Marshall Papers, Marshall Research Foundation, Lexington, Va. (hereafter cited as GMP); Hershey to Marshall, 15 Sept. 1942, HP; Peggy Bush interview of Hershey, 28 May 1971, HP.

42. Albert A. Blum, *Drafted or Deferred* (Ann Arbor: University of Michigan Press, 1967), p. 23; Wamsley, *Selective Service*, p. 73; U.S. Congress, Senate, Military Affairs Committee, *Hearings on Universal Service*, 77th Cong., 2nd sess., 26 Oct. 1942, p. 60; O'Sullivan questionnaire, 13 Nov. 1974, GF.

43. Carlton Dargusch interview.

44. Hershey to George C. Marshall, 3 Apr. 1941, HP.

45. Robert Patterson to Hershey, 26 Jan. 1942, Bush file, HP; Edwin M. Watson to Hershey, 13 Feb. 1942, box 2, OF 1413, FDR; Henry Stimson to Hershey, 8 Mar. 1942, Bush file, HP; Hershey to Stimson, 16 July 1942, ibid.; SD, 11 Aug. 1942.

46. Blum, *Drafted or Deferred*, p. 44. See ch. 5, below, for a discussion of race and the draft.

47. Hershey speech to National War College, 17 Apr. 1947, carton 65, RG 147, NA.

48. Blum, *Drafted or Deferred*, p. 33; Byron Fairchild and Jonathan Grossman, *The Army and Industrial Manpower* (Washington: Department of the Army, 1959), pp. 47–49.

49. U.S. Congress, House, Military Affairs Committee, *Hearings on Liability*, 77th Cong., 1st sess., 13 Dec. 1941, pp. 7–8; Senate, ibid., 14 Oct. 1942, p. 69; Stimson memo to George C. Marshall, 2 Oct. 1942, box 140, Henry Stimson Papers, Sterling Library, Yale University, New Haven, Conn. (hereafter cited as SP); Senate, Committee on Agriculture, *Hearings on Food Supply*, 78th Cong., 1st sess., 18 Feb. 1943, pp. 142, 156; quote in House, Committee on Appropriations, *Hearings*, 78th Cong., 2nd sess., 30 Mar. 1944, p. 354.

50. Hershey to Rear Admiral C. W. Nimitz, 1 July 1941; Hershey to Secretary of War, 22 July 1941; Hershey to Major General Holcomb, 2 Aug. 1941, all HP.

51. Hershey to Secretary of War, 17 Dec. 1941; Hershey to President, 20 Dec. 1941, White House file; Hershey to Secretary of Navy, 12 Jan. 1942; Hershey to Secretary of Navy, 12 Jan. 1942; Hershey to Carl Vinson, 4 Mar. 1942, Congressional file, all ibid.; *NYT*, 22 Dec. 1941, p. 10; 20 Jan. 1942, p. 21; Admiral Arleigh Burke explained that, whenever Hershey put pressure on draftees, many good people volunteered for the navy; Burke interview.

52. *NYT*, 12 Aug. 1942, p. 7; 20 Aug. 1942, p. 12; Hershey to Representative Thomas E. Martin, 23 Oct. 1942, HP; SD, 4 Dec. 1942, 41: 77; Albert Blum, "Sailor or Worker," *Labor History* 6 (Fall 1965), 235; Hershey to Byrnes, 20, 23 July 1944, HP; Hershey interview, 11 Sept. 1976, ibid.

53. L. B. Hershey, "We Must Improve Our Youth," *NYT Magazine*, 10 Feb. 1946, pp. 10–11; see also Selective Service System, *Physical Examination of SS Registrants During W.W. II*, Special Monograph #17 (Washington: U.S. Government Printing Office, 1947).

54. Hershey, "SS and Its Relationship to Nutrition," 27 May 1941, speech file, HP; *NYT*, 28 May 1941, p. 12; 30 May 1941, p. 10.

55. *SS*, 1 June 1941; U.S. Congress, Senate, Military Affairs Committee, *Hearings on Age Deferment*, 77th Cong., 1st sess., 5 June 1941, pp. 8, 14–15, 19.

56. Hershey to Frederick Osborn, 21 July 1941, HP.

57. Hershey to Mrs. Roosevelt, 23 Sept. 1941, box 2, OF 1413, FDR; "Selective Service and Its Relation to Nutrition," 27 May 1941, speech file, HP.

58. SD, 3 Oct. 1941, 6 Oct. 1941, 22 Oct. 1941.

59. Hershey to Roosevelt, 10 Oct. 1941, box 2, OF 1413, FDR; Hershey to F. J. Bailey, 24 Nov. 1941, HP.

60. Hershey to President, 27 Oct. 1941, box 2, OF 1413, FDR; Hershey to Lauchlin Currie, 6 Nov. 1941, White House file, HP; *NYT*, 16 Nov. 1941, p. 40.

61. Hershey to Henry Stimson, 26 Mar., 4 Apr. 1942; Stimson to Hershey, 3 June 1942, all HP.

62. Hershey to President, 5 June 1943, OF 1413F, FDR; *NYT*, 29 Feb. 1944, p. 1; White House hearings, 7 Jan. 1944, cont. 5, OF 1413, FDR.

63. U.S. Congress, House, Committee on Appropriations, *Hearings on War Agencies Appropriation*, 78th Cong., 2nd sess., 30 Mar. 1944, p. 355.

64. U.S. Congress, Senate, Committee on Education and Labor, *Hearings on War-*

time Health and Education, 78th Cong., 2nd sess., 10 July 1944, pp. 1613, 1616, 1619–23.

65. Colonel Leonard G. Roundtree, "Mental and Personality Disorders in Selective Service Registrants," *Journal of the American Medical Association* (11 Aug. 1945), 1084–87; U.S. Congress, House, Committee on Interstate and Foreign Commerce, *Hearings on Neuropsychiatric Center,* 79th Cong., 1st sess., 19 Sept. 1945, pp. 36, 54; Senate, *Hearings on Wartime Health,* 78th Cong., 2nd sess., 10 July 1944, p. 1841.

66. Hershey to Henry Stimson, 27 Feb., 25, 26 Sept. 1943, 13 Feb. 1945; Minutes of State Directors' Conference, 13 Nov. 1943, HP.

67. *Gallup Poll,* I, 441, 448; U.S. Congress, House, Committee on Appropriations, *Hearings,* 78th Cong., 2nd sess., 30 Mar. 1944, pp. 356–57; *NYT,* 30 Mar. 1944, p. 1; 8 Apr. 1944, p. 1; 11 Apr. 1944, p. 13; 5 May 1944, p. 1; FDR press conferences, 28 Mar. 1944, vol. 23: 123–25, FDR.

68. Minutes of State Directors' Conference, 19 Nov. 1944, HP.

69. Robert Patterson memo to Hershey, 16 Oct. 1942, box 183, RPP; Hershey to Major E. L. MacLean, 16 Jan. 1942, HP.

70. Hershey to Henry Stimson, 21 Sept. 1943, HP.

71. Notes of cabinet meeting, 18 Feb. 1944, box 172, SP; Minutes of State Directors' Conference, 8 May, 16–18 Nov. 1944, HP.

72. Conference minutes, 4 Feb. 1942, MD, 492: 99, 102, FDR.

73. Hershey to Frank Knox, 7 Apr., 24 Nov. 1941, and 18 Mar. 1942; Hershey to Dr. J. W. Barker, 25 Aug. 1942, both HP.

74. Hershey to Dr. J. W. Barker, 23 Sept. 1942; Hershey to Secretary of Navy, 27 Nov. 1942, ibid.

75. MD, 15 Dec. 1943, 684: 119, 121, 123, FDR.

76. Millard G. White to Hershey, 12 Feb. 1944, OP, HP.

77. Blum, *Drafted or Deferred,* pp. 125–32; SD, 13 Mar. 1944.

78. Hershey press conference, 17 Feb. 1944, carton 65, RG 147, NA; quote from U.S. Congress, House, Committee on Appropriations, *National War Agencies Appropriation, 1945,* 78th Cong., 2nd sess., 30 Mar. 1944, p. 350. Hershey invited the navy to join the army in taking 30,000 Puerto Ricans who were single and eligible to fill the gap. Many of these men had navy job deferments. See Hershey to Vice Admiral Randall Jacobs, 1 Mar. 1944, OP, HP.

79. Millard G. White to Hershey, 7, 11 Apr. 1944, War Department file, HP; TAG to CO, Service Commands, 7 Apr. 1944, ibid.; *NYT,* 9 Apr. 1944, p. 1; Gareth N. Brainerd and William S. Iliff interviews.

80. *NYT,* 6 May 1944, p. 7; 9 Sept. 1944, p. 1.

81. Hershey to Gen. Lucius Clay, 29 Dec. 1944, White House file, HP; Henry Stimson memo, 11 Jan. 1945, box 172, SP; Blum, *Drafted or Deferred,* pp. 43–44; *NYT,* 12 Jan. 1945, p. 1.

82. *SS,* Jan. 1945. See Flynn, *Mess in Washington,* pp. 98–102, for the confused military performance in early 1945.

CHAPTER V

1. Radio address, 23 June 1941, *Congressional Digest,* 20: 203.

2. Hershey speech, 20 June 1941, speech file, HP; radio address, 23 June 1941, *Congressional Digest,* 20: 203; Hershey to Mrs. Aaron Kinsey, 8 Apr. 1942, HP.

3. *NYT,* 17 Jan. 1941, p. 10. For all references to the law, see U.S. *Statutes at Large* 54 (16 Sept. 1940), 885–97.

4. *NYT,* 17 Jan. 1941, p. 10; 18 Jan. 1941, p. 7; Governor Culbert L. Olson to Chairman Ralph B. Elm, 20 Jan. 1941, strikers' file, KP; O'Sullivan questionnaire, 13 Nov. 1974, GF.

5. SD, 18 Jan. 1941.

6. Albert A. Blum, *Drafted or Deferred* (Ann Arbor: University of Michigan Press, 1967), pp. 198–99; *NYT*, 10 June 1941, p. 1; Henry Stimson to Wayne Coy, 29 Sept. 1941, OP, HP.

7. Telephone memo, Paul G. Armstrong to Hershey, 13 June 1941, carton 65, RG 147, NA.

8. Allan S. Haywood to Hershey, 14 Aug. 1941, labor file, HP; Richard Polenberg, *War and Society* (Philadelphia: Lippincott, 1972), p. 156.

9. Hershey to Allan S. Haywood, 29 Aug. 1941, labor file, HP; telephone memo, Hershey to Col. Bloomer, 3 Aug. 1941, carton 65, RG 147, NA; Merrill C. Meigs to Robert Patterson, 26 Oct. 1942, cont. 183, RPP; *NYT*, 12 Aug. 1941, p. 12; 13 Aug. 1941, p. 15; Hershey news release, 24 Oct. 1941, OP, HP; U.S. Congress, Senate, Military Affairs Committee, *Hearings on Liability Extension*, 77th Cong., 1st sess., 15 Dec. 1941, p. 26.

10. Hershey to William Green, 5 Jan. 1942, HP; Hershey to John Green, draft, n.d., ibid.; press conference, 21 Feb. 1942, carton 65, RG 147, NA; *NYT*, 25 Sept. 1942, p. 42.

11. Polenberg, *War and Society*, pp. 161–69; Oscar Cox to Harry Hopkins, 4 June 1943, cont. 324, manpower file, HHP; Isador Lubin to Hopkins, 22 June 1943, ibid.

12. O'Sullivan questionnaire, 13 Nov. 1974, GF; Hershey to Warner F. Woodring, 27 June 1943, HP; Hershey to Representative Andrew J. May, 22 Apr. 1943, congressional file, ibid.

13. Hershey to Col. William Leitch, 14 Aug. 1943, misc. file, HP; Hershey to Henry Stimson, 27 Dec. 1943, ibid.; Blum, *Drafted or Deferred*, p. 203; *NYT*, 6 Aug. 1944, p. 30; Hershey to Governor Frank J. Lausche, 22 Jan. 1945, OP, HP; Robert Patterson to Hershey, 3 Mar. 1945, War Department file, ibid.; Hershey to California State Director, telegram, 7 May 1945, ibid.; *NYT*, 4 July 1945, p. 14.

14. Minutes of State Directors' Conference, 12 Nov. 1943, HP; SS, Aug. 1942; Jonathan Daniels, *White House Witness, 1942–1945* (New York: Doubleday, 1975), p. 37.

15. Joel Seidman, *American Labor from Defense to Reconversion* (Chicago: University of Chicago Press, 1953), p. 157; Hershey interview, 1975, MHI. Statistics on deferments can be found in Selective Service System, *Selective Service and Victory* (Washington: U.S. Government Printing Office, 1948), appendix 62.

16. *NYT*, 2 Mar. 1941, p. 12; 17 May 1941, p. 8; SS, May 1941; Hershey to Col. Arthur F. Doran, 20 Oct. 1941, HP.

17. Press conference, 11 Dec. 1941, carton 65, RG 147, NA; *Congressional Digest*, 3 Feb. 1942, 21: 293; *NYT*, 6 Feb. 1942, p. 1; 19 Feb. 1942, p. 32; 23 Mar. 1942, p. 6; 12 May 1942, p. 20; Hershey to Franklin K. Lane, 19 Dec. 1941, HP; Hershey to Paul V. McNutt, 12 Sept. 1942, ibid.; speech, 15 Sept. 1942, speech file, ibid.

18. Hershey press release, 21 Feb. 1942, K. D. Pulcipher Papers, MHI; Blum, *Drafted or Deferred*, p. 93; Minutes of State Directors' Conference, 18 Nov. 1944, HP.

19. Hershey to Judge Patterson, 23 Sept. 1942, HP; Packinghouse Workers of America to Roosevelt, 12 Mar. 1945, box 10, OF 1413–45, FDR; *Monthly Labor Review*, May 1943, p. 1025; speech to Industrial College of Armed Forces, 15 Apr. 1948, speech file, HP; U.S. Congress, House, Military Affairs Committee, *Hearings on Lowering Draft Age*, 77th Cong., 2nd sess., 15 Oct. 1942, p. 108.

20. Speech to Industrial College of Armed Forces, 6 Feb. 1947, carton 65, RG 147, NA.

21. Radio address, 23 June 1941, *Congressional Digest*, 20: 202; U.S. Congress, Senate, Military Affairs Committee, *Hearings on Liability Extension*, 77th Cong., 1st sess., 16 Dec. 1941, pp. 90, 65.

22. *NYT*, 11 Jan. 1942, sec. 4, p. 8; 13 Jan. 1942, p. 20; Hershey to Col. Kramer, 2 Mar. 1942, HP; *NYT*, 21 Mar. 1942, p. 30; George H. Gallup, *The Gallup Poll: Public Opinion, 1935–1971*, 3 vols. (New York: Random House, 1972), I, 326; Hershey to President, 28 Mar. 1942, White House file, HP.

23. Speech, 12 Apr. 1942, Pulcipher File, MHI; War Manpower Commission, minutes, 13 May, 26 Aug. 1942, RG 211, NA; *NYT*, 15 May 1942, p. 15; MD, 26 Aug. 1942, 562: 153; *Business Week*, 12 Sept. 1942, p. 45.

24. *Gallup Poll*, I, 347; *NYT*, 14 Sept. 1942, p. 1; *SS*, Sept. 1942.

25. U.S. Congress, Senate, Military Affairs Committee, *Hearings on Lowering Draft Age*, 77th Cong., 2nd sess., 14 Oct. 1942, pp. 38–39, 57–58; House, ibid., 15 Oct. 1942, pp. 90, 94, 97, 118–19, 127–28.

26. Selective Service System, *Selective Service as the Tide of War Turns* (Washington: U.S. Government Printing Office, 1945), pp. 134–36; Blum, *Drafted or Deferred*, p. 57.

27. *NYT*, 9 Dec. 1943, p. 1; 12 Dec. 1943, p. 7; Hershey to staff, 11 Dec. 1943, speech file, HP.

28. *SS*, Jan., Feb. 1944; *Gallup Poll*, 9 Mar. 1944, I, 435; Hershey press conference, 17 Feb. 1944, carton 65, RG 147, NA.

29. *Selective Service and Victory*, appendix 62, pp. 114, 484; see also Albert A. Blum, "The Farmer, the Army and the Draft," *Agricultural History* 38 (Jan. 1964), 34–42.

30. Hershey press conference, 15 Jan. 1941, speech file, HP; *NYT*, 26 May 1941, p. 8; U.S. Congress, House, Military Affairs Committee, *Hearings on Selective Service Law*, 77th Cong., 1st sess., 16 June 1941, p. 37.

31. *SS*, 1 Sept. 1941, p. 4; *NYT*, 30 Sept. 1941, p. 10.

32. U.S. Congress, House, Military Affairs Committee, *Hearings on Liability Extension*, 77th Cong., 1st sess., 13, 15 Dec. 1941, pp. 13–16.

33. Blum, *Drafted or Deferred*, p. 85, blames Hershey for much of the problem; Hershey statement to House, Committee Investigating National Defense Migration, 3 Feb. 1943, copy in KP; *NYT*, 24 Feb. 1942, pp. 1, 12; Hershey to M. C. Tarver, 17 Feb. 1942, HP.

34. Hershey to Secretary of Agriculture, 18 Feb. 1942, HP; *NYT*, 18 Feb. 1942, p. 15; press conference, 21 Feb. 1942, carton 65, RG 147, NA; Hershey telegram to State Director, Bismarck, N.D., 21 July 1942, HP; Hershey to Kenneth W. Hones, 3 Sept. 1942, ibid.

35. Joseph H. Ball et al. to Hershey, 8 Oct. 1942, Presidential correspondence file, HP; *NYT*, 10 Oct. 1942, p. 1; U.S. Congress, Senate, Military Affairs Committee, *Hearings on Lowering Draft Age*, 77th Cong., 2nd sess., 14 Oct. 1942, p. 51; House, ibid., 15 Oct. 1942, pp. 88–89, 99, 104, 122; Hershey to A. G. Halifax, 17 Oct. 1942, HP.

36. Deferment of agricultural workers file, Oct. 1942, KP; *NYT*, 19 Oct. 1942, p. 12; *Selective Service as the Tide of War Turns*, pp. 110–11; Frank V. Keesling interview.

37. U.S. Congress, House, Committee on Military Affairs, *Hearings on H.R. 1730*, 78th Cong., 1st sess., 11, 15, 17 Feb. 1943, pp. 9, 16; Senate, Committee on Agriculture, *Hearings on Food Supply*, 78th Cong., 1st sess., 18 Feb. 1943, pp. 134–38, 146–47.

38. U.S. Congress, Senate, Committee on Agriculture, *Hearings*, 78th Cong., 1st sess., 18 Feb. 1943, pp. 147–48; 150–51, 154; *NYT*, 19 Feb. 1943, p. 12.

39. Edwin M. Watson to Hershey, 19 Feb. 1943, box 12, OF 1413B, FDR; Hershey to President, 19 Feb. 1943, White House file, HP.

40. Hershey to Executive Director, WMC, 22 Feb. 1943, HP; Hershey to Senator Robert R. Reynolds, 1 Mar. 1943, congressional file, ibid.; *NYT*, 2 Mar. 1943, p. 12; Hershey to Millard Tydings, 10 Mar. 1943, agricultural deferment file, KP.

41. Harry S Truman to Ruby M. Hulen, 6 May 1943; Hulen to Truman, 27 Apr. 1943, both in senatorial file, box 160, Truman Papers, Harry S Truman Library, Independence, Mo. (hereafter cited as HST).

42. Hershey to President, 27 Apr. 1945, White House file, HP; *NYT*, 26 Feb. 1944, pp. 1, 3; Blum, *Drafted or Deferred*, p. 82.

43. *Selective Service and Victory*, pp. 113, 483; U.S. Congress, House, Committee on Merchant Marine and Fisheries, *Hearings on Manpower Shortage*, 78th Cong., 2nd

sess., 21 Mar. 1944, p. 92; House, Committee on Appropriations, *War Agencies*, 78th Cong., 2nd sess., 30 Mar. 1944, pp. 341–42; Minutes of State Directors' Conference, 8 May 1944, HP.

44. Hershey to General Lucius D. Clay, 29 Dec. 1944, White House file, HP.

45. James Byrnes to Hershey, 2 Jan. 1945, Bush file, HP; *NYT*, 4 Jan. 1945, p. 1.

46. O'Sullivan questionnaire, 13 Nov. 1974, GF.

47. *NYT*, 17 Jan. 1945, p. 1; 20 Jan. 1945, p. 12.

48. Hershey to state directors, 22 Jan. 1945, state directors file, KP; *NYT*, 23 Jan. 1945, p. 11; Hershey to Robert A. Taft, 31 Jan. 1945, HP.

49. Hershey to Kentucky State Director, 27 Jan. 1945, HP; Hershey to Charles W. Holman, 11 Jan. 1945, ibid.; radio address, 1 Feb. 1945, speech file, ibid.; *NYT*, 6 Feb. 1945, p. 20; 19 Feb. 1945, p. 18.

50. Herman M. Somers, *Presidential Agency* (Cambridge: Harvard University Press, 1950), p. 158; Frank Keesling to Adolph J. Sabath, 4 May 1945, agriculture deferment file, KP.

51. HST to L. H. Yates, 26 Aug. 1944, senatorial file, 161, HST.

52. U.S. Congress, House, Committee on Appropriations, *National War Agencies*, 79th Cong., 1st sess., 26 Apr. 1945, pp. 50–51; Hershey to President, 27 Apr. 1945, White House file, HP; Minutes of State Directors' Conference, 30 Apr. 1945, ibid.; Somers, *Presidential Agency*, p. 161; Hadley Cantril, *Public Opinion, 1935–1946* (Princeton: Princeton University Press, 1951), pp. 462–63, 466, 467, 468. Most public opinion polls during the war revealed a high percentage of public approval of the way the draft was handled, but farm opinion was always suspicious.

53. On the debate over the impact of the war, see Polenberg, *War and Society*; Richard Lingeman, *Don't You Know There's a War On?* (New York: Putnam, 1970); Geoffrey Perrett, *Days of Sadness, Years of Triumph* (New York: Coward, McCann & Geoghegan, 1973); William Manchester, *The Glory and the Dream*, 2 vols. (Boston: Little, Brown, 1973), I, 355; John M. Blum, *V Was For Victory* (New York: Harcourt Brace Jovanovich, 1976).

54. For a discussion of women at war, see William Chafe, *The American Woman* (New York: Oxford University Press, 1972); Leila Rupp, *Mobilizing Women for War* (Princeton: Princeton University Press, 1978); and Karen Anderson, *Wartime Women* (Westport, Conn.: Greenwood, 1981).

55. FDR to Molly Dewson, 7 Nov. 1940, box 2, OF 1413, FDR.

56. Hershey to Minnie L. Maffett, 9, 30 Dec. 1940; Hershey to Sara H. Horn, 16 Dec. 1942, HP.

57. *Washington Evening Star*, 27 May 1941; "Women's Part in National Defense," 26 May 1941, speech file, HP; Hershey to United Spanish War Veterans, 18 Aug. 1941, ibid.

58. Hershey to Eleanor Roosevelt, 23 Sept. 1941, box 2, OF 1413, FDR.

59. *NYT*, 27 Jan. 1942, p. 18; Hershey to John J. Corson, 7 Mar. 1942, HP; U.S. Congress, House, Military Affairs Committee, *Hearings on Lowering Draft Age*, 77th Cong., 2nd sess., 14, 15 Oct. 1942, p. 136.

60. *Gallup Poll*, I, 316, 327, 406, 420, 435, 438–39, 485.

61. Press conference, 15 Jan. 1941, speech file, HP; U.S. Congress, House, Military Affairs Committee, *Hearings on Extending Liability*, 77th Cong., 1st sess., 13 Dec. 1941, p. 35; Hershey memo to Roosevelt, 8 Apr. 1942, box 2, OF 1413, FDR.

62. Roosevelt memo to Secretary of War, 11 Apr. 1942, box 2, OF 1413, FDR; Hershey to Grenville Clark, 16 Apr. 1942, HP; Hershey to F. J. Bailey, 25 May 1942, ibid.

63. *Atlanta Constitution*, 29 May 1943; Hershey to Assistant Chief of Staff, G-1, 25 Jan. 1944, HP; Hershey to Andrew J. May, 26 July 1944, congressional file, ibid.

64. Jesse Covell to Hershey, 22 June 1919, GF.

65. Ellen to Lewis, 27 July 1919, GF; HD, 5 Feb. 1919, 25 Dec. 1920, ibid.

66. Selective Service System, *Special Groups*, Special Monograph no. 10, 2 vols. (Washington: U.S. Government Printing Office, 1953), I, 41; Public Law No. 783, 16 Sept. 1940, *Statutes at Large*, 54 (1940), 885. For a fuller discussion see Richard M. Dalfiume, *Desegregation of the U.S. Armed Forces* (Columbia: University of Missouri Press, 1969), ch. 3.

67. James Rowe to FDR, 6 Sept. 1940, box 16, OF 1413A, FDR.

68. Hershey to Reverend A. L. Gilmore, 8 Oct. 1940, carton 65, RG 147, NA; Hershey to T. C. McFall, 22 Sept. 1940, ibid.

69. FDR to Robert Patterson, 4 Oct. 1940, box 1, OF 1413, FDR; Patterson to William White, 7 Oct. 1940, ibid.

70. Telephone transcript of Hershey to Dozier (S.C.), Metts (N.C.), Fleming (La.), Collins (Fla.), Edwards and Howard (Tex.), Byrd (Ark.), Jones (Miss.), Means (Mo.), all on 27 Sept. 1940, in carton 65, RG 147, NA.

71. *Special Groups*, I, 45; James Rowe to President, 18 Oct. 1940, box 12, OF 1413B, FDR; *SS*, Sept. 1968.

72. *SS*, Oct. 1968; Frank V. Keesling interview; C. A. Dykstra to James M. Nabrit, 26 Oct. 1940, KP; *Special Groups*, I, 29–30. Johnson stayed on with SS until his death in 1968.

73. *Special Groups*, I, 36; Campbell Johnson to Director, 6 Dec. 1940, OP, HP.

74. Hershey to Mr. Thomas, 9 June 1941; Hershey to Prof. J. W. Seabrook, 24 Feb. 1942; Hershey to Tin, 29 Mar. 1942; Hershey to Roscoe Carroll, 6 Aug. 1942; Carroll to Hershey, 22 July 1942; Hershey to Edward N. Wilson, 27 July 1944, all HP.

75. Hershey to A. A. Liveright, OP, ibid.; *Special Groups*, I, 33, 34; Minutes of State Directors' Conference, 21 Mar. 1947, HP; Lewis Hershey interview, Sept., 1974, OHC.

76. For statistics on blacks in World War II, see *Special Groups*, II, 99–115, appendix 43; also Minutes of State Directors' Conference, 21 Mar. 1947, HP.

77. Transcript, University of Chicago Roundtable, 1940, speech file, HP; *Special Groups*, I, 45.

78. George C. Marshall to President, 25 Oct. 1940, box 1, OF 1413, FDR; *Special Groups*, I, 46.

79. George C. Marshall to President, 25 Oct. 1940, box 1, OF 1413, FDR.

80. *Special Groups*, I, 89–90.

81. Baird V. Helfrich to Paul G. Armstrong, 2 Dec. 1940, *Lynn* v. *Downer* file, HP.

82. Ibid.; *Special Groups*, I, 46.

83. William Averill interview; Hershey to Carlton Dargusch, 20 Feb. 1942, HP; Col. M. B. Bell to Hershey, 31 May 1941, ibid.

84. *Special Groups*, I, 25; P. L. Prattis to Roosevelt, 25 Sept. 1941, box 12, OF 1413, FDR; Roosevelt to Prattis, 7 Oct. 1941, ibid.; Hershey to President, 4 Oct. 1941, White House file, HP; Hershey to Henry Stimson, 18 Sept. 1941, ibid.; General E. S. Adams to Hershey, 11 Oct. 1941, ibid.

85. Campbell Johnson to Hershey, 6 Jan. 1942, *Lynn* v. *Downer* file, HP.

86. Hershey to Paul McNutt, 7 Jan., 30 July 1943, ibid.; State Directors' Advice, 6 Nov. 1942, ibid.

87. Hershey to Henry Stimson, 4 Oct. 1944, War Department file, HP; Stimson to Hershey, 14 Oct. 1944, ibid.

88. *Special Groups*, I, 71–72.

89. Ibid., I, 71–79; Hershey to Secretary of War, 19 July 1944, War Department file, HP.

90. For a review of cases dealing with judicial review of Selective Service, see Lewis Hershey, *Legal Aspects of Selective Service* (Washington: U.S. Government Printing Office, 1969), pp. 52–54, 306. See also *Estep* v. *U.S.*, 327 U.S. 114 (1946).

91. *Special Groups*, I, 49–50; FBI memo, 11 Dec. 1942, *Lynn* v. *Downer* file, HP; J. E. Hoover to General George V. Strong, 11 Dec. 1942, ibid.; for briefs, see *U.S. ex rel Lynn* v. *Downer*, 140 Fed. (2) 397 (2 Feb. 1944).

92. Hershey to Paul McNutt, 30 Dec. 1942, *Lynn* v. *Downer* file, HP; Hershey memo to Executive Director, WMC, 7 Jan. 1943, ibid.

93. Robert M. Hedrick to Hershey, 9 Feb. 1944, *Lynn* v. *Downer* file, ibid.; *Special Groups*, I, 49–50.

94. Hedrick to Hershey, 26 Aug. 1943, HP; *Special Groups*, I, 50; Hershey to Francis Biddle, 25 Aug. 1944, Pulcipher file, HP.

95. *Statutes at Large*, 1940, p. 889. The official history of alternate service is found in Selective Service, *Conscientious Objection*, Special Monograph no. 11, 2 vols. (Washington: U.S. Government Printing Office, 1950); the standard history is Mulford Q. Sibley and Philip E. Jacob, *Conscription of Conscience: The American State and the Conscientious Objector, 1940–1947* (Ithaca: Cornell University Press, 1952).

96. Hershey essay on moral pathology, 1918, GF; HD, 10 Aug. 1917, 6 June, 12 Dec. 1920, ibid.

97. Roger Baldwin to Henry Stimson, 27 Aug. 1940, box 5A, RG 147, NA; for polls see Hadley Cantril, *Public Opinion, 1935–1946* (Princeton: Princeton University Press, 1951), p. 135.

98. U.S. Congress, House, Military Affairs Committee, *Hearings on Selective Service Bill*, 76th Cong., 3rd sess., 24 July 1940, p. 126; Hershey interview, 7 May 1975, HP.

99. Hershey to Morris Sheppard, 8 Aug. 1940, box 3C, RG 147, NA; Sibley and Jacob, *Conscription of Conscience*, p. 116; Hershey to Leverett Saltonstall, 13 Apr. 1945, HP; Mennonite Central Committee, news release, 27 May 1977, GF.

100. Sibley and Jacob, *Conscription of Conscience*, pp. 115–18.

101. Roosevelt to Harold Smith, 21 May 1941, OF 1413, box 2, FDR; Hershey to President, 22 Nov. 1941, HP; EO 8675 (6 Feb. 1941); *Conscientious Objection*, II, 7; Frank Keesling memo for Edwin M. Watson, 18 Oct. 1940, OF 1413A, box 8–9, FDR; Hershey to David Miloserdoff, Walter Shinen, John K. Berkoff, 16 Oct. 1940, KP.

102. Sibley and Jacob, *Conscription of Conscience*, pp. 56, 110, 123; *SS*, 1 Feb. 1941.

103. Hershey to Fred Kosch, 9 Apr. 1941, HP.

104. *Conscientious Objection*, I, 142–45; II, 37–55; Sibley and Jacob, *Conscription of Conscience*, p. 77; Hershey to Attorney General, 27 Jan. 1943, HP; on local boards, see Kenneth M. Dolbeare and James W. Davis, Jr., *Little Groups of Neighbors: The Selective Service System* (Chicago: Markham, 1968); *SS*, 1 Apr. 1941; Hershey to Roger Baldwin, 22 Nov. 1941, HP.

105. Sibley and Jacob, *Conscription of Conscience*, p. 68; Clyde E. Jacobs and John F. Gallagher, *The Selective Service Act* (New York: Dodd, Mead, 1967), p. 24; *Conscientious Objection*, I, 79–80; Col. John D. Langston to Hershey, 27 Oct. 1941, congressional file, HP; Hershey to Chairman, Planning Council, 31 Oct. 1941, ibid.

106. Sibley and Jacob, *Conscription of Conscience*, p. 68; Hershey to James Rowe, 5 Mar. 1942, White House file, HP; Hershey to U.S. Attorney Mathias F. Correa, 16 Nov. 1941, box 4A, RG 147, NA; U.S. Congress, House, Committee on Appropriations, *Hearings*, 78th Cong., 2nd sess., 30 Mar. 1944, p. 397.

107. Sibley and Jacob, *Conscription of Conscience*, pp. 75–80; *Conscientious Objection*, I, 137–38, 152.

108. Hershey to Secretary of Interior, 24 Feb. 1941; Hershey to Quartermaster General, 9 Apr. 1942; Hershey to Walter W. Van Kirk, 9 Nov. 1940; Hershey to E. K. Burlew, 16 Feb. 1942; Hershey to Mrs. Franklin D. Roosevelt, 4 May 1944, all HP.

109. *Conscientious Objection*, I, 173–74; II, 184–204, 283; Hershey to Secretary of Agriculture, 9 Apr. 1942, HP; Hershey to President, 3 Sept. 1942, 21 July 1943, ibid.; U.S. Congress, House, Committee on Appropriations, *Hearings*, 78th Cong., 2nd sess.,

30 Mar. 1944, pp. 383–86. At the end of the war Hershey recommended that, in future programs, some pay and compensation be given to CO's.

110. Hershey to Reverend Harold James, 9 June 1943, HP; Hershey to C. Wayland Brooks, 14 May 1945, ibid.; Sibley and Jacob, *Conscription of Conscience*, p. 297. For descriptions of projects, see *Conscientious Objection*, I, 209–25; II, 189–204.

111. Clarence E. Pickett to Roosevelt, 18 May 1943, OF 1413B, box 12, FDR; Hershey to Ernest Angell, 25 Oct. 1943, HP; Hershey to Secretary of Interior, 26 Oct. 1944, legal file, ibid.; Oswald G. Villard to Roosevelt, 15 May 1944, OF 1413B, box 12, FDR; Francis Biddle to President, 2 June 1945, OF 111, box 526, HST.

112. See Sibley and Jacob, *Conscription of Conscience*, p. 438; *Rodenko v. U.S.* 147 F. 2d 752 (1944), and *White v. U.S.*, 215 F. 2d 782 (9 Cir. 1954); Hershey to Ernest Angell, 25 Oct. 1943, HP; Hershey to Secretary of Interior, 26 Oct. 1944, legal file, ibid.; U.S. Congress, Senate, Military Affairs Committee, *Hearings on CO's*, 78th Cong.,1st sess., 17 Feb. 1943, pp. 17–18.

113. Angell, Jones, and Lawrence to Roosevelt, 8 Mar. 1944, White House file, HP; Oswald G. Villard to President, 17 May 1944, OF 1413B, box 12, FDR; Hershey to Secretary of War, 10 May 1944, White House file, HP; Roosevelt to National Committee on Conscientious Objectors, ACLU, 25 May 1944, ibid.; Roosevelt to Villard, 14 June 1944, ibid.

114. Hershey to Mrs. Estelle H. Cannon, 8 June 1942, HP; U.S. Congress, House, Committee on Appropriations, *Hearings*, 78th Cong., 2nd sess., 30 Mar. 1944, pp. 388, 392; Senate, Military Affairs Committee, *Hearings on CO's*, 78th Cong., 1st sess., 17 Feb. 1943, p. 14; *NYT*, 14 Apr. 1943, p. 1; Hershey memo for Stephen Early, 9 June 1943, White House file, HP.

115. U.S. Congress, Senate, Military Affairs Committee, *Hearings on CO's*, 78th Cong., 1st sess., 17 Feb. 1943, p. 15; Hershey to L. Taylor Krawczyk, 21 Oct. 1941, White House file, OP, HP.

116. *Conscientious Objection*, I, 260–64. Sibley and Jacob, *Conscription of Conscience*, p. 332, disputes the official figures. Hershey to Attorney General, 17 Sept. 1946, legal file, HP; Hershey to J. Edgar Hoover, 8 Mar. 1944, war file, OP, ibid.; Hershey to Attorney General, 19 Dec. 1945, 20 Jan. 1946, legal file, ibid.

117. Hershey to Jonathan Daniels, 10 Apr. 1945, White House file, HP; Hershey to General Harry Vaughan, 1 Apr. 1945, OF 111, box 526, HST; Hershey to Secretary of War, 28 May 1945, War Department file, HP; *Conscientious Objection*, I, 291, 303.

118. Francis Biddle to President, 2 June 1945, and Samuel Rosenman to President, 13 June 1945, OF 111, box 426, HST.

119. Sibley and Jacob, *Conscription of Conscience*, p. 239; Hershey to Harry Vaughan, 1 Apr. 1945, OF 111, box 426, HST; Hershey to Senator Francis J. Myers, 29 Oct. 1945, HP; Hershey to Robert Patterson, 12 July 1945, War Department file, ibid.; *NYT*, 13 June 1945, p. 17; *Conscientious Objection*, I, 304.

120. Hershey to J. Parnell Thomas, 12 July 1945; Hershey to Louis Ludlow, 14 July 1945; Hershey to Margaret Chase Smith, 17 July 1945; Hershey to Robert Patterson, 12 July 1945, War Department file, all HP.

121. Sibley and Jacob, *Conscription of Conscience*, p. 239; Hershey to J. Leroy Johnson, ? July 1945; Hershey to Thomas E. Martin, 10 Oct. 1945; Hershey to Francis J. Myers, 29 Oct. 1945; Hershey to C. W. Bishop, 19 Oct. 1945; Hershey to John W. Brynes, 1 Oct. 1945, all in HP; Hershey to General Vaughan, 1 Apr. 1945, OF 111, box 526, HST; Robert Patterson to Hershey, 4 Aug. 1945, War Department file, HP; *Conscientious Objection*, I, 305–6.

122. Cantrill, *Public Opinion, 1935–1946*, p. 135; Hershey to Dewey Short, 29 Mar. 1946, congressional file, HP; Hershey to General Vaughan, 1 Apr. 1946, OF 111, box 526, HST; *Conscientious Objection*, I, 310–12.

CHAPTER VI

1. Speech file, 20 May 1945, HP.
2. Speech to American Legion Convention, 18–21 Nov. 1945, speech file, ibid.; *SS*, Nov. 1945; Minutes of State Directors' Conference, 7 Nov. 1945, HP; Hershey to Indiana Society of Chicago, 15 Dec. 1945, speech file, ibid.; Hershey to Alice, 17 Dec. 1945, alpha file, ibid.
3. Hershey speech, 11 Jan. 1944, speech file, HP; speech to UAW-CIO, 6 Apr. 1944, ibid.; *NYT*, 7 Apr. 1944, p. 13.
4. *NYT*, 21 Apr. 1944, p. 1; 22 Aug. 1944, p. 8; 27 Aug. 1944, sec. 4, p. 10; *Baltimore News and Post*, 9 Aug. 1944; L. B. Hershey, "Ex-GI Joe," *Rotarian*, Sept. 1944, pp. 12–13; *SS*, Aug. 1944.
5. *NYT*, 1 Oct. 1944, p. 1; Lewis to Ellen, 18 Sept. 1944, GF; *Indianapolis News*, 24 Aug. 1944.
6. SD, 11 Oct. 1943, 29 Sept. 1944; Henry Stimson memo of talk with Marshall, 27 Dec. 1944, folder 12, box 171, SP.
7. Carlton Dargusch interview; Hershey to Roosevelt, 13 Oct. 1944, box 12, OF 1413B, FDR.
8. Henry Stimson memo, 27 Dec. 1944, box 172, SP; Roosevelt to Hershey, 1 Dec. 1944, White House file, HP; Hershey to President, 5 Dec. 1944, ibid.
9. Radio script, 27 May 1944, carton 65, RG 147, NA. In an article, "Selective Service—Today and Tomorrow," 16 Feb. 1944, Hershey stressed three remaining tasks: 1) maintain armed forces until the war is over; 2) provide deferments to workers in critical industry and agriculture; 3) aid in the reemployment of veterans. See speech file, HP.
10. *NYT*, 13 July 1944, p. 19; Hershey, "Selective Service—Today and Tomorrow," Aug. 1944, speech file, HP; Hershey, "Jobs for the Veterans," 28 Sept. 1944, ibid.
11. Selective Service System, *Selective Service and Victory* (Washington: U.S. Government Printing Office, 1948), p. 235; *NYT*, 25 Aug. 1941, p. 1; 2 Sept. 1941, p. 28; Herbert B. Swope to Hershey, 25 Aug. 1941, HP.
12. *Selective Service and Victory*, p. 241; Hershey to John H. Hancock, 1 Dec. 1943, HP.
13. Davis R.B. Ross, *Preparing for Ulysses* (New York: Columbia University Press, 1969), pp. 148–57.
14. *SS*, Oct. and Nov. issues, 1944; *NYT*, 27 Sept. 1944, p. 23; 28 Sept. 1944, p. 13; Hershey to Graham A. Harden, 22 Feb. 1944, congressional file, HP; Local Board memo 190A, 20 May 1944, Yale alumni file, KP.
15. Hershey to Frank T. Hines, 15 Mar. 1944, OP war file, HP; U.S. Congress, House, Committee on Appropriations, *National War Agencies*, 78th Cong., 2nd sess., 30 Mar. 1944, p. 379.
16. Minutes of State Directors' Conference, 17 Nov. 1944, HP.
17. Samuel Rosenman to President, 12 Oct. 1944; Roosevelt to Rosenman, 1 Nov. 1944; Rosenman memo for files, 20 Nov. 1944, all in box 12, OF 1413B, FDR; *SS*, Oct. 1944; *NYT*, 29 Oct. 1944, p. 42; Hershey to Daniel Tracy, 19 Jan. 1945, legal file, HP; Hershey to Frank T. Hines, 20, 25 Jan. 1945, ibid.
18. *Selective Service and Victory*, pp. 233–34; Hershey to Frank T. Hines, 8 Apr. 1945, HP.
19. Hershey to Dean Dinwoodey, 14 Feb. 1945, HP; *NYT*, 24 Sept. 1945, p. 1; William Averill interview; *Selective Service and Victory*, p. 234.
20. Hershey to Thomas B. Martin, 29 Oct. 1945, HP.
21. Hershey speech, 6 Apr. 1944, speech file, HP; Frances Perkins to Hershey, 25 Sept. 1944, legal file, ibid.
22. *NYT*, 7 Apr. 1945, p. 18.

23. *SS*, Apr. 1945. This entire issue was devoted to the reemployment question.

24. Walter Reuther to Hershey, 14 May 1945, Bush file, HP; Town Hall Meeting of the Air, 26 July 1945, speech file, ibid. See also *NYT*, 27 July 1945, p. 16; American Forum of the Air debate, 31 July 1945, speech file, HP.

25. Minutes of State Directors' Conference, 30 Apr. 1945, HP; Hershey to Theodore F. Green, 24 July 1945, ibid.; *NYT*, 28 June 1945, p. 27.

26. Smith Presidential Conferences, 5 Sept. 1945, FDR; U.S. Congress, House, Committee on Appropriations, *Supplemental Appropriations Bill*, 79th Cong., 1st sess., 10 Sept. 1945, pp. 161–67.

27. Hershey to President, 25 Oct. 1945, White House file, HP; Smith Presidential Conferences, 30 Oct. 1945, FDR; HST to Hershey, 2 Nov. 1945, Bush file, HP; HST to General Omar Bradley, 8 Nov. 1945, White House file, ibid.

28. Hershey to Gilbert, 14 May 1942, HP; Alma to Lewis, 19 July 1942, GF; Hershey to G. F. Lichtey, 20 July 1942, HP; Hershey to Dr. Raymond Waggoner, 29 July 1942, ibid.; Hershey to Florence, 7 Aug. 1942, ibid.; Hershey to Mother Dygert, 1 Nov. 1942, ibid.

29. Hershey to Alma Richardson, 9 Mar. 1942; Hershey to Una Ashley, 19 June 1942; Hershey to Alma, 12 July 1942, all HP; Major J. W. Mollaun to Hershey, 17 June 1943, GF; Hershey to Mother, 27 June 1943, HP; Hershey to Alma, 4 July 1943, ibid.

30. Hershey to Florence Dygert, 14 May 1942; Hershey to Gilbert, 17 May 1942; Hershey to George, 3 Aug. 1942; Hershey to Leonard Hicks, 27 Aug. 1942; Hershey to Gilbert, 12 Oct. 1942, all HP.

31. *NYT*, 19 Apr. 1942, p. 20; Hershey to Dr. Burton Handy, 1 Apr. 1942, HP; Hershey to Florence, 14 June 1942, ibid.; Hershey to Dr. Bevis, 18 May 1942, ibid.; Navy Distinguished Service Medal Citation, 3 May 1946, GF; *NYT*, 4 May 1946, p. 13; Army Distinguished Service Medal Citation, 21 Jan. 1946, GF; Peggy Bush interview of Hershey, 28 May 1971, HP; Harry H. Vaughan interview; *NYT*, 6 June 1946, p. 21; *SS*, Feb.-Apr. 1947.

32. *Washington Daily News*, 23 Feb. 1942; Hershey scrapbook, 9 Sept. 1943, GF; *WP*, 22 Mar. 1942; Hershey to Elmer Davis, 30 Nov. 1942, HP.

33. Hershey to Elmer Davis, 30 Nov. 1942, HP; George Gallup, *The Gallup Poll: Public Opinion, 1935–1971*, 3 vols. (New York: Random House, 1972), I, 333, 355, 511; *SS*, May, Oct. 1942. In June 1945, 79 percent thought the system was fair. See Hadley Cantrill, *Public Opinion: 1935–1946* (Princeton: Princeton University Press, 1951), p. 462.

34. John J. O'Sullivan, "From Voluntarism to Conscription: Congress and Selective Service, 1940–1945" (Ph.D. dissertation, Columbia University, 1971), p. 316.

35. Ibid., p. 249; Hershey to Senator Robert R. Reynolds, 8 May 1944, Congressional file, HP.

36. Speech to Industrial War College, 10 Apr. 1946, speech file, HP; Hershey, "We Must Improve Youth," *NYT Magazine*, 10 Feb. 1946, p. 54.

37. Speech to National War College, 17 Apr. 1947, carton 65, RG 147, NA; speeches to Industrial College of the Armed Forces, 10 Apr. 1946 and 5 Jan. 1949, speech file, HP.

38. Speech to Industrial College of Armed Forces, 15 Apr. 1948, speech file, HP; Hershey to Federal Security Administrator, 20 Sept. 1946, legal file, ibid.

39. *NYT*, 8 Aug. 1943, p. 30; Hershey speech, 24 Apr. 1944, speech file, HP.

40. U.S. Congress, Senate, Committee on Education and Labor, *Hearings on Neuropsychiatric Institute Act*, 79th Cong., 2nd sess., 7 Mar. 1946, p. 47; House, Committee on Agriculture, *School Lunch Program*, 79th Cong., 1st sess., 27 Mar. 1945, pp. 46–48.

41. Hershey interview, Sept. 1974, MHI; memo for Chief of Staff by H. Merrill Pasco, 8 Oct. 1945, Hershey file, GMP.

42. General Thomas T. Handy to TAG, 31 May 1945, Hershey 201 file, ARC; Lt.

General Joseph T. McNarney to TAG, 30 June 1942, ibid.; General J. Van B. Metts to Senator Clyde R. Hoey, 26 Nov. 1945, GF.

43. W. S. Paul to Hershey, 12 Apr. 1946, Hershey 201 file, ARC; Gilbert Hershey interview, 8–15 Aug. 1977; *NYT*, 10 Oct. 1946, p. 29; O'Sullivan questionnaire, 13 Nov. 1974, GF.

44. Proceedings of Army Retirement Board, 20 Nov. 1946, Hershey 201 file, ARC.

45. Ibid.

46. May to Surgeon General, 27 Nov. 1946, ibid.; Col. James Gillespie to TAG, 29 Nov. 1946, ibid.; War Department Letter Order, 19 Dec. 1946, ibid.; Hershey to President, 2 Jan. 1947, White House file, HP.

47. U.S. Congress, House, Committee on Appropriations, *Supplemental Appropriations*, 79th Cong., 1st sess., 10 Sept. 1946, pp. 164–68.

48. Minutes of State Directors' Conference, 30 Apr., 7 Nov. 1945, HP.

49. John W. Barber interview, 6 Aug. 1977; Gilbert Hershey interview, 8–15 Aug. 1977; General Henry M. Gross interview, n.d., MHI.

50. Louis H. Renfrow interview, 15 Mar. 1971, HST; John W. Barber interview, 29 Dec. 1978; Bernard Franck interview; Bush interview of Hershey, 28 May 1971, HP; Harry H. Vaughan interview; Vaughan to President, 13 Aug. 1945, OF 400, box 288, HST; Hershey to President, 16 Apr. 1945, GF.

51. *NYT*, 22 Jan. 1946, p. 20; *SS*, Jan. 1946; Harry H. Vaughan interview; E. D. Ingold interview.

52. Hershey to Chief of Staff, 3 Jan. 1946, War Department file, HP.

53. Hershey to Judge Rosenman, 30 Aug. 1945, White House file, HP; James M. Gerhardt, *The Draft and Public Policy* (Columbus: Ohio State University Press, 1971), p. 46.

54. Smith Presidential Conferences, 4 Jan. 1946, FDR; Truman speech to SSS, 21 Jan. 1946, GF.

55. *NYT Magazine*, 10 Feb. 1946, p. 10; Smith Presidential Conferences, 4 Jan. 1946, FDR.

56. Hershey to F. J. Bailey, 8 May 1946, congressional file, HP; Minutes of State Directors' Conference, 6 May 1946, ibid.

57. *NYT*, 19 Sept. 1946, p. 15; 3 Oct. 1946, p. 8; speech, 2 Oct. 1946, speech file, HP.

58. Minutes of State Directors' Conference, 20–22 Nov. 1946; Hershey to Dr. Karl P. Compton, legal file; Hershey to Secretary of War, 21 Feb. 1947, War Department file, all HP.

59. Truman statement, 9 May 1945, Zimmerman files, box 9, HST; Hershey speech, 25 June 1945, speech file, HP.

60. Elbert D. Thomas to Truman, 11 Aug. 1945, White House file, HP; *NYT*, 15 Aug. 1945, p. 13; 27 Aug. 1945, p. 1; Truman to Representative Andrew J. May, 27 Aug. 1945, SS extension file, KP; *NYT*, 27 Aug. 1945, p. 12; Gerhardt, *Draft and Public Policy*, pp. 38–39.

61. Hershey to John W. Snyder, 11 Aug. 1945, White House file, HP; Snyder to Hershey, 8 Sept. 1945, ibid.

62. Hershey to Chairman Andrew J. May, 7 Jan. 1946, congressional file, ibid.; Hershey to John W. Snyder, 17 Jan. 1946, OP, ibid.

63. U.S. Congress, Senate, Military Affairs Committee, *Hearings on Demobilization*, 79th Cong., 1st and 2nd sess., 18 Jan. 1946, pp. 408, 410, 421–22; *NYT*, 19 Jan. 1946, p. 7; *SS*, Jan. 1946.

64. Dwight D. Eisenhower to Hershey, 21 Jan. 1946, War Department file, HP; *SS*, Feb. 1946.

65. Dwight D. Eisenhower to Hershey, 21 Jan. 1946, War Department file, HP; Minutes of State Directors' Conference, 6 May 1946, ibid.

66. Robert Patterson to Hershey, 16 Oct. 1946, War Department file, HP.

67. Robert Patterson to Hershey, 5 Dec. 1946, ibid.; Minutes of State Directors' Conference, 20–21 Mar. 1947, ibid.

68. U.S. Congress, Senate, Military Affairs Committee, *Selective Service Extension*, 79th Cong., 2nd sess., 5 Mar. 1946, pp. 3–6.

69. Ibid.

70. Gerhardt, *Draft and Public Policy*, pp. 42, 51–52; *Gallup Poll*, I, 566; Hershey to Thomas G. Abernathy, 18 Mar. 1946, congressional file, HP; Hershey to Andrew J. May, 19 Mar. 1946, ibid.; *NYT*, 20 Mar. 1946, p. 1.

71. Gerhardt, *Draft and Public Policy*, p. 42; U.S. Congress, House, Military Affairs Committee, *Selective Service Extension*, 79th Cong., 2nd sess., 21 Mar. 1946, pp. 2–10; Senate, *Selective Service Extension*, 79th Cong., 2nd sess., 5, 28 Mar. 1946, pp. 17–19.

72. Senate, *Selective Service Extension*, 28 Mar. 1946, pp. 17, 20–22, 25–28.

73. Ibid., pp. 39–43; *NYT*, 29 Mar. 1946, p. 13.

74. Hershey to John C. Cochran, 29 Mar. 1946, congressional file, HP; *The Reviewing Stand* (Northwestern University), 31 Mar. 1946, carton 65, RG 147, NA; *NYT*, 19 Apr. 1946, p. 7; radio debate on draft, 28 Apr. 1946, congressional file, HP.

75. Minutes of State Directors' Conference, 6–9 May 1946, HP.

76. *Selective Service and Victory*, p. 289; *SS*, Apr.-May 1946; Hershey to Truman, 16 May 1946, box 44, OF 242A, HST; Truman statement to press, 16 May 1946, ibid.; *U.S. News and World Report*, 24 May 1946, p. 28.

77. *Selective Service and Victory*, pp. 290–92.

78. Major General Harry H. Vaughan to Colonel Louis Renfrow, 11 July 1946, box 44, OF 242A, HST; Hershey to President, 11 July 1946, White House file, HP.

79. *SS*, Dec. 1946; W. S. Paul to Hershey, 5 Dec. 1946, OP, HP.

80. Hershey to John Steelman, 27 Nov. 1946, legal file, HP; Hershey to Truman, 5 Dec. 1946, White House file, HP; Hershey to Frank Keesling, 16 Dec. 1946, status of Hershey file, KP; Hershey to President, 29 Jan. 1946, White House file, HP.

CHAPTER VII

1. Robert Patterson to President, 21 Jan. 1947, box 32, White House central files, HST.

2. Robert Patterson to President, 31 Jan. 1946, ibid.; James Forrestal to Clark M. Clifford, n.d., box 97, G. M. Elsey Papers, HST.

3. George C. Marshall to President, 6 Feb. 1947, box 97, G. M. Elsey Papers, HST.

4. Director of the Budget to Clark Clifford, 12 Feb. 1947, ibid.

5. George M. Elsey to Major Mitchell, 26 Feb. 1947, ibid.; memo for record by Dr. J. R. Steelman, 4 Mar. 1947, box 288, OF 440, HST; Truman quoted in James M. Gerhardt, *The Draft and Public Policy* (Columbus: Ohio State University Press, 1971), pp. 56, 58.

6. Hershey to James E. Webb, 3 Mar. 1947, RG 147, NA; Hershey to President, 6 Mar. 1947, White House file, HP.

7. U.S. Congress, Senate, Armed Services Committee, *Establishing OSSR*, 80th Cong., 1st sess., 11 Mar. 1947, pp. 20–24; Harry H. Vaughan to Robert Patterson, 24 Mar. 1947, box 288, OF 440, HST; Patterson to Vaughan, 31 Mar. 1947, ibid.

8. Minutes of State Directors' Conference, 20–21 Mar. 1947, HP.

9. *SS*, Feb.-Apr. 1947; Hershey to local boards, 21 Apr. 1947, RG 147, NA; U.S. Congress, Senate Committee on Appropriations, *Deficiency Appropriations*, 80th Cong., 1st sess., 9 May 1947, p. 24; 19 July 1947, p. 150.

10. *Congressional Record*, 80th Cong., 1st sess., 12 Mar. 1947, p. 1981.

11. Truman press release, 10 Mar. 1947, box 288, OF 440, HST; U.S. Congress, Senate, Armed Services Committee, *Establishing OSSR*, 80th Cong., 1st sess., 11 Mar. 1947, pp. 3, 9–19.

12. Minutes of State Directors' Conference, 6 May 1946, 20–21 Mar. 1947, HP; Hershey interview, Sept. 1974, MHI.

13. Minutes of State Directors' Conference, 20–21 Mar. 1947, HP; John W. Barber, interview, 29 Dec. 1978; Charles H. Grahl interview; O'Sullivan questionnaire, 13 Nov. 1974, GF; Hershey memo on Berlin crisis, 14 Apr. 1972, Bush file, HP.

14. Hershey to Lt. Col. L. R. Salisbury, 11 Sept. 1947, congressional file, HP; John H. Ohly to Hershey, 21 Apr. 1947, OP, ibid.; Hershey to President, 20 July 1947, misc. file, ibid.

15. "American Forum of the Air" transcript, 17 June 1947, speech file, ibid.

16. *NYT*, 11 Oct. 1947, p. 8; "American Forum of the Air" transcript, 11 Nov. 1947, GF.

17. Walter Millis, *Arms and the State* (New York: Twentieth Century Fund, 1958), p. 203.

18. Hershey to President, 4 Nov. 1947, Renfrow file, HP; Millis, *Arms and the State*, pp. 200–201.

19. U.S. Congress, House, Committee on Appropriations, *Independent Offices*, 80th Cong., 2nd sess., 9 Jan. 1948, pp. 370–415.

20. U.S. Congress, Senate, Committee on Appropriations, *Independent Offices*, 80th Cong., 2nd sess., 4 Mar. 1948, pp. 172–89; Hershey to Ellen, 2 Mar. 1948, GF; Hershey to Elmer B. Staats, 31 Mar. 1948, War Department file, HP.

21. Millis, *Arms and the State*, p. 208; Gerhardt, *Draft and Public Policy*, p. 83; Walter Millis, ed., *The Forrestal Diaries* (New York: Viking, 1951), pp. 375–76.

22. Millis, ed., *Forrestal Diaries*, p. 373.

23. Millis, *Arms and the State*, pp. 210–13.

24. Gerhardt, *Draft and Public Policy*, p. 88; *NYT*, 18 Mar. 1948, p. 2; George Gallup, *The Gallup Poll: Public Opinion, 1935–1971*, 3 vols. (New York: Random House, 1972), I, 724.

25. U.S. Congress, House, Armed Services Committee, *Hearings on Selective Service*, 80th Cong., 2nd sess., 21 Apr. 1948, pp. 6514–15; Minutes of State Directors' Conference, 26 May 1948, HP; Senator James Wadsworth to A. G. Thacher, 4 May 1948, WP; Chan Gurney to Hershey, 8 July 1949, GF; *NYT*, 28 Apr. 1948, p. 18; Bernard Franck interview.

26. See Public Law 759 (24 June 1948), *Statutes at Large*, 62: 604–25. For criticism of the bill, see Gerhardt, *Draft and Public Policy*, pp. 114–15, 119–22.

27. Minutes of Planning Group, 20 Jan. 1948, OP, HP; *NYT*, 7 Apr. 1948, p. 4; 14 Apr. 1948, p. 2; Minutes of Selective Service Army Area Conference, Fort Leavenworth, Kans., 8–22 May 1948, misc. file, HP.

28. Bernard Franck notes, 22 Mar. 1948, congressional file, HP; HST to Arthur M. Hill, Chairman, NSRB, 5 Apr. 1948, box 44, OF 242A, HST.

29. Hershey to Secretary of Defense, 21 Apr. 1948, OP-War file, HP; Hershey speech to Industrial College of Armed Forces, 15 Apr. 1948, speech file, ibid.; Minutes of State Directors' Conference, 27 May 1948, HP.

30. *NYT*, 18 July 1948, p. 1; Harry H. Vaughan interview; Clare Boothe Luce to Hershey, 21 July 1948, alpha file, HP; *NYT*, 9 Aug. 1948, p. 2; presidential appointment certificate, 29 Jan. 1949, GF.

31. Hershey memo on Berlin crisis, 14 Apr. 1972, Bush file, HP. Hershey later argued that the blockade helped pass the 1948 law, but the bill passed a month before the full blockade. Soviet harassment, however, had begun in April and probably did generate

some enthusiasm for military preparedness. See *Gallup Poll*, I, 737, 751.

32. Robert J. Donovan, *Conflict and Crisis* (New York: Norton, 1977), pp. 390–91; *NYT*, 18 July 1948, p. 36; Hershey to Secretary of Defense, 20 May 1949, photocopy file, HP; Barton J. Bernstein and Allen J. Matusow, *The Truman Administration* (New York: Harper Colophon, 1966), p. 111.

33. *NYT*, 20 July 1948, p. 1; 22 July 1948, p. 1; interview with Tyrrell Krum, 24 July 1948, misc. file, HP.

34. Kenneth McGill interview; William Averill interview; copy of EO 9988, 20 Aug. 1948, presidential correspondence file, HP; Minutes of State Directors' Conference, 1 Dec. 1948, ibid.

35. Interview with Tyrell Krum, 24 July 1948, misc. file, HP; speech to Commerce and Industry Association, 4 Aug. 1948, speech file, ibid.; Minutes of State Directors' Conference, 1–3 Dec. 1948, ibid.; Jean Carper, *Bitter Greetings* (New York: Grossman, 1967), p. 36.

36. Gerhardt, *Draft and Public Policy*, pp. 122, 125; quoted in Robert Liston, *Greetings* (New York: McGraw-Hill, 1970), p. 47; *NYT*, 14 Jan. 1949, p. 16.

37. *Current Biography*, 1951, p. 271; *NYT*, 2 Sept. 1948, p. 9; speech to Industrial College of Armed Forces, 5 Jan. 1949, speech file, HP.

38. *NYT*, 28 Apr. 1949, p. 1; Hershey to Dr. John R. Steelman, NSRB, box 288, OF 440, HST.

39. Hershey to Truman, 9 Sept. 1949, ibid.

40. Hershey to Secretary of Defense, 28 July 1948, DOD file, HP.

41. *Gallup Poll*, I, 758; *NYT*, 12 Nov. 1948, p. 5; 28 Aug. 1942, p. 2; speech to SS area conference, 7–21 May 1949, HP; Hershey speech, 11 Apr. 1949, ibid.; Hershey speech to Association of American Medical Colleges, 3 Nov. 1948, speech file, ibid.

42. U.S. Congress, House, Committee on Appropriations, *Hearings*, 81st Cong., 2nd sess., 10 Jan. 1950, pp. 141–49.

43. Adjutant General to Hershey, n.d. [ca. 1949], Hershey 201 file, ARC; Lewis to Ellen, 10 Jan. 1940, GF; Hershey medical exam, 31 Oct. 1948, Hershey 201 file, ARC; Lewis to Ellen, 7 Feb. 1949, GF; Raymond E. Willis to Hershey, 29 Dec. 1948, Bush file, HP; Selective Service Training Conference, Newburgh, N.Y., 10 June 1950, ibid.

44. Louis Johnson to Hershey, 8 Aug. 1949, DOD file, HP; *NYT*, 15 Oct. 1941, p. 5; James E. Webb to Johnson, PSF general file, box 136, HST.

45. Gerhardt, *Draft and Public Policy*, p. 127; Gallup Poll, II, 889; *New Haven Journal Courier*, 4 Jan. 1950; *Waterbury Republican*, 20 Dec. 1949; *NYT*, 4 Jan. 1950, p. 28.

46. U.S. Congress, House, Armed Services Committee, *Selective Service Act*, 81st Cong., 2nd sess., 26 Jan.1950, pp. 5186–90.

47. Louis Johnson to Carl Vinson, 24 Jan. 1950, OF 440, box 288, HST; John R. Steelman to President, n.d., PSF general file, box 36, ibid.

48. B. Frank to Hershey, 15 Mar. 1950, congressional file, HP; Omar N. Bradley speech, 2 May 1950, OP, ibid.

49. U.S. Congress, Senate, Armed Services Committee, *Selective Service Extension*, 81st Cong., 2nd sess., 1 June 1950, pp. 21–24; *NYT*, 2 June 1950, p. 3; Gerhardt, *Draft and Public Policy*, pp. 128–29.

50. Minutes of State Directors' Conference, 26 June 1950, HP; Gerhardt, *Draft and Public Policy*, p. 129; U.S. Congress, House, Armed Services Committee, *Selective Service Extension*, 81st Cong., 2nd sess., 26 Jan. 1950, pp. 5195, 5212.

51. Minutes of State Directors' Conference, 26–29 June 1950, HP.

52. Ibid., 28 June 1950.

53. Memo to local boards, 31 Dec. 1950, OP, HP; *NYT*, 11 July 1950, p. 1; Minutes of State Directors' Conference, 14–17 Nov. 1950, 9 May 1969, HP; Hershey to Col. Mark E. Smith, 16 Oct. 1950, official correspondence, ibid.

54. U.S. Congress, Senate, Armed Services Committee, *Doctors' Draft*, 81st Cong., 2nd sess., 22 Aug. 1950, p. 36; Hershey to Chairman, National Security Resources Board, 15 Sept. 1950, ODM file, HP; *U.S. News and World Report*, 29 Sept. 1950, pp. 35–37; *Time*, 15 Oct. 1950, p. 19; *NYT*, 9 Oct. 1950, p. 17; 13 Oct. 1950, p. 1; *Washington Star*, 23 Oct. 1950; speech, 6–7 Oct. 1950, educational deferment file, HP; William M. Boyle, Jr., to Matthew J. Connelly, 1 Nov. 1950, OF 440, box 288, HST.

55. Selective Service System, *Selective Service under the 1948 Act Extended* (Washington: U.S. Government Printing Office, 1953), pp. 240–41.

56. Hershey to Chairman, National Security Resources Board, 15 Sept. 1950, ODM file, HP; *U.S. News and World Report*, 29 Sept. 1950, pp. 34, 38; *NYT*, 27 Sept. 1950, p. 35.

57. *NYT*, 19 Jan. 1951, clipping in Dan Omer files, Washington, D.C.; *NYT*, 18 July 1950, p. 11; 21 July 1950, p. 38; *U.S. News and World Report*, 29 Sept. 1950, pp. 36–37; *NYT*, 30 Sept. 1950, p. 1; 6 Oct. 1950, p. 16; 16 Oct. 1950, p. 9; *Time*, 16 Oct. 1950, p. 19. See Joseph C. Goulden, *Korea: The Untold Story of the War* (New York: New York Times/Quadrangle, 1982), for a critical account of MacArthur's leadership.

58. Interagency committee minutes, 4 Aug. 1950, OP, HP; Liston, *Greetings*, p. 50; U.S. Congress, Senate, Armed Services Committee, *Doctors' Draft*, 81st Cong., 2nd sess., 22 Aug. 1950, pp. 31–35; Truman to Hershey, 6 Oct. 1950, Renfrow file, HP; *NYT*, 7 Oct. 1950, p. 1; *Washington Star*, 23 Oct. 1950; *Newsweek*, 16 Oct. 1950, p. 56; Gerhardt, *Draft and Public Policy*, pp. 224–25.

59. Hershey to President, 14 Nov. 1950, Renfrow file, HP. A summary of NSC-68 can be found in Cabell Phillips, *The Truman Presidency* (Baltimore: Penguin, 1969), pp. 306–8.

60. *NYT*, 8 Dec. 1950, p. 22; 12 Dec. 1950, p. 22; 13 Dec. 1950, p. 1.

61. Memo by President Harry S Truman to Hershey et al., 5 Dec. 1950, White House correspondence, HP; *NYT*, 13 Dec. 1950, p. 20; Gerhardt, *Draft and Public Policy*, p. 146; Marshall for Secretaries of Army, Navy, Air Force, etc., 28 Dec. 1950, science manpower file, HP.

62. *NYT*, 11 Jan. 1951, p. 1; Sam Stavisky, "Who Will Be Drafted This Time?" *Saturday Evening Post*, 20 Jan. 1951, p. 29; *NYT*, 12 Jan. 1951, p. 9; Hershey interview with John Edwards, 1 Feb. 1951, carton 65, RG 147, NA; transcript of Georgetown Forum of the Air, ibid.; *NYT*, 13 Feb. 1951, p. 15; 20 Feb. 1951, p. 8; *Selective Service under the 1948 Act Extended*, p. 10.

63. *Gallup Poll*, II, 965–66, 978; Stavisky, "Who Will Be Drafted?" pp. 28–29.

64. U.S. Congress, Senate, Armed Services Committee, Preparedness Subcommittee, *Universal Military Training*, 82nd Cong., 1st sess., 18 Jan. 1951, pp. 505–11.

65. Ibid., pp. 534–36. The Senate approved the bill on 9 March by a vote of 79–5.

66. Bernard Franck to Hershey, 30 Jan. 1951, congressional file, HP.

67. U.S. Congress, House, Armed Services Committee, *Universal Military Training*, 82nd Cong., 2nd sess., 30 Jan. 1951, pp. 189–92, 220–22.

68. Ibid., pp. 217, 219, 226–27, 246.

69. Ibid., pp. 195, 224, 236–40, 242–43, 245–46.

70. U.S. *Statutes at Large*, vol. 65, 1951, pp. 75–88; Gerhardt, *Draft and Public Policy*, pp. 160, 183, 221; Roger W. Little, ed., *Selective Service and American Society* (New York: Russell Sage Foundation, 1969), p. 43.

71. *NYT*, 14 Feb. 1951, p. 6.

72. Stavisky, "Who Will Be Drafted?" p. 97; *U.S. News and World Report*, 29 Sept. 1950, p. 36; *NYT*, 8 May 1951, p. 63; 18 May 1951, p. 43; 3 July 1951, p. 6.

73. Ellen Hershey Diary, 1951, and HD, Aug.-Sept. 1951, GF.

74. *SS*, Oct. 1951; *NYT*, 4 Nov. 1951, pp. 35, 72; Minutes of State Directors' Conference, 21 Nov. 1951, HP; Hershey to James W. Wadsworth, 17 Dec. 1951, congressional file, ibid.; Hershey speech, 28 Nov.1951, speech file, ibid.

75. Hershey to Truman, 30 Nov. 1951, presidential correspondence, HP.

76. *Annual Report of the Director of Selective Service, 1952* (Washington: U.S. Government Printing Office, 1953), pp. 61–63.

77. U.S. Congress, Senate, Armed Services Committee, *Manpower Utilization Hearings*, 82nd Cong., 2nd sess., 24 Jan. 1952, p. 10; Hershey to Anna Rosenberg, 21 Nov. 1951, Renfrow file, HP.

78. Hershey to Secretary of Defense, 18 Feb. 1952, presidential correspondence, HP; Anna Rosenberg to Truman, PSF general file, box 36, HST; Robert B. Landry to President, 21 Feb. 1952, PSF, general file, box 136, ibid.

79. David H. Stowe to President, 26 Feb. 1952, PSF, box 136, HST.

80. *Annual Report of the Director of Selective Service, 1953* (Washington: U.S. Government Printing Office, 1954), p. 83; Hershey to Anna Rosenberg, 21 Nov. 1951, Renfrow file, HP.

81. U.S. Congress, House, Committee on Appropriations, *Hearings on Independent Offices Appropriations*, 82nd Cong., 2nd sess., 17 Jan. 1952, pp. 307–12, 316–17, 318–19.

82. U.S. Congress, Senate, Armed Services Committee, *Manpower Utilization*, 82nd Cong., 2nd sess., 24 Jan. 1952, pp. 1–3, 6–7, 17–18, 20, 24.

83. *Washington Daily News*, 13 June 1952; *NYT*, 12 June 1952, p. 12.

84. Hershey speech to Industrial War College, 15 Sept. 1952, speech file, HP.

85. Ibid.

86. *NYT*, 5 Aug. 1952, p. 22; *Gallup Poll*, II, 1067.

87. *Colliers*, 13 Sept. 1952, p. 78; Minutes of State Directors' Conference, 1 Dec. 1952, HP.

88. Gilbert Hershey interview, 8–15 Aug. 1977; Dad to Pete [Mrs. Gilbert Hershey], 3 Oct. 1952, GF; *NYT*, 20 Dec. 1952, p. 11.

89. Hershey speech, 6 Mar. 1952, speech file, HP; *SS*, Mar. 1952.

90. Arthur H. Sulzberger to Hershey, 25 Sept. 1952, GF; Hershey to Sulzberger, 3 Oct. 1952, ibid.; news clipping, n.d., KLF; speech to War College, 15 Sept. 1952, speech file, HP.

91. *SS*, Feb. 1952; memo to local boards, 31 Dec. 1950, OP, HP; Minutes of State Directors' Conferences, 24 May, 21 Nov. 1951, ibid.

92. Minutes of State Directors' Conference, 21 Nov. 1951, ibid.

93. *NYT*, 29 Aug. 1952, p. 8; *SS*, Mar., Apr., June 1952; Minutes of State Directors' Conference, 1 Dec. 1952, HP.

CHAPTER VIII

1. Truman to Hershey, 19 Jan. 1953, presidential correspondence, HP.

2. *NYT*, 1 Feb. 1953, p. 49; E. D. Ingold interview; Gilbert Hershey interview, 8–15 Aug. 1977; John W. Barber interview, 29 Dec. 1978; Carlton Dargusch interview; Daniel Omer interview.

3. For a history of McCarthyism see Robert Griffith, *The Politics of Fear* (Lexington: University of Kentucky Press, 1970), and Athan Theoharis, *Seeds of Repression* (New York: New York Times/Quadrangle, 1971).

4. Minutes of State Directors' Conference, 25–28 May 1953, HP.

5. *SS*, July 1953, pp. 1–2; Hershey to Col. James E. Hatcher, CSC, 6 May 1955, in U.S. Congress, Senate, Committee on Post Office and Civil Service, *Federal Employees' Security Program*, 84th Cong., 1st sess., 2 Dec. 1955, pp. 1177, 1180.

6. Robert A. Divine, *Eisenhower and the Cold War* (New York: Oxford University Press, 1981), pp. 27–31; Peter Lyon, *Eisenhower: Portrait of a Hero* (Boston: Little, Brown, 1974), pp. 468–71, 535–43.

7. *Annual Report of the Director of Selective Service, 1953* (Washington: U.S. Government Printing Office, 1954), p. 89.

8. George Gallup, *The Gallup Poll: Public Opinion, 1935–71*, 3 vols. (New York: Random House, 1972), II, 1124–25.

9. Minutes of State Directors' Conference, 15–18 May 1953, HP.

10. *NYT*, 21 July 1953, p. 5; 22 July 1953, p. 4; 28 July 1953, p. 9; *Newsweek*, 5 Oct. 1953, p. 24; *SS*, Sept. 1953, p. 1.

11. Fiscal year totals and monthly averages for draft: 1954, 251,000/20,916; 1955, 211,000/17,583; 1956, 136,000/11,333; 1957, 161,000/13,416; 1958, 124,958/10,413; 1959, 109,000/9,083; 1960, 89,500/7,458. See *Annual Report of the Director of Selective Service, 1953–1960* (Washington: U.S. Government Printing Office, 1954–1961), appendices.

12. Hershey, "Selective Service and College Personnel," 6 Feb. 1941, Pulcipher file, MHI; Hershey, "The Selective Service Act and the College Student," 5 Apr. 1941, speech file, HP; Hershey, "Selective Service and Colleges," 29 Mar. 1941, ibid.

13. Hershey to Edwin M. Watson, 11 Aug. 1941, OF 1413, box 1, FDR; Hershey to Grenville Clark, 23 Aug. 1941, HP; U.S. Congress, House, Military Affairs Committee, *Hearings on Extending Liability*, 77th Cong., 1st sess., 13 Dec. 1941, pp. 9, 24, 30; Stephen Early to Hershey, 13 Dec. 1941, OF 1413, box 2, FDR.

14. Quote in Hershey to Fred Engelhardt, U. of New Hampshire, 8 Oct. 1942, HP; *NYT*, 15 Apr. 1942, p. 18; Hershey to Clarence A. Dykstra, U. of Wisconsin, 6 Aug. 1942, HP; Hershey to Paul McNutt, 25 Mar. 1942, ibid.; Hershey to Dr. Remsen Bird, Occidental College, 30 July 1942, ibid.

15. U.S., *Statutes at Large* 62 (24 June 1948), 612.

16. *Selective Service under the 1948 Act Extended* (Washington: U.S. Government Printing Office, 1953), p. 47.

17. Robert Patterson to Hershey, 10 Oct. 1945, box 44, OF 242A, HST; U.S. Congress, Senate, Military Affairs Committee, *Hearings on Draft Extension*, 79th Cong., 2nd sess., 28 Mar. 1946, pp. 36–37; John R. Steelman to Hershey, 29 July 1946, legal file, HP.

18. E. D. Ingold interview; *Gallup Poll*, I, 737; *NYT*, 5 Aug. 1946, p. 11; Minutes of State Directors' Conference, 2 Dec. 1948, HP; *Statutes at Large*, 62: 605.

19. Col. Renfrow to Hershey, 20 Apr. 1948, congressional file, HP; Renfrow interview, 15 Mar. 1971, HST; Hershey to Truman, 3 Aug. 1948, box 36, PSF general file, HST.

20. John W. Barber interview, 29 Dec. 1978; Hershey to Truman, 3 Aug. 1948, box 36, PSF general file, HST; Jean Carper, *Bitter Greetings* (New York: Grossman, 1967), p. 72; Hershey to Charles E. Odegaard, 28 Oct. 1948, specialized personnel file, HP; Lewis F. Kosch to Social Science Research Council, 26 Aug. 1948, ETS file, ibid.

21. Membership on the Scientific Advisory Committee of Selective Service including the following: 1) Agricultural and Biological Sciences: Lewis J. Stadler, Elmer G. Butler, John S. Nichols; 2) Engineering: Steven L. Kyler, George M. Bailey, Carl R. Soldberg; 3) Humanities: Berthold L. Ullman, Earl Swisher, Charles Odegaard; 4) Healing Arts: Stockton Kimball, Donald G. Anderson, Walter R. Kill, R. McFarland Tilley; 5) Physical Sciences: Thomas B. Noland, Roswell C. Gibbs, Henry Barton, George C. Kearney, Samuel S. Wilkes; 6) Social Sciences: Charles W. Cole, J. Kenneth Galbraith, Malcolm Willey, Everett L. Kelley.

22. James M. Gerhardt, *The Draft and Public Policy* (Columbus: Ohio State University Press, 1971), pp. 154–56; Hershey to Dr. Charles Cole, 18 Oct. 1948, specialized personnel file, HP; Lewis F. Kosch to Professor Everett L. Kelley, 28 Oct. 1948, ibid.

23. M. H. Trytten to Hershey, 21 Dec. 1948, OP misc., HP.

24. Gerhardt, *Draft and Public Policy*, p. 156; Hershey to Truman, 3 Mar. 1949, ETS file, HP.

25. Gerhardt, *Draft and Public Policy*, p. 154; Resolution by AAU, 4 Dec. 1948, spe-

cialized personnel file, HP; Hershey to Industrial College of Armed Forces, 5 Jan. 1949, speech file, ibid.

26. Minutes of Interagency Evaluation Committee, 14 July 1950, OP, HP.

27. Ibid., 21 July 1950.

28. Minutes of Scientific Advisory Committee, 30 July 1950, educational deferment file, HP.

29. Minutes of State Directors' Conference, 14 Nov. 1950, HP.

30. *NYT*, 7 Oct. 1950, p. 1; *U.S. News and World Report*, 29 Sept. 1950, p. 35; quote on "justice" in *Time*, 16 Oct. 1950, p. 19; Minutes of Scientific Advisory Committee, 18 Dec. 1950, HP.

31. Henry Chauncey to Hershey, 21 Dec. 1950, ETS file, HP; *Gallup Poll*, II, 966. For a defense of the plan, see M. H. Trytten, *Student Deferment in the Selective Service* (Minn.: University of Minnesota Press, 1952), pp. 128–30, and National Manpower Council, *Student Deferment and National Manpower Policy* (New York: Columbia University Press, 1952), pp. 3, 97.

32. Louis Renfrow to Col. Irvin, 19 Jan. 1951, ETS file, HP; Hershey to Mr. Millard, 8 Jan. 1951, misc. file, ibid.; U.S. Congress, Senate, Armed Services Committee, *Universal Military Training Act*, 82nd Cong., 1st sess., 18 Jan. 1951, pp. 514, 519–21, 526, quote on 531–32.

33. U.S. Congress, House, Armed Services Committee, *Universal Military Training Act*, 82nd Cong., 1st sess., 30 Jan. 1951, pp. 196–97, 253–54, 255–56.

34. Hershey to Homer Capehart, 5 Mar. 1951, Renfrow file, HP; U.S. Congress, Senate, Select Committee on Small Business, *Industrial Manpower*, 82nd Cong., 1st sess., 7 Mar. 1951, pp. 59–61; quote on p. 62.

35. *NYT*, 8 Apr. 1951, p. 34; Hershey to Carl Vinson, 14 Mar. 1951, congressional file, HP; *Selective Service under the 1948 Act Extended*, pp. 50–52, contains a description of the plan; see also Gerhardt, *Draft and Public Policy*, pp. 157–58.

36. *NYT*, 13 Apr. 1951, p. 11; 9 Apr. 1951, pp. 1, 5; Renfrow interview, 15 Mar. 1971, HST.

37. Sam Stavisky, "Who Will Be Drafted This Time?" *Saturday Evening Post*, 20 Jan. 1951, p. 96; Hershey to Senator Dennis Chavez, 23 May 1951, misc. file, HP.

38. Hershey to Charles G. Ralls, 24 May 1951, Renfrow file, HP; Hershey speeches, "Youth and Draft," 8, 29 Apr. 1951, speech file, ibid.

39. Hershey to Mrs. J. W. Biddle, 17 Apr. 1951, misc. file, HP; interview by Richard Harkness, 5 Apr. 1951, speech file, ibid.; quote in "Youth and Draft," 15 Apr. 1951, ibid.

40. Hershey interview, 5 Apr. 1951, speech file, HP.

41. See *Selective Service under the 1948 Act Extended*, pp. 52–53, for eligibility requirements; "Youth and the Draft," transcripts, 15, 29 Apr., 20 May 1951, misc. file, 1950's, HP; *NYT*, 1 Apr. 1951, p. 1.

42. Hershey speech, 4 June 1951, OP, HP.

43. *NYT*, 3 Apr. 1951, p. 6; 2 May 1951, p. 37; Hershey to Charles J. Turck, 25 Apr. 1951, ETS file, HP.

44. A statistical review of the SSCQT for the 1950's is very revealing:

Fiscal year	Number taking test	Percentage passed
1951	335,837	63.0
1952	77,528	58.2
1953	69,035	56.7
1954	54,728	67.2
1955	27,654	83.3
1956	17,003	83.9

Fiscal year	Number taking test	Percentage passed
1957	11,122	85.2
1958	5,403	79.2
1959	5,257	82.3
1960	3,316	85.0
Totals	606,883	64.4

See *Selective Service Annual Report, 1960* (Washington: U.S. Government Printing Office, 1961), p. 23.

45. Hershey to Senator William F. Knowland, 14 Sept. 1951, ETS file, HP; Lyndon B. Johnson to Hershey, 13 June 1951, ibid.; Hershey to Johnson, 19 June 1951, Renfrow file, HP; Hershey to Johnson, 15 June 1951, ETS file, ibid.

46. Minutes of State Directors' Conference, 27 Nov. 1951, HP; John W. Barber interview, 29 Dec. 1978.

47. *Gallup Poll*, II, 1067.

48. Gerhardt, *Draft and Public Policy*, pp. 227–28.

49. First quote, U.S. Congress, Senate, Armed Services Committee, *Manpower Utilization Hearings*, 82nd Cong., 2nd sess., 24 Jan. 1952, p. 27; second quote, U.S. Congress, House, Committee on Appropriations, *Hearings*, 82nd Cong., 2nd sess., 17 Jan. 1952, p. 321; third quote, Hershey speech, 6 Mar. 1952, speech file, HP; fourth quote, ibid.; fifth quote, Minutes of State Directors' Conference, 1 Dec. 1952, ibid.; *Washington Evening Star*, 5 Oct. 1952; *NYT*, 5 Oct. 1952, p. 18.

50. *NYT*, 31 Jan. 1953, p. 12; Farrington Daniels to Hershey, 10 Feb. 1953, educational deferment file, HP; recommendations of Scientific Advisory Committee, 19–20 Feb. 1953, science advisory file, HP.

51. M. H. Trytten to Hershey, 25 Feb. 1953, HP.

52. Wilton B. Persons to Shanley, 10 Feb. 1953, box 663, OF 133-G-1, Dwight D. Eisenhower Papers, Eisenhower Library, Abilene, Kans. (hereafter cited as EP); Bryce Harlow to General Persons, 2 Mar. 1953, box 664, OF 133, K-2, ibid.; Hershey to Steven B. Derounian, 16 Feb. 1953, educational deferment file, HP.

53. *Washington News*, 26 Feb. 1953; *SS*, Mar. 1953; *NYT*, 10 Apr. 1953, p. 22; *Daily Northwestern*, 10 Mar. 1953.

54. Hershey to Arthur S. Fleming, 5 Mar. 1953, Scientific Advisory Group file, HP; Hershey to General Persons, 6 Mar. 1953, 1950's misc. file, ibid.

55. Hershey to Arthur S. Fleming, 22 Apr. 1953, OP, HP; J. D. Griffing to Hershey, 21 Apr. 1953, ibid.

56. Minutes of State Directors' Conference, 25 May 1953, HP.

57. Hershey to M. H. Trytten, 24 Aug. 1953, educational deferment file; Ralph E. Cleland to Hershey, 28 Sept. 1953; Trytten to Hershey, 6 Oct. 1953, all ibid.

58. Hershey speech to AAAS, 23 Dec. 1953, scientific personnel file, HP.

59. H. A. Meyerhoff to Louis Renfrow, 10 Mar. 1954, Renfrow file, HP; *NYT*, 27 June 1954, p. 29; *SS*, Aug. 1954.

60. Hershey to H. A. Meyerhoff, 3 Nov. 1954, Scientific Advisory Committee file, HP; *NYT*, 27 June 1954, p. 29; Hershey to Alden H. Emery, 17 June 1954, OP, HP.

61. *NYT*, 9 Apr. 1954, p. 15; speech to ICAF, 21 Sept. 1954, speech file, HP.

62. Draft calls in 1955–56 went from a high of 23,000 per month in Jan. 1955, to a low of 8,000 in Apr. 1956. They usually averaged 10,000 until Jan. 1956, when they dropped to 6,000.

63. *SS*, Mar. 1955; H. A. Meyerhoff to Arthur S. Fleming, 14 Mar. 1955, box 665, OF 133-K-2, EP.

64. *SS*, Dec. 1954, Mar. 1955; *NYT*, 2 Feb. 1955, p. 10; U.S. Congress, Senate, Armed

Services Committee, *Hearings on Draft Extension*, 82nd Cong., 1st sess., 10 June 1955, p. 224.

65. *WP*, 2 Feb. 1955; Gerhardt, *Draft and Public Policy*, p. 223.

66. Gerhardt, *Draft and Public Policy*, p. 223; quotes, Senate, Armed Services Committee, *Hearings on Draft Extension*, pp. 232–33, 236–37, 238–40, 241–43, 249.

67. Hershey to Dr. Herbert R. Appell, 23 Feb. 1955, alpha file, HP; Gerhardt, *Draft and Public Policy*, implies that the change was sudden from 1955 to 1958 (pp. 233, 358). Several other studies of the draft also emphasize the newness and illegality of the channeling function. See Carper, *Bitter Greetings*, p. 84; Lawrence Baskir and William Strauss, *Chance and Circumstance* (New York: Knopf, 1978), p. 15; Harry A. Marmion, "Critique," in Sol Tax, ed., *The Draft* (Chicago: University of Chicago Press, 1967), p. 60; Kenneth M. Dolbeare and James W. Davis, Jr., *Little Groups of Neighbors: The Selective Service System* (Chicago: Markham, 1968), p. 154.

68. Quote in *SS*, July 1956; Hershey interview, 7 May 1975, HP; E. D. Ingold interview.

69. Hershey to Dr. Willard F. Libby, 13 Dec. 1955, OP, HP; Hershey to Arthur B. Fleming, 29 Nov. 1955, ODM file, ibid.; *NYT*, 23 Nov. 1955, p. 25.

70. Proceedings, Engineer Joint Council, 26–28 Jan. 1956, speech file, HP; *NYT*, 27 Jan. 1956, p. 11.

71. *SS*, Aug. 1957; memo for record by R. H. Rankin, 5 Dec. 1957, Committee on Specialized Personnel, HP; *U.S. News and World Report*, 10 Jan. 1966, p. 41.

72. *SS*, Jan. 1958; U.S. Congress, House, Committee on Appropriations, *Independent Offices*, 82nd Cong., 2nd sess., 22 Jan. 1958, p. 201; Senate, Committee on Appropriations, *Hearings*, 85th Cong., 2nd sess., 29 Apr. 1958, pp. 6, 11.

73. Quoted in *SS*, May 1958.

74. Minutes of 3rd meeting of National Selective Service Scientific Advisory Committee, 18 Dec. 1958, scientific advisory file, HP.

75. *Gallup Poll*, II, 1448–49, 1452; *SS*, July 1958; Gerhardt, *Draft and Public Policy*, p. 244; U.S. Congress, House, Committee on Appropriations, *Hearings*, 85th Cong., 2nd sess., 22 Jan. 1958, p. 198; Lewis to Ellen, 19 Aug. 1958, GF.

76. Minutes of Interagency meeting, 26 Sept. 1958, OP, HP; *SS*, Nov. 1958.

77. Minutes of Interagency committee, 26 Sept. 1958, OP, HP; Roger W. Jones to General Andrew J. Goodpaster, 30 Sept. 1958, box 664, OF 133-K-5, EP; Selective Service notes on extension, 21 Oct., 13, 14, 21, 26 Nov. 1958; quote in 17 Dec. 1958 notes, all in OP, HP.

78. U.S. Congress, House, Armed Services Committee, *Hearings on Draft Extension*, 86th Cong., 1st sess., 28 Jan. 1959, pp. 83–84; Senate, Armed Services Committee, *Hearings on Draft Extension*, 86th Cong., 1st sess., 5 Mar. 1959, p. 188; House, Committee on Appropriations, *Hearings*, 85th Cong., 2nd sess., 22 Jan. 1958, p. 218.

79. U.S. Congress, Senate, Armed Services Committee, *Hearings on Draft Extension*, pp. 191–97.

80. For this novel interpretation of powers, see U.S. Congress, House, Committee on Appropriations, *Hearings, Independent Offices Appropriations*, 86th Cong., 1st sess., 26 Jan. 1959, pp. 29–30; Senate, Armed Services Committee, *Hearings on Extension of the Draft*, 86th Cong., 1st sess., 5 Mar. 1959, p. 191; House, *Hearings on Draft Extension*, pp. 80, 103–4; Gerhardt, *Draft and Public Policy*, p. 226.

81. *SS*, July 1959; Hershey to Dr. Carmichael, 12 May 1959, scientific advisory file, HP; *Army–Navy–Air Force Register and Defense Times*, 22 Aug. 1959; U.S. Congress, House, Committee on Appropriations, *Hearings*, 86th Cong., 2nd sess., 18 Jan. 1960, p. 38.

82. Quote in Hershey draft article for *Look*, 15 Oct. 1951, speech file, HP; interviews

with Joseph Tiagno and Henry Willis; Hershey, "Obligation to Service," *Scholastic Life*, June 1954, p. 36.

83. Hershey tour notebook and diary, 1957, Europe, GF; *SS*, Dec. 1957.

84. *SS*, Dec. 1957. Hershey took another tour of Europe in late 1959 and returned with similar observations. See *SS*, Jan. 1960.

85. *SS*, Jan. 1957; Minutes of State Directors' Conference, 16 May 1960, HP; Hershey interview in *Army–Navy–Air Force Register and Defense Times*, 22 Aug. 1959.

86. *Army–Navy–Air Force Register and Defense Times*, 22 Aug. 1959; *SS*, Jan. 1959, Oct. 1960; quote in *SS*, Oct. 1954; Minutes of State Directors' Conference, 16 May 1960, HP.

87. Hershey family correspondence, 1950's, GF; Kathryn Hershey Layne interview; Gilbert Hershey interview, 14–15 Nov. 1977; William Averill interview; Hershey 201 file, ARC.

88. *SS*, July, Sept. 1953, Mar. 1958; news clipping, 23 Feb. 1958, alpha file, HP.

89. George N. Craig to President, 26 Nov. 1954, Hershey 201 file, ARC; A. D. Surles to Col. Schulz, 6 Dec. 1954, box 230, OF 47, EP; Robert L. Schulz to Staff Secretary, 11 Dec. 1954, ibid.; Col. A. J. Goodpaster to Schulz, 22 Dec. 1954, ibid.

90. Bernard Franck interview; Chester J. Chastek to Warren G. Magnuson, 20 Apr. 1956, GF; Paul G. Armstrong to Everett M. Dirksen, 1 June 1956, ibid.; Wilber Brucker to President, 6 June 1956, Hershey 201 file, ARC; *NYT*, 7 June 1956, p. 63.

91. Eisenhower to Hershey, 20 Dec. 1960, presidential correspondence, HP.

CHAPTER IX

1. On Kennedy's foreign policy outlook, see Roger Hilsman, *To Move a Nation* (New York: Doubleday, 1967); Richard J. Walton, *Cold War and Counter-Revolution: The Foreign Policy of John F. Kennedy* (Baltimore: Penguin, 1972), pp. 65–66; Jim Heath, *Decade of Disillusionment* (Bloomington: Indiana University Press, 1975), p. 10.

2. Hershey to General Wilton B. Parsons, 6 Jan. 1961, presidential correspondence, HP; Bernard Franck interview; John Sparkman to Walter H. Thompson, 23 Mar. 1961, GF; Hershey to Lawrence F. O'Brien, 9 Jan. 1961, presidential correspondence, HP; Hershey to Walter Jenkins, 21 Oct. 1964, GF.

3. Hershey to President, 30 Jan. 1961, presidential correspondence, HP; Kenneth O'Donnell to Hershey, 10 May 1961, box 179, FG 282, John F. Kennedy Papers, Kennedy Library, Boston, Mass. (hereafter cited as JFK); Kennedy remarks, 23 May 1962, name file, box 1202, ibid.; Kennedy to State Directors, 8 Oct. 1962, FG 282, box 179, ibid.

4. *Annual Report of the Director of Selective Service, 1964* (Washington: U.S. Government Printing Office, 1965), pp. 66–67.

5. James M. Gerhardt, *The Draft and Public Policy* (Columbus: Ohio State University Press, 1971), p. 255; *NYT*, 21 July 1961, p. 1.

6. *NYT*, 21 July 1961, p. 1; *Newsweek*, 7 Aug. 1961, pp. 12, 16; *U.S. News and World Report*, 4 Sept. 1961, p. 65; *NYT*, 7 Aug. 1961, p. 12.

7. *NYT*, 29 Aug. 1961, p. 17; *SS*, Sept. 1961; quote in *U.S. News and World Report*, 4 Sept. 1961, p. 63.

8. U.S. Congress, House, Armed Services Committee, *Military Reserve Posture Hearings*, 87th Cong., 2nd sess., 24 May 1962, p. 6126.

9. Gerhardt, *Draft and Public Policy*, p. 265; U.S. Congress, House, Committee on Appropriations, *Hearings*, 87th Cong., 2nd sess., 17 Jan. 1962, p. 56; *SS*, Mar. 1963, Apr. 1962; House, Armed Services Committee, *Military Reserve Posture Hearings*, 87th Cong., 2nd sess., 24 May 1962, pp. 6135–36; House, Committee on Appropriations, *Hearings*, 88th Cong., 1st sess., 21 Jan. 1963, p. 4.

10. Kennedy to Hershey, 19 Aug. 1963, SS file, JFK; Hershey to President, 30 Aug. 1963, ibid.

11. C. V. Clifton memo to President, 4 Sept. 1963, FG 282, box 179, JFK; Norbert A. Schlei memo to President, 9 Sept. 1963, ND 9–4, box 606, ibid.; EO 1119, 10 Sept. 1963, SS file, ibid.; *Washington Daily News*, 10 Sept. 1963; Gerhardt, *Draft and Public Policy*, p. 269; Hershey to Representative Bob Casey, 24 Oct. 1963, FG 282, box 179, JFK.

12. U.S. Congress, House, Armed Services Committee, *Military Reserve Posture Hearings*, 87th Cong., 2nd sess., 24 May 1962, pp. 6127–30, 6132–33; memo for record by Frank Keesling, 24 July 1962, Status of Hershey file, KP; Major William T. Armstrong to Keesling, 28 Sept. 1962, ibid.

13. John W. Barber interview, 29 Dec. 1978; Frank Kossa interview; William Averill interview; Hershey to David E. Bell, 31 Mar. 1961, FG 282, box 179, JFK.

14. Hershey to David E. Bell, 31 Mar. 1961, FG 282, box 179, JFK; B. O. B. revisions on SS, EO, 16 Nov. 1961, ibid.; Nicholas Katzenbach to AG, 15 Dec. 1961, ibid.; Kennedy to James P. Ringley, 5 Jan. 1962, ibid.; *Annual Report of the Director of Selective Service, 1962* (Washington: U.S. Government Printing Office, 1963), p. 8.

15. U.S. Congress, House, Committee on Appropriations, *Hearings*, 87th Cong., 1st sess., 20 Mar. 1961, pp. 267, 270; Senate, Committee on Appropriations, *Hearings*, 87th Cong., 2nd sess., 13 Aug. 1962, p. 948; House, ibid., 17 Jan. 1962, p. 43; and 88th Cong., 1st sess., 21 Jan. 1963, pp. 6, 19, 28.

16. SS, July 1962; U.S. Congress, House, Committee on Appropriations, *Hearings*, 88th Cong., 1st sess., 21 Jan. 1963, pp. 4, 7–8.

17. *NYT*, 2 Mar. 1963; Roger W. Little, ed., *Selective Service and American Society* (New York: Russell Sage Foundation, 1969), p. 17; U.S. Congress, House, Armed Services Committee, *Hearings to Extend Induction*, 88th Cong., 1st sess., 1 Mar. 1963, pp. 85, 87, 94; Harry A. Marmion, *Selective Service* (New York: John Wiley, 1968), p. 1; *NYT*, 12 Mar. 1963, p. 4; 16 Mar. 1963, p. 1; 30 Mar. 1963, p. 7. The draft call for Feb. 1963 was for only 4,000.

18. Annual medical examination, 13 Nov. 1962, Hershey 201 file, ARC.

19. SS, Apr., June 1962.

20. SS, May 1962, July 1963; Hershey to E. Roland Harriman, 7 May 1962, name file, Hershey, box 1202, JFK; SS, Jan. 1961; *U.S. News and World Report*, 4 Sept. 1961, p. 67. For an excellent discussion of the idea of community in America, see Thomas Bender, *Community and Social Change in America* (Baltimore: Johns Hopkins University Press, 1978).

21. Report to Superintendent of Schools from Special Committee on Group Activities, Jan. 1963, HP.

22. For the youth revolt, see Irwin Unger, *The Movement* (New York: Dodd, Mead, 1974).

23. Hershey to President, 3 Dec. 1963, GF; Bernard Franck interview; Frank M. Slatinshek interview.

24. E. D. Ingold interview; Daniel Omer interview; Johnson to General and Mrs. Hershey, 29 Nov. 1967, Hershey name file, box 275, Lyndon Johnson Papers, Johnson Library, Austin, Tex. (hereafter cited as LBJ).

25. George C. Herring, *America's Longest War: The United States and Vietnam, 1950–1975* (New York: John Wiley, 1979), p. 108.

26. Clipping of *NYT*, 2 Oct. 1963, newspaper file, HP.

27. U.S. Congress, Senate, Committee on Appropriations, *Hearings*, 88th Cong., 2nd sess., 18 Aug. 1964, p. 546.

28. SS, Sept. 1964; *News Notes: Central Committee for Conscientious Objectors*, Mar.-Apr. 1964, newspaper file, HP, provides extensive press bibliography of draft criti-

cism. See also *WP*, 6 Dec. 1964; E. D. Ingold interview, 20 Feb. 1972, transcription, HP.

29. Hershey memo to President, 30 Aug. 1963, ND 9–4, box 606, JFK; Kennedy to James G. Patton, 6 Sept. 1963, ibid.

30. U.S. Congress, Senate, Committee on Labor and Public Welfare, *Nation's Manpower Revolution*, 88th Cong., 1st sess., 22 Nov. 1963, pp. 2817–24.

31. *Annual Report of the Director of Selective Service, 1964* (Washington: U.S. Government Printing Office, 1965), p. 11; George Gallup, *The Gallup Poll: Public Opinion, 1935–1971*, 3 vols. (New York: Random House, 1972), III, 1853; Kenneth M. Dolbeare and James W. Davis, Jr., *Little Groups of Neighbors: The Selective Service System* (Chicago: Markham, 1968), pp. 162–63; Walter Jenkins to Hershey et al., 8 Apr. 1964, EX FG 282, cont. 303, LBJ.

32. *NYT*, 16 Apr. 1964, p. 32; Hershey memo, 21 Apr. 1964, appointment file, HP; Department of State to Ambassadors, NATO (aerogram), 23 Apr. 1964, White House correspondence, ibid.

33. U.S. Congress, House, Committee on Appropriations, *Hearings*, 88th Cong., 2nd sess., 21 Apr. 1964, pp. 201–2; Senate, ibid., 7 May 1964, pp. 636–38; Hershey to Carl Vinson, 6 May 1964, congressional file, HP.

34. Hershey to Ralph A. Dungan, 5 Mar. 1964, White House correspondence, HP.

35. *SS*, Feb. 1961; *NYT*, 7 Mar. 1961, p. 1; 17 Apr. 1961, p. 33; O'Sullivan questionnaire, 13 Nov. 1974, GF; R. Sargent Shriver to L. Mendel Rivers, n.d., congressional file, HP; Hershey to Rivers, 23 Apr. 1965, ibid.

36. *Annual Report of the Director of Selective Service, 1964*, p. 61; Gerhardt, *Draft and Public Policy*, p. 265.

37. Hershey to Representative Carl D. Perkins, 22 Aug. 1961, congressional file, HP; Hershey to Timothy J. Reardon, 4 Aug. 1961, White House correspondence, ibid.; *SS*, Dec. 1961.

38. Hershey to State Directors, 1 Nov. 1963, ND 9–4, box 606, JFK. The Cassius Clay case proved particularly embarrassing to the administration.

39. Lyndon Johnson memo for Secretaries of Labor, HEW, and Defense, and Director of SS, 9 May 1964, White House file, HP.

40. Hershey to Secretary of Defense, 10 Jan. 1964, box 606, ND 9–4, JFK; Proceedings of Ad Hoc Committee on Manpower Conservation, 27 Jan. 1964, SS records, ibid.; *News and Notes: Central Committee for Conscientious Objectors*, Mar.-Apr. 1964, newspaper file, HP; Gilbert Hershey interview, 8–15 Aug. 1977.

41. Johnson memo for Director of SS, 3 Feb. 1964, EX FG 282, cont. 303, LBJ; *NYT*, 18 Feb. 1964, p. 17; *SS*, Feb. 1964.

42. Hershey to State Directors, 20 Feb. 1964, SS file, JFK; *SS*, Apr. 1964.

43. U.S. Congress, Senate, Committee on Appropriations, *Hearings, Independent Offices Appropriations*, 88th Cong., 2nd sess., 7 May 1964, pp. 617–25.

44. *SS*, Mar. 1965; U.S. Congress, Senate, Committee on Appropriations, *Hearings, Supplemental Appropriations Bill*, 88th Cong., 2nd sess., 18 Aug. 1964, pp. 529–43.

45. *NYT*, 6 Apr. 1966, p. 8; 25 Aug. 1966, p. 1; Charles C. Moskos, "The Negro and the Draft," in Little, ed., *Selective Service*, p. 155; *SS*, Oct. 1966; U.S. Congress, House, Armed Services Committee, *Review of Selective Service*, 89th Cong., 2nd sess., 23–24 June 1966, pp. 9647, 9705; *NYT*, 15 Dec. 1966, p. 22.

46. Hershey to Colonel Irvin, 23 Sept. 1964, alpha file, HP; *SS*, Nov. 1964.

47. Hershey to William Moyers, 23 Nov. 1964, GF; *Washington Evening Star*, 8 Dec. 1964.

48. Joseph Califano to William Moyers, 22 Jan. 1965, EX Le, cont. 3, LBJ.

49. Lyndon B. Johnson, *The Vantage Point* (New York: Holt, Rinehart & Winston, 1971), p. 122.

50. Ibid., p. 142; for a discussion of this escalation, see Herring, *America's Longest War*, pp. 133–44.

51. Johnson, *Vantage Point*, pp. 146–48; *Annual Report of the Director of Selective Service, 1966* (Washington: U.S. Government Printing Office, 1967), p. 86.

52. Hershey speech to 37th National Convention of ROA, Miami, n.d., HP; Hershey to Hugh B. Hester, 12 July 1966, alpha file, ibid.

53. Quote in Hershey to National Press Club, 12 Mar. 1968, speech file, HP; O'Sullivan questionnaire, 13 Nov. 1974, GF; Gilbert Hershey interview, 8–15 Aug. 1977; Arleigh Burke interview.

54. Herring, *America's Longest War*, p. 141; Roger Little, "Procurement of Manpower," in Little, ed., *Selective Service and American Society*, p. 5; Hershey to Cloyd T. Caldwell, 30 June 1965, alpha file, HP.

55. *NYT*, 30 July 1965, p. 1; Gerhardt, *Draft and Public Policy*, p. 273; *Annual Report of the Director of Selective Service, 1966*, p. 86.

56. *NYT*, 30 July 1965, p. 4; *U.S. News and World Report*, 16 Aug. 1965, p. 21; *Washington Sunday Star*, 8 Aug. 1965; *San Francisco Chronicle*, 31 Aug. 1965.

57. *U.S. News and World Report*, 10 Jan. 1966, p. 41; *SS*, Mar., July 1966; *NYT*, 10 Jan. 1966, p. 3; *Washington Sunday Star*, 16 Dec. 1965; U.S. Congress, House, Committee on Appropriations, *Hearings*, 89th Cong., 2nd sess., 1 Feb. 1966, p. 1.

58. Godfrey Hodgson, *America in Our Time* (New York: Vintage, 1976), p. 296. For the youth protest and the draft, see Unger, *The Movement*, pp. 41–42, 141; William L. O'Neill, *Coming Apart* (New York: New York Times/Quadrangle, 1971), p. 287; Michael Useem, *Conscription, Protest, and Social Conflict* (New York: John Wiley, 1973).

59. U.S. Congress, House, Armed Services Committee, *Hearings on Card Destruction*, 89th Cong., 1st sess., 6 Aug. 1965, pp. 3129–32; *NYT*, 1 Sept. 1965, p. 17.

60. Hershey to Col. Caldwell, 29 Nov. 1965, alpha file, HP.

61. *Columbus Dispatch*, 29 Oct. 1965; *NYT*, 5 Dec. 1965, p. 70; *WP*, 15 Dec. 1965, 2 Dec. 1966.

62. Quote from Jean Carper, *Bitter Greetings* (New York: Grossman, 1967), p. 130; *U.S. News and World Report*, 10 Jan. 1966, p. 43.

63. *San Francisco Chronicle*, 31 Aug. 1965; *Washington Sunday Star*, 16 Dec. 1965; *NYT*, 24 Oct. 1965, p. 75.

64. *NYT*, 28 Jan. 1966, p. 46; *WP*, 15 Dec. 1965; *Christian Century*, 16 Mar. 1966, p. 325; *NYT*, 26 Nov. 1965, p. 8; 17 Dec. 1965, p. 4; 23 Dec. 1965, p. 1.

65. George E. Reedy to President, 16 Dec. 1965, National Security-Defense, cont. 148, LBJ.

66. *Omaha World Herald*, n.d., 1966, newspaper file, HP; *NYT*, 12 Jan. 1966, p. 1; 15 Jan. 1966, p. 6.

67. Hershey interview, May 1975, OHC, MHI; *NYT*, 22 Dec. 1965, p. 3; *U.S. News and World Report*, 10 Jan. 1966, pp. 39, 42, 43; *The Nation*, 3 Jan. 1966, inside cover; *NYT*, 12 Jan. 1966, p. 8. Despite his rejection of the criminal analogy, Hershey did occasionally slip into the trap. When discussing deferments he remarked, "If you want to call it a parole, they have violated the terms of their parole and they have no business to have a deferment after that" (see *Washington Sunday Star*, 16 Dec. 1965).

68. J. Starr, "How Fair Is the Draft?," *Look*, 19 Apr. 1966, p. 26; U.S. Congress, House, Committee on Appropriations, *Hearings*, 89th Cong., 2nd sess., 1 Feb. 1966, p. 77; Hershey to Meyerhoff, 5 Apr. 1966, alpha file, HP.

69. *NYT*, 8 Dec. 1965, p. 17; U.S. Congress, Senate, Committee on Appropriations, *Hearings*, 89th Cong., 2nd sess., 25–26 May 1966, pp. 1206, 1222; *NYT*, 18 Feb. 1966, p. 10; Starr, "How Fair Is the Draft?" p. 26.

CHAPTER X

1. *SS*, Aug. 1965; *NYT*, 21 Oct. 1965, p. 1; *Washington Sunday Star*, 8 Aug., 16 Dec. 1965; *SS*, June 1966.

2. Kenneth McGill interview; Arleigh Burke interview; quote in *Washington Star*, 13 Apr. 1966; *NYT*, 18 Mar. 1966, p. 28; quote in *Washington Daily News*, 12 Dec. 1966; Hershey interview, Sept. 1974, MHI.

3. Total draft calls: 1965, 101,300; 1966, 336,530; 1967, 288,900. The calls did rise to 343,300 in 1968, but dropped immediately to 266,900 in 1969 and to 209,300 in 1970. See *Semi—annual Report of the Director of Selective Service, 1 January—30 June 1970* (Washington: U.S. Government Printing Office, 1970), p. 52.

4. George H. Gallup, *The Gallup Poll: Public Opinion, 1935–1971* (New York: Random House, 1972), III, 2016; *SS*, Mar. 1968.

5. *Annual Report of the Director of Selective Service, 1966* (Washington: U.S. Government Printing Office, 1967), p. 17.

6. *Gallup Poll*, III, 2017, 2032.

7. *Omaha World Herald*, n.d., newspaper file, HP; Jean Carper, *Bitter Greetings* (New York: Grossman, 1967), p. 22.

8. Johnson to Col. E. S. Stephenson, telegram, 6 Oct. 1965, GF.

9. Joseph Califano to President, 20 June 1966, National Secretary of Defense, cont. 148, LBJ; James M. Gerhardt, *The Draft and Public Policy* (Columbus: Ohio State University Press, 1971), p. 308.

10. Eric Goldman, *The Tragedy of Lyndon Johnson* (New York: Knopf, 1969), pp. 295, 494–95; Joseph Califano to President, 25 June 1966, FG 698, LBJ; interview with E. D. Ingold.

11. EO 11289, 2 July 1966, Legal Background of Selective Service, cont. 1, LBJ; Califano to President, 28 July 1966, FG 698, ibid.; Harry A. Marmion, *Selective Service* (New York: John Wiley, 1968), p. 77.

12. *SS*, Aug. 1966; Hershey to all Local and Appeal Boards, 23 Sept. 1966, Legislative Background of Selective Service, cont. 1, LBJ.

13. William Hogan interview; Hershey to Mendel Rivers, 27 Jan. 1966, congressional file, HP; Ted Kennedy to Hershey, 10 June 1966, GF.

14. *NYT*, 12 Jan. 1966, p. 1; 2 Mar. 1966, p. 9; *WP*, 13 Mar. 1966; Marmion, *Selective Service*, p. 22.

15. Carper, *Bitter Greetings*, p. 17; U.S. Congress, House, Armed Services Committee, *Review of Selective Service Administration*, 89th Cong., 2nd sess., 22 June 1966, pp. 1615, 9656, 9907.

16. House, *Review of Selective Service Administration*, pp. 9689, 9698.

17. Ibid., pp. 9633, 9639–40, 9652, 9666, 9696, 9698.

18. Ibid., pp. 9669, 9680, 9691, 9700.

19. Ibid., pp. 9635, 9638, 9654, 9658, 9662, 9676, 9714, 9720.

20. Draft calls for the rest of 1966 fluctuated: July, 28,500; Aug., 36,600; Sept., 37,300; Oct., 49,200; Nov., 37,600; Dec., 12,100. Calls dropped off considerably after November. See *Annual Report of the Director of Selective Service, 1967* (Washington: U.S. Government Printing Office, 1968), p. 86.

21. E. D. Ingold interview; Marmion, *Selective Service*, p. 77.

22. Harry A. Marmion, "Critique of Selective Service," in Sol Tax, ed., *The Draft* (Chicago: University of Chicago Press, 1967), p. 55; Richard W. Boone and N. G. Kirkland, "Freedom," ibid., p. 271; Bruce Chapman, "A Proposal to Replace the Draft," ibid., p. 217; Geoffrey C. Hazard, Jr., "Charge to the Conference," ibid., p. 293.

23. Hershey, "Fact Paper," ibid., p. 3; E. D. Ingold, ibid., pp. 302–5, 313; Hershey to Laura, 27 Dec. 1966, alpha file, HP.

24. The major recommendations of the commission were as follows: elimination of all student deferments, except ROTC; elimination of all other deferments except hardship; induction of men on a youngest-first basis beginning at age nineteen; selection of men through a random system; reorganization of the system to reduce the number of local boards from over 4,000 to 300 under centralized control, with ten regional offices and professional classifiers acting according to national and uniform criteria and using computers. See report of the National Advisory Commission on Selective Service, *In Pursuit of Equity: Who Serves When Not All Serve?* (Washington: U.S. Government Printing Office, 1967), pp. 3–10. For more information on the elite character of local boards, see Kenneth M. Dolbeare and James W. Davis, Jr., *Little Groups of Neighbors: The Selective Service System* (Chicago: Markham, 1968), p. 26; see also Gerhardt, *Draft and Public Policy*, pp. 321, 323–25, 327.

25. Joseph Califano to President, 11 Jan. 1967; Bradley H. Patterson, Jr., to Califano, 17 Jan. 1967, both FG 698, LBJ.

26. Joseph Califano to President, 23, 26 Feb. 1967, ibid.

27. Hershey interview, May 1975, OHC, MHI.

28. Gerhardt, *Draft and Public Policy*, pp. 331–32; *SS*, Apr. 1967.

29. Joseph Califano to Hershey, 8 Apr. 1967, EX FG 282, cont. 303, LBJ; Hershey to Califano, 14 Apr. 1967, White House correspondence, HP; *SS*, Apr. 1967.

30. *U.S. News and World Report*, 20 Mar. 1967, p. 70; *NYT*, 12 Mar. 1967, p. 52; 13 Mar. 1967, p. 29.

31. Marmion, *Selective Service*, p. 96; U.S. Congress, Senate, Committee on Labor and Public Welfare, Subcommittee on Employment, *Hearings on Manpower Implications of Selective Service*, 90th Cong., 1st sess., 20 Mar. 1967, pp. 1, 11, 13, 17, 21, 29; quote on p. 12.

32. For the scope of protest against the draft in its various forms, see Lawrence Baskir and William Strauss, *Chance and Circumstance: The Draft, the War and the Vietnam Generation* (New York: Knopf, 1978), which is excellent on draft evasion but inaccurate on Hershey.

33. Betty M. Vetter to Hershey, 22 Mar. 1967, alpha file, HP; *NYT*, 16 Mar. 1967, sec. 4, p. 10; 29 June 1967, p. 5.

34. Minutes of State Directors' Conference, 1–5 May 1967, HP; quote, Hershey note, 9 Feb. 1967, in Daniel Omer files, Alexandria, Va.; *The Diamondback* (University of Maryland), 24 Feb. 1967, alpha file, HP; Hershey to Valerie Wiener, 12 June 1967, ibid.

35. *SS*, Feb. 1967; *Gallup Poll*, III, 2065.

36. U.S. Congress, Senate, Armed Services Committee, *Amending and Extending the Draft Law*, 90th Cong., 1st sess., 19 Apr. 1967, pp. 609, 626; House, Armed Services Committee, *Extension of UMT and SS Act*, 90th Cong., 1st sess., 10 May 1967, p. 2629.

37. Ibid., pp. 2513, 2612.

38. Ibid., pp. 2640, 2657.

39. Ibid., pp. 2663, 2674–75; Senate, *Amending and Extending the Draft Law*, pp. 261, 655.

40. Ibid., pp. 630, 637–38.

41. Ibid., pp. 636, 649, 653, 654; House, *Extension of UMT and SS Act*, pp. 2624, 2633, 2661.

42. Ibid., pp. 2618, 2619, 2633, 2645–47; Senate, *Amending and Extending the Draft Law*, pp. 613, 639, 656.

43. Hershey to Commodore Mark L. Hershey, 27 Mar. 1967, alpha file, HP; Minutes of State Directors' Conference, 1–5 May 1967, HP.

44. Johnson speech to State Directors, 3 May 1967, EX FG 282, cont. 303, LBJ.

45. *U.S. Statutes at Large* 81 (1967): 100–105.

46. Ibid.

47. Joseph Califano to President, 12, 29 June 1967, Califano file, cont. 55 (1757), LBJ.

48. U.S. Congress, Senate, Committee on Judiciary, *On Right of Counsel to Draftees*, 90th Cong., 2nd sess., 16 May 1968, p. 27.

49. Carter B. Magruder interview, 28 Dec. 1972, OHC, MHI.

50. Robert McNamara, Charles Schultze, and Hershey to President, 9 Jan. 1968, EX FG 600, cont. 367, LBJ.

51. Ibid.; Joseph Califano to Johnson, 19 Jan. 1968, ibid.; Charles Schultze to President, 9 Jan. 1968, ibid.; Minutes of State Directors' Conference, 22–26 Apr. 1968, HP.

52. Joseph Califano to Hershey, 23 Jan. 1968, EX FG 600, cont. 367, LBJ; *Washington Daily News*, 30 Apr. 1968; *NYT*, 3 May 1968, p. 46.

53. *Omaha World Herald*, 3 Mar. 1966; *NYT*, 5 Dec. 1966, p. 53.

54. Hershey to Johnson, 30 Jan. 1964, GF; *SS*, Sept. 1967; *Fort Lauderdale News*, 24, 25 May 1968; *NYT*, 18 Sept. 1967, p. 17; *Washington Evening Star*, 1 July 1968.

55. "Aspects of Human Equality," 13 Apr. 1956, speech file, HP.

56. *NYT*, 26 May 1956, p. 41; Hershey to Major General Wilton B. Persons, 26 Sept. 1956, OF 133-K, box 664, EP.

57. *NYT*, 22 Sept. 1956, p. 38; 4 Oct. 1956, p. 22; Hershey to Earl Goodwin, 25 Sept. 1956, OF 133-K, box 664, EP.

58. The charges that the armed forces discriminated against blacks are still being debated in the literature. For a discussion, see Baskir and Strauss, *Chance and Circumstance*, p. 8, and Charles C. Moskos, "Negro and the Draft," in Roger W. Little, ed., *Selective Service and American Society* (New York: Russell Sage Foundation, 1969), pp. 143–45, 159, who insist that Negroes were more likely to be drafted than whites. Dolbeare and Davis, *Little Groups of Neighbors*, p. 16, qualify this contention; Neil D. Fligstein, "Who Served in the Military, 1940–1973," *Armed Forces and Society* 6 (Winter 1979): 297, disputes it and states that the draft was not unfair to blacks or the poor. This last study emphasizes that more education meant a greater chance of being drafted. Blacks were less likely to serve than whites, and the American farmer was the least likely to serve in all periods of conflict from World War II through Vietnam.

59. Kenneth McGill, in an interview, admitted some footdragging in the system over integration. See also *WP*, May 1966, newspaper file, HP; *WP*, 6 Sept. 1968; Tax, ed., *The Draft*, p. 308; J. A. Willenz, ed., *Dialogue on the Draft* (Washington, D.C.: American Veterans' Committee, 1966), p. 64.

60. Joseph Califano to Johnson, 28 June 1967, EX FG 282, cont. 303, LBJ.

61. Hershey to President, 31 Aug. 1967, ibid.; Hershey to Clifford L. Alexander, 29 June 1967, alpha file, HP; Hershey to Joseph Califano, 13 Nov. 1969, ibid.; *SS*, Oct. 1968.

62. *SS*, Jan., Feb., July 1969, Feb 1970; Hershey to Laynes, 1 May 1970, KLF.

63. *Semi-annual Report of the Director of Selective Service, 1 July to 31 December 1967* (Washington: U.S. Government Printing Office, 1968), p. 13; *NYT*, 24 Feb. 1968, p. 10; 19 Sept. 1967, p. 13; William Averill interview.

64. William O'Neill, *Coming Apart* (New York: New York Times/Quadrangle, 1971), pp. 340–42; *WP*, 17 Oct. 1967; Daniel Omer interview.

65. *SS*, Mar. 1967; Joseph Califano to President, 12 June 1967, Legislative background of SS, cont. 2, LBJ; Johnson to Ramsey Clark, 20 Oct. 1967, alpha file, HP. Johnson's initiation of Hershey's actions is confirmed by Hershey's own testimony and that of others, including Califano. Larry Levinson to Califano, 8 Nov. 1967, Califano file, cont. 55, LBJ; Kenneth McGill interview; Bernard Franck interview; Jonathan Rose interview.

66. Local Board Memorandum No. 85, 24 Oct. 1967, Califano files, cont. 55, LBJ; Hershey to State Directors, 25 Oct. 1967, ibid.

67. Hershey to Members of SS, 26 Oct. 1967, ibid.

68. Hershey to All Government Appeal Agents, 26 Oct. 1967, EX FG 282, cont. 303, LBJ; Daniel Omer interview; William Averill interview.

69. Hershey to Charles Schultze, 27 Oct. 1967, Califano file, cont. 55, LBJ.

70. Larry Levinson to Joseph Califano, 8 Nov. 1967, ibid.; Memo of staff comments by Bureau of Budget, 8 Nov. 1967, ibid.; Califano to President, 14 Nov. 1967, ibid.; *U.S. News and World Report*, 20 Nov. 1967, p. 6.

71. Joseph Califano to President, 14 Nov. 1967, cont. 55, Califano files, LBJ; Califano to President, 18 Nov. 1967, Hershey name file, ibid.

72. *WP*, 14 Dec. 1967; *NYT*, 12 Nov. 1967, p. 2; *Washington Evening Star*, 17 Nov. 1967; *The Nation*, 18 Dec. 1967, p. 643.

73. Jim Gaither to Joseph Califano, 29 Nov. 1967, Hershey name file, box 265, LBJ; Douglass Cater to President, 16 Nov. 1967, Califano file, cont. 55, ibid.; *NYT*, 18 Nov. 1967, p. 14; 24 Dec. 1967, p. 48; *U.S. News and World Report*, 25 Dec. 1967, p. 23; *The New Republic*, 2 Dec. 1967, p. 7; *The Nation*, 18 Dec. 1967, pp. 642–43; K. Sperry, "Draft Statement," *Science*, 15 Dec. 1967, p. 1434.

74. *San Francisco Chronicle*, 26 Dec. 1967; *NYT*, 7 Dec. 1967, p. 46.

75. *WP*, 14 Dec. 1967; *Time*, 22 Dec. 1967, p. 19.

76. Hershey to John E. Moss, 21 Nov. 1967; Moss to Hershey, 22 Nov. 1967; Hershey to Moss, 27 Nov. 1967; Moss to Hershey, 5 Dec. 1967; Hershey to Moss, 13, 20 Dec. 1967; all in congressional file, HP; *NYT*, 15 Dec. 1967, p. 13.

77. L. Hershey, "The Ephemeral Criticism of the October Letter," *Forensic Quarterly* 42 (May 1968), copy in RG 147, NA; Veterans' organizations to President, 7 Dec. 1967, newspaper file, HP; *New York Daily News*, 25 Nov. 1967.

78. Hershey to Senator Mike Monroney, 29 Nov. 1967, congressional file, HP; *SS*, Dec. 1967; Hershey to Bruce Comly French, 21 Nov. 1967, alpha file, HP; Hershey to Gen. Carlton Dargusch, 21 Nov. 1967, ibid.

79. Hershey to Ramsey Clark, 1 Mar. 1967, GF; Clark to Hershey, 7 Mar. 1967, ibid.; Hershey interview, Sept. 1974, MHI. His relationship with Attorney General Ramsey Clark went back several years. Hershey was an old friend of Justice Tom Clark, Ramsey's father. After Johnson appointed Ramsey as attorney general in 1967, Hershey wrote his congratulations and added, "I have great confidence that you will meet the difficult challenges of your office in these perilous times." Ramsey replied: "It is a privilege to serve with you, General." From this point everything went sour.

80. *Washington Daily News*, 6 May 1967; *SS*, Apr. 1968; Frank M. Slatinshek interview; F. Edward Hebert interview.

81. Hershey memo to L. E. Levinson, 26 Sept. 1968, GF; Johnson to Ramsey Clark, 20 Oct. 1967, EX FG 282, cont. 303, LBJ; Clark to Johnson, 6, 16 Nov. 1967, ibid. Many years later Clark admitted that his department was probably "soft on Selective Service prosecutions" (Clark to author, 14 July 1980).

82. *NYT*, 8 Nov. 1967, p. 1; 9 Nov. 1967, p. 3; 10 Nov. 1967, p. 1; 11 Nov. 1967, p. 5; *SS*, Dec. 1967.

83. *NYT*, 3 Dec. 1967, p. 26; Joint Statement by Attorney General Ramsey Clark and Director Lewis B. Hershey, n.d., alpha correspondence, White House file, HP; *NYT*, 10 Dec. 1967, p. 1.

84. Ramsey Clark to author, 14 July 1980; *NYT*, 12 Dec. 1967, p. 16; clipping from *Forensic Quarterly*, May 1968, RG 147, NA.

85. Joseph Califano to Johnson, 11 Dec. 1967, EX ND 9-4, LBJ; Warren Christopher to Califano, 29 Dec. 1967, EX FG 282, cont. 303, ibid.; *NYT*, 31 Dec. 1967, p. 5.

86. Minutes of State Directors' Conferences, 24 May, 21 Nov. 1951, HP; Hershey to Earl Warren, 12 Oct. 1953, GF.

87. *SS*, Jan. 1968; Hershey speech to National Press Club, 12 Mar. 1968, speech file, HP; *SS*, July 1968.

88. *WP*, 21 May 1968; *Los Angeles Times*, 7 Sept. 1968; *NYT*, 19 May 1968, p. 74.

89. Hershey to Lewis Kosch, 31 May 1968, alpha file, HP; Minutes of State Directors' Conference, 22–26 Apr. 1968, HP; *NYT*, 19 May 1968, p. 74.

90. See *Oestereich* v. *Local Board 11*, 393 U.S. 233 (1968); *NYT*, 25 Jan. 1970, clipping, HP; *Los Angeles Times*, 17 Dec. 1968.

91. George C. Herring, *America's Longest War* (New York: John Wiley, 1979), pp. 202–4.

92. Quoted ibid., p. 205.

CHAPTER XI

1. Hershey editorial draft, 14 Aug. 1968, alpha file, HP; *NYT*, 23 Apr. 1968, p. 1.

2. Hershey to Marine Corps Hersheys, 26 May 1968, GF; interview with General Henry M. Gross, OHC, MHI; *NYT*, 14 May 1968, p. 95; 16 May 1968, p. 51; J. Edgar Hoover to Hershey, 5 Apr. 1968, GF; FBI report, 29 Mar. 1968, ibid.

3. *SS*, June 1969; *Knickerbocker News*, n.d., newspaper file, HP; *Fort Lauderdale News*, 24 May 1968; *Memphis Press Scimitar*, 10 Dec. 1968; *SS*, Aug. 1968; Hershey to Valeri Wiener, 25 Nov. 1968, alpha file, HP.

4. *SS*, Sept. 1968; Hershey to National Press Club, 12 Mar. 1968, speech file, HP; Minutes of State Directors' Conference, 22–26 Apr. 1968, HP.

5. Lewis Hershey, "The Ephemeral Criticism of the October Letter," *Forensic Quarterly* 42 (May 1968), copy in RG 147, NA; *SS*, Feb. 1968; *Christian Century*, 3 Jan. 1968, p. 3; *WP*, 6 Sept. 1968.

6. *Editor and Publisher*, 12 Oct. 1968; *NYT*, 8 Mar. 1968, p. 7; Minutes of State Directors' Conference, 22–26 Apr. 1968, HP; Hershey to National Sheriffs' Association, July 1968, speech file, ibid.; *SS*, May, Nov. 1968.

7. Gilbert Hershey interview, 8–15 Aug. 1977; *NYT*, 7 Jan. 1968, p. 1; 21 Mar. 1968, p. 37; 20 May 1968, p. 33; 3 Aug. 1968, p. 11; 6 Aug. 1968, p. 21.

8. *NYT*, 1 Aug. 1968, p. 17; 3 Aug. 1968, p. 11; *Washington Star*, 8 Aug. 1968.

9. *Washington Star*, 8 Aug. 1968; Hershey interview, Sept. 1974, MHI.

10. *WP*, 18 Aug. 1968; *SS*, Mar. 1969.

11. Nixon to Hershey, 16 Sept. 1955, presidential correspondence, HP; Hershey to Vice-President, 26 May 1955, Bush file, ibid.; Nixon to Hershey, 15 Aug. 1956, ibid.; Lewis to Ellen, 15 Feb. 1958, GF; Gilbert Hershey interview, 8–15 Aug., and 14 Nov. 1977; Lewis Hershey interview, 9 June 1975, OHC, MHI.

12. *Memphis Press Scimitar*, 10 Dec. 1968; *Prince George's Sentinel*, 8 Feb. 1969; Daniel O. Omer to Charles S. Murphy, 7 Jan. 1969, EX FG 282, cont. 304, LBJ; Arleigh Burke interview.

13. Jonathan Rose interview; *National Review*, 17 Dec. 1968, p. 1254; George Gallup, *The Gallup Poll: Public Opinion, 1935–1971*, 3 vols. (New York: Random House, 1972), III, 2180.

14. E. D. Ingold interview, 20 Feb. 1972, OHC, MHI; William Averill interview; David R. Gergen interview; Minutes of State Directors' Conference, 8 May 1969, HP; *WP*, 31 Jan. 1969.

15. *Indianapolis Star*, 12 Apr. 1969; *WP*, 3 Mar. 1969; Nixon press release, 13 May 1969, White House correspondence, HP.

16. Nixon press release, 13 May 1969, White House correspondence, HP; Col. Franck to Hershey, 13 May 1969, GF; *NYT*, 14 May 1969, p. 1.

17. *Gallup Poll,* III, 2016–17; *WP,* 11 May 1968.

18. Minutes of State Directors' Conference, 5, 9 May 1969, HP; Hershey to Joseph A. Califano, 13 Nov.1969, alpha file, ibid.; *NYT,* 20 May 1969, p. 1.

19. Hershey to Charles B. Wilkinson, 1 July 1969, White House correspondence, HP; Bernard Franck interview; *NYT,* 7 June 1969, p. 2; *WP,* 7 June 1969.

20. Hershey memo to L. E. Levinson, 26 Sept. 1968, GF; Harry A. Marmion, *Selective Service: Conflict and Compromise* (New York: John Wiley, 1968), p. 53; *Current History,* July 1968, p. 4; *U.S. News and World Report,* 21 Apr. 1969, p. 78; Hershey interview, 7 May 1975, OHC, MHI; Minutes of State Directors' Conference, 8 May 1969, HP.

21. *WP,* 18 Oct. 1968; *NYT,* 20 Oct. 1968; *Gallup Poll,* III, 2090.

22. *SS,* Apr. 1969. In fact, the Gates report of early 1970 gave a ringing endorsement to the feasibility of an all-volunteer armed force. See Commission on an All-Volunteer Armed Force, *Report* (Washington: U.S. Government Printing Office, 1970).

23. Interview with John W. McClellan; Hershey to BG Hugh B. Hester, 12 July 1966, alpha file, HP; Gilbert Hershey interview, 8–15 Aug. 1977; quote in *SS,* Jan. 1967; Hershey memo to L. E. Levinson, 26 Sept. 1968, GF.

24. *U.S. News and World Report,* 21 Apr. 1969, pp. 76–79; *Current History,* July 1968, p. 5.

25. *SS,* Sept. 1969; Las Vegas *Review Journal,* 27 June 1969; speech to National Press Club, 12 Mar. 1968, speech file, HP; Hershey interview in *U.S. News and World Report,* 21 Apr. 1969, p. 79.

26. Minutes of State Directors' Conference, 9 May 1969, HP; *Prince George's Sentinel,* 8 Feb. 1969; Raleigh *News and Observer,* 3 May 1969.

27. *SS,* May 1969; Hershey editorial, 16 May 1969, alpha file, HP.

28. Helena *Independent Record,* 11 July 1969; *Prince George's Sentinel,* 8 Feb. 1969; Greensboro *Daily News,* 4 May 1969; Hershey to Rick Layne, 13 July 1969, KLF; *SS,* Aug. 1969.

29. *NYT,* 18 Sept. 1969, pp. 12, 46; *SS,* Oct. 1969.

30. *NYT,* 21 Sept. 1969, p. 1; 24 Sept. 1969, p. 46.

31. *Washington Star,* 5 Aug. 1969; *NYT,* 30 Aug. 1969, p. 8.

32. Jonathan Rose interview; E. D. Ingold interview; F. Edward Hebert interview; Gilbert Hershey interview, 8–15 Aug. 1977; *Time,* 22 Dec. 1967, p. 20.

33. Jonathan Rose interview; Bernard Franck interview; Frank M. Slatinshek interview; David R. Gergen interview; quote from *NYT,* 19 Oct. 1969, sec. 4, p. 3; Nixon was sensitive to charges that he had dumped Hershey because of protesters; he ordered Peter Flanigan to counter such reports being spread by Dan Rather and others. See *NYT,* 1 Nov. 1973, p. 34.

34. Hershey interview, May 1975, MHI; Hershey to Pete Taylor, 22 Oct. 1969, alpha file, HP; Hershey to Joan Hershey, 21 Sept. 1969, JH.

35. Bernard Franck interview; Nixon statement, 10 Oct. 1969, GF; *NYT,* 11 Oct. 1969, p. 1. After some opposition from the Pentagon, Hershey was promoted with a date of rank of 23 Dec. 1969.

36. *Washington Sunday Star,* 12 Oct. 1969; Hershey to Col. Robert B. Coons, 24 Oct. 1969, alpha file, HP; Hershey to Joan Hershey, 12 Oct. 1969, JH; Hershey interview, May 1975, MHI; Juel Peeke and Clark Smith interviews.

37. *NYT,* 1 Oct. 1969, p. 11.

38. U.S. Congress, House, Armed Services Committee, *Hearings on Random Selection,* 91st Cong., 1st sess., 1 Oct. 1969, pp. 4518–25.

39. Ibid., pp. 4526–42; *NYT,* 17 Oct. 1969, p. 23; Frank M. Slatinshek interview.

40. U.S. Congress, Senate, Committee on Judiciary, Subcommittee on Administration, *Selective Service System, Hearings,* 91st Cong., 1st sess., 23 Oct. 1969, pp. 1, 85, 87, 91, 93, 94, 97.

41. U.S. Congress, Senate, Armed Services Committee, *Hearings on Random Selection*, 91st Cong., 1st sess., 14 Nov. 1969, pp. 18, 23; Hershey to Rick, 4 Nov. 1969, KLF.

42. *WP*, 16 Nov. 1969; Hershey to Rick, 16 Nov. 1969, KLF.

43. President Nixon remarks, n.d., White House correspondence, HP.

44. James M. Gerhardt, *The Draft and Public Policy* (Columbus: Ohio State University Press, 1971), pp. 343–44.

45. Hershey interview, 28 May 1971, Bush file, HP; *Newsweek*, 15 Dec. 1969, pp. 37–38.

46. Hershey to Joan, 7 Dec. 1969, JH; *Chicago Tribune*, 30 Dec. 1969. According to one participant, the lottery was mishandled. Capsules were inserted in chronological order and the subsequent mixing proved inadequate. As Jan. dates went in first and Dec. dates last, these two months produced a majority of the low and high numbers respectively (David R. Gergen interview). For a statistical analysis which proved the selection was not random, see Art Berman, "Statistician Brands Lottery Unfair," *Los Angeles Times*, 3 Dec. 1969.

47. Hershey to Ehrlichman, 21 Nov. 1969, White House correspondence, HP; Hershey to Nixon, 1 Dec. 1969, GF; Hershey to Flanigan, 6 Feb. 1970, ibid.

48. *National Observer*, 16 Feb. 1970, p. 7; *Time*, 2 Mar. 1970, p. 14; *NYT*, 12 Feb. 1970, p. 1.

49. *NYT*, 17 Feb. 1970, p. 30; news clipping, n.d., alpha file, HP.

50. Frank Kossa interview; E. D. Ingold interview, 20 Feb. 1972, OHC, MHI; David R. Gergen interview; Hershey interview, May 1975, OHC, MHI; Curtis Tarr to ___, 14 Apr. 1970, alpha file, HP. For a self-serving view of the Tarr regime see Curtis Tarr, *By the Numbers: The Reform of the Selective Service System, 1970–1972* (Washington, D.C.: National Defense University Press, 1981).

51. Daniel Omer interview; Henry A. Carlson to Director, 20 July 1970, and Keith E. McWilliams to State Director, California, 23 July 1970, both in Daniel Omer files, Alexandria, Va. (private).

52. John J. McCloy to Hershey, 28 Oct. 1969, alpha file, HP; Lawrence Spivak to Hershey, 14 Oct. 1969, ibid.

53. F. Edward Hebert interview; guest list for dinner, 17 Feb. 1970, GF; Nixon to Hershey, 16 Feb. 1970, Presidential correspondence file, HP; John W. McClellen interview.

54. *Chicago Tribune*, 19 Jan. 1968; *SS*, Jan. 1968; Kathryn Hershey Layne interview; Hershey to Kathryn, 13 Nov. 1964, KLF; Gilbert Hershey interview, 8–15 Aug. 1977.

55. *Washington Sunday Star*, 12 Oct. 1969; Gilbert Hershey interview, 8–15 Aug. 1977; Hershey interview, May 1975, MHI; Hershey to Joseph Califano, 13 Nov. 1969, alpha file, HP.

56. Hershey to Hugh B. Hester, 12 July 1966, alpha file, HP; *SS*, July 1965; Apr. 1966; S. McBeen, "Riots," *Life*, 20 Aug. 1965, p. 29; O'Sullivan questionnaire, 13 Nov. 1974, GF.

57. *NYT*, 1, 14 May 1969, p. 20; Hershey to Rick Layne, 1 May 1967, KLF.

58. Richard M. Bateman to all personnel, Selective Service Headquarters, 9 Dec. 1969, newspaper file, HP; John W. McClellan interview.

CHAPTER XII

1. *WP*, 12 Apr. 1970; Hershey to Col. James T. Coatsworth, 25 Sept. 1972, alpha file, HP, MHI.

2. Nixon to Congress, 23 Apr. 1970, in *Semi-Annual Report of the Director of Selective Service, 1 Jan.-30 June 1970* (Washington: U.S. Government Printing Office, 1970), pp. 45–48. Yet the problems of Vietnam delayed Nixon's program. Not until 27 Jan. 1973 did

Secretary of Defense Melvin Laird announce that inductions were ending. The authority to induct expired in July 1973.

3. Hershey memo to Peter Flanigan, 26 Mar. 1970, GF; Hershey memo to President, 30 Mar. 1970, ibid.; Hershey memo to National Security Council, 23 Mar. 1970, ibid.; Salt Lake City *Deseret News*, 13 Oct. 1970.

4. Hershey to National Security Council, n.d., DF.

5. E. Grayson Swailes to Commander Elizabeth Denny, 14 Sept. 1970, DF; Denny to Swailes, 22 Sept. 1970, ibid.; Denny interview; transcript of UCLA talk, 9 Oct. 1970, HP.

6. Hershey to President, 19 Aug. 1971, GF; Curtis W. Tarr to Hershey, 19 Aug. 1971, biography file, HP.

7. Hershey to President, 2 Jan. 1973, GF; Hershey interview, May 1975, OHC, MHI.

8. Hershey to Col. McLean, 29 May 1973, alpha file, HP; Jonathan Rose interview; Elizabeth Denny interview; Nixon to Hershey, 14 Feb. 1973, GF.

9. Denny interview; Hershey to Col. Averill, 12 Apr. 1973, alpha file, HP; Hershey to President, 14 Feb. 1973, GF; Nixon to Hershey, 16 Mar. 1973, ibid.

10. News clipping, AP wire story, 27 Mar. 1973, GF; Elizabeth Denny interview; Hershey 201 file, ARC; *NYT*, 28 Mar. 1973, p. 43.

11. Hershey physical examination, 8 Mar. 1973, GF.

12. Hershey daily diaries, 1973–76, on loan to author from Col. John W. Barber; Kathryn Hershey Layne interview; Arleigh Burke interview; Frank Kossa interview; Juel Peeke and Clark Smith interviews; John W. McClellan interview.

13. Gilbert Hershey interview, 8–15 Aug. 1977; Kathryn Layne interview; Hershey to K. D. Pulcipher, 9 May 1975, Pulcipher Papers (private), Denver, Colo.; Hershey interview, Sept. 1974, MHI.

14. Hershey to Dr. Wayne Davis, 26 May 1972, GF; Hershey interviews, Sept. 1974 and 7 May 1975, MHI.

15. *Indianapolis Star Magazine*, 23 July 1972; Hershey to Leo A. Bouret, 28 Nov. 1972, DF; Hershey interview, May 1975, MHI; transcription of speech, 11 Sept. 1976, GF.

16. Kathryn Layne interview; *NYT*, 24 Feb. 1977, p. 46; 25 Feb. 1977, sec. 2, p. 16; Gilbert Hershey interview, 8–15 Aug. 1977; Jimmy Carter to Hershey, 14 Apr. 1977, KLF; Arleigh Burke interview.

17. Gilbert Hershey interview, 8–15 Aug. 1977; John W. McClellan interview; Ruby Hershey interview; *NYT*, 21 May 1977, p. 1.

18. Hershey had some $150,000 in a variety of savings accounts, most paying very low interest. He always kept several thousand dollars in his checking account. His annual salary during the last ten years of his life rose from $20,000 to $36,000 in 1970. His will divided all property equally among his children. Hershey notebooks, GF; Hershey will, 4 June 1936, ibid.; Gilbert Hershey interview, 8–15 Aug. 1977.

19. Hershey to Joan Hershey, 10 Nov. 1968, JH.

20. Gary L. Wamsley, *Selective Service and a Changing America* (Columbus: Charles Merrill, 1969), p. 42; Roger W. Little, ed., *Selective Service and American Society* (New York: Russell Sage Foundation, 1969), pp. xv, 22; James Fallows, *National Defense* (N.Y.: Random House, 1981). Lawrence Baskir and William Strauss, in *Chance and Circumstance* (New York: Knopf, 1978), p. 6, emphasize the Darwinian aspect of the draft but confuse people drafted with those inducted and seeing combat.

21. Gary L. Wamsley, "Decision-Making in Local Boards," in Little, ed., *Selective Service and American Society*, pp. 106–7. See also Wamsley, *Selective Service*, pp. 54–55; Daniel Omer interview; Charles H. Grahl interview; Gareth N. Brainerd and William S. Iliff interviews.

22. Gilbert Hershey interview, 14 Nov. 1977; Kathryn Hershey Layne interview; Kenneth McGill interview; Joseph Tiagno and Henry Willis interviews; E. D. Ingold interview; William Averill interview.

23. Henry M. Gross to Hershey, 11 Dec. 1970, Gross Papers, MHI; Minutes of State Directors' Conference, 16 May 1960, HP; William Averill interview.

24. Minutes of State Directors' Conferences, 26 June 1950, 21–25 May 1962, HP; Elizabeth Denny interview.

25. Louis Galambos, "The Emerging Organizational Synthesis in Modern American History," *Business History Review* 44 (Aug. 1970), 279–90.

26. Otis L. Graham, Jr., *Toward a Planned Society: From Roosevelt to Nixon* (New York: Oxford University Press, 1976), p. 80.

27. For a discussion of the two models of bureaucracy, see Douglas Yates, *Bureaucratic Democracy: The Search for Democracy and Efficiency* (Cambridge: Harvard University Press, 1982).

28. Graham, *Toward a Planned Society*, p. 143.

29. On his political performance before Congress, see Frank M. Slatinshek and William Hogan interviews. These two men served as general counsels for the House Armed Services Committee. See also Wamsley, *Selective Service*, pp. 186, 215.

30. See Thomas Bender, *Community and Social Change in America* (New Brunswick, N. J.: Rutgers University Press, 1978), pp. 143–50, for a discussion of the survival of community in the twentieth century.

31. Minutes of State Directors' Conference, 29 June 1950, HP.

32. See Samuel P. Huntington, *The Soldier and the State* (Cambridge: Harvard University Press, 1957), ch. 9, for the evolution of military professionalism.

Essay on Sources

A study of the life of Lewis B. Hershey is also a study of the American draft system. This essay on sources, however, will concentrate on the material found useful in explaining Hershey's own development and character as director of the draft. For those readers interested primarily in the institution of conscription, I recommend beginning with Martin Anderson, ed., *Conscription: A Select and Annotated Bibliography* (Stanford: Hoover Institution Press, 1976), the current standard in the field.

In dealing with contemporary figures the historian must rely upon the cooperation of many individuals. The interview becomes an invaluable (although treacherous) source of information. The following individuals provided excellent cooperation:

William Averill, Tupelo, Miss., 27 July 1978.
John W. Barber, Arlington, Va., 6 Aug. 1977; San Francisco, 29 Dec. 1978.
Gareth N. Brainerd, Denver, Colo., 25 Aug. 1978.
Arleigh Burke, Bethesda, Md., 26 Aug. 1977.
Ramsey Clark, letter to author, 14 July 1980.
Carlton Dargusch, Columbus, Ohio, 22 Nov. 1977.
Elizabeth Denny, Vienna, Va., 16, 22 Aug. 1977.
Lynn W. Elston, Fort Wayne, Ind., 17 Nov. 1977.
Bernard Franck, Arlington, Va., 1 Sept. 1977.
David R. Gergen, Washington, D.C., 30 Aug. 1977.
Charles H. Grahl, Bethesda, Md., 26 Aug. 1977.
F. Edward Hebert, New Orleans, La., 19 July 1978.
Gilbert Hershey, Jacksonville, N.C., 8–15 Aug. 1977 and 14–15 Nov. 1977.
Lewis B. Hershey, Bethesda, Md., 26 May 1975.
See also interviews of Hershey dated 26 May 1971, Sept. 1974-May 1975, and 11
    Sept. 1976, Oral History Collection, MHI.
Ruby Hershey, Angola, Ind., 19 Nov. 1977.
William Hogan, Washington, D.C., 31 Aug. 1977.
William S. Iliff, Denver, Colo., 25 Aug. 1978.
E. D. Ingold, Alamagordo, N.M., 15–16 Aug. 1978.
Frank V. Keesling, San Francisco, Calif., 28 Dec. 1978.
Frank Kossa, Jeffersonville, Ind., 26 July 1978.
Teresa Kundred, Angola, Ind., 19 Nov. 1977.
Kathryn Hershey Layne, Washington, D.C., 7 Aug. 1977.
John W. McClellan, Angola, Ind., 18 Nov. 1977.
Kenneth McGill, Abilene, Kans., 17 Aug. 1978.
Daniel Omer, Alexandria, Va., 28, 30 Aug. 1977.
Juel Peeke, Takoma Park, Md., 24 Aug. 1977.
K. D. Pulcipher, Denver, Colo., 26 Aug. 1978.
Jonathan Rose, Alexandria, Va., 16 Nov. 1977.
Margaret Rowdybush, Cape Coral, Fla., 21–22 July 1978.
Frank M. Slatinshek, Alexandria, Va., 31 Aug. 1977.
Clark Smith, Takoma Park, Md., 24 Aug. 1977.

Joseph Tiagno, Angola, Ind., 18 Nov. 1977.
Harry H. Vaughan, Alexandria, Va., 29 Aug. 1977.
Henry Willis, Angola, Ind., 18 Nov. 1977.

Of major importance for the book were several manuscript collections. The Lewis Hershey Papers, MHI, are voluminous (over 1,000 boxes) but still lacking in systematic arrangement. The folders of correspondence, in chronological order, and the minutes of state directors' conferences were most useful, as were several other files listed in the appropriate footnotes. For Hershey's career before 1940 it was necessary to consult the papers held by his son, Gilbert Hershey, at his home in Jacksonville, North Carolina. Colonel Hershey allowed me to transport several large cartons of papers back to Lubbock, Texas, for research. The Gilbert Hershey collection includes private diaries by both Lewis and Ellen Hershey and voluminous correspondence. Ellen kept almost every letter Lewis wrote her during their long marriage. Gilbert's file also contains dozens of volumes of newspaper clippings, plus a fine collection of photographs and tape recordings.

Several other private collections were also useful. Hershey's daughter, Mrs. Kathryn Hershey Layne, who lives in Washington, opened her records to me and provided encouragement for the project. Colonel Frank Keesling of San Francisco managed to take his papers with him when he left Selective Service after World War II, and he allowed me free access to these. They proved very useful in understanding problems during the war. Colonels John Barber and Daniel Omer also kept many files from their service under Hershey and made them available. K. D. Pulcipher's private papers proved useful for understanding the work of the Joint Army-Navy Selective Service Committee.

The official files of the Selective Service System were important in understanding Hershey's leadership. Thanks to the fine cooperation of archivist Fred W. Pernell, I was able to make good use of Record Group 147 (Selective Service System), and the records of the Joint Army-Navy Selective Service Committee. Also useful were records of the Office of the Secretary of War, Record Group 107, National Archives.

Because Hershey served under six different presidents, it was necessary to consult their various libraries. The outstanding staff at the Franklin D. Roosevelt Library at Hyde Park, New York, provided keys to several important collections, including the papers of Harry Hopkins, Henry Morgenthau, and Harold Smith. In Independence, Missouri, I was assisted through the Harry S Truman Papers by a very cooperative staff. The Dwight David Eisenhower Library in Abilene, Kansas, proved rather sparse in Hershey material; the same was true of the John F. Kennedy Papers, at that time housed in Waltham, Massachusetts. By contrast, the Lyndon B. Johnson Papers in Austin, Texas, were filled with information on the draft during the hectic 1960's. The files of Joseph Califano proved especially useful.

Several other smaller collections were also enlightening. Hershey's military personnel records were voluminous, as one might expect from someone who had spent a long life in the army. Thanks to the cooperation of Gilbert Hershey, I was able to examine records housed at the National Personnel Records Center (Military Personnel Branch) in St. Louis. The Henry Stimson Diary and Papers at the Yale University Library were invaluable for my research on World War II. Also useful for this same period were the papers of Robert Patterson and James W. Wadsworth, both housed at the Manuscript Division, Library of Congress. The George C. Marshall Research Library at Lexington, Virginia, was kind enough to make a small file on Hershey available.

Despite his long tenure, Hershey was not a prolific author. He did write editorials for a monthly newsletter entitled *Selective Service*, which ran from 1941 to 1969. These columns were helpful in determining his attitude toward shifting currents in international affairs. He also appears frequently in print through the reports of his speeches or testimony before Congress. Several articles bear his personal style and reflect his ideas at different times. During World War II he wrote for *Survey Graphic* (July 1941), *Aviation* (Feb. 1942), and the *Rotarian* (Sept. 1944). More elaborate articles appeared later in *The Annals* of the American Academy of Political and Social Sciences (Sept. 1945), *New York Times Magazine* (10 Feb. 1946), *Current History* (July 1968), and in Sol Tax, ed., *The Draft: A Handbook of Facts and Alternatives* (Chicago: University of Chicago Press, 1967).

In his capacity as director, Hershey submitted periodic reports on Selective Service operations. The first five reports had individual titles: *Selective Service in Peacetime, 1940–1941* (1941); *Selective Service in Wartime, 1941–42* (1943); *Selective Service as the Tide of War Turns, 1943–44* (1945); *Selective Service and Victory, 1944–1947* (1948); *Selective Service under the 1948 Act Extended* (1953). After the first five volumes, annual reports were issued until 1967, when semiannual reporting went into effect. The earlier volumes are filled with the chronological high points of the draft and with information and statistics on a wide variety of topics. The later volumes are smaller but still useful, especially for statistical information. Also useful was *Special Groups*, Special Monograph no. 10, 2 vols. (1953).

Perhaps the most fulsome record of Hershey in action can be found in hundreds of pages of congressional testimony. Few men have testified as often as Hershey did in his thirty years of government service. Listing each hearing would prove a burdensome and perhaps useless task; the preceding footnotes provide a guide to the relevant material. Readers interested in perusing the testimony are encouraged to consult *Witness Index to U.S. Congressional Hearings, 25th through 89th Congress* (Westport, Conn.: Greenwood, 1974; microfiche), as well as the *Cumulative Index of Congressional Committee Hearings, 1935–1967*, 3 vols. (Washington: Government Printing Office, 1959, 1963, 1967). Not surprisingly, the hearings of the armed services committees, formerly the military affairs committees, proved most useful. *The Congressional Digest* and *Vital Speeches* also provided reports on Hershey's remarks.

For easily accessible biographical information on Hershey several sources may be consulted. The genealogy of the Hershey family in America is traced in exhaustive detail through Henry Hershey, comp., *Hershey Family History* (Scottdale, Pa.: Mennonite Publishing House, 1929) and Scott F. Hershey, *History and Records of the Hershey Family from the Year 1600* (New Castle, Pa.: Petite Book Co., n.d.). See also Richard F. Seiverling, *Lewis B. Hershey: A Pictorial and Documentary Biography* (Hershey, Pa.: Keystone Enterprises, 1969), which is a celebration rather than a critical study, but useful for dates and pictures. Hershey sketches at various times in his career also appear in the following: Edward R. Murrow, *This I Believe* (New York: Simon & Schuster, 1952); *Current Biography* (June 1941 and 1951); Dorothea F. Fisher, *American Portraits* (New York: Holt, 1946); *Generals of the Army and the Air Force and Admirals of the Navy* 2 (Feb. 1954): 10–12.

Hershey appeared in the popular press as the draft became more visible. His career can be traced partially through newspapers, especially the *New York Times*, and, for his early career, the *Steuben Republican* (Angola, Ind.). The following periodicals covered Hershey as the draft became more controversial: *Colliers, Time, The Nation, The Saturday Evening Post, Life, Look, Newsweek, The New Republic, Commonwealth, The Christian Century, The National Review*, and, above all, *U.S. News and World Report*.

For a proper appreciation of Hershey's career, one must also be aware of the draft as part of America's overall defense policy. No book is more useful on this topic than James M. Gerhardt, *The Draft and Public Policy: Issues in Military Manpower Procurement, 1945–1970* (Columbus: Ohio State University Press, 1971). Also useful, but limited by a confusing citation system, is Albert A. Blum, *Drafted or Deferred: Practices Past and*

Present (Ann Arbor: University of Michigan Press, 1967). Several documentary collections were helpful: John W. Chambers, *Draftees or Volunteers: A Documentary History of the Debate over Military Conscription in the United States, 1787–1973* (New York: Garland, 1975), and John O'Sullivan and Alan M. Meckler, eds., *The Draft and Its Enemies* (Urbana: University of Illinois Press, 1974). During the 1960's controversy over the draft, several studies appeared. Some of the less shrill and more useful include the following: Harry A. Marmion, *Selective Service: Conflict and Compromise* (New York: John Wiley, 1968); Gary L. Wamsley, *Selective Service and a Changing America* (Columbus: Charles Merrill, 1969); Roger W. Little, ed., *Selective Service and American Society* (New York: Russell Sage Foundation, 1969). Less useful were Clyde E. Jacobs and John F. Gallagher, *The Selective Service Act: A Case Study of the Governmental Process* (New York: Dodd, Mead, 1967), and John R. Graham, *A Constitutional History of the Military Draft* (Minneapolis: Ross & Haines, 1971). Sol Tax, ed., *The Draft: A Handbook of Facts and Alternatives* (Chicago: University of Chicago Press, 1967), came out of a conference on the draft held in Chicago in 1966. For additional works on the 1960's draft, see below, under President Johnson.

Several outstanding studies cover special aspects of the draft and its operations; all of these provide insights into how Hershey functioned as director. Mulford Q. Sibley and Philip E. Jacob, *Conscription of Conscience: The American State and the Conscientious Objector, 1940–1947* (Ithaca: Cornell University Press, 1952), details the operations of the alternate service program during World War II from a point of view sympathetic to CO's. For the treatment of the black American see especially Richard M. Dalfiume, *Desegregation of the U.S. Armed Forces* (Columbia: University of Missouri Press, 1969), and Charles C. Moskos, Jr., "The Negro and the Draft," in Roger W. Little, ed., *Selective Service and American Society* (1969). Martha Derthick, *The National Guard in Politics* (Cambridge: Harvard University Press, 1965), is informative on that organization and the drive for conscription.

No related subject aroused more controversy than the deferment policy which Hershey directed. The best study of the operation of the local boards in classifying draftees is Kenneth M. Dolbeare and James W. Davis, Jr., *Little Groups of Neighbors: The Selective Service System* (Chicago: Markham, 1968). Additional information on deferments for special groups can be found in the following articles: Harry A. Marmion, "A Critique of Selective Service with Emphasis on Student Deferment," in Tax, ed., *The Draft*; Albert A. Blum, "Sailor or Worker: A Manpower Dilemma during the Second World War," *Labor History* 6 (Fall 1965), and Blum, "The Farmer, the Army and the Draft," *Agricultural History* 38 (Jan. 1964). The latest word on how deferments did or did not discriminate in American society is Neil D. Fligstein, "Who Served in the Military, 1940–1973," *Armed Forces and Society* 6 (Winter 1979).

The secondary literature dealing with each president under whom Hershey served was of only marginal significance. Hershey's obscurity in the official literature may reflect his success in adopting the role of "a faceless bureaucrat" who still wielded enormous power. The literature of the Franklin D. Roosevelt era continues to grow. For Hershey and the draft, the following were informative: Byron Fairchild and Jonathan Grossman, *The Army and Industrial Manpower* (Washington: Department of the Army, 1959); George Q. Flynn, *The Mess in Washington: Manpower Mobilization in World War II* (Westport: Greenwood, 1979); Davis R. B. Ross, *Preparing for Ulysses* (New York: Columbia University Press, 1969); Herman M. Somers, *Presidential Agency: OWMR, Office of War Mobilization and Reconversion* (Cambridge: Harvard University Press, 1950); and John J. O'Sullivan, "From Voluntarism to Conscription: Congress and Selective Service, 1940–1945" (Ph.D. dissertation, Columbia University, 1971). On the broad social history of the home front, the best work is Richard Polenberg, *War and Society: The United States, 1941–1945* (Philadelphia: Lippincott, 1972). Also useful is John M. Blum, *V Was for Victory: Politics and American Culture during World War II* (New York: Harcourt Brace Jovanovich, 1975). More popular treatments include A. A. Hoehling, *Home Front, USA* (New York: Crowell, 1966); Richard Lingeman, *Don't You Know There's a War On?* (New York: Putnam, 1970); and Geoffrey Perrett, *Days of Sadness, Years of Triumph* (New York: Cowa 1, McCann & Geoghegan, 1973).

Scholarly secondary material is still growing on the postwar period. Otis Graham, *Toward a Planned Society: From Roosevelt to Nixon* (New York: Oxford University Press, 1976) is a fine work, but many manuscript collections remain partially closed, and journalism takes over. Several good studies of the Truman administration are noted in Richard Kirkendall, ed., *The Truman Period as a Research Field: A Reappraisal, 1972* (Columbia: University of Missouri Press, 1974), and in his similar earlier book (1967). To understand the Truman presidency, see especially two volumes by Robert J. Donovan, *Conflict and Crisis* (New York: Norton, 1977) and *The Tumultuous Years* (New York: Norton, 1982). Also useful is the older work by Cabell Phillips, *The Truman Presidency* (Baltimore: Penguin, 1969). Barton J. Bernstein and Allan J. Matusow, *The Truman Administration: A Documentary History* (New York: Harper Colophon, 1966), provides contemporary evidence. Specific studies which discussed the draft as part of American defense policy include two works by Walter Millis, *Arms and the State: Civil Military Elements in National Policy* (New York: Twentieth Century Fund, 1958), and an edited work, *The Forrestal Diaries* (New York: Viking, 1951). On the student deferment problem of the 1950's see M. H. Trytten, *Student Deferment in the Selective Service* (Minneapolis: University of Minnesota Press, 1952), which is a defense of the policy by a leading author of the idea, and National Manpower Council, *Student Deferment and National Manpower Policy* (New York: Columbia University Press, 1952).

Literature dealing with the draft under Eisenhower is very sketchy. The following biographical works were useful: Peter Lyon, *Eisenhower: Portrait of a Hero* (Boston: Little, Brown, 1974); Herbert S. Parmet, *Eisenhower and the American Crusade* (New York: Macmillan, 1972). Charles C. Alexander, *Holding the Line: The Eisenhower Era, 1952–1961* (Bloomington: Indiana University Press, 1975), provides a useful sketch of the major events and a good bibliography. Robert A. Divine, *Eisenhower and the Cold War* (New York: Oxford University Press, 1981), is a recent and positive evaluation.

The increased draft calls during the 1960's generated more studies of the draft and of Hershey's role. For overall views of the decade the following books proved informative: Jim Heath, *Decade of Disillusionment: The Kennedy-Johnson Years* (Bloomington: Indiana University Press, 1975); Godfrey Hodgson, *America in Our Time* (New York: Vintage, 1976); William L. O'Neill, *Coming Apart: An Informal History of America in the 1960's* (New York: New York Times/Quadrangle, 1971). Hershey hardly appears in the literature of Kennedy's presidency, but the draft became more important under Johnson. Johnson's autobiography, *The Vantage Point* (New York: Holt, Rinehart & Winston, 1971), contains information on the escalation of the draft but must be used with caution. Of some use on the reform of the draft was Eric Goldman, *The Tragedy of Lyndon Johnson* (New York: Knopf, 1969), written by an historian and administration liberal.

Several studies of the draft and youth appeared during the 1960's. Many of these are adversarial in tone, but Irwin Unger, *The Movement: A History of the American New Left, 1959–1972* (New York: Dodd Mead, 1974) is an excellent survey. Lawrence Baskir and William Strauss, *Chance and Circumstance: The Draft, the War and the Vietnam Generation* (New York: Knopf, 1978), is informative but marred by factual errors concerning Hershey. Michael Useem, *Conscription, Protest, and Social Conflict* (New York: John Wiley, 1973), makes good use of interviews with protesters. George C.

Herring, *America's Longest War: The United States and Vietnam, 1950–1975* (New York: John Wiley, 1979), is a recent and well-balanced survey of that conflict. Of the many antidraft publications spawned by the 1960's protests, Jean Carper, *Bitter Greetings: The Scandal of the Military Draft* (New York: Grossman, 1967), and Robert Liton, *Greetings: You Are Hereby Ordered for Induction: The Draft in America* (New York: McGraw-Hill, 1970), are representative. Very useful for understanding the attempted reforms under Johnson is the National Advisory Commission on Selective Service, *In Pursuit of Equity: Who Serves When Not All Serve?* (Washington: U.S. Government Printing Office, 1967). A defense of Hershey's draft of protesters can be found in C. W. Schiesser and Daniel H. Benson, "The Legality of Reclassification of Selective Service Registrants," *American Bar Association Journal* (Feb. 1967).

Hershey's long tenure with the draft would have been impossible without consistent support from the American public. The degree of the draft's public popularity can be traced through two excellent collections: Hadley Cantrill, *Public Opinion, 1935–1946* (Princeton: Princeton University Press, 1951), and George H. Gallup, *The Gallup Poll: Public Opinion, 1935–1971*, 3 vols. (New York: Random House, 1972).

Index